JOSEPH GOEBBELS

DESCRIBES IN HIS OWN WORDS
THE FINAL AGONY OF THE REICH

"CONVEYS A SHARP SENSE OF IMMEDIACY . . . an intimate glimpse of how one of the brutal regime's leaders views the Nazi *Gotterdammerung*. . . . Goebbels petty scorn spares practically none of his colleagues. . . . Even Hitler is not immune." *Time*

"ONE OF THE MOST EERY AND ENGROSSING BOOKS OF THE SEASON. . . . The significance of FINAL ENTRIES lies in the candor with which the minister shared the truth day by day about events and people as he saw them. . . his diaries depict the realities of the Nazis' doom." *Newsday*

"AN ABSORBING ACCOUNT of the Third Reich in its last paroxysm, seen through the daily diary entries of the man who was the most gifted, most loyal, and most revolutionary of Hitler's followers . . . a fascinating picture of Goebbels' attempts to get rid of the incompetent and defeatist party leaders, to arouse new energies in an increasingly lethargic Führer, and to radicalize the war effort for a struggle to the bitter end. A document of major historical importance." Gordon Craig

"A UNIQUE PICTURE OF THE LAST WEEKS of the war as seen from a Nazi viewpoint in Berlin. . . . Prefaced by an excellent biographical essay on Goebbels by Hugh Trevor-Roper."
The New York Times Book Review

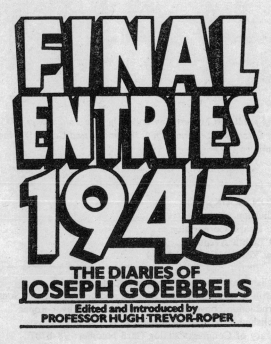

FINAL ENTRIES 1945

THE DIARIES OF JOSEPH GOEBBELS

Edited and Introduced by
PROFESSOR HUGH TREVOR-ROPER

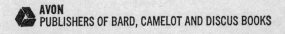

AVON
PUBLISHERS OF BARD, CAMELOT AND DISCUS BOOKS

First published in Germany under the title *Tabebucher 1945:
Die Letzen Aufzeichnungen C Hoffmann und Campe Verlag,*
Hamburg 1977

AVON BOOKS
A division of
The Hearst Corporation
959 Eighth Avenue
New York, New York 10019

English translation of text copyright © 1978 by
Martin Secker & Warburg Limited and G. P. Putnam's Sons
Introduction copyright © 1978 by Hugh Trevor-Roper
Published by arrangement with G. P. Putnam's Sons
Library of Congress Catalog Card Number: 78-6707
ISBN: 0-380-42408-8

First Avon Printing, April, 1979

AVON TRADEMARK REG. U.S. PAT. OFF. AND IN
OTHER COUNTRIES, MARCA REGISTRADA, HECHO EN
U.S.A.

Printed in the U.S.A.

CONTENTS

THE DIARY

CONTENTS

CONTENTS

CONTENTS

CONTENTS

CONTENTS

CONTENTS

CONTENTS

CONTENTS

CONTENTS

INTRODUCTION

Hugh Trevor-Roper

Joseph Goebbels has been described as "the only really interesting man in the Third Reich beside Hitler." The other Paladins of Nazism who, like him, were with the Fürher from beginning to end—Göring, Himmler, Bormann, Ley—were made by Hitler's power. In themselves they were, at best, commonplace men. Without them, Hitler and Nazism would probably have been the same, for substitutes would have been found. Goebbels was different. Although he needed Hitler in order to rise, he also contributed significantly to Hitler's power. He transformed his image, gave him public appeal, his charisma. He also sought to perpetuate that appeal for posterity. He set out to predetermine the future history of Nazism, its myth. Even after its complete failure, historians will still have to contend with that myth.

To those who lived through the years of Nazism, Goebbels will always be remembered as Hitler's "Minister for Propaganda and Enlightenment," the unscrupulous propagandist whose shameless brilliance as a mob orator and a manipulator of the news vindicated the statement of Hitler, in *Mein Kampf*, that the greater the lie, the more chance it had of being believed. First as a demagogic speaker at Party functions, then as an organiser of censorship and propaganda, finally as master of the media throughout the Reich, he saw to it that nothing was heard or seen on party platforms, on the radio, in the cinema, or in the press, except what he judged useful for immediate political purposes. Moreover, this uniform propaganda, disseminated at every level and through all the media, was not dull and predictable. Though crude and violent in form, utterly unscrupulous in substance and quite indifferent to truth, it was managed with an agility and a sophistication which exhorted a reluctant admiration even from its enemies and its victims. There was nothing dead or mechanical about it: with its un-German clarity, its accurate assessment of the potentialities of the medium, the need of the moment, and the taste of the audience, it became a deadly and flexible instrument of power. In this it accurately reflected the mind of its director. Goebbels was an impresario of genius, the first man to realise the full potentialities of mass media for political purposes in a dynamic totalitarian state.

But if this was the public image of Goebbels in his lifetime, it does not represent the sum of his contribution to Nazism. His importance was greater than this. He was also an efficient administrator, a radical political adviser to Hitler, and, to historians, an important (though dangerous) source.

Perhaps the best account of Goebbels' services to the Nazi movement was given by himself. On 12 December 1941, when victory on all fronts still seemed likely, Goebbels told his assistants in the Ministry of Propaganda that he had vitally strengthened that movement in four decisive ways. First, as leader of the National Socialists in Rhine and Ruhr, he had converted Nazism from a middle-class nationalist movement, based on Munich, into a Socialist working-class party, able to capture and hold the workers of the industrial Rhineland. Secondly, he had won Berlin and thereby prepared the way for the "seizure of power" in the Reich; for "without control of Berlin the Party would have remained a provincial movement." Thirdly, he had worked out the style and technique of the Party's public ceremonies: the mass demonstrations, the marches with standards, the ritual of the great Party occasions. Anyone, he remarked, could measure that achievement by comparing the annual commemorative gatherings in the beercellar at Munich with the giant demonstrations in the Sportpalast in Berlin. Finally, he had created the "myth" of the Führer. He had given to Hitler "the halo of infallibility," the charisma which enabled him to rise above the Party and be "the Führer," blindly followed by the German people.*

It is difficult to fault this complacent claim by Goebbels. That lucid mind, which seldom unconsciously deceived, was accurate even in self-perception. To the end, he could distinguish the objective truth from his own propaganda. To the end, he combined fanaticism with detachment: a politically calculated fanaticism with an intellectual detachment. That indeed is why his propaganda was so effective.

The character of Goebbels is clearly revealed by his early history, a vital part of which is illustrated by his personal diary: for throughout his life he was a compulsive diarist. A Rhinelander, the son of devout Catholic parents from the lower middle class, handicapped from childhood by a club-foot, he showed early intellectual promise and acquired —thanks to a Catholic charitable organisation—a university education. He had intellectual and literary ambitions, and at first sought self-expression by writing novels and plays, in which however there is no substance, only self-idealisation, romantic attitudes—and a streak of nihilism. Failing to make any mark at the university, blaming the Jewish monopoly for his inability to prosper in literature, he toyed with one political *credo* after another and then, early in 1925, joined the Nazi Party in the Rhineland. That branch of the Party was controlled by the most radical of the early Nazi leaders, Gregor Strasser.

---

* Rudolf Semler, *Goebbels, The Man next to Hitler* (1947) p. 56. I have not hesitated to cite Semler as a source in spite of Mr. David Irving's judgment (*Hitler's War*, p. xx) that his diaries are "phony." Mr. Irving bases this judgment on one entry—an account of a visit by Hitler to the Goebbels family on 12 January 1945—which is clearly misdated in the printed text. Semler's dates are not always reliable, but his matter remains valid. The visit itself is confirmed by Werner Naumann, who was there (Roger Manvell and Heinrich Fraenkel, *Dr. Goebbels*, 1960, p. 262). Other entries by Semler have been confirmed in detail by documents unavailable at the time of publication, including the Goebbels Diaries. In my opinion Semler's notes are authentic, although perhaps not kept in diary form.

Goebbels was in one sense always true to his origins. He was always a radical in the Party, and there remained always in him a recurrent streak of nihilism, arising, originally, from hatred of the society around him and from a certain inner emptiness: for he was a man of postures, not ideas or beliefs. However, he had also another characteristic, which would also serve him well: opportunism. With his complete freedom from conviction, and his remarkable mental agility, he was able to anticipate events and change course with great dexterity and to justify the change by nimble arguments. An occasion to exercise these gifts arose within a year of his joining the Party. It was to have a decisive influence on his career.

The matter at issue was the compensation or the expropriation of the Hohenzollern princes. The Munich party, led by Hitler, who had been chastened by the failure of his 1923 Putsch, urged compensation; the Rhineland party, led by Strasser, demanded expropriation. The battle became fierce, and Goebbels committed himself entirely to Strasser's camp. He attacked the Munich party, and Hitler personally, in violent terms. At one time he is said to have demanded that "the petty bourgeois Adolf Hitler be expelled from the Nazi Party." However, at a meeting at Bamberg, Goebbels was won over by Hitler and soon he would dramatise his conversion, or apostasy. Hitler would become, to him, "the creative instrument of Fate and Deity," a man who had "everything to be King," "a born tribune of the people, the coming dictator." From now on, Goebbels would be faithful to Hitler, building up his image as the man of destiny. Hitler, and the cult of Hitler, would supply him with the central ideal, the necessary conviction which was lacking in his own mentality, and around which the brilliant impresario could organise the ritual of devotion. For Hitler was power, and Goebbels, as his biographers have written, "was always loyal to power."* Gregor Strasser he would leave to be murdered, with his fellow "radicals," in the great purge of 30 June 1934.

* Manvell and Fraenkel, op. cit., p. 134.

Goebbels was rewarded for his "apostasy" by being made Gauleiter of Berlin, and this office he held to the end, for nearly twenty years. An able and vigorous administrator, he soon captured the capital for Nazism. He did so by his usual combination of ruthlessness and skill. He purged the local party, streamlined the administration, and maintained Nazi power in the city by effective propaganda, frightening demonstrations of power and unscrupulous persecution of chosen scapegoats. At first he had affected not to wish for the post; but he was too intelligent not to see its value. "Whoever can conquer the streets," he wrote, "will one day conquer the State, for every form of power politics and any dictatorially run state has its roots in the streets." Besides, in the jungle of the Nazi Party, Berlin was a great fief: whoever ruled it could hold his own against any other of the great feudatories. By combining it with the command of the media, which he used to denigrate and destroy those who resisted his power, he had—at least during the years of struggle, the "*Kampfzeit*"—a stronger base than any of them.

Once in control of the Party in Berlin, Goebbels never allowed that control to slacken. He reinforced it by continual demonstrations and organised, almost ceremonial violence. "We cannot have enough of demonstrations," he wrote, "for that is far and away the most emphatic way of demonstrating one's will to govern." Some of his demonstrations were notorious: the funeral of Horst Wessel, a radical Nazi student killed in a brawl in 1930; the exploitation of the Reichstag Fire in February 1933; the barbarous ceremony of "the burning of the books" on 10 May 1933; and, on 9 November 1938, the so-called *Kristallnacht*, an allegedly "spontaneous" outburst of anti-semitism in which the windows of all Jewish shops in Berlin were smashed— with disastrous financial consequences to good Aryan insurance companies. Some of these demonstrations were counter-productive: the burning of the books outraged foreign opinion at a time when it was being wooed, and the *Kristallnacht* was deplored by other Nazi leaders, like Himmler, who wanted silent elimination of the Jews, not spectacular pogroms. But Goebbels never lost Hitler's support as Gauleiter. In 1942 Hitler paid a notable tribute to his achievement. Goebbels, he wrote, was the man for whom he had long been waiting; he was the ideal man for that difficult task; he had "worked like an ox" to destroy opposition; "I have never regretted giving him the powers he asked for. When he started, he found nothing particularly efficient as a political organisation to help him; nevertheless, in the literal sense of the word, he captured Berlin."*

In the autumn of 1939, when Hitler prepared to launch his war, Goebbels was among those who sought to avert it. As he had no positive ideals, Hitler's vast plans of Eastern empire made no special appeal to him: it was not for them that he had joined the Party. Albert Speer tells us that "we who were members of Hitler's personal circle considered him, as well as Goering, who also counselled peace, as weaklings who had degenerated in the luxury of power and did not want to risk the privileges they had acquired."† Moreover, with the outbreak of war, Goebbels' position necessarily shrank. Hitler himself (we are told) declared that, for the duration of the war, the Propaganda Minister must be kept in the background.‡ Of course Berlin still had to be controlled and propaganda still had to be made. But military victory ensured the loyalty of Berlin and spoke louder than any propaganda. In those years of victory, therefore, Goebbels ceased to make the pace. He became a mere commentator, carried with the tide. In his radio programmes, his victory films, his own paper *Der Angriff*, and his regular leading articles in the Party organ *Das Reich*, he celebrated the triumph of German arms, ridiculed the enemy, and built up the picture of Hitler, not now as a revolutionary leader but as a national hero, the reincarnation of Frederick the Great, "the greatest warlord of all time." He also organised victory parades and enjoyed a life of feverish activity as the advertiser, friend

* *Hitler's Table Talk* (ed. H. Trevor-Roper, 1953), p. 532.
† Albert Speer, *Inside the Third Reich* (1970), pp. 162–3.
‡ Alfred Rosenberg, *Politische Tagebuch*, 3 September 1939.

and counsellor of the dictator whose frequent dilettantism and uncertainty he did so much to disguise.

Goebbels' routine as propagandist during the war is shown by the minutes of the regular, almost daily conferences in which he gave directives to his officials. As a minister, his activity was incessant. Constant action was a psychological necessity to him—again, it seems, an escape from inner emptiness—and no detail was too small for his attention. Often he laid down his general rules. "The fundamental principle of all propaganda," he declared, was "the repetition of effective arguments"; but those arguments must not be too refined—there was no point in seeking to convert the intellectuals. For intellectuals would never be converted and would anyway always yield to the stronger, "and this will always be the man in the street."* Arguments must therefore be crude, clear and forcible, and appeal to emotions and instincts, not to the intellect. Truth was unimportant, and entirely subordinate to tactics and psychology, but convenient lies ("poetic truth," as he once called them) must always be made credible. In accordance with these general directives, precise instructions were issued. Hatred and contempt must be directed at particular individuals; only such expressions were to be used as would generate the required emotion; specific lies were to be disseminated. These instructions were mandatory: officials who failed to follow them were regularly threatened with the concentration camp.

Meanwhile Goebbels sought to ensure that the exigencies and distractions of war did not weaken his influence at court. Here he had one great advantage, for although never one of Hitler's intimate circle, he was closer to him than any other of the old guard of Nazism. Hitler used Göring, Bormann, Himmler, but he was never familiar with them, never relaxed in their company or revealed to them his unguarded thoughts. He saw himself as a universal genius, an artist as well as a statesman, and he was impatient of that philistine, froth-blowing, class-bound world of early

---

* Manvell & Fraenkel, op. cit., pp. 14, 24, 294.

Nazism. Hence his affection for Speer, his architect, who, because of his "artistic" interests, could claim to be his only friend. Among politicians, Goebbels, with his command over the media, came closest to Speer. He could supply Hitler with films and film-actresses, he could talk of art and music, and, like Speer, he came from an educated background. It was he who, externally at least, had raised Hitler above the vulgar level of his first associates in the beer-halls of Munich. In fact, of course, Goebbels was not a cultivated man. He had no aesthetic interests. He burned the German classics and destroyed "decadent" art. He closed the Berlin theatres during the war. He was indifferent to the State Opera. He never went to concerts. His tastes were as banal and trivial as those of Hitler himself. But to Hitler he counted as an intellectual. Besides, Hitler liked presentable, admiring women. Frau Goebbels was an elegant woman from a rich family; she worshipped Hitler; and Hitler was glad to have her worship. Hitler had been best man at Goebbels' marriage, and when that marriage nearly broke down, owing to Goebbels' numerous amours with actresses and secretaries, Hitler positively forbade divorce and personally imposed a reconciliation.

In private life, Goebbels again separated himself from the other old Nazis and sought to advertise his superior character as an intellectual. He was fastidious in his dress, wore well-cut clothes, and kept a huge wardrobe. His palatial residence near the Brandenburg Gate in Berlin and his villa at Schwanenwerder on the Wannsee were luxuriously furnished; but the luxury was combined with a certain austerity. He hated the gross display of opulence made by some of the Party bosses, and particularly by that greatest of vulgarians and *faux bonhommes*, "the Reich Marshal," Hermann Göring, whose extravagance of dress and gluttony for material things only aggravated, in Goebbels' eyes, his crime of inefficiency as Commander-in-Chief of the Luftwaffe. Goebbels' outward life, was, by contrast almost puritanically simple. The frugality of his entertainment was notorious, and much resented by his officials who expected something better from their tyrannical and exacting master.

This very austerity was to serve him well and to provide him with a programme in the later years of the war. The earlier years had been the years of victorious *Blitzkrieg*, when all Germany grew fat on the spoils of Europe and Göring stacked his palaces with the most priceless treasures and the costliest wines looted from the conquered West. But after the winter of 1941 the conditions of war changed, and by the end of 1942 it was clear that the years of easy victory were over. Germany had now roused against itself a world coalition. Its armies were on the defensive on three fronts. They had been defeated in Africa, halted in Russia, and feared invasion in the West. Then came the disaster at Stalingrad: the encirclement and, in the end, the capture of the entire 6th Army, whose generals, to make the disgrace even more bitter, instead of committing suicide according to their instructions, surrendered and, in captivity, became propagandists for the Russians, broadcasting to the German troops and urging universal surrender. This was a great humiliation to the master propagandist in Berlin: a humiliation made worse by the fact that victory at Stalingrad had been confidently predicted and elaborate arrangements had been made to celebrate its fall.

The disasters of the winter of 1942–43, which transformed the character of the war, brought Goebbels back into the forefront of German politics. Hitherto much of his energy had been devoted to the suppression rather than the publication of the radical doctrines and policies which he secretly favoured, and his instructions to his own officials were often negative. The euthanasia programme, for instance, was never to be mentioned by the media. The war against the Church, unseasonably pressed by the fanatical anti-Christian Martin Bormann, was to be put off till after victory. The Final Solution of the Jewish Problem, which Goebbels himself supported, "whatever the cost," was similarly under a strict taboo. And it was hardly possible to make propaganda to the Russian people by describing German war aims in the East since those war aims were simply conquest, extermination and exploitation. As Goebbels himself remarked with cynical candour, even the German people would never have voted for the Nazis if it had known what they intended to do. However, the disasters of the second Russian winter marked a change. Damaged by defeat, the Party leadership had to reassert itself and command new efforts by the German people. This return to the spirit of the *Kampfzeit* gave the minister a new opportunity to deploy his old arts and to raise his old voice: the arts of the impresario, the virtuoso master of ceremonies; the voice of radicalism, nihilism, destruction.

For a long time Goebbels had been the prophet of "total war." Unlike Hitler, who remained emotionally wedded to the concept of the Blitzkrieg and who had never envisaged, or prepared for, a long struggle, Goebbels, with the absolutism of the intellectual, retained a lifelong preference for radical measures and had advocated, in particular, the mobilisation of women. Periodically he had convinced Hitler, but always, when his back was turned, Hitler had relapsed into his old habit. Now, in defeat, Goebbels saw his chance. He returned to the attack. Hitler was by this time entirely surrounded by a "Committee of Three" consisting of Bormann, Lammers and Keitel—which meant, effectively, Bormann; but in December 1942 Goebbels broke through this ring and submitted a memorandum to Hitler proposing measures of total mobilisation. In the exigency of the time, Hitler approved the memorandum and next month signed a decree accordingly.

Goebbels now threw himself into action. He saw Stalingrad as Germany's Dunkirk and he tried to rouse in Germany the same spirit as Churchill had roused in Britain after Dunkirk. "At that time," Goebbels declared, "Winston Churchill displayed admirable frankness in drawing the necessary conclusions and telling the British people the absolute truth. At the time, we did not understand this"— and indeed, he did not, for at that time he had ordered all broadcasts to Britain to be prefaced by the "catchy slogan," "Churchill is a fool"—but with these tactics Churchill had aroused the nation. Now Nazi Germany must do the same. Only, he added, we must not seem to be imitators: "Churchill's slogan of 'blood, sweat and tears' must not be taken up: we must think of a slogan of our own."*

It is pleasant to see the great master of the lie suddenly discovering the tactical advantages of "absolute truth." Goebbels' first application of this novel doctrine was a frank admission of the catastrophic nature of the German defeat. On 3 February 1943, he ordered three days of national remembrance for Stalingrad. All places of entertainment were to be shut, and there was to be a complete standstill of traffic for one minute on the first and last day. There was to be no mourning, no sentimentality, only a dignified and resolute devotion to further effort. Goebbels even ordered—again a new departure—that the press should not publish cartoons which belittle the enemy: "we have no reason at the present moment to portray our opponents as being smaller than in fact they are."†

Meanwhile Goebbels was exploiting to the full Hitler's decree ordering "the extreme totalisation of the war which he, the minister, has been demanding for the past eighteen months." On 18 February he mounted a great demonstration in the Sportpalast in Berlin. He himself made one of his most famous speeches, in which he demanded even greater efforts and promised that blood, sweat and tears (though not of course in those words) would bring ultimate victory. In the course of the speech he gave vent to the usual hysterical radicalism. Speer, who was there, afterwards said that he had never seen an audience so effectively roused to fanaticism. Goebbels pulled out all the old stops and screamed abuse at the Jews who, he declared, were behind all Germany's enemies. Implicitly, he also used his opportunity to show his rivals at court that he could direct against them the terrible engine of a fanatical mob. At the climax of the speech, he posed ten carefully prepared questions and extracted (with the aid of canned applause on gramophone records) a hideous chorus of rhythmical assent. After his speech, he was carried shoulder-high from

* *The Goebbels Diaries*, ed. P. Lochner (1948), p. 322.
† Ibid., p. 329.

the hall; then he relaxed in the company of Albert Speer who was ultimately to be the effective organiser of the total war of which Goebbels was merely the trumpeter. To Speer's astonishment, Goebbels quietly and complacently analysed, as a purely technical exercise, the speech which, at the time, had seemed a spontaneous emotional outburst. Even at his most fanatical, Goebbels was always the dispassionate realist, observing, with detached, professional expertise, the effect of his own carefully rehearsed mob-oratory.*

Having thus whipped up the radicalism of the masses, Goebbels turned, by natural instinct, to acts of destruction. As Gauleiter of Berlin, he ordered the closure of all expensive restaurants. This, predictably, led to a clash with Göring, who was a regular patron, and protector, of the most famous and luxurious of such restaurants, Horcher's in the Lutherstrasse. Göring attempted to exempt Horcher's from what he called "the crazy Goebbels regulations," and provided a guard to defend the place. Thereupon Goebbels organised a "spontaneous" demonstration. The windows of the restaurant were smashed; Goebbels refused the proprietor's request for police protection, and after long and bitter recriminations Göring was obliged to yield—for a time. This minor "Kristallnacht" was Goebbels' one concrete contribution to the "totalisation of the war."

Like so many of his gestures, it was ill-timed; for precisely at this moment Goebbels needed, or thought that he needed, the help of Göring. In the excitement generated by the new programme of total war, Goebbels and Speer, now closely allied ("Speer is entirely mine," wrote Goebbels) believed that, with Göring's help, they might displace Bormann's "kitchen cabinet," the Committee of Three. Goebbels himself had hopes of replacing Ribbentrop, the asinine Foreign Minister whom Hitler persisted in regarding as a second Bismarck. So, for a few weeks, there was a buzz of high-powered intrigue. In the interest of the new alliance, the Horcher affair was redressed: the

* Speer, op. cit., p. 257.

restaurant was reopened as a Luftwaffe club under the high patronage of the Reich Marshall as Commander-in-Chief; and Goebbels suddenly found himself praising Göring's open-hearted geniality. "His dress," he admitted, "is somewhat baroque, and would, if one did not know him, strike one as almost laughable. But that's the way he is, and one must put up with his idiosyncracies; they sometimes even have a charm about them."*

The attempt by Speer and Goebbels to use Göring and oust Bormann from the centre of power was a complete failure. In fact, as Speer afterwards discovered, it had been doomed from the start, for Bormann had already seduced Göring with a gift of six million marks from Party funds. So Göring sank back into his usual self-indulgent lethargy, from which (as Speer writes) "he only awoke at Nuremberg." Goebbels had to admit defeat and settle for a *modus vivendi* with Bormann. It was an uneasy settlement: Goebbels privately referred to Bormann as "a primitive OGPU type"; but in view of Bormann's absolute control over access to Hitler it was a necessity; and Goebbels kept it, reluctantly, to the very end.

However Goebbels did not give up his ambitions of greater political power, and with each new misfortune he tried to reassert the necessity of greater radicalism in all things, and of himself as the director of it. In pursuit of such aims he was forced into alliance not only with the hated Bormann but also with the equally hated Reichsführer of the SS, Heinrich Himmler. Being himself, in his own view, "a man of fine feeling," Goebbels could not bear the "inartistic" Himmler, with his "Asiatic" slanting eyes, his short fat fingers, his dirty nails.† Still, he was attracted by the radicalism and the brutality of that terrible ogre who had built (as he remarked) "the greatest power organisation that one can imagine"; he approved whole-heartedly of the extermination of the Jews which Himmler was so efficiently carrying out; and he followed his own infallible

* *The Goebbels Diaries*, p. 197.
† Semler, op. cit., p. 96.

nose for power. By July 1943 Goebbels went so far as to urge Hitler to replace Göring as Commander-in-Chief of the Luftwaffe—only to incur a rebuff: to his disgust, Hitler absolutely refused to dismiss his old comrade.

As the war news worsened—when the Allies invaded Italy and Mussolini was overthrown—Goebbels even turned against Hitler himself. As in 1925, he began again to think that "the petty bourgeois Adolf Hitler" was not radical enough, and he blamed himself for having built up his image and created the legend of his infallibility. One of his assistants noted that he now mentioned the Führer less often. "He feels himself superior to Hitler: he cannot admit any longer the sole and unconditional authority of a man whom he himself made great." He no longer thought Hitler capable of mastering the difficulties of the time, and regularly sighed that "if I were the Führer," things would be different. Rumours were put about that he was to be Vice-Chancellor or Prime Minister. However, this mood did not last. As in 1925, Hitler's powerful personality, and Goebbels' own inner emptiness, would once again bring him round. He needed an object of devotion and could not long reject the idol he had made. So, as the clouds gathered more thickly around its base, he would build up the image of the Führer higher than ever, to tower above them.

This psychological process was described by one of Goebbels' assistants. "Whenever Goebbels goes to Hitler's headquarters," wrote Rudolf Semler, "he starts off full of distrust of the Führer's genius, full of irritation, criticism and hard words. Each time he is determined to tell Hitler just what he thinks. What happens in their talks, I don't know; but every time that Goebbels returns from these visits, he is full of admiration for the Führer and exudes an optimism which infects us all."

The political post which Goebbels coveted for himself most of all was that of Foreign Minister, and in April 1944 he once again sought to attain it. By now he despaired of winning the war and looked to diplomacy to save something from the wreck. But on which front, he asked, could peace be made? Since Churchill and Roosevelt seemed implacable, he argued that attempts should be made to buy off Russia. He therefore wrote a forty-page memorandum urging a return to the position of 1939–40 under the Nazi–Soviet Pact, and submitted it to Hitler. In the present parlous conditions, when the life of Germany was at stake, it would be wrong, he said, to let ideology lead us into ruin, and he proposed to surrender to Russia all Eastern Europe from North Norway to Greece inclusive. So radical a change in foreign policy, he admitted, would entail changes at the Foreign Office. Ribbentrop, as the man responsible for Germany's present diplomatic isolation, must go. Goebbels then assured Hitler of his own disinterested loyalty and offered to shoulder the heavy burden of this daring experiment in foreign policy.*

Having submitted his memorandum, he waited anxiously for a call to the Führer's Headquarters. It was strangely delayed. When it did come, Hitler never mentioned the memorandum. Finally Goebbels asked him about it. "What memorandum?" asked Hitler. After a search, it was found, buried in Bormann's in-tray.† Bormann had suppressed it because it was contrary to Party doctrine. Hitler was committed to a policy of Eastern conquest and could hardly be expected to go suddenly into reverse. Goebbels, who was committed to no doctrine, was capable of greater flexibility. To the very end he would be willing to make peace—of a kind—with Russia rather than with the West; but to the very end Ribbentrop would remain Foreign Minister of the Reich.

Three months later Goebbels made another, and this time a decisive, intervention in politics. On 20 July 1944 a group of conspirators in the Army General Staff sought to assassinate Hitler by placing a bomb under the conference table at his headquarters at Rastenburg in East Prussia. The attempt failed, but the conspirators went ahead: they announced his death and in the confusion which followed they might still have succeeded in seizing power in Berlin.

* Semler, op. cit., pp. 119–121.
† Ibid, pp. 122–3.

The crucial moment came when a crack regiment of guards was ordered to cordon off the Ministries of the Reich and effectively imprison the government. The commander of the regiment, Major Remer, a loyal Nazi, had his doubts and took the precaution of making contact with the Gauleiter, Goebbels. Goebbels informed him that Hitler was alive and then, to prove that this time he was telling the truth, telephoned to the Führer's Headquarters. Hitler spoke personally to Remer and told him to place himself under Himmler's orders and suppress the revolt ruthlessly. From that moment, the revolt was doomed. Goebbels himself addressed the troops in his office garden. Remer accepted his new duties with alacrity and led his troops to capture not the Reich government but the War Ministry, the headquarters of the conspirators. By the evening all was over. Goebbels' prompt action had saved the day, and Nazism itself, for another nine months.

It also enabled Goebbels to gratify once again his taste for revenge and destruction. That same night he turned his house into "a prison, headquarters and court rolled into one"; Goebbels himself headed a commission of investigation; and he and Himmler cross-examined the arrested generals throughout the night. Those condemned, then or thereafter, were executed with revolting cruelty. They were hanged from meat-hooks and slowly strangled. Goebbels ordered a film to be made of their trial and execution; it was to be shown, *in terrorem*, to Wehrmacht audiences. However, the reaction of the first audience was so hostile that it had to be suppressed.* The purge spread throughout Germany, and some of the victims were still being executed in the last days of the Reich.

Goebbels also exploited the Plot to demand, once again, a totalisation of war. He went himself to Rastenburg and told Hitler that it was partly the faults of the leadership which had led the Plot; that the war could not go on in the present desultory way; and that there was now no alternative to total war. Once again he offered himself to

---

* J. W. Wheeler Bennett, *The Nemesis of Power* (1953), p. 684.

undertake the thankless task, and guaranteed in three months to raise a new army of a million men. Hitler agreed. He appointed Goebbels Reich Commissioner for Total Mobilisation of Resources for War. As he travelled back by train to Berlin, Goebbels said to his assistant, "if I had received these powers when I wanted them so badly"— that is, in January 1943—"victory would be in our pockets today and the war would probably be over. But it takes a bomb under his arse to make Hitler see reason."*

Once again, Goebbels' measures were largely negative. While Speer streamlined the armaments industry, Goebbels imposed restrictions on travel, closed theatres and luxury shops, stopped publications. He also organised violence against defeatism and preached nihilism, "scorched earth," self-immolation. As the war became more desperate, he positively gloated in the destruction of German cities—the less we possess, he cried, the freer we are to fight. Meanwhile, all traitors must be rooted out and all restraints on the savagery of war removed. He called for more and more executions. He urged Hitler to use a deadly poison-gas, Tabun;† and in February 1945 he proposed that he denounce the Geneva Convention and order that all British and American pilots in prisoner-of-war camps be shot. This, he said, would both stop the Allied bombing and deter German soldiers from surrendering in the West, lest they be treated likewise. Those already captured, apparently, could be written off. At the same time he was still seeking to enlarge his own political power. He would have Ribbentrop removed, Göring tried before a People's Court, and would himself take over complete control. He would raise armies, re-create the extinct Luftwaffe. Why should he not rule all Germany as he ruled Berlin? He would be Prime Minister, Foreign Minister, Chancellor of the Reich . . .‡

In the end he would obtain his wishes. Hitler would dismiss Göring. He would drop Ribbentrop. He would give

---

* Semler, op. cit., p. 147.
† Speer, op. cit., p. 413.
‡ Semler, op. cit., pp. 179–80.

Goebbels full power to reform the Luftwaffe. He would appoint him Chancellor of the Reich. But by then it would all be too late, far too late. For months the great realist had been the victim of his own propaganda. He had believed that, somehow, the war could still be won.

How was it to be won? Not militarily: that was now clearly impossible. With the enemy advancing from East and West, and in complete command of the air, Germany was overpowered. But if only the fronts could hold out a little longer, perhaps diplomacy would succeed where arms could not. Had not Frederick the Great, Hitler's hero and therefore also his own, once been in precisely such a position? And had he not, by holding firm, even when the military situation seemed hopeless, in the end, by an unpredictable diplomatic revolution, snatched victory from the jaws of defeat? That revolution, "the miracle of the House of Brandenburg," had been the death of the Czarina, Elizabeth, which had caused Russia to abandon the coalition against Prussia. And then there was the second Punic War, 2000 years earlier, when Hannibal, having crossed the Alps, and won the battles of Trasimene and Cannae, was at the gates of Rome, and yet Rome, by playing for time, had in the end defeated him and so gone on to rule the world . . . Such were the hopes on which Goebbels, in the last months of the war, fed Hitler, the German people, and himself.

From 16 January 1945, when Hitler returned to Berlin after directing the Ardennes offensive, the last German counter-attack in the West, Goebbels had regular access to the Führer and was able to exert all his personal influence on him. That is, he was able to encourage him in his fantasies of victory, and give to those fantasies the gloss and edge of his own. So, in the intervals of denouncing his own rivals for their incompetence or defeatism, he read Carlyle's *Life of Frederick the Great*, Dr. Frank on the second Punic War, the history of Prussia's fight against Napoleon. From history, or his own news-bulletins, he snatched at every straw of comfort and often stopped to hear, and admire, the echo of his own propaganda. To infect Hitler with his own radicalism he pressed upon him photographs of bombed cities and ruined architectural monuments—for Hitler himself had never visited a bombed city. He urged Hitler, who had fallen silent since 20 July 1944, to address the nation. He demanded a new diplomatic initiative. The war, he insisted, would go on for a long time: why should not Russia be detached from the enemy alliance and converted into an ally to roll back the Western front? Meanwhile, he looked forward to the future. Publicly, he assumed that it would be a Nazi future. But even if that should fail, it must be a future that would be interested in Nazism, a future which would be reached by his own propaganda, and would see Hitler, and Nazism, and himself, through his eyes.

So he continued to write. Even in the last weeks of the war, when the enemy armies were closing in, he was still writing: books, articles, diaries. In March 1945 we find him correcting the proofs of a new book, *The Law of War*. Even later, he is writing an article on *History as Teacher*—no doubt on the Punic War or Frederick the Great. And every day, now as before, he dictated his diary: that diary that was to be—and will still be, in spite of everything—a primary source for the detailed history of the years of Nazism.

The documentary history of Goebbels' diary is told, in this volume, by Peter Stadelmayer. Some of it—a discontinuous part of it embracing the years 1942–43—is already in print. Much more of it now exists in typescript. This volume contains the last surviving part of it. It begins before the Western Allies had crossed the Rhine and when Hitler could still hope to counter-attack against the Russians in Hungary. It ends with the evident collapse of Nazism, hostile armies in the heart of the Reich, and Hitler relying, since all else had failed, on horoscopes and his star.

There is no need for me to summarise the dramatic history of those six weeks, or Goebbels' reactions to them. The diary is here, and it needs no commentary. I will only observe that Goebbels, on every page, is true to himself. Here we see his opportunism, his radicalism, his nihilism, his hatred of humanity; but also his incredible mental energy, his unfailing flair for propaganda, and his personal courage. Most prominent of all, perhaps, is his passion for destruction. In these last weeks, he is still raging against Göring and Ribbentrop, denouncing those who—like Speer —wish to save anything of Germany independently of Nazism, castigating whole classes, whole groups, whole nations: the miserable bourgeoisie, the generals, the Luft-waffe, the Churches, the Jews, the Swiss, the Swedes. In particular, it is Göring, Ribbentrop and the generals whom he detests: Göring for his sybaritic indolence, which has left Germany helpless in the air, Ribbentrop for his diplo-matic uselessness which has allowed the world to unite against it, the generals for treasonable reluctance to fight a revolutionary war. Why, he asks, did we not shoot the generals instead of the SA in 1934! Stalin was right: he purged his entire General Staff. Stalin indeed is the only man to be praised in these pages. Fortunately, Hitler now agrees that peace should be made with Stalin. Stalin at least is a realist. Of course, the Führer admits, we could not now attain our war-aims of 1941—the permanent occupa-tion of Russia up to the Urals, the total demolition of Leningrad and Moscow—but we would settle for Hungary, Croatia and half of Poland, and then join Russia to destroy the West . . . "This programme," comments Goebbels, "is grandiose and persuasive. The only objection is that there is no means of achieving it." Goebbels is at least more realistic than the Führer.

Perhaps it is not saying much. The reader of these diaries is more likely to be struck by the unreality than the reality of Goebbels' mental picture of the war. Everywhere he sees the liberated countries of the West about to revolt against their liberators, preferring German domination. The French, he says, are listening as eagerly to German as formerly to English broadcasts: already Europe regrets us. Industrial action is paralysing the West: we "must hang on till all Europe sinks in chaos." The Anglo-Americans are hopelessly incompetent: they understand neither war psychology nor war propaganda; how silly of the German people (and Himmler) to prefer them to the Russians! Stalin must be our model: the worse the military situation, the more ruthlessly the Party must secure its control over the whole country. Meanwhile there is room for diplomacy. Goebbels shows no inkling of an understanding of the plain fact that German diplomacy had lost all credibility, thanks to its control by the Nazi Party. It was not merely Ribbentrop who had failed: Nazism was now totally bankrupt. As Speer wrote, "there were differences of degree in the flight from reality," and Goebbels was "many times closer to recognizing actualities" than the other leaders; "but these differences shrink to nothing when we consider how remote all of us . . . were from what was really going on."*

On 6 April, when Goebbels' own commentary on events breaks off, he is still hoping against hope for a miraculous break-up of the enemy alliance. A week later he believed that such a break-up was imminent. On the evening of 13 April the news came that President Roosevelt had died. Goebbels was away from Berlin at the time, visiting the headquarters of General Busse's Ninth Army. There he had assured the officers that, if only the German army and people stood firm, a miracle might yet save them, like "the miracle of the House of Brandenburg" in 1762. The officers, it seems, had been sceptical: what kind of a miracle, they asked, could be expected now? On his return to Berlin, Goebbels was told the news. He was overjoyed. This, he declared, was the turning-point! . . . It was like the death of the Empress Elizabeth in the Seven Years War. He telephoned Busse's headquarters to rub home his point. He and Hitler were both, for a time, in ecstasy. They now looked to see America withdraw from the war. Goebbels told the Press to do nothing to irritate the new President: "our rejoicing at Roosevelt's death we must keep to ourselves."†

* Speer, op. cit., p. 291.

† This episode is described in the diary of Count Lutz Schwerin von Krosigk (cited in my *The Last Days of Hitler*) and, independently, by Semler, op. cit., pp. 190–3.

These hopes were quickly dashed. Roosevelt's death, it soon became clear, made no difference to American policy, and the armies of East and West closed remorselessly in on German soil. Four days later Goebbels had given up hope of miracles and decided to prepare for the end. But even the end must be dramatised, turned into propaganda. On 17 April Goebbels summoned his staff together. Some fifty men were there, and many of them were demanding to be released to the fighting forces in order to escape from the doomed capital. Goebbels spoke to them about a new colour-film *Kolberg*, which had recently been released. Then he spoke of another even more splendid colour-film which would be shown a hundred years hence. It would be the film of the Twilight of the Gods in Berlin in 1945. Did they not wish to appear with credit in that film? "I can assure you it will be a fine and elevating picture, and for the sake of this prospect it is worth standing fast. Hold out now, so that a hundred years hence the audience does not hoot and whistle when you appear on the screen!" His staff were not impressed by these heroic gestures. They looked at him with amazement and concluded that he had gone off his head.*

Five days later, on 22 April 1945, when the Russians had almost encircled Berlin, the Propaganda Ministry, like other government offices, broke up. Those who did not wish to feature posthumously in Goebbels' imaginary film flew to Obersalzberg in order to fall into Western hands. Goebbels himself, after dictating his last (and now lost) diary entry, moved into the Führerbunker under the Reich Chancellery, thence to direct the last battles of Hitler's war and his own propaganda. There, with Martin Bormann, his uneasy partner to the end, he witnessed the last convulsions of Nazism and attended to its last ceremonies: the marriage of Hitler and Eva Braun, their suicide, the lurid funeral in the Chancellery garden. Then, with all his family, he too committed suicide, having first seen to it that a manifesto should reach the world to put the correct

* Semler, op. cit., pp. 193–4.

propagandist gloss on this final gesture of annihilation. He destroyed himself, typically, in the shadow of his leader, whose votive lamp he had tended, making himself visible only by its rays.

For Goebbels was essentially a man of words, images, gestures. He had no ideas, no beliefs of his own. Positive aims he had none: even the positive aims of Nazism— race, blood, an empire in the East—meant nothing to him. His life consisted entirely of reactions, not actions. Hence his need of perpetual motion. He depended on external stimulus because he had no inner impulse, and needed incessant activity as an escape from inner emptiness. Hence also his intellectual and political agility. He piqued himself on his objectivity, his freedom from prejudice; but his very freedom from prejudice was a function of his own lack of beliefs, and he valued his perception of reality only as a means towards its distortion. The ideas which he assumed were entirely borrowed. Until he discovered Hitler, he lived in a void, clutching at changing ideologies, feeding on nihilism and resentment. Thereafter, he lived on Hitler, and although he could detach himself from Hitler, and the image of Hitler which he had created, he could not detach himself for long: his own essential nullity always drove him back. Even the trappings of his intellectual world were imitated from Hitler: he, the university graduate, the doctor of philosophy, would read and quote only the books, or the subjects, recommended by that self-taught genius: Schopenhauer, Frederick the Great, the Punic War. Left to himself, his only ideal was destruction. His great theatrical gestures were always an incitement to destruction: hymns of hate against the bourgeoisie, the bolsheviks, the Jews. His chosen form of action was destructive violence: organised street-riots, broken plate-glass windows, bonfires of books. His chosen ceremonial was the funeral: the funeral of Horst Wessel, regular funerals of SS-men, the funeral-march for Stalingrad. His funeral oratory was proverbial: he was known as "the Reich Funeral Master." In the last months, it was natural that he should direct his destructive spirit against Germany itself; that his last ceremony should be the funeral of Hitler; and that then, when the necessary host had gone, the parasite should quietly extinguish itself. He would happily have extinguished Germany too. After the extinction of its ruling class, he said, the German people could not live. As Hitler himself said, it was not worthy to live.

THE STORY OF THE
1945 GOEBBELS DIARIES

Peter Stadelmayer

Up to 8 July 1941 Goebbels wrote his diary entries in manuscript. From 9 July onwards the "stenographer at the Minister's disposal" took down the entries, which were dictated at high speed, transcribed them on a "Continental" typewriter with specially large type (one carbon, both sheets of same quality) and was responsible for safe keeping.

These entries begin with 9 July 1941 and, like the manuscript diaries, invariably deal with events of the previous day, starting with "Military Situation," the basis of which was the briefing by the Wehrmacht Liaison Officer from OKW [Oberkommando der Wehrmacht—High Command of the German Armed Forces]. This briefing was given every morning to a small circle in the Minister's study, occasionally—and towards the end of the war invariably—with the stenographer present: it differed from the "Situation Report" given at the subsequent Minister's conference in that it gave a less varnished account. The "Military Situation" paragraphs reproduced in this book were drafted by the OKW liaison officer and the stenographer.

Entries dictated by the Minister were taken down word for word. They were intended as raw material for subsequent publications and were not, therefore, in final form. According to both his stenographers, Goebbels never asked to see the transcripts of his dictated entries and so made no amendments to them. This explains many of the careless errors which the author would certainly have corrected when revising for publication. It is both specially valuable and specially fascinating for the present-day reader to be able, so to speak, to listen to the most articulate of the Third Reich's leaders dictating a rough draft. One suspects, for instance, that, had Goebbels read through his dictation with pencil in hand, the Bourbon Princess who suggested that people clamouring for bread should eat cake, would turn back into the Habsburg Princess Marie-Antoinette who was married to a Bourbon.

Towards the end of the war dictated diary entries, by this time a considerable pile, together with the black oil-cloth manuscript diaries, were in the Reich Propaganda Ministry's safes. During the last months of the war various official agencies in Berlin "microcopied" their most important files and at this time Richard Otte, the stenographer who kept the diaries, was ordered to direct and supervise microcopying of the Goebbels diaries. By this time the permanent diary stenographer was Otto Jacobs. Richard Otte had been temporarily seconded in 1938 from the German News Agency (DNB) to the Reich Ministry for Popular Enlightenment and Propaganda where he joined the Minister's stenographic service and was used to take minutes at conferences; in 1941 he became "stenographer at the Minister's disposal" with the rank of Regierungstrat [lowest rank in the Higher Civil Service]. By contrast Otto Jacobs, who was also seconded to the Ministry in 1941, retained his professional connection with the German News Agency during those years. After the war Otte and Jacobs worked in the Federal Republic as parliamentary and diplomatic stenographers, Richard Otte initially in the Lower Saxony Landtag, later in the German Bundestag and Bundesrat. Until 1974 Otto Jacobs was head parliamentary stenographer of the Hamburg Municipality, for which he still works in retirement.

Otte and Jacobs worked in Goebbels' Ministry until 22 April 1945, the Sunday on which the Goebbels family moved into the Reich Chancellery bunker. Otto Jacobs remembers taking diary dictation and transcribing it up to 22 April. Apart from the extracts now produced here for the first time, however, all other entries in Goebbels' diary of 1945 must be considered to have vanished.

Otte and Jacobs have done a great deal of work on the material now published unabridged in this book. Jacobs recognised his own orthography of the time, for instance his preference for "ss" as opposed to the German "ß," and Otte recognised his handwriting in notes for the photographer doing the microcopying. The publisher is grateful to both these gentlemen for their help in checking passages which were difficult to read.

To judge from the notes referred to above, microcopying was done at that time on "plates" each capable of "taking" 45 DIN A4 sheets at a time in 5 rows each of 9 sheets. The fragment produced here begins with page 52, entry dictated on 28 February 1945, and in the top left-hand corner is the figure "41" in Otte's handwriting. It may be supposed that for purposes of microcopying page 1 of the entry for 1 January 1945 was given the figure 1 and therefore that diary entries filling 40 plates for the 59 days of the first two months of 1945 averaged about 30 pages ($40 \times 45 = 1800$, $1800 = 59 \times 30$ approx.). This corresponds to the volume of the dictation published here.

Initially we were uncertain whether the first entry reproduced here should be dated 27 or 28 February; the nearest number (42) which, at the normal rate of 45 sheets per plate, would not be found until 38 pages after page 59, is to be found on page 1 of the entry for 1 March. Plate 41, therefore, may have contained an entry for a further day consisting of 37 pages. The diary of Linge, Hitler's valet, however, shows that Goebbels visited Hitler at 6:45 p.m. on 27 February. Since all Goebbels' diary entries refer to the previous day, in all probability pages 52–9 were dictated on 28 February.

Study of the lay-out of plates also leads to the conclusion that Plate 70, which has vanished taking with it parts of the entries dictated on 2 and 3 April, contained the last 25 pages (pp. 21–45) for 2 April and the first 20 pages of 3 April (25 plus 20 = 45 = 1 plate).

So far neither the originals nor the plates of the 1945 transcripts have been found. The material published here has been compiled from a film copy on perforated microfilm, Type ORWO S NP 15, originating from East Germany. This copy is part of the voluminous material offered to Hoffmann & Campe in October 1972 by the journalist Erwin Fischer and handed over shortly thereafter for publication purposes.

Parts of Goebbels' diaries have already appeared in print. After the "Seizure of Power" (30 January 1933) Goebbels himself incorporated extracts from his 1932/3 diaries in his book *Vom Keiserhof zur Reichskanzlei* (Munich 1934). Shortly after the war Louis P. Lochner, the American journalist, published a selection of fragments from the 1942/3 diaries; these were from the actual originals, the existence of which had become known by devious means to the American occupation authorities in Berlin at or shortly after the end of the war and which had been placed in safe custody by them (*The Goebbels Diaries* 1942–43, Hamish Hamilton, London 1948).

In 1960 Helmut Heiber, the German historian, published through the Institut für Zeitgeschichte an annotated edition of fragments from the manuscript diaries of 1925/6.

The originals of the entries for 1942/3 and 1925/6 are in the Hoover Institution in Stanford, California. Photocopies of these are kept in the Institut für Zeitgeschichte, Munich, which also has a small stock of hitherto unpublished originals of 1942/3; to some extent these overlap with the film material available to the present publishers.

It is known from books, and has been and still is confirmed by surviving members of Goebbels' staff, that he regarded his diaries, which he kept with astounding regularity, as his most valuable possession. The conscientious process of microcopying also proves that he wanted them to be preserved.

Wilfred von Oven, one of Goebbels' last two Press Officers, maintains in his diary (*Mit Goebbels bis zum Ende*, 2 vols., Buenos Aires 1948/50; single-volume new edition entitled *Finale Furioso*, Tübingen 1974) that several photocopies of the diaries were made and buried in various places. Richard Otte corrects this statement, which may be based on rumour, as follows: "I made only one micro-

copy of the diaries, a negative on plates. The Ministry did not want a positive (contact print) to be made although it would have required less storage space than the plates. As the situation in Berlin became critical, it was intended that the originals should be taken to the 'Alpine Fortress.' After being microcopied they were packed in metal containers ('officers' chests') and presumably (I was not responsible for this stage) taken to the Reich Chancellery. Their move to the 'Alpine Fortress' never took place because, with the Americans and Russians meeting on the Elbe, the road to Bavaria was closed."

Wilfred von Oven says that the documents were buried some days before 18 April 1945. Otte remembers being present about the middle of April when an "officer's chest" containing the photographic plates of the microcopy was buried to a depth of three feet in the wood between Michendorf and Caputh not far from the autobahn.

- 52 -

Wir müssen so sein, wie Friedrich der Grosse gewesen
ist, und uns auch so benehmen. Der Führer stimmt mir
völlig zu, wenn ich ihm sage, dass es unser Ehrgeiz
sein soll, dafür zu sorgen, dass, wenn in Deutsch-
land einmal in 150 Jahren eine gleich grosse Krise
auftaucht,unsere Enkel sich auf uns als das heroische
Beispiel der Standhaftigkeit berufen können. Auch
die stoisch-philosophische Haltung zu den Menschen
und zu den Ereignissen, die der Führer heute ein-
nimmt, erinnert stark an Friedrich den Grossen. Er
sagt mir zum Beispiel, dass es nötig sei, für sein |
             dass
Volk zu arbeiten, aber daß auch das nur begrenztes
Menschenwerk sein könne. Wer wisse, wann wieder einmal ein Mondeinbruch in die Erde stattfinde und diese.

Yelena Rshevskaya, the Russian historian, says in her book *Hitlers Ende ohne Mythos* (Deutscher Militärverlag, East Berlin 1967) that, when working as an interpreter with a special detachment in early May 1945, she had to "sift innumerable papers and documents" in the bunker of the Reich Chancellery; they included Goebbels' diaries. She says: "One of our most important discoveries was Goebbels' diaries, a dozen thick folders, closely written in a close perpendicular hand—difficult to read. The first folios referred to 1932, when the fascists were not yet in power; the last ended in mid-1941 . . . I wrote a short summary of contents and then they were sent to Front Headquarters."

The Polish historian Juliusz Stroynowski, now living in the Federal Republic, told the publishers that in 1967 he stumbled across several stacked folders containing Goebbels' diaries in the archives of the Russian Ministry of Defence. He was allowed to examine this material in connection with his research work but was not allowed to take photocopies.

Readers of Albert Speer's *Spandau Diaries* will perhaps wonder about "the last entry in Goebbels' diary" copied out by Speer on 13 May 1947 and quoted in that book. Speer found this quotation, as he was good enough to tell us, in the *Nürnberger Nachrichten* of 6 May 1947, where it was given without reference to source. It was not in fact a quote from Joseph Goebbels, but fiction. The newspaper was quoting faithfully from a book *Wie konnte es geschehen— Auszüge aus den Tagebüchern und Bekenntnissen eines Kriegsverbrechers* [How could it happen—Extracts from the Diaries and Confessions of a War Criminal] by Max Fechner (J.H.W. Dietz II GmbH, Berlin 1946). The author, at one time Deputy Chairman of the Socialist Unity Party with Walter Ulbricht, wrote in his "Afterword" to these fictitious records by Dr. Joseph Goebbels: "This is how he ought to have written, had he been honest. But he was a great liar and remained so until he took his poison. We have accordingly taken the pen from his hand."

The present publishers [Hoffmann & Campe] have available copies of nearly 16,000 pages of the diaries from the years 1924 to 1945 together with other written material from Goebbels' papers. Over 4,000 pages are in manuscript and over 11,000 typewritten. The total volume is approximately equivalent to 20,000 of the diary pages reproduced in facsimile on p. xlvi.

The Annexes to the present book contain a selection of documents from the days for which no diary entries by Goebbels are available. The "Chronology" extends beyond the death of Hitler and Goebbels to the end of the Third Reich.

As this first volume appears the publishers express the hope that other possessors of originals or copies will assist in completing Goebbels' literary estate and will make available to them further material for the publication of his records.

Translator's Note

Peter Stadelmayer explains that Goebbels dictated his diary entries, invariably referring to events of the previous day. The question therefore arose whether entries should be headed with the date of dictation or the date referred to; the German edition uses the date of dictation. However, this produces certain ostensibly erroneous statements. In this translation, therefore, the dates of entries are those on which the events in question occurred, not the dates on which the entry concerned was dictated. The word "yesterday" has been omitted from the "Military Situation" subheadings and on the comparatively rare occasions on which it appeared in the text.

Front lines of Allied Armies
at the dates shown

1st. Nov. 1944.
16th. April 1945

D.J.C.

1

- 8 -

[Dieseceächte haben augenblicklich für uns nur
och Spott und Hohn übrig. Sie fühlen sich auf der
Höhe der Situation und tun so, als hätten sie den
Krieg bereits gewonnen. Sie halten unsere Moral für
stark angeschlagen und geben uns keinerlei Siegeg-
aussichten mehr. Der Volkssturm ist nach ihren Dar-
stellungen eine müde Altemänner-Garde. Die Bevölke-
rung der besetzten Gebiete habe schon vom national-
sozialistischen Regime und von der nationalsozialisti-
schen Führung Abschied genommen; sie lege ihnen ge-
genüber eine devote Unterwürfigkeitanden Tag, die
geradezu peinlich wirke. Von einer geordneten deut-
schen Verwaltung könne weder in den besetzten noch
in den unbesetzten Gebieten sehr dieRede sein. Das

TUESDAY 27 FEBRUARY 1945

(pp. 52–59 of dictation transcript, pp. 1–51 missing)

We must be as Frederick the Great was and act as he did. The Führer agrees with me entirely when I say to him that it should be our ambition to ensure that, should a similar great crisis arise in Germany, say in 150 years' time, our grandchildren may look back on us as a heroic example of steadfastness. The stoic philosophical attitude to people and events adopted by the Führer today is very reminiscent of Frederick the Great. He says to me, for instance, that it is essential to work for one's people but that there is a limit to what men can do. Who knows when the moon may not crash into the earth and this whole planet go up in flames and ashes. Nevertheless, he says, it must be our mission to do our duty to the last. In these matters the Führer too is a stoic and a complete disciple of Frederick the Great whom, consciously and unconsciously, he emulates. That must be a model and an example to us all. How gladly would we wholeheartedly copy this model and example. If only Göring was not so completely out of line. He is no National-Socialist but a sybarite and certainly no disciple of Frederick the Great. In contrast what a fine imposing impression is made by Dönitz.* As the Führer told me he is the best man in his whole arm of the service. Look at the invariably gratifying results he has achieved with the Navy. Raeder was also a man of the highest class,

---

* Grand Admiral Dönitz had replaced Grand Admiral Raeder as Commander-in-Chief, German Navy, in 1943. He was a strong Nazi (see below p. 225). As such, Hitler would designate him, in his will, as his successor as President (but not Führer) of the Reich.

1

the Führer says; he had shown unwavering loyalty to the Führer and had instilled into his arm of the service a spirit which had enabled it today to erase the stain on the German Navy left by the World War. It is a pity that the Party is represented, not by a man like that but by Göring, who has as much to do with the Party as a cow with radiology. But, as I have said, this problem must now be solved. It is no longer any good skating over these things and it is of no help to the Führer if one tries to spare him by holding one's tongue.

The discussion which I had with the Führer over this, in my view, completely fundamental problem of our war leadership was very dramatic and heated. But the Führer agreed with me on every point. I feel in fact that he is annoyed that things should have gone so far, not that I spoke so bluntly and frankly. On the contrary he complimented me on it, took my side openly and unreservedly and expressed his pleasure that I for one made no bones about my views. I told him that I had recently been reading Carlyle's book on Frederick the Great. The Führer knows the book very well himself. I repeated certain passages from the book to him and they affected him very deeply. That is how we must be and that is how we will be. If someone like Göring dances totally out of line, then he must be called to order. Bemedalled idiots and vain perfumed coxcombs have no place in our war leadership. Either they must mend their ways or be eliminated. I shall not rest or repose until the Führer has put this in order. He must change Göring both inside and outside or show him the door. For instance it is simply grossly bad style for the senior officer of the Reich, in the present wartime situation, to strut round in a silver-gray uniform. What effeminate behaviour in face of present developments! It is to be hoped that the Führer will succeed in turning Göring into a man again. The Führer is glad that Göring's wife has now moved to the Obersalzberg because she was a bad influence on him. Anyway Göring's whole entourage is not worth a row of beans. It encouraged instead of restraining his tendency to effeminacy and pleasure-seeking. By contrast the Führer

2

had high praise for the simplicity and purity of my family life. This is the only way to meet the demands of the present times.

I have the very definite impression that this discussion with the Führer made a real impact. It was necessary and the timing was entirely right. We argued so loudly that the aides outside could hear what we said through the door. They were extremely pleased. These splendid young men are interested solely in seeing the Party led back to its true essence and nature since only in this way can the fortunes of this war be turned. All these young people are on my side and look upon me as their mouthpiece since I can say to the Führer point-blank what has to be said. Round the dinner-table in the Reich Chancellery there sits a worn-out collection of officers. I barely say "good evening" to them. These people are as foreign to me as men can be.

Back at home I have a mountain of work to deal with. But I can now get on with it very quickly and energetically since I have got a real burden off my chest.

In the evening we have the regulation Mosquito raid on Berlin once more.

The situation in the West causes me great anxiety. What will happen if the enemy really makes a break-through here? But we will not assume the worst. The great thing is that I have at last succeeded in hacking my way through this fundamental question of our war leadership.

During the night the cursed Englishmen return to Berlin with their Mosquitos and deprive one of the few hours' sleep which one needs more than ever these days.

WEDNESDAY 28 FEBRUARY 1945

(pp. 1–33)
Military Situation.

In Hungary no special developments. In Slovakia several violent enemy attacks at Altsohl were repulsed. In the entire Silesian sector as far as the area south of Breslau no fighting of significance. An enemy salient at Schwarzwasser was eliminated in one of our attacks. Apart from a break-in at Lauban numerous enemy attacks between Strehlen and Görlitz were repulsed. The enemy succeeded in penetrating into the northern outskirts of Lauban. Enemy attacks near Goldberg were very heavy but all were repulsed. Street fighting continues on the outskirts of Breslau. Local Soviet attacks on Forst and Guben failed. In the Oder sector the Bolshevists were able to expand their bridgehead at Lebus slightly by means of a local attack. A strong local enemy attack south of Pyritz was repulsed. In the area between Rummelsburg and Neustettin the Bolshevists were able to increase the depth of their break-in. They took Neustettin and pushed on a few kilometres farther west to the Neustettin–Kolberg and Neustettin–Falkenburg railway. An enemy attempt to advance from Bublitz towards Köslin was frustrated. From Pollnow the enemy succeeded in advancing as far as Latzig heading for Schlawe. In this sector the emergency defence unit from an air base at Stolp was sent into action at Pollnow; it had 15 *Panzerfaust* and destroyed 11 enemy tanks, losing only one man in the process. In the sector northwards from Konitz to the Vistula numerous local enemy attacks were repulsed, particularly at Heiderode; the enemy succeeded in breaking in north of Konitz. In East Prussia fighting was generally not quite so severe as on previous days, but particularly violent attacks took place north of Zinten. Our defence was again entirely successful. In Courland too violent enemy attacks were once more repulsed.

On the Western Front the British and Canadians made only small local gains of ground despite violent attacks southwards from Goch. Most of the attacks were repulsed. In the area of the major American offensive the enemy has now deployed all his reserves of armour and is attempting to push on eastwards. So far he has nowhere achieved a break-through or operational freedom of movement but his gains of ground have not been insignificant nevertheless. He pushed farther along the railway from Erkelenz towards Rheydt and along the road from Erkelenz to München-Gladbach. Here fighting is taking place some 3–5 km west and south-west of the suburbs of Rheydt. German units are everywhere offering stiff resistance and inflicting severe losses on the enemy. In the sector north-east and east of Julich the enemy was also able to gain ground. His leading units are now in the Erft valley on the west bank of the Erft. He has thus covered half the distance from Jülich to Köln. South of this he reached the Düren–Köln road in the area of Blatzheim. Severe fighting also continues on the Eifel front. Here the enemy has deployed an additional division withdrawn from Hagenau and replaced there by a French division. In the Bitburg depression the enemy is clearly trying to make progress towards Wittlich. North of Bitburg he has advanced farther towards the River Kyll. He succeeded in moving into Bitburg from the south. North of Welschbillig he crossed the Bitburg–Trier road. South of Trier, where the Americans advanced to Zerf, they increased the depth of their break-in, almost reaching the Ruwer valley. Enemy dispositions lead one to suspect that he will swing his flank units southwards from Bitburg and northwards from Zerf in order to capture Trier.

No operations of particular importance have been reported from the Italian front.

Enemy air activity in the East was fairly heavy. The

Soviets deployed a total of some 1200 aircraft, the majority in the area of the offensive in Pomerania. Our own air activity too was fairly heavy and successful. Once more numerous enemy tanks and assault guns were destroyed and his columns shot up. Our fighter-bombers sank an enemy torpedo-boat near Polangen.

In the West, owing to unfavourable weather enemy low-level and twin-engine bomber activity was somewhat smaller than usual.

Over Reich territory 1100 four-engined American bombers with strong fighter escort attacked transport installations at Halle and Leipzig. In the afternoon 150 British bombers with fighter escort attacked transport targets in Dortmund, Castrop-Rauxel and Recklinghausen. Some 300 British bombers made a raid on Mainz. Flying from Italy, 600 four-engined American bombers attacked industrial and transport targets in the Augsburg area. Some 80 aircraft from this formation made a subsidiary attack on Salzburg. So far 20 aircraft have been reported shot down. During the night two harassing raids were made on Berlin, in each case by some 70 Mosquitos.

The British and Americans are at present spreading horror stories about the situation in the West. They maintain that they have achieved a breakthrough all along the line and—as Montgomery in particular emphasises—are henceforth compelled to impose a news black-out so that no information of any value can reach us. The Americans specifically boast that they are only 15 km from Köln and that it is now only a trifling matter for them to reach the Rhine. During the day, however, these views have had to undergo fundamental revision. The resistance offered by our troops is so immense that even the enemy has had to admit that there is not the remotest question of a collapse of the German front.

By the evening their tone was much more subdued. British headquarters in particular stress most explicitly that there can be no talk of a break-through. Clearly they have overcalled their hand; they took our outpost position for the main front and only then did they encounter vast resistance which is now making it hard work for the enemy assault divisions. Enemy casualties are enormous. The Americans report mountains of dead and they no longer make any secret of the fact in their press. In addition there are the very high casualties they are suffering on the island of Iwo Jima. In short we are at the moment in a stage of the war when, by causing the enemy maximum casualties, we can exact the most respect from him. Undoubtedly this makes a very deep impression on Anglo-American public opinion.

In the evening it was suddenly stated in London that Rundstedt* had changed his tactics, that he was not giving battle on the forward line but trying to draw the attacking British and Americans on against lines farther in rear and that the effect of this would be highly disadvantageous for the attacking troops.

A debate is taking place in the Commons about the Crimea Conference.† A number of opposition Tory MPs have put down an amendment to the motion of confidence approved by the government and its implications for the relationship between England and her allies will be fairly embarrassing. The battle is over this amendment. The Churchill government is opposing its acceptance tooth and nail and the opposition naturally does not dare force matters as far as a public vote of no confidence. In his speech during the debate Greenwood, the deputy leader of the Labour Party, criticised most sharply the treatment meted out to the Poles at the Crimea Conference; on the Conservative side too severely critical speeches were to be heard. Without a doubt, however, Churchill will emerge from this debate unscathed. England is too weak to be able to afford a government crisis, particularly at this stage of the war. She went along with the rest, she will be

* Commander-in-Chief West.
† i.e. the Allied Conference at Yalta, 4–12 February 1945.

7

carried along with the rest and she will hang with the rest. She has started on the downward path and must now stew in her great dilemma.

Criticism of the Yalta decisions comes primarily from Tory circles. The group of Tories forming the inner circle has long been at work either to bring Churchill back onto the right course or to bring him down. In these circles people talk of Poland when of course they mean Germany. But at the moment this opposition is of no great importance to us. It cannot really get going for the reasons just described.

Churchill's remarks on the shipping situation produced great alarm. In addition a government spokesman in the Lords stated that the Allies had never had as much shipping as they have now but that there had never been such an extraordinary shortage of shipping. If our new U-boat operations can cash in on this situation they may, under the circumstances, have a disastrous effect on Anglo-American strategy.

Eden has let it be known to a private circle in the Commons that Churchill did not conclude a secret agreement in Yalta, as has been suspected. This question is of vital importance for the conduct of the debate in the Commons.

We hear from American sources that in November 1940 Pétain concluded a secret treaty with England to the effect that France would re-enter the war against Germany at a favourable moment. The treaty was concluded behind Laval's back. I think this entirely possible. Pétain has duped us and Laval too probably knew all about it. As the Anglo-American invasion proceeded they both expressed a wish to remain in Paris—and for good reason. I do not think they would have had to face trial for treason.

The strike movement in the USA appears to be growing and it is especially noticeable in the armaments sector. Such developments are now the order of the day in England and America. They are symptomatic of the profound political crisis prevalent in Western enemy countries.

The well-known American journalist von Wiegandt has

written an article about the worldwide threat of bolshevism; it follows preceisely the line of his last article headed "The Year 2000." Being published in the entire Hearst newspaper chain, this von Wiegandt article has created a real press sensation. The extent to which our theories are repeated in this article is truly astounding. The Hearst chain has always been anti-bolshevist but the fact that it has stuck its neck out so far in the present war situation seems to me of some significance. In any case, if Roosevelt now faces the American public, he will meet strong opposition.

The struggle over the Radescu* cabinet goes on in Rumania. The Bolshevists apparently intend to make *tabula rasa.* They are demanding Radescu's resignation and the instalment of a democratic people's government as they call it, in other words of a Soviet bolshevist regime. Vyshinsky,† the notorious bolshevist mass butcher, has now arrived in Bucharest. He will certainly do a proper job.

Innumerable reports of bolshevist atrocities are now coming in. They are horribly realistic and quite indescribable. I intend to give international publicity to these atrocity reports. I shall do this at a reception for the home and foreign press at which Colonel-General Guderian‡ will read out Zhukov's order to Soviet troops before their break-out from the Baranov§ bridgehead. To some extent this order gave the signal for bolshevist atrocities. Though I do not anticipate any immediate political repercussions, it will certainly have some long-term effect.

At midday I had a prolonged discussion with General Vlasov.¶ He is an extremely intelligent and energetic

---

* General Nicolae Radescu was the last non-communist Prime Minister of Rumania. He had been appointed by King Michael in December 1944.

† Stalin's Acting Commissar for Foreign Affairs.

‡ Chief of Army General Staff.

§ Marshal Zhukov, recently appointed commander of the Russian armies heading for Berlin, had issued a bloodthirsty order of the day, announcing a "cruel revenge" on "Hitler's cannibals."

¶ A captured Russian general who had deserted to the Germans in 1942 and was put in command of the "National Army of Liberation": Russian soldiers prepared to fight for Germany against Stalin.

Russian army commander and he gave me an impression of great reliability. We talked first about the general relationship between the Russian and German peoples. His view is that Russia can only be saved if she can be liberated from bolshevist ideology and adopt an ideology similar to that given to the German people by National-Socialism. He describes Stalin as an extraordinarily cunning, indeed jesuitical, being, not a word of whose utterances is to be believed. Up to the outbreak of war bolshevism had only comparatively few conscious fanatical adherents among the Russian people. As we advanced into Soviet territory, however, Stalin succeeded in turning the war against us into a holy patriotic struggle and this was of decisive importance. Vlasov described to me the days in Moscow in late autumn 1940* when the city was threatened with encirclement. The entire Soviet top level had lost their nerve at that time; Stalin was the only one to insist on continued resistance, though even he was very depressed. The situation at that time was not unlike ours at this moment. With us it is the Führer who preaches resistance at all costs and carries all the others along with him over and over again.

For me this conversation with General Vlasov was most encouraging. I deduce from it that the Soviet Union has had to weather precisely the same crises as we are now facing and that there is always a way out of these crises if one is determined not to knuckle under to them.

We then discussed the methodology of our anti-bolshevist propaganda. Vlasov emphasised—in my view rightly—that bolshevist propaganda is extraordinarily adroit and dangerous. Propaganda is in fact the strongest aspect of bolshevist political activity. This also explains why the bolshevist regime attacks German propaganda with special violence. After the Führer I am the one who is criticised with the greatest violence and hostility in the bolshevist press. Our propaganda to the Russian people—and here I agree with Vlasov—should be roughly along the lines laid

* Presumably a slip for 1941.

down by Vlasov in his famous proclamation. We might have achieved much with our eastern policy if in 1941 and 1942 we had acted on the principles advocated here by Vlasov. But it is very difficult now to make good our failures in this respect.

I have already emphasised that Vlasov seems to me to be an outstanding brain. His knowledge of bolshevist ideology and practice can be very valuable to us. He has with him General Shilenkov who at one time played a decisive role in the bolshevist party in Moscow. I intend to receive General Vlasov again next week in order to discuss with him certain practical questions concerning our propaganda. Vlasov's information about internal goings-on in the bolshevist hierarchy is of particular interest. In practice Stalin rules Russia with dictatorial plenary powers. He is trying to exploit the Jews for his own purposes while the Jews are trying to exploit him for theirs. Even if Stalin pledges his word he is by no means to be trusted. Stalin is an extremely cunning sly peasant who works on the principle that the end justifies the means. Compared to him what a piteous spectacle the Duce is, for instance. He now lets it be known through his newspapers that fascism intends to revert to a two-party system. This is again some new quirk of fascist intellectualism which is totally off the rails and now, to cap it all at this stage of the war, is saying farewell to its own principles.

I discussed with the Berlin Defence Council problems of the defence of the capital. In this connection I can make use of General Vlasov's revelations. General von Hauenschild* is now losing most of the troop units from Berlin, in particular the schools and the cadets. As a result he is short of men everywhere. We must therefore call up the second Volkssturm levy and if necessary even proceed to form women's battalions. I even proposed the constitution of strictly supervised units formed of the less serious criminals from the prisons and concentration camps. As General Vlasov had told me, this method proved extraor-

* Commander of the Berlin district.

dinarily successful during the defence of Moscow. At that time Stalin had asked him whether he was prepared to form a prisoners' division. He had constituted it on the condition that amnesty would be granted for deeds of bravery. The prisoners' division had fought outstandingly well. In the present emergency why should not this be done here?

Once more a series of very heavy air raids thundered down on the western areas of the Reich throughout the day. It is hardly possible to record them individually. We are completely defenceless against this raging enemy air war.

I am now in process of working out a new system of call-up into the Wehrmacht. Previous methods have proved too complicated for the present phase of the war. The postal service does not function and most card-indexes have been destroyed—in short we must now use some more rough and ready procedure to avoid men released as fit for service in the Wehrmacht waiting sometimes four or five weeks before being called into barracks. Graf Krosigk, the Finance Minister, has written me a most instructive letter on this subject. He has found out that men released for service from his offices have sometimes waited over a month before being called up.

In addition I am carrying out a thorough check of the Wehrmacht Construction Troops. At present there are still 250,000 men in this corps, of whom at least half are totally superfluous. The Todt Organisation* can take over their duties in many cases and so these Construction Troops can be released.

I am very pleased that the newspaper *Front und Heimat* [Front and Home] is now reaching the front-line troops in far larger quantities. Previous transport difficulties have largely been overcome. A proposal has been made to me that the paper should now appear three times a week; I

---

* This organisation, founded by Fritz Todt, was responsible for all military construction—roads, fortresses, communications, etc. After Todt's death in an air-crash in February 1942, his organisation, and his Ministry of Munitions, were taken over by Albert Speer.

think this is also necessary but unfortunately it will probably founder on the paper problem. Re-establishment of our troops' morale and will to resist is now of decisive importance.

My speech was carried over the radio at 7:00 p.m. I listened to it again. Delivery and style are excellent and I anticipate at least some effect, although naturally I was in no position to produce concrete victories as the best arguments. But people are pleased if one gives them an hour's encouraging talk these days. I shall hear more about its effect out in the country during the next few days. The speech was heard, thank God, without serious disturbance from the air, though just at the end we had the regulation Mosquito raid on Berlin once more. Fortunately it was finished just in time.

The evening situation report announces that our troops in the West have again succeeded in bringing the Anglo-American advance to a halt. Though under very severe pressure they have maintained their positions throughout the day. The enemy has made no progress anywhere. There is definitely no question of a break-through. Today, therefore, we have scored an enormous defensive victory. Very heavy tank casualties have been inflicted.

The situation in the Bitburg area, on the other hand, has developed unfavourably. Counter-measures are being taken, however, which will probably relieve the pressure.

In East Pomerania also the enemy has been unable to make progress. We attacked his leading elements on both flanks so that they were forced to halt to avoid being cut off from their communications. It is hoped to clear up this somewhat critical situation. Violent attacks took place in the whole area of Army Group Vistula.* They were repulsed, thank God. Elsewhere no developments of special importance to report except that the fighting in Breslau is slowly nearing the city centre and is most bitter.

The Führer has instructed me to publish long articles on

---

* A new Army Group, set up in January 1945, under the command of Himmler, to defend the area between the Vistula and the Oder.

the Punic Wars in the German press. In addition to the Seven Years War the Punic War was the great example which we can and must follow today. In fact it fits our situation better than the Seven Years War since the Punic War was more decisive in a world-historical sense and its effects were felt over several centuries. Moreover the quarrel between Rome and Carthage, just like the present-day dispute over Europe, was not settled by a single war; the question whether the resulting ancient world was to be led by Rome or Carthage depended upon the courage of the Roman people and its leaders.

THURSDAY 1 MARCH 1945

(pp. 1–22)
Military Situation.
The main centre of activity on the Eastern Front was in
East Prussia where the Soviets again attacked in large
numbers but without success.

In Slovakia attacks on Altsohl were less violent. On the
Silesian front the enemy is regrouping. He made various
unsuccessful battalion-strength attacks between Strehlen
and Görlitz. Fighting round Lauban was particularly severe.
Fierce house- and street-fighting continues on the southern
outskirts of Breslau. No special developments on the Neisse
front apart from attacks on Guben where fighting is taking
place on the northern and eastern outskirts of the town.
In the Oder sector an enemy break-in at Görlitz was dealt
with. In Pomerania the Soviets attacked northwards in
strength between Arnswalde and Kallies. At the same time
they renewed their attack on Pyritz where they were repulsed. They made minor break-ins between Arnswalde and
Kallies. This may be the start of a major offensive aiming
at a break-through but probably the object is to tie down
our forces to prevent the situation in the Neustettin–
Rummelsburg area being cleared up. The break-in was
localised by occupying switch positions to east and west and
the enemy could make no further progress northwards.
More detailed reports of the progress of our counter-
measures are not yet available. Local enemy attacks between Heiderode and the Vistula were unsuccessful. Offensive activity in Courland was reduced.

On the Western Front the enemy was again unsuccessful

in the area south of Goch. Penetrations were dealt with by counter-attacks.

The major American offensive between Aachen and Köln is now at its height. The enemy has committed all his available forces. Our own troops' conduct is exemplary; not only are they defending themselves stubbornly but in numerous sectors they have also carried out successful counter-attacks to eliminate enemy penetrations. The enemy only gained an insignificant amount of ground yesterday. The fighting is taking place some 12 km west and 3 km south-west of München-Gladbach, also some 5 km south of Rheydt and 3 km west of Grevenbroich. Counter-attacks are in progress between Rheydt and Grevenbroich. On the Erft all enemy attacks failed with heavy losses. Here too counter-attacks were made at numerous points. In the sector east of Düren the enemy has now reached the Steffel stream and south of Düren he is some 6 km north-west and 9 km west of Zülpich. In the area of the main offensive about 200 American tanks were destroyed yesterday. In the area either side of Prüm local fighting was renewed. Numerous attacks were repulsed and counter-attacks made. The enemy was able to cross the Prüm at one or two points south of the town. In the Bitburg area the enemy was able to push on farther towards the Kyll at one or two points between Bitburg and Welschbillig. Here too break-ins were halted in stiff fighting and in some cases driven back by counter-attack. The centre of activity in this area moved southwards and equally in the area between the Saar and the Ruwer the enemy turned north indicating his clear intention to capture Trier. On the Zerf–Trier road the enemy reached Pellingen.

In Italy local fighting took place in the mountains south-east of Bologna.

In the East there was again heavy enemy air activity over East Prussia. Our own air action in the Breslau area and over the break-in at Rummelsburg was successful.

In the West there was heavy low-level and fighter-bomber air activity mainly directed on Münsterland and

Rhineland-Westphalia. Our anti-aircraft shot down 10 enemy planes.

Kassel and the Westphalian area were raided by 1100 four-engined bombers. A smaller British force attacked the Ruhr area and targets in the region of Gelsenkirchen and Essen. There are no reports of enemy casualties yet.

Harassing raids on Berlin by 70 Mosquitos at night. Some 10 Mosquitos were over Nuremberg and the Munich area.

During February our naval forces, primarily submarines, sank 41 ships totalling 200,480 GRT and in addition 5 destroyers and 6 escort vessels; 13 ships totalling 75,900 GRT and 3 escorts were torpedoed. The Navy evacuated 651,000 refugees to the Reich during February.

———

The enemy are now taking a somewhat more sceptical view of the possibilities and prospects of the British-American offensive in the West. They are primarily both surprised and astonished at the stiff resistance offered by our troops to the American advance in the München-Gladbach–Rheydt area. There is talk of fanatical fighters outbidding each other in courage and determination. Even General Montgomery has become much more cautious in his estimates. In his usual way he shot off his mouth a few days ago and now has to eat his words in some embarrassment.

The debate on the Crimea Conference is still going on in the Commons. It seems to be a very heated one. Churchill is faced with considerable opposition even though at the moment it cannot be politically active. There is widespread fear among the public of the increase of bolshevism. People dare not refer to this openly, however, for fear of offending Stalin and the Kremlin. As a result the amendment to the motion of confidence in Churchill put forward by certain Tories, referring to the Polish problem in critical terms, was lost by 396 votes to 25. This means, in other words, that over 200 MPs abstained; they probably belong to the opposition mentioned but at the moment do not dare come forward publicly. The Commons is again bowing the knee to its allies, both the Americans and more particularly the Soviets. Only a few isolated voices are to be heard such as that of an influential Conservative MP who openly declares that at the Crimea Conference Churchill led Britain into a political Dunkirk and that Europe is heading straight for domination by bolshevism. Unfortunately, as I have said, these can only be described as lone voices and at the moment they cannot do anything practical. One Conservative MP has resigned his seat because he can no longer go along with and support Churchill's policy.* As I have said, however, we have no reason at the moment to pin any hopes on this development.

Eden had to attempt to pacify the restive opposition in a speech following that of Churchill. It was made in remarkably subdued tones. He stammered out one excuse after another, particularly on the Polish question. He maintained that Britain had reserved her position regarding the Lublin Committee and proposed to wait and see what it did. Eden's statement was contemptible twaddle and illustrates Britain's impotence in the present phase of the war. This is solely due to Churchill's mistaken strategy and war policy. Nevertheless he got his vote of confidence—and by 403 votes to nil. I have the impression, however, that he has won a Pyrrhic victory, for again there were evidently some 200 abstentions in the Commons and criticisms of the Yalta decisions has become so severe both among the British public and in particular in the Commons that it is fair to assume that many MPs only vote for Churchill to avoid a wartime political upheaval in Britain.

The opposition referred to above is growing not only in London but also in Washington. Certain members have voiced the general discontent in Congress over the Yalta decisions. Once more it must be emphasised that, although

---

* This is incorrect. A Conservative MP, Mr. W. Petherick (Penryn and Falmouth) proposed an amendment on Poland, which was defeated by 396 votes to 25; but there were no resignations.

people only refer to the Polish question, in reality they mean bolshevism on the one hand and Germany on the other. Roosevelt is now being reminded that Wilson too pursued a similar policy binding on America and that this was later rejected out of hand by Congress. At a press conference Roosevelt was forced meekly to admit that at the Yalta Conference there had been no discussion at all about Japan. I think this may easily be true. Stalin may have refused point-blank to be dragged into the East Asian conflict. At Roosevelt's press conference, moreover, a few guarded friendly words were addressed to us but I think the motives behind them were propagandist rather than genuine.

Meanwhile in Rumania the Kremlin is largely disregarding the Yalta decisions and attempting to create *faits accomplis*. Following the resignation of the Radescu cabinet, the bolshevists, as they admit in their press, are trying to clear matters up as quickly as possible using draconian methods. In view of Soviet pressure Radescu's resignation was unavoidable and we must now wait to see how the King with his court clique handles the Rumanian conflict. Anyway Radescu's resignation has produced sensation and embarrassment in the British-American press. Even *The Times* is becoming somewhat impatient and takes a hard line over the Kremlin's policy. I fancy that *The Times* will frequently have occasion to complain of the Kremlin's high-handedness.

I have in front of me an order to Soviet troops from Marshal Koniev. It deals with the increase in looting by Soviet soldiers in the eastern German territories. He cites a number of instances which tally exactly with the information we have. In these territories the Soviet soldiers are laying hands mainly on spirits; they drink themselves silly, put on civilian clothes, including top hats, and set off eastwards on bicycles. Koniev orders commanders to take the sternest measures against such cases of indiscipline. He also forbids arson and looting except when ordered. His description of what is going on is remarkably informative. One deduces that, in the Soviet soldiery, we are faced with the offscourings of the steppes. We have similar reports of atrocities from the eastern territories. They are truly horrifying. They cannot be repeated in detail. From Upper Silesia in particular information coming in is shattering. In certain towns and villages all women between the ages of 10 and 70 were raped innumerable times. This seems to have been done on orders from above, since the behaviour of the Soviet soldiery leads one to think that there is a definite system.

We shall now launch our major campaign against all this both at home and abroad. Colonel-General Guderian has said that he is prepared to read Marshal Zhukov's famous order in front of the home and foreign press and then publicly interrogate a number of officers who have returned to our lines from Poznan and have seen the devastation and atrocities with their own eyes on innumerable occasions.

In Spain Falangism is on the upgrade. One or two communists murdered by Falangists have been buried. The Spanish press has seized on the occasion to launch a very definite anti-bolshevist campaign. But of course there is no serious political move behind this. Franco is a pompous ass; he puffs himself out like anything when the moment seems favourable but when the moment has passed he becomes timorous and meek again.

Obergruppenführer Steiner* has been commissioned by Himmler to move all units now in the home area to the rear areas of the Eastern and Western fronts. In addition he is to form a new Ninth Army from the units which I have combed out from the Replacement Army. This is a large-scale project to which I will give my warmest support. It is nonsense that there should still be Wehrmacht units under training today in Nuremberg or Bayreuth for in-

---

* Steiner, one of Himmler's closest subordinates in the SS, had founded the "Viking division," the first SS division of European volunteers. He was one of the only three SS generals (apart from Himmler) to command an army. The others were Sepp Dietrich (see below p. 28) and Paul Hausser. In the end, Hitler would expect him to relieve Berlin. Obergruppenführer=full general in the SS.

stance. The right course is to locate them behind the front in Brandenburg or Pomerania so that, should the Soviets break through anywhere, they are ready to act. If as a result these areas necessarily become overpopulated, I would be quite prepared to reduce or even totally evacuate the civil population; our women would certainly prefer to leave their towns and villages to make room for German rather than Soviet solders. Steiner, moreover, makes an excellent impression on me. He is energetic and purposeful and is attacking his job with great verve.

In addition we propose to cram the rear areas of the fronts, not only in the East but also in the West, as full as we can with units due for training. Then we shall at least have something available in the event of dire emergency.

The air war has now turned into a crazy orgy. We are totally defenceless against it. The Reich will gradually be turned into a complete desert. Responsibility for this lies at the door of Göring and his Luftwaffe. It is absolutely not in any position to put up any form of defence.

We are already being forced to make extraordinarily severe reductions in the food ration and shall soon be compelled to make even more. The loss of the eastern territories is now making itself most painfully felt. Backe is in no position to draw up even a conservative ration scale since he does not know what is available at the moment or what will be available in future. We shall very soon be forced to reduce by 35–50% the ration of the most important items, fat and bread. As a result they will fall below the tolerable minimum subsistence level. In some cases reductions must be made straight away, in others we can allow ourselves until 9 April. One can imagine what the effect on the public will be. Even if we reconquer our eastern territories we shall not avoid severe shortages. To all our people's miseries that of hunger will now be added. But, as we know, in this struggle there is nothing for it but to try to hold out bravely.

Reactions to my radio speech differ. The public naturally expected something more positive, in other words that I might be in a position to offer the people some real hope rather than harping on its courage. Sadly I am not in a position to do that. If, for instance, my speech is criticised because I only made vague statements about the air war, the fault lies with Göring not with me. I would have preferred to say something positive about the Luftwaffe if the Luftwaffe had been in a position to do anything positive. I think, moreover, that in the near future the speech will have a greater and more profound effect. The arguments used were directed to those in the country whose hearts are strong. Provided we can persuade them to give unreserved support to the decision to fight on, they will carry the broad mass of the people along with them.

The situation this evening is again rather more critical. The enemy has attacked in the West with the greatest violence. Admittedly he has now thrown in all his reserves but he has made considerable progress. He is now in Rheydt, my home town, and on the edge of München-Gladbach. His armour has exerted enormous pressure. It has already reached the outskirts of Grevenbroich and formed bridgeheads over the Erft which we had planned as our new defence line. The enemy has suffered very heavy losses but he can accept them provided he makes progress. He has also advanced in the Prüm and Trier areas and he is now 6 km from Trier. In the next 24 hours the city may be in danger. The bright spot in this depressing news is that nowhere has he achieved a break-through. That is, after all, the deciding factor.

In the East two major offensives have now opened, in the Zobten area and in eastern Pomerania. As far as the latter is concerned the enemy has made some deep penetrations in the Arnswalde area. It looks as if the Führer's theory, which is also my own, is being confirmed: that the Soviets do not intend to drive on towards Berlin in the first instance but to split up and cut off Pomerania. At Neustettin too the enemy has advanced farther north. We are trying to attack his flanks but forces available are not large. Very severe street fighting is raging in Breslau. We propose to assist with airborne troops. In East Prussia our troops scored another clear defensive victory.

Heavy air raids all day over the whole Reich, in particular on Vienna, Ulm and Augsburg. The less said on the question of the air war the better. One can only say with Hamlet: "The rest is silence."

FRIDAY 2 MARCH 1945

(pp. 1–32)
Military Situation.
Fighting in the East again centred on the Neustettin–Rummelsburg area where enemy armoured advanced guards, moving north-west and north along the Bublitz–Köslin and Bublitz–Schlawe roads, reached points south of Köslin and Schlawe. Our own attacks from the Rummelsburg area, aiming to cut off the enemy forces which had broken through, gained some ground but could not get through. To divert our counter-attacks the enemy attacked in a northerly direction north of Schlochau and pushed forward a few kilometres towards the Rummelsburg–Bütow road.

The second main centre of activity was in East Prussia where Soviet attacks were beaten off once more. Our troops fought all day under the most difficult conditions and their achievement was outstanding.

On the remaining front two enemy penetrations to a depth of 10 km between Reetz and Kallies are worthy of note. Otherwise no changes in the situation.

In the Canadian-British sector of the Western Front the enemy advanced a few kilometers farther south and was held on the line Sonsbeck–Kevelaer. In the sector of the American offensive fighting was centred on the Gladbach–Rheydt area where the enemy is attempting to push farther north-eastwards. Our troops occupied a defence line between Venlo and Dülken as northern flank-guard. The Americans advanced into München-Gladbach and Rheydt and are now between Rheydt and Neuss engaged with

24

German troops moving up to counter-attack. Neuss and Düsseldorf are under enemy artillery fire. The enemy scored only local successes in the Erft sector. East of Düren the Americans were able to gain further ground towards the Erft valley. Köln is also under enemy artillery fire.

In the Bitburg area the Americans made only minor local gains. In the area south of Trier they advanced north and succeeded in reaching the eastern edge of the city.

Over the Reich some 1200 American bombers attacked targets in south and south-west Germany. A large British formation attacked places in west Germany, Mannheim, Ludwigshafen and the Dortmund area. Throughout the day there was heavy enemy fighter-bomber activity along the central Rhine and in the Rhine-Westphalian industrial zone.

Some 800 American four-engined bombers from Italy raided Moosbierbaum with a subsidiary attack on Marburg. Harassing raids were made on Berlin and Erfurt during the night. Reports of aircraft shot down are not yet available.

The situation in the West is increasingly menacing. The enemy is again extravagantly jubilant. On the other hand Stimson, the American Secretary of War, has been compelled to admit quite frankly that American losses during the present operations have been extraordinarily high. He says that our men have been fighting like savage fanatics and that at present there can definitely be no question of German resistance slackening. If in the West we could not hold out at least on the Rhine, that would be very bad. Any futher advance by the Americans would very largely upset our whole political concept. We are now at a stage of this gigantic struggle in which everything is on a knife-edge and the fate of the Reich sometimes seems to hang by a thread.

The debate in the Commons is now finished. In his closing speech Eden made yet another appeal to the so-called Austrian people to secede from the German Reich; he then executed a real sword-dance round the question of Poland. He blandly states that the Lublin Committee* has not been recognised by the British and that the representatives of this Committee made an extraordinarily bad impression when they visited London recently. In Yalta the British were allegedly against the Lublin Committee. On the other hand he does not refer to Stalin in this connection. In London people are exasperated that the Lublin Committee should quite simply have arrested members of the families of Poles exiled in London, the wife of Arziszewski, the Polish Premier-in-exile, for instance. Eden declares that Britain proposes to discuss with the USA what to do next. Nothing will be done of course since Britain is in no position to do anything. What matters now is not what Britain wants but what Britain can do and that is nothing at all. Anyway the result of the debate was that, as he left the House, Churchill was clapped on the shoulder by several MPs. This of course he is broadcasting all over the world through Reuters. He has need of it since, despite his vote of confidence, his situation is extraordinarily precarious.

In the Lords too the Yalta talks were thoroughly well criticised. The Poland affair is, so to speak, the test case for British credibility throughout the world. Churchill is now under notice that the vote of confidence given him was not a blank cheque for his policy of servility to the Kremlin. It seems to me, however, that at the moment all this is mere talking round the problem. For the present no political move is to be expected from England, still less from the United States.

Roosevelt is now facing Congress. His speech is a hotch-potch of phrases and repetitious mouthing of his old slogans from which it is impossible to extract anything concrete about the Yalta decisions. He talks about the prospective world peace and the Atlantic Charter, on which he still

---

* The committee of Polish communists which Stalin recognised as the government of Poland, instead of the exiled Polish government in London.

insists; he says that the enemy's task is first to knock out
the Reich and only then deal with other problems, that
the knock-out blow can be administered with few losses,
that complete unity must prevail on the enemy side, that
co-ordination of military operations was most definitely
achieved at Yalta and that the United States still adheres
to the principle of unconditional surrender. The enemy,
he says, has no wish to victimise the Germans, but Nazism
and militarism must be eradicated and then Germany is
entitled to a good life in association with the other peoples
of the world. To cut a long story short we have here a fresh
edition of the seductive verbiage invariably employed by
Roosevelt when he is trying to achieve some political success. It is mere insolence when Roosevelt says that he has
seen the devastation in Sebastopol. His conclusion is that
between Christian decency and Nazism there is a great
gulf fixed. Of the frightful destruction wrought daily by the
American Air Force on unfortified and undefended German
towns he naturally says nothing at all. In short it is hardly
worth while scrutinising this Roosevelt speech. It is too
mendacious and too insolent for polemics to be initiated
against it. I now definitely take the view that German
publicity should concern itself somewhat less with foreign
statesmen's speeches. They deluge the world daily with
fresh statements and, if we take issue with them, we are
indirectly making propaganda for them. The only interesting point in Roosevelt's speech is that he referred to a
prolonged war against Japan. So he is preparing the
American public for the fact that they have still got to
make considerable sacrifices to satisfy his megalomania.

King Michael of Rumania has now commissioned Prince
Stirbey to form a new cabinet. Prince Stirbey was the man
who conducted the preliminary negotiations with the Anglo-
Americans for Rumania's withdrawal from our coalition.*

* Prince Barbu Stirbey, a veteran Rumanian politician (he had
been Prime Minister for a brief period in 1927), had visited Cairo in
March 1944 in an attempt to negotiate an armistice through the
Western Allies.

Clearly the Rumanian court clique is now at its wits' end and is turning to the Anglo-Americans for protection against the Soviets.

I talked to Sepp Dietrich* and he told me of the next assignment given him by the Führer. He hopes to be able to start the operations in Hungary, which have so often been mooted, in about six days' time. He reckons that these operations will last some 10 to 12 days. If all goes well we can anticipate enormous success. Then, he thinks, he will be available for further operations in east Germany in 14 days. So far we have successfully concealed 6 SS Panzer Army's concentration in Hungary from the enemy; at least no counter-measures by him have been reported for the moment. In general terms, therefore, we can count on major operations in the east German area being possible by the end of March. We have a long hard row to hoe till then, however.

Dietrich quite openly criticised measures taken by the Führer. He complains that the Führer does not give his military staff a sufficiently free hand and that this tendency has now become so pronounced that the Führer even lays down the employment of individual companies. But Dietrich is in no position to judge. The Führer cannot rely on his military advisers. They have so often deceived him and thrown dust in his eyes that he now has to attend to every detail. Thank God he does attend to them, for if he did not, matters would be even worse than they are anyway.

From a detailed report on the situation in Silesia I infer that Schörner† has succeeded in re-establishing a semi-solid defence line. It is clear, however, that at very many points our forces are too weak to initiate any counter-measures. In this area the Soviets are using their old tactics and

---

* An old Nazi stalwart, commander of SS Leibstandarte (Life Guards), now commanding the (Waffen SS) 6th Panzer Division, which had been transferred from the West to Hungary.

† Col.-Gen. Ferdinand Schörner was the most Nazi of the generals and as such Hitler would designate him, in his will, as Commander-in-Chief of the Army. For his methods, see below, pp. 96, 98–100, 125–6, 304, 346.

concentrating their effort at different points, so that there is always a danger of them making a break-through.

In general the Soviet situation is described somewhat as follows: their troops are extraordinarily well equipped but they are suffering from an increasing shortage of man-power. The attacking infantry is composed largely of workers swept up from our eastern territories and Poles. Rations are described as semi-sufficient. The Polish attitude to the Soviets in the Government General is hostile. They know well enough what hangs over them once the Soviets have got a free hand. In general terms discipline in the Soviet armoured forces is said to be good. The main body of infantry, however, is in pretty miserable shape. The Soviet soldier is war-weary. He can only be kept going by the hope that he will soon be in Berlin and so the war will come to an end.

It is reported from Rumania that the entire population looks back with nostalgia to the time when the country was occupied by Germans. Unhappily the realisation comes too late. Meanwhile the Iron Guard* has set to work. As developments in Rumania itself prove, however, the Soviets are keeping a very close watch on them.

The air war is still the great tale of woe in the present situation. The Anglo-Americans have again made very heavy raids on western and south-eastern Germany with damage quite impossible to set out in detail. The situation becomes daily more intolerable and we have no means of defending ourselves against this catastrophe.

Evacuation is now proceeding in a semi-orderly manner. The question is whether we can actually transport great masses of German refugees to Denmark as the Führer wishes. There is no knowing how this will develop in the immediate future.

We shall make a start, however, with a gradual reduction

---

* Horia Sima's fascist organisation in Rumania. It had been opposed to the pro-German regime of Marshal Antonescu, but had enjoyed the support of Himmler and the SS. After the overthrow of Antonescu in August 1944, the Germans pinned their hopes on the "legionaries" of the Iron Guard.

of population density, in Berlin at least. Should the capital's situation become precarious, we shall at least have removed a portion of the population from the city.

As a result of the war, specially the air war, some six million dwellings have so far been totally destroyed in the Reich. This is a horrifying percentage of the total of 23 million dwellings possessed by the Reich in 1939. In general it can be said at the moment that in Germany over-all there is a shortage of nine million dwellings. After the war, therefore, we shall face a monumental task in this field. Nevertheless I believe that with modern building methods we can achieve a great deal. Before the war one reckoned that one building worker erected one dwelling per year; it should be possible to halve this percentage by rationalisation of the process. This means, therefore, that if we have to erect nine million dwellings and employ one million building workers, it should be possible to solve the entire housing problem in some four to five years.

Stuckart* tells me that OKW [Oberkommando der Wehrmacht—High Command of the German Armed Forces] and OKH [Oberkommando des Heeres—High Command of the Army] have commandeered quarters in Thuringia— enough for 54,000 men. How can command be exercised by a military machine with so many men on its strength? The deadweight of such manpower makes it so cumbersome that it is in no position to improvise.

As far as the German home front is concerned the following observations are to hand: in general the people remain comparatively solid. There is too much grumbling about the officers however. People try to lay the blame for all setbacks on them and this naturally leads to a noticeable reduction of their authority among the troops. It is too facile to ascribe the defeats of the last two years to sabotage by officers. Things are not as simple as that. I have therefore decided that at the next opportunity—perhaps during a visit to the front—I shall say a word in public to extricate

* State-secretary in Ministry of the Interior. (The Minister was Himmler.)

officers from this situation; there is no point now, when this struggle has reached a critical stage, in starting to enquire who is really to blame. The visible relaxation of saluting discipline shows that in the long run such debates only demoralise the troops. The scandal of desertions has seriously increased. It is suspected that there are tens of thousands of soldiers in the major German cities who are supposedly stragglers but in practice are evading service at the front. I am urging as hard as I can that all leave for the Wehrmacht now be stopped. In this critical situation no soldier has the right to go on leave; it is the duty of all to fight.

In the letters I receive there is much criticism of our war leadership in general and it is now also directed at the Führer personally. People see no way out of the present dilemma. In particular they fear that with the loss of our eastern provinces rationing restrictions will be necessary very soon, which is in fact the case. We must probably anticipate the most dangerous problems here.

Greiser's* behaviour is most severely criticised in a whole series of letters. He is a real disgrace to the Party.

Masses of letters continue to arrive containing high praise for my journalistic and oratorical activity. In general my last speech has made a good impact. Naturally it could not have an enormous effect since I could cite no military victories, only setbacks. On the one hand people particularly appreciate the calm with which I made my statements, on the other I am occasionally urged to put more verve into it. I think, however, that most people are now best addressed in a relaxed rather than a hysterical tone.

Speer† is now at work re-establishing the transport network. He has put 80,000 men on to repair of marshalling yards, primarily in the West. If we can once succeed in clearing the marshalling yards, traffic will run smoothly again and the numerous stranded trains can get on the move once more. This is the nub of the problem as far as

---

* Gauleiter of Wartheland.
† Albert Speer, Hitler's architect, who succeeded Todt as Minister of Munitions, was now the economic dictator of the Reich.

our run-down transport system is concerned. In this instance Speer is the right man in the right place. He knows how to get to the root of enormously difficult problems. Moreover Speer has come out one hundred per cent in favour of the financial reforms proposed by Krosigk and that is quite right. We must get our feet on the ground again as regards the money problem.

I am reading memoranda by Gneisenau and Scharnhorst about preparations for expansion of the people's war in 1808. At that time things were precisely as they are today and we must defend ourselves against the enemy using the same methods as were in vogue before the wars of liberation.

In Berlin we are faced with exceptional difficulties owing to shortage of energy. Power stations in Berlin itself, but also long-distance power lines, have been very heavily damaged with the result that there is large-scale unemployment in the capital including even the most important armament industries. The effect on the air raid alert system is very bad. At the moment we are unable to put the system into action at all.

Fuel for the capital is also very short. As Schach rightly remarks, we are now hardly able to fill our cigarette lighters.

A long walk with Gauleiter Eggeling* who spoke of his worries about the leadership of the Reich. Everything to which his criticisms of detail were directed is well known to me. He can add nothing new. His remarks were directed primarily against Göring and he expressed surprise that the Führer still had not thrown him on the scrap-heap. The Gauleiters are in despair over the Führer's lack of decision on the most vital personnel problems and they implore me —as Eggeling does now—to do urgent and ceaseless battle with the Führer in order to persuade him to make some change, at least in the command of the Luftwaffe and the conduct of German foreign policy.

I am very vexed with the newspaper *Das Reich*. Once again it has published an article by Schwarz van Berk which

---

* Gauleiter of Halle-Merseburg.

runs directly counter to our general theme. *Das Reich*'s main characteristic is that it plays the role of a sort of outsider. I shall now take energetic steps to stop this. Instead the duty of *Das Reich* is to advocate our general theme with the greatest possible degree of intelligence, perspicacity and emphasis, not to go its own way.

The situation this evening is not reassuring. The enemy has forced his way into Krefeld. He is now just outside Neuss and so has made considerable gains of ground in this area which is vital for us. The Erft sector, thank God, has in general held. There is no question of a break-through at the moment. But the situation has become very precarious. We shall probably have to withdraw in the Venlo area, otherwise our troops are in danger of being cut off. The city of Trier is now surrounded. In general the outlook for the next few days is gloomy.

In the East too operations have not gone through as we expected, in particular those initiated in order to cut off the leading Soviet armoured advanced guards in eastern Pomerania. So far they have met with no success. The enemy is pouring forces through the gap and taking no notice of our counter-attacks. At Arnswalde the enemy succeeded in making a deep penetration. His advance at Zobten, on the other hand, was driven back.

I have had sad news. Eugen Hadamovsky, a member of my staff and an old friend, has been killed leading his company in an attack. He was shot through the heart and died instantly. In him I have lost a fellow-traveller who has accompanied me tirelessly and faithfully for many years. I shall treasure his memory. How much valuable blood has been spilt in this war! But if one sits back and looks at the world crisis which we are going through at this moment, one may perhaps think that Hadamovsky is to be envied for the fate he chose.

SATURDAY 3 MARCH 1945

(pp. 1–30 + 14a)
Military Situation.
In the East the centre of activity is still in Pomerania where
the enemy has massed in an attempt to break up and drive
in our northern flank. Between Köslin and Schlawe the
enemy reached the Köslin–Stolp road at the crossing of the
Grabow. A German counter-attack south-west from the
Rummelsburg area recaptured Rummelsburg itself and
pushed on south for 10 km but then met very strong
resistance and could not penetrate further. Our line now
runs some 10 km north-west and west from Rummelsburg
and then east through Heiderode to the Vistula. The left
flank of the enemy salient in the Neustettin–Bublitz–Köslin
area runs north some 30 km west of Neustettin. Here again,
after initial gains of ground, our counter-attacks could not
progress further. A second focal point is the break-in area
north of Reetz. Here the enemy attacked northwards with
armour and his leading tanks reached the Stargard–Köslin
road and railway south of Labes. Other enemy forces north
of Reetz swung west towards Stargard. At the same time
the Soviets attacked northwards from the Arnswalde area
and crossed the Stargard–Reetz railway at Zachan. In the
Pyritz area and also west therefrom between Pyritz and
Bahn the enemy attacked towards Stettin and penetrated
to a depth of 6–8 km. Pyritz fell into enemy hands.

In Slovakia the enemy continued his heavy local attacks
south of Schemnitz and east of Altsohl. Nothing of significance on the remaining front as far as Breslau. Attacks on
the Zobten position were somewhat less intense and were

all driven off. Between Löwenberg and Lauban and between Lauban and the area north-east of Görlitz we gained as much as 8 km in a northerly and north-westerly direction. No special developments on the Oder or Neisse fronts. South of Küstrin, however, the enemy succeeded in widening his bridgehead west of Görlitz by a few hundred yards reaching the high ground. Violent Soviet attacks in East Prussia once more failed against the unflinching resistance of our defences. Only near Zinten did the enemy succeed in making a minor penetration. In Courland the day was quieter.

In the West the main pressure of the great American offensive is in the area between Neuss, Krefeld and Venlo. On the previous day the enemy had reached the edge of Neuss and yesterday he pushed through Neuss to the Rhine bridges. North of this he advanced some 10 km along the Neuss–Moers road. At Krefeld he reached the railway station on the southern edge of the town. Severe street fighting is in progress. From the Venlo area the enemy reached the Niers south-west of Kempen. At the same time the British and Canadians continued their attack south from Goch but without achieving any noticeable success. The main pressure was directed on Xanten. Enemy attempts to penetrate our new line from Sonsbeck to Kevelaer failed. The main fighting is now in the wooded area west of Xanten. In the Erft sector and the area south of Düren the enemy continued to attack with extraordinary violence but there was no major change in the situation. We counter-attacked the enemy flank between Neuss and Grevenbroich along the Jülich–Neuss road. The enemy succeeded in penetrating into Grevenbroich and gaining some ground south of it. In the Erft sector itself enemy attacks were repulsed; one or two penetrations were dealt with by counter-attacks. North of Zülpich the enemy was able to push on farther towards Bonn. Our troops are still west of the Erft in this area. In the Eifel violent enemy attacks took place on either side of Prüm but with only minor local penetrations. In the Trier area the enemy increased his north–south pressure; he was held on a line about 4–5 km north and north-west of the city. From Trier the enemy succeeded in reaching the southern bridge over the Moselle. In the Zerf sector enemy pressure was maintained; all attacks were repulsed however.

Nothing special reported from Italy.

In the area immediately behind the Western Front there was very heavy enemy air activity yesterday. Main targets for enemy fighter-bombers and twin-engined formations were Münsterland, the Rhine–Main area, the Rhineland and Westphalia.

Over Reich territory some 1250 American four-engined bombers with strong fighter escort attacked Dresden, Schwarzheide, Böhlen, Espenheim, Chemnitz and Magdeburg. About 150 British bombers with fighter escort attacked transport targets in the Koblenz–Neuwied area. According to reports so far fighters and anti-aircraft shot down 35 enemy aircraft.

Some 350 American four-engined aircraft from Italy attacked Linz. A few scattered bombs were dropped on Villach and Graz.

A less numerous British air formation mined the Skagerrak at night. Harassing raids were made on Berlin and Kassel. Three Mosquitos were shot down.

———

At the moment we are having an extraordinarily hard time in the West. The situation, as it has developed, gives rise to the greatest anxiety and it may well be necessary to withdraw to the Rhine unless there are reasonable prospects of holding out in the Erft sector. We had never really visualized such a course of events, although against this it must not be forgotten that the Rhine is the best conceivable defence line for us. We do not lose much armaments potential in this area since the existing potential had already been largely destroyed by enemy air attacks. In itself this development is obviously pretty miserable but it is no good moaning about it. We must try to hold out at some point, no matter where, to await the further course of political developments. They, at least, give cause for greater hope.

Real wartime experience has now become the order of the day in the USA which naturally does not please the Americans very much. As certain informers tell us, the war has now become a day-to-day phenomenon in the United States. Nevertheless the American people do not face it with the genuine resolution shown by, for instance, the German or Russian peoples. One strike succeeds another and this time it is the miners' turn.

In England too strike fever has reasserted itself again. Labour in the docks and ports stops work for trivial reasons. One does not have to look far to detect political reasons behind these strikes. The Kremlin is taking a hand in the game.

The *Daily Mail* has just made a truly sensational admission; it says that for two years now I have been the only person to analyse the case of Poland correctly and forecast accurately the way in which England would succumb to the Kremlin. Churchill comes in for criticism of rare severity. In general terms the *Daily Mail* entirely supports our viewpoint in its estimate of the Polish problem and accuses Churchill of mere monotonous repetition of the battle-cry "Beat the Huns," what time England is slowly going to the dogs.

I am happy to say that at present my rating is extraordinarily high both with the neutral and even with the enemy press. Neutral papers, the social-democrat press in Stockholm for instance, praise my last radio speech to high heaven; they describe me as a magician of political psychology and the most adroit propagandist in the world today. It is a fact that, at the present stage of the war, vast adaptability is required to talk both to one's own people and the world and on the one hand tell the truth and on the other avoid prejudicing German faith in victory.

In his recent speech to the French National Assembly de Gaulle simply whined and lamented. He laid the blame unequivocally on the Allies for the miserable situation prevailing in France at this moment. France, he says, cannot live and cannot die. There is mass unemployment in France such as has never been known before in French history.

Belgium is in a similar situation, moreover. Starvation stalks the country. The Belgian government too reproaches the Western Allies in the strongest terms but they are in no position to make even the smallest tonnage available to supply the peoples of Western Europe.

Developments in Rumania proceed precisely as the Kremlin wants. The nomination of Prince Stirbey as Minister-President* was a desperate attempt on the part of the Royal House to save the situation. The purpose was to reinforce links to the Anglo-Americans. The Kremlin, however, put a red pencil through this scheme in that Vyshinsky, Stalin's representative in Rumania, turned Prince Stirbey's candidature down flat and paved the way for Petru Groza to become Rumanian Minister-President. Groza is confirmed intellectual left-wing radical. So there is no further question of a Kerensky; the term to use now is little Lenin. It will not be long now before the treacherous Rumanian Court and its boy-king Michael are removed and Rumania itself incorporated into the Soviet Union as a new republic.

In Poland the Americans would like to make a leader of the Polish church into Prime Minister. I reckon that the Kremlin will laugh itself silly over this proposal, for Stalin has never for a moment thought either of reforming or dropping the Lublin Committee. That was merely a little birthday present for the Yalta Conference which was quietly withdrawn by the donor as soon as the conference was over.

The Soviet advance in eastern Pomerania has once more put us in a critical situation. We had not expected it but should have done so because we are too weak on all sectors of the front. It is therefore quite easy for the Soviets to concentrate somewhere and then break through; we have to shuffle our units about to the hot spots like a fire brigade

* See above p. 27.

in order to plug the holes as best we can, suffering severely in the process.

Alarming news comes out of Finland via Sweden. The Soviets are now said to have stopped all traffic abroad from Helsinki, an indication that they propose to repeat the Rumanian pattern in Finland. The situation has become very acute and it has aroused great indignation in London. The situation in Finland has reached a stage when there could well be an explosion very soon. In Stockholm there is consternation; the Swedes have no reason to put on an air of surprise, however, for they were the people who continually advised the Finns to embark on the fateful path of collaboration with the Soviet Union.

At midday I had a long discussion with Stuckart about the evacuation problem. He reported measures already taken in this connection, those ready and prepared and those still to be taken. In the Reich overall some 17 million people have now been evacuated. This is a really horrifying percentage. One can imagine the resultant conditions. At least we have the advantage that our standard of accommodation before the war was luxurious. Stuckart was compelled to evacuate large sections of the East Pomeranian population helter-skelter and overnight. Some 800,000 people were set on the move in this area. They had to be evacuated largely by sea since the Soviets had already cut the roads as they advanced. The Reich has now become fairly constricted. We have therefore decided to carry out no more evacuations from the West. Even if the Anglo-Americans advance in the West, people must look after themselves. If we were to clear the western population out entirely, the interior of the Reich would be so congested that it would be impossible to accommodate people in practice.

I discussed with Stuckart a provisional reduction in numbers and an emergency evacuation of women and children from Berlin. He has already taken the necessary measures so that we have available billets for a total of 1.5 million people. It would be good if we never had to proceed to this measure at all, but it is best to be prepared for the worst; we shall make all the greater effort to ensure that the worst does not happen.

Stuckart also tells me officially that, should Berlin be attacked or surrounded, he is firmly determined to remain in the city himself; the same has been said to me by a whole number of other Ministers and State Secretaries. All are clear that a battle for Berlin will be decisive in this fateful struggle by our people.

I had a most serious showdown with Sparing, chief editor of *Das Reich*, concerning the recent *faux pas* of which the paper has been guilty. These will now definitely cease. I have no intention of allowing *Das Reich* gradually to degenerate into a defeatist newspaper. It must do justice to its name. Above all it must present a bellicose aspect at this time and fly the flag of our resistance. During our people's present battle for freedom and equality of status *Das Reich* should fulfil the same function as did the *Angriff* during our struggle for power at home. As a result it is intolerable that *Das Reich* should continue to give vent to intellectual tittle-tattle. It should present the German war themes in the most intelligent, radical, intellectual and inspiring form.

Captain Klaas reports to me concerning his measures for distribution to the front of the paper *Front und Heimat*. In one respect it is now easier to get this newspaper into the hands of the troops but in another it is harder. It is easier since distances to the front have now become shorter, harder because routing has now become extraordinarily complicated owing to the destruction of transport communications. Nevertheless we must do our utmost to ensure that the men have a good political newspaper available twice and if possible three times per week. In this connection I get very little support from the WPR Section [Wehrmacht Presse Referent—Armed Forces Press Office] of OKW. The section has just been examined by a commission for the introduction of total war measures and it emerges that some 550 officers and men can be released from it. I intend to concentrate all Wehrmacht propaganda in a new section of the Propaganda Ministry and leave only a small residual section in OKW; its duty would be to take the necessary technical and organisational steps following the issue of political propaganda guidelines by the Wehrmacht Propaganda Section in the Ministry of Propaganda. In this way I have killed two birds with one stone: in the first place I have released considerable manpower for the front; secondly I have at last achieved co-ordination of political and military propaganda which is urgently required and really should have been done on the outbreak of war.

The enemy air terror has again raged over German territory. Dresden, Chemnitz, Magdeburg and Linz were attacked. Up to 70 aircraft are reported shot down. This is obviously nothing like enough to dissuade the enemy from overflying German territory, but it is better than nothing. Recently hardly any aircraft have been reported shot down.

I have been discussing with my staff a problem concerning the initiation of total war which will be of decisive importance for the system of personnel replacements in the Wehrmacht. All over Germany people are complaining that thousands of soldiers are travelling hither and thither by train, some with movement orders, some without. These men represent a considerable slice of our fighting manpower and on evidence so far available it is practically impossible to catch them out. The arrangement henceforth will be as follows: at the front there should be only one commanding general with the right to give a man a movement order for the interior; in addition we propose to intercept at railway stations all soldiers without movement orders and form them into new divisions. I believe the number of troops we shall make available thereby will be astonishing. In addition my view is that we must take stricter measures, not only in this but also in other fields in order to constitute new formations. The present organisation of the German Wehrmacht originates from the good old days when we could afford to employ men lavishly. That time is now finally past and even the Wehrmacht is compelled to draw the consequences from our new circumstances.

During the afternoon I was busy with the proofs of my

new book *Das Gesetz des Kriegs* [The Law of War]; a very large edition is to be published in handy form. The book contains no topical articles but rather basic studies on war, its philosophy and fundamental theory which I published in previous years in *Das Reich* or the *Völkischer Beobachter*. The foreword, written by Model,* is excellent and very flattering to me.

News from the West this evening is sparse. Pressure in the area of the American offensive has noticeably increased. We are trying to reduce it by counter-measures. By midnight there were still no reports of gains or losses of ground.

In eastern Pomerania the situation has deteriorated further. The Soviets have swung around in a pincer movement on either flank and are clearly planning an encirclement. We are carrying out a relieving operation in the threatened area to disrupt the Soviet plan. Schievelbein has been lost. Our troops are fighting excellently. There is no question of the present crisis being due to demoralisation.

There has been no change on the Oder front. At Zobten all attacks were repulsed and at Görlitz we even scored a modest offensive victory.

The Führer has paid a visit to I Corps on the Eastern Front, primarily to the "Döberitz" and "Berlin" divisions. The effect of the Führer's visit both on officers and men was enormous. I think it right that the Führer should now pay more frequent visits to the front to put an end to the nauseating rumour-mongering that he does not pay sufficient attention to the front. He does so, but in a way unimaginable to the simpler military minds. Nevertheless, on psychological grounds it is essential for the Führer to show himself in person, as he is doing.

This evening a speech by Gauleiter Hanke† from the

* Field Marshal Walter Model (now commanding Army Group B in France) was one of the generals whom Hitler trusted most cf. below p. 304. When encircled and forced to surrender, he would (unlike Paulus) commit suicide.

† Gauleiter of Lower Silesia. A sound Nazi, he would be nominated by Hitler, in his will, as Reichsführer SS in place of the dismissed Himmler. For Goebbels' confidence in him, see below pp. 77, 224, 333, 371, 399.

encircled fortress of Breslau was carried over the radio. It was movingly impressive, demonstrating an acme of political morale worthy of admiration. If all our Gauleiters in the East were like this and acted like Hanke, we should be in better shape than we are. Hanke is the outstanding personality among our eastern Gauleiters. One can see that he was brought up in Berlin.

In the evening we again had the regulation Mosquito raids on Berlin. The population of the capital is gradually becoming habituated to the necessity of spending one or two hours every evening in the air-raid shelters.

SUNDAY 4 MARCH 1945

(pp. 1–44 + 7a)
Military Situation.

In Pomerania heavy fighting continues against Soviet forces advancing north. From his break-in zone between Dramburg and Labes the enemy advanced to a line just south of Regenswalde and Schievelbein. East of Schievelbein he crossed the Schievelbein–Bad Polzin railway. Enemy advanced guards are some 20 km south-east of Naugard. From the Arnswalde area the enemy advanced towards Stargard and drove us back to a line just east and south of the town. Between Pyritz and Bahn the Bolshevists reached an area 15 km east of Greifenhagen. The enemy was able to advance farther west from his break-in in the Bublitz–Rummelsburg area where our counter-attacks were unsuccessful. He is now some 10 km south-east and north-east of Belgard and is also between Köslin and Schlawe. Farther east the enemy gained a few kilometres along the road to Bütow. From this point the front is continuous; it runs some 20 km south of Bütow in a general south-easterly direction towards Newe. In fierce fighting the enemy penetrated deeper into Graudenz which his artillery has set on fire. In East Prussia he continued his attacks north of Zinten but without success. Heavy attacks on Königsberg from the north were also repulsed. In Samland we gained further ground in local offensive operations. At Preekuln several enemy regimental-strength attacks were defeated. We must reckon on a resumption of the enemy's major offensive in the next few days.

No special developments on the Oder or Neisse fronts. Enemy bridgeheads north of Fürstenberg and south of Guben were further reduced by counter-attacks. Local gains of ground were made between Görlitz and Löwenberg. Heavier enemy attacks southwards from Goldberg and against Zobten were repulsed and enemy concentrations broken up by artillery fire. Heavy Soviet attacks on Breslau both from north and south failed. An enemy bridgehead south of Oppeln was driven in further. Soviet troop concentrations were observed east of Schwarzwasser.

In Slovakia the enemy succeeded in driving our line back a little south of Schemnitz and east of Altsohl.

In the West British and Canadian divisions continued their attacks between the Meuse and the Rhine but without success. South-west of Xanten they were driven back by our counter-attacks. The Americans advanced farther between Krefeld and Geldern. Here the enemy is some 5 km east of Geldern. He succeeded in crossing the Krefeld–Geldern road east of Kempen. Violent fighting is taking place between Kempen and Mörs. We are still holding a bridgehead on the west bank of the Rhine at Oberkassel opposite Düsseldorf. A frontal attack by the enemy on the Köln area was held along the Grevenbroich–Köln road some 6 km south-east of Grevenbroich. The Americans crossed the Erft valley either side of the Jülich–Köln road and headed for Köln. Here they are some 20 km north-west and south-west of Köln and engaged in severe fighting with our troops. Between Düren and Euskirchen the enemy captured Zülpich. In the Eifel local fighting continued on either side of Prüm but with no great change in the situation. East of Bitburg the enemy crossed the Kyll at two points. North of Trier enemy armour advanced to Ehrang on the Kyll. Street fighting is taking place in the eastern quarter of Trier. Local engagements only in the Forbach area.

No special news from the Italian front.

On the eastern front there was heavy enemy air activity in Pomerania and the Oder sector. Our own air effort was concentrated in Silesia.

In the West enemy twin-engined bombers, fighter-bombers and low-flying aircraft were active throughout the day, concentrating mainly on the central Rhine, Münsterland and the Rhineland-Westphalian industrial area. Raids were made on Stuttgart and Wiesbaden.

Some 1100 American four-engined bombers with strong fighter escort carried out raids on central, western and north-west Germany, including Chemnitz, Magdeburg, Hannover, Brunswick, Bielefeld, Hildesheim, Schwarzheide, Gütersloh, Erfurt, Plauen, Nienburg, Peine and Nienhagen. According to reports so far fighters and anti-aircraft shot down 20 enemy aircraft. During the night some 500 British four-engined bombers raided Dortmund and the Dortmund–Ems canal. Harassing raids were made on Berlin, Würzburg and Emden. So far 14 aircraft reported shot down.

A difficult problem is now arising in that the population of the western districts conquered by the Anglo-Americans is giving them a comparatively good reception. This I had really not expected. Moreover I had thought that the Volkssturm [Home Guard] would fight better than in fact it has. It must always be taken into consideration, however, that these people have been totally worn down by the air war and the severe hardships they have suffered. It may be assumed, therefore, that when they have recovered somewhat they will revert to their old attitude. The Anglo-Americans are naturally giving extraordinary publicity to the welcome they are receiving. They are clear, nevertheless, that the friendship shown them is somewhat hypocritical.

Among our Western enemies extraordinarily severe criticism of the Yalta decisions is to be heard. It is continually on the increase both in England and in the United States as well. Mistrust of the Kremlin persists and is fed by developments in Rumania and Finland. A number of

U.S. senators have spoken out against Roosevelt's policy without mincing their words. I can only emphasise once again, however, that these indications of incipient recognition of the situation are of no political significance for the present.

The workers' strikes now flaring up both in England and the USA, however, are more important. One may conclude that in both these enemy countries morale is sinking noticeably, particularly among the working class. The strikes are generally started for trivial reasons—proof that the guiding hand of the Kremlin is behind them.

The situation in Serbia is also described in extraordinarily gloomy terms by British and American correspondents. Tito is working industriously to shift the whole Serbian area into the Kremlin's sphere of influence. The starvation prevailing in Serbia provides him with the best possible conditions.

A remarkable statement has been issued by the U.S. State Department: that the United States henceforth recognises the Baltic States and is granting their diplomatic representatives extraterritorial rights. This declaration by the United States is barely comprehensible. The entire wartime political situation borders on insanity. It is full of hysterical improbabilities no longer comprehensible to the outsider.

Meanwhile, however, Stalin is creating military *faits accomplis*, giving him an edge over Roosevelt and Churchill. A truly desperate situation for us has developed in Pomerania. The position gives rise to the greatest apprehension. Our front there has been split wide open and for the moment it is impossible to see how we can re-establish a firm defence line. A number of our best formations have either been cut off or even surrounded in this area. We shall naturally try to move up to the front anything which can be spared from Berlin; but that again will merely be an invitation to Stalin to risk an offensive on Berlin as soon as possible.

Matters have now moved so far in Finland that the Finnish government has declared war on Germany. So the sequence of events is: Mannerheim* capitulates to take Finland out of the war; then the national ruling caste is slowly killed off; now Stalin cuts Finland's communications with the outside world; finally Finland has to re-enter the war on the opposite side. Such is the result of Mannerheim's policy. Such is the far-sightedness of a Marshal when he embarks on the slippery slope of politics.

Rumania too is heading straight for chaos and I do not think that Finland will be far behind Rumania. The Soviets are now demanding that the remaining Finnish resistance leaders be handed over and they are hard at work sidetracking Ryti.

Horrible weather over Germany at the moment—snow, rain, cold and an icy wind. I make use of Sunday to get some rest but naturally work must go on.

Unfortunately there have been very heavy air raids on Germany in the last 24 hours. They can no longer be recorded in detail. The Americans overfly German territory practically unresisted and are destroying one town after another; the damage done to our armaments potential is quite beyond repair.

Around midday I have an opportunity to do some reading. I am now immersed in Carlyle's book on Frederick the Great. What an example to us and what comfort and consolation in these dark days! One's heart lifts as one reads this account. There have been periods in Prussian-German history when the fate of the country and the people has been on an even sharper knife-edge than it is now. Then there were a few great men who saved the people and the country; it must be the same again now.

Nevertheless military developments are such that it sometimes seems as if we had little hope of achieving anything noticeable in this field. During this Sunday the enemy reached the Rhine at several points and we blew up the Rhine bridges. The bridgehead which we proposed to form

* Field Marshal Carl Gustav von Mannerheim was President and Commander-in-Chief of Finland. He had led Finland's resistance to Russian aggression in "the Winter War" of 1939–40 and had brought Finland into the war against Russia in 1941.

around Neuss seems to have taken a battering already. The enemy is now only 8 km from Köln. Admittedly since the beginning of his offensive he has lost 960 tanks; but what does he care with his material superiority! He is always able to replace material losses. We can only hurt him by inflicting casualties on him.

The situation in the East is even worse. There has been an extraordinary deterioration especially in the Pomeranian area. The penetration, or rather the break-through, which the enemy has made here is disastrous. Soviet tanks are already outside Kolberg. Our position in Pomerania may be said to have disintegrated totally. The enemy's two pincers have met and inside them are large German forces which the enemy is now in the process of splitting into three disastrous pockets. This is a truly shattering development. In addition the enemy has made most violent attacks on Breslau and has now reached the city centre. In the Lauban area our counter-attack has unfortunately been halted once more. In addition we anticipate an early large-scale Soviet offensive in the Mährisch–Ostrau* area. Here we really must be able to counter an enemy offensive successfully, for if we lost the Mährisch–Ostrau industrial zone we must visualize our armaments capacity being unable to meet even emergency demands.

This evening I had a long interview with the Führer. In contrast to last time I found him somewhat depressed— understandable in the light of the military developments. Physically too he is somewhat hampered; I noticed with dismay that the nervous twitch of his left hand had greatly increased. His visit to the front last Saturday went off very well. The general officers put on a good show and the soldiers cheered the Führer. Unfortunately, however, the Führer refuses to issue a press announcement about his visit to the front. Today it is as essential as our daily bread.

As far as the position in the East is concerned the Führer still hopes to clear up the situation in Pomerania. He is moving up large formations which should provide a breath-

* Now Moravska Ostrava, in Czechoslovakia.

ing space. I fear, however, that these units will not be
adequate to counter the Soviet assault effectively. It is
extraordinarily difficult to reorganise a front once it has
disintegrated. In addition Himmler is now laid low with
some infectious disease; he is still commanding his Army
Group from his bed but one knows very well how difficult
that is.

The Führer points out once more that, in contrast to the
General Staff, he had always expected the Soviets to move
on Pomerania first and not on Berlin. So once again the
Führer was right in his forecast. In spite of this the General
Staff disposed our forces wrongly, concentrating them in
the Oder area in front of Berlin. Himmler also took the
view that the first offensive would be against Berlin. The
Führer says that he allowed himself to be talked around by
the General Staff. Now it is too late, however, to repair the
error. We are now forced yet again to plug holes as best
we can. It is incomprehensible to me why, when the Führer
is so clear in his mind, he does not insist on his views being
adopted by the General Staff; after all he is the Führer and
it is for him to give the orders. The Führer is right when
he says that we must view the situation in the East in per-
spective, comparing it with the position we were in, say,
four weeks ago. To this extent he is right when he says that
the situation is easier nevertheless. Four weeks ago the
situation was such that the majority of military experts had
given us up for lost. As the Führer rightly observes, people
had turned up their toes in Berlin and given the capital up
for lost. If the Führer had not come to Berlin then and
taken a grip of things, we should probably be on the Elbe
today.

I tell the Führer in detail about my talk with General
Vlasov, specially about the methods he used on Stalin's
orders to save Moscow in late autumn 1941. The Soviet
Union was then in exactly the same situation as we are
today. At that time she took decisive measures which
various important people on our side have neither the nerve
nor the energy to take today. I submit to the Führer my plan
to intercept soldiers on the move and form them into new

regiments. The Führer approves this plan. He also agrees that we should now form women's battalions in Berlin. Innumerable women are volunteering to serve at the front and the Führer is of the opinion that, provided they volunteer, they will undoubtedly fight fanatically. They should be placed in second line; then the men in the front will lose all desire to withdraw.

As far as the Silesia front is concerned the Führer regards it as temporarily stabilised. He is very pleased with the work done here by Schörner. He also has high praise for Hanke's activities. He had heard Hanke's speech on the radio and had been very pleased with it.

The Führer is somewhat worried about the Mährisch–Ostrau industrial zone. The Soviets have concentrated very heavily in this area and an enemy offensive in this area is expected in a few days. The Führer is determined to make a stand in this area under all circumstances, always provided that our forces are adequate. Our blow in Hungary is due to fall on 6 March, in other words this coming Tuesday. The Führer is afraid that the enemy already knows all about our concentration in this area and has made the necessary preparations. Nevertheless he hopes that our measures will lead to complete victory. We have assembled first-class troops under command of Sepp Dietrich for our offensive here.

The General Staff now sees the necessity for our offensive in Hungary. Previously it had fought tooth and nail to prevent priority being given to this area. Now it realises that the petrol supply question is overriding and that we must under all circumstances hold in Hungary if motorised warfare is not to come to a complete standstill. The Führer is right when he says that Stalin has a whole number of outstanding army commanders but no strategist of genius; had he had one, the Soviet offensive would have taken place in Hungary, not from the Baranov bridgehead. Had we lost the Hungarian and Viennese oil we should have been totally incapable of conducting a counter-offensive, as we are planning to do in the East.

The Führer is naturally very worried about the situation

in the West. Here too the front may be regarded as largely disrupted. Nevertheless the Führer is of the opinion that we must succeed in holding the Rhine since it provides us with an outstanding defensive obstacle. He has ordered that under all circumstances operations must provide for the retention of certain bridgeheads west of the Rhine. In the West we are shorter of equipment than of troops. The Führer, however, agrees with me that we must call up and train as many men as possible since shortage of weapons naturally does now relieve us of the necessity to prepare troop units for possible emergencies.

To some extent Model has lost control in the West. But he cannot be blamed for doing so. The West was too thinly manned. As I impressed urgently on the Führer, if we can really no longer hold out in the West, then our last political war plan collapses, for if the Anglo-Americans reach central Germany, they would not have the smallest reason to enter into talks with us.

Our task now is to stay on our feet whatever happens. The crisis in the enemy camp is admittedly growing to a considerable magnitude but it is still questionable whether the blow-up will come so long as we are still able to put up even a partial defence. The only hope for a successful end to the war is that the split in the enemy camp becomes irreparable before we are flat on the floor.

The Führer again gives vent to very severe criticism of the General Staff. I put to him, however, the question: what good does that do him? He should consign the General Staff to the devil if it creates so many difficulties for him. The Führer counters by quoting Bismarck who is once supposed to have said that he could deal with the Danes, the Austrians and the French but not with the German bureaucracy. Bismarck, however, did not possess the power which the Führer has today. The Führer is of course right when he says that army reform in France was carried out not during the French Revolution but during the Napoleonic wars. Stalin, on the other hand, put through his army reform in good time and is now reaping the reward. If our defeats now force us to do likewise, it will come very late in the day to produce ultimate success. The Führer's view, however, still is that we must somehow succeed in holding firm in the West and the East. For the moment, however, he is not clear himself exactly how this is to be done.

The Führer is violently opposed to any steps being taken to assist Anglo-American prisoners of war now in process of transfer from the East to the neighbourhood of Berlin. There are some 78,000 of them and they can no longer be properly fed; they are riddled with lice and many of them are suffering from dysentery. Under present circumstances there is little one can do for them. Perhaps it would be possible to call in the Red Cross to help in producing a semi-human existence for them.

The Führer takes a very hopeful view of the political situation. He too has noticed with satisfaction that the political crisis in the enemy camp is growing. I point out to him, however, that its progress is too slow from our point of view. The question is whether we have the time to wait for this crisis to develop fully. The Führer is right when he says that England is very war-weary. He too had been struck by the Washington report that the USA was recognising the Baltic States. It seems that a serious quarrel between the Anglo-Americans and the Soviets is going on behind the scenes. But, as I emphasise over and over again, the dispute is not deep-rooted enough to afford us any relief at the moment.

The Führer is convinced that, if any country on the other side is willing to take the initiative in opening talks with us, it will be the Soviet Union. Stalin is having the greatest difficulties with the Anglo-Americans and his is now one of the countries hoping to take some loot home from the war, just like us. As a result the moment will come one day when he will be sick of quarrelling eternally with the Anglo-Americans and will look round for other possibilities. His tactics in Rumania and Finland, the Führer stresses, are really alarming to the Anglo-Americans, to say nothing of the Polish problem. The Führer forecasts that San Francisco will be something of a diplomatic fiasco. But before we can start talks either with one side or the other, it is essential that we score some military success. Even Stalin must first lose a few tail feathers before he will have anything to do with us.

The Führer is right when he says that Stalin is in the best position to do an about-turn in war policy, since he need take no account of his public opinion. It is rather different with England. It is quite immaterial whether Churchill wants to pursue a different war policy; even if he did, he couldn't; he is too dependent on internal political forces which are already semi-bolshevistic in character, to say nothing of Roosevelt, who shows not the smallest sign of any intention to change course.

The objective which the Führer has in mind is to discover some possibility of an accommodation with the Soviet Union and then to pursue the struggle against England with brutal violence. England has always been the mischiefmaker in Europe; if she was finally swept out of Europe, then we should have peace and quiet, at least for a time.

Soviet atrocities are of course frightful and are a severe handicap to the Führer's concept. But the Mongols once ravaged Europe as the Soviets are doing today without preventing political progress in settling the disputes of those days. Storms from the East come and go and Europe must cope with them.

I submit to the Führer my propaganda plan for publicising Soviet atrocities and my intention to use Guderian in this connection. The Führer is in full agreement with this plan. He approves the idea that prominent National-Socialists should be kept somewhat in the background in publicising these atrocities since our information will acquire greater international credibility thereby. In any case it is essential that people should be absolutely clear on what they think of bolshevism. The atrocities are so appalling that the people cannot be left in ignorance. One's heart misses a beat as one reads the reports. But what good is it to moan about it! We must try to get out of our dilemma somehow; it has now reached such proportions as to be truly horrifying.

I then revert to the subject of the Luftwaffe. The Führer gives vent to the most violent criticism of Göring and the Luftwaffe. He regards Göring as the real scapegoat for the collapse of the Luftwaffe. I put to him the question: why then has there been no change in command of the Luftwaffe? The Führer opines that there is no suitable successor. Industry's experts, he says, are miles superior to those of the Luftwaffe. No outstanding brain has emerged from the Luftwaffe itself. The Me 262s have been in action as fighters for the first time and achieved considerable success. The Führer is somewhat hesitant, however, about using the Me 262s for fighter defence on a large scale. He sees some hope here. Otherwise he regards the Luftwaffe merely as a great junk-shop. But we have all known this for a long time and we have all repeatedly put the problem to the Führer; yet no change has been made in the command of the Luftwaffe and this is the reason for its decay.

I tell the Führer that Hadamovsky has been killed on the eastern front and he is greatly shocked. He asks me to ensure that Dr. Naumann* does not go to the front under any circumstances. We must keep our top level men together as far as possible now, since we may have urgent need of them in this time of crisis.

I can add some additional details to the story of the Dresden catastrophe. The Führer tells me that Frau Raubal† has written him a letter bursting with fury and indignation. She behaved with extraordinary courage during the Dresden catastrophe.

In this connection I tell the Führer that Magda‡ and the children wish to remain with me whatever happens, even if Berlin is attacked and surrounded. After some hesitation the Führer approves.

---

* Goebbels' State Secretary in the Ministry of Propaganda. He would stay in Berlin to the end.

† Angela Raubal, *née* Hitler, Hitler's widowed half-sister, who had kept home for him from 1925 to 1936.

‡ Frau Goebbels.

I raise the case of Fromm* with the Führer. Having been guilty of cowardice in the face of the enemy, namely the 20 July putschists, Fromm undoubtedly deserves the death sentence, but with the Peoples Court being run as it is at present no death sentence is to be anticipated. The Führer reverts to the idea of appointing Frank† as President of the Peoples Court. He would not be an ideal figurehead but is nevertheless a political jurist. Apart from him we have no one available and I cannot put forward any other name as a candidate.

In general the Führer gives me a very stalwart impression once more. He is totally unshaken by the fearful blows to which we are now subjected. His steadfastness is admirable. If anyone can master this crisis, he can. Throughout the length and breadth of the land there is no one who can hold a candle to him.

In any case our guiding principle must now be this: whatever happens we are going to get the better of this crisis; if this is not possible, however, we must endure it with dignity. We do well to visualise everything and burn our bridges behind us. That way we are most likely to lead our banners to victory.

I then have a short talk with Ambassador Hewel.‡ He tells me that Ribbentrop is now very busy trying to forge links to the West but that for the moment there is no prospect of success. There is not the smallest reciprocity either from the British side or the American. Churchill's and

* Col.-Gen. Friedrich Fromm, C-in-C Replacement Army, had been compromised in the plot to assassinate Hitler on 20 July 1944. Once the plot had failed, he covered his traces by ordering the instant court martial and execution of the conspirators, including Stauffenberg; but suspicion later fell on him and he was now in prison. For his fate, see below, pp. 110–11, 156.

† Hans Frank, Minister of Justice and former Governor-General of Poland. He was an old Nazi, who had been Hitler's personal lawyer. An appointment was necessary because the notorious President of the People's Court, Roland Freisler, had been killed by a bomb dropped on his court on 3 February.

‡ Ribbentrop's liaison officer at Hitler's HQ. He had the title but not the function of an ambassador.

Roosevelt's attitude is completely negative. This has been made plain as possible to us by our contacts both in Stockholm and The Vatican. It is clear that, until we can chalk up some military success, there is nothing to be done politically at the moment. One might well repeat the cry: A kingdom for a victory! As regards initiation of political measures to bring the war to an end, at present it is too late on the one hand and too early on the other. The present situation offers no prospects. Hewel also takes the view that our U-boat successes are no longer making an impression on the enemy; they came too late. Both the British and Americans are still determined to annihilate us first and then to see what happens. Hewel tells me that on various occasions in 1941/2 Ribbentrop proposed to the Führer that peace be concluded with Moscow, since in a year's time at latest the American armaments potential would make itself felt on the battlefield; the Führer, however, turned the suggestion down flat. I do not believe this is true. In any case Ribbentrop would have been at fault in not ensuring that he had adequate support for this plan from other members of the Führer's entourage. He has turned foreign policy into an occult science which only he is supposed to understand and now he is reaping the reward of his own ideas. Hewel thinks that there is no prospect of doing anything political to ensure success. I am still of the opinion that the blame lies primarily at Ribbentrop's door. When Hewel tells me that Ribbentrop is totally discouraged at the moment, this makes not the smallest impression on me. Ribbentrop deserves more severe punishment than depression and discouragement. He has been the Führer's evil genius driving him on from one reckless adventure to the next.

The general mood in the Reich Chancellery is pretty dismal. I would rather not go there again because the atmosphere is infectious. The generals hang their heads and the Führer alone holds his head high.

I drive home late in the evening and plunge into work. It is still the best medicine.

MONDAY 5 MARCH 1945

(pp. 1–26, p. 19 overlaid)
Military Situation.
In eastern Slovakia all enemy attacks in the areas Schemnitz, Altsohl and Nikolas failed apart from some minor penetrations. No special activity on the entire Oder front as far as Goldberg. In the Breslau area the enemy is regrouping. Our own attack at Lauban gained further ground at low cost; in the Oder valley there was only local fighting round the bridgeheads without change in the situation.

Mobile operations are now in progress in Pomerania. In detail the Soviets gained ground north of Pyritz, drove into Stargard from the north-east but were then held on the line Plathe–Raugard. Kolberg is surrounded. Street fighting is taking place in Köslin. Between Belgard and Kolberg our troops withdrew from Greifenberg on orders. The northward Soviet advance in central Pomerania was held south-west of Bütow, at Schlawe and west thereof. Heavy Soviet troop concentrations in the Heiderode area. Mass attacks by a Soviet Army west of Grosswollental were held on the main defence line and driven back. Very fierce fighting is raging round the fortress of Graudenz.

In East Prussia battalion-strength attacks were repulsed all along the front.

In Courland too violent Soviet attacks at Preekuln and south-east of Frauenburg failed in face of successful counter-attacks.

In the West the British continued their mass attacks and reached the Geldern–Wesel railway line. Leading elements of the forces which have been attacking from Venlo for some days reached the area north-west of Mörs some 6 km west of the Xanten–Mörs road. On the Rhine attacks on the bridgeheads at Homberg and north of Düsseldorf were repulsed. The Rhine bridges were blown at Duisburg, Krefeld and Düsseldorf. Between Düsseldorf and Köln strong enemy forces reached the Neuss–Köln railway line with their leading troops despite tenacious resistance by our troops. Fluctuating fighting is in progress immediately west of Köln. Strong enemy forces attacked towards Euskirchen from the Zülpich area. At the Urit valley dam the enemy seized Gemünd. Counter-attacks are being made south of this point and also in the Euskirchen area and west of Köln. In the Prüm sector American attacks gained some ground and drove our lines back a few kilometres. The enemy succeeded in forming small bridgeheads across the Kyll valley. Violent fighting continues in Trier. Local actions only in the Zerf area, at Forbach and at Reipertsweiler.

In Italy fighting for individual mountain peaks continues. Enemy attacks were repulsed along the Senio and at Faenca.

Owing to unfavourable weather, air activity on both fronts was somewhat less than on previous days.

Over Reich territory 900 American four-engined aircraft with strong fighter escort made daylight raids on transport and industrial targets and airfields in south-western and southern Germany. A smaller British formation attacked industrial and transport targets in the Gelsenkirchen area. A large American four-engined bomber formation from the south attacked Austrian industrial and transport targets in the Wiener-Neustadt area. The German Bight was mined during the night. In addition harassing raids were made on Berlin and Bremen by high-speed aircraft.

In the last few days the daily OKW reports have been presenting a dismal picture. At the moment we have no specially favourable news to give regarding the situation either in Pomerania or the West. Quite the contrary. One can imagine the effect of this on the German people who are anyway very depressed over the severe blows we have suffered in recent weeks. It is urgently necessary for us to be able to report a success at least somewhere. I hope that this will be the case in the Hungarian area in the next few days. But this is not of great interest to the German people, although it is of decisive importance for the war; how decisive it is difficult to make clear to the German people, surrounded as they are by enemies. Otherwise practically every OKW report gives the public an enormous shock. Although people have largely got used to the fact that we have to endure very heavy blows at the moment, in the long run this engenders not fanaticism but a sort of fatalism. It does not lead people, thank God, to neglect their everyday duties either at the front or at work.

Naturally our western enemies' flags are flying high. People are jubilant that Eisenhower has succeeded in driving our front back to the Rhine. The news that the town of Rheydt received the Americans with white flags makes me blush. I can hardly realise it, especially not the fact that one of these white flags flew from the house where I was born. At the moment, however, I do not even know who is living in the house and I can only suppose that this deed of madness was done by evacuees or people who had been bombed out. It makes a first-class sensation for the Americans of course, just as it is shameful and humiliating to me. If we ever return to Rheydt, however, I shall try to clear the matter up.

Otherwise, however, our Western enemies are clear that our withdrawal across the Rhine was carried out in an orderly manner and that Eisenhower has not succeeded in disrupting our front or annihilating our armies. They realise that the Rhine is an extraordinarily difficult and dangerous defensive barrier, particularly if we succeed in gaining sufficient time to put it into a proper state of defence. In any case they are quite clear that German resistance in the West can in no way be regarded as crushed.

Eisenhower is now enjoying himself offering terms of surrender to those towns west of the Rhine which we still hold and are proposing to defend. These terms are naturally being rejected with scorn.

Reuters have published a long significant article to the effect that our situation is nothing like so catastrophic as is generally assumed in London. We can still produce an adequate supply of weapons, it says, and our manpower potential is by no means exhausted. There can therefore be no question of an early end to the war. The heart of Germany has not been affected by our recent set-backs. Reuters foresee that our only major difficulty will be the food sector, which in fact is the case. Here we must anticipate an extraordinarily severe crisis in the next three to four months.

For the second time German high-speed aircraft have been over London at night and this has naturally created a great stir among the British public. It has not been thought possible that we were in any position to do this. The British Home Secretary has been compelled to re-impose the black-out in the London area which naturally does not contribute to an improvement of morale among the British people.

I set great store by the miserable conditions in the Anglo-American rear areas. Food shortages in France and Belgium, for instance, have reached a really grotesque level. The British and Americans are now so short of shipping that they cannot spare even one or two ships for food supply to the countries of the West. If our U-boats can really be effective in this strained shipping situation, the war in the West might take on a very different aspect. Once again the OKW report shows that 44,000 tons of British and American shipping have been sunk.

Development in the countries occupied by the Soviets proceed precisely according to plan, in Finland, in Rumania and now also in Serbia. As far as Serbia is concerned the Soviets are relying initially on the increasing food shortage to make the people ripe for bolshevisation. In Rumania things have gone further. Here the Iron Guard is dealing out terror and provocation and the Soviets are concluding therefrom that they must make *tabula rasa* in Rumania. There is talk of fascist impudence, the worst vice in Soviet eyes, and Rumanian politicians who tried to make common cause with the British and Americans are being accused of this. There is little love lost between the Russians and London over all this, but the British are now too intimidated and too impotent to dare oppose the Soviets openly.

As far as the situation in the Soviet Union itself is concerned great war-weariness is prevalent. People really wanted to put an end to the war after the success of the Baranov offensive but—so confidential reports tell us— Stalin is now completely in the grip of victory hysteria. He is holding the Seydlitz Committee* ready so that he can perhaps install it as a provisional German government provided a psychological opportunity presents itself and he can risk so open a provocation of the British and Americans.

Japan is hoping that Soviet neutrality in the Pacific conflict will be maintained. The Japanese argument is that the Soviets are being compelled to withdraw so many troops from the Manchurian front that they cannot risk entry into the Pacific war.

Certain influential politicians in Tokyo are working to overthrow the present Koiso cabinet and adopt a policy of greater compromise. For the moment, however, they have no prospect of coming anywhere near doing so.

Fear of the Soviets is growing in Western countries particularly among the military leaders. Eisenhower, for instance, recently said to an agent that if the British and Americans did not succeed in making a definitive breakthrough in the West, they would have lost the war in Europe politically.

The situation in Pomerania naturally gives rise to the greatest anxiety, although Guderian is still of the opinion that we can succeed in clearing it up by counter-attacks.

---

* The "Free Germany" committee of captured German officers, headed by Field Marshal Paulus and General von Seydlitz, who broadcast to Germany for Russia.

On the map the position is simply terrible but one cannot judge a situation solely from the map.

Dr. Fischer, our former Governor of Warsaw, has fallen into Soviet hands as a prisoner of war. A fearful fate undoubtedly awaits him. I had never expected that he would have the strength of character to commit suicide in order to escape the consequences now threatening him.

Roatta, the former Italian Chief of Staff, has escaped from the military prison in Rome. A price of a million lire has been put on his head. This traitor is now being attacked by both sides. His treachery is costing him dear.

Limitless terror from the air! It is quite impossible to record the results in detail. The eternal question everyone asks is: Where are our fighters? It is raised with increasing urgency both at command level and among the public. One . . .

[Gap in text; clearly p. 19 of the original was inadvertently overlaid with another page during copying]

. . . go to the rear, form themselves into groups and simply tell the checkpoints that their officers have left them in the lurch. They are merely trying to create an alibi for their own cowardice.

At a meeting of the Berlin Defence Council there was a considerable rumpus with General Schönfeld, deputising for General Hauenschild who is sick; he gave vent to unacceptable criticism of the construction of defence works now in progress on the authority of the Wehrmacht. It is now the fashion with the Wehrmacht to lay the blame for anything that goes wrong on to the political agencies. It happened in this case. I countered this tactless and somewhat insolent way of going about things with vigour, putting forward weighty arguments. I am now demanding weekly progress report on the defences of Berlin with clear answers to the questions how much food, how much petrol, how many weapons, how much ammunition and how many fit men we have available for the defence of the capital at any one time. I find myself compelled to demand such a report every week since there is naturally considerable fluctuation in these basic ingredients of the capital's defence and I must be and intend to be in a position to intervene energetically should this fluctuation assume dangerous proportions. The Wehrmacht is most unwilling to give me the figures since it means that they must balance their books. They will not be able to evade this requirement of mine however.

Now that Speer has taken the railways under his wing he is refusing to release any more railwaymen for service and is even demanding release of men from the Wehrmacht. I had anticipated these difficulties; nevertheless the construction control commissions initiated for the Reichsbahn will continue their work.

We have made no progress in controlling the innumerable number of soldiers on the move. It is very difficult to find a simple but effective procedure.

A vast amount of work today.

The evening situation report shows no major change as far as the Western Front is concerned except that the enemy is now along broad stretches of the west bank of the Rhine. Thank God, however, we succeeded in blowing the Rhine bridges in good time wherever they were immediately threatened. The picture in the West is obviously anything but pleasant but at the moment we can flatter ourselves that we shall be able to hold the Rhine as a firm defensive obstacle without the British and Americans being able to form bridgeheads across it. In fact we intend to hold such bridgeheads ourselves on the left bank.

As regards the situation in the East our offensive in the Lauban area is going well. We have made no great gains of ground but we have inflicted severe losses on the Soviets. We have even created a small pocket, though on a modest scale. The Soviets are now withdrawing troops and equipment from the Fürstenberg area, in all probability destined for Upper Silesia. The offensive on Mährisch–Ostrau already forecast by the Führer seems imminent. So there is no direct threat to Berlin at the moment. The situation in Breslau has not changed noticeably. Developments in

Pomerania, on the other hand, are dramatic and unpleasant. The enemy has captured Belgard and Köslin. The military Commandant of Kolberg—if he can so be called—made a proposition to the Führer that the town be surrendered without a fight. The Führer immediately removed him and put a younger officer in his place. Have these degenerate generals no sense of history or of responsibility? Does a present-day Military Commandant of Kolberg nurture the ambition to emulate a Loucadou rather than a Gneisenau?

We are now at work preparing large-scale counter-measures for the Pomeranian area. I hope they can be set in motion soon. Our offensive in Hungary is expected on Tuesday. If both these operations succeed, we should of course emerge in good shape. But it is too much to hope that both will be fully successful. The situation has become somewhat acute in East Prussia in that the Soviets have made a number of deep penetrations. It is hoped, however, to deal with them.

In the evening we are again confined to the air raid shelters for hours. Berlin is raided by Mosquitos. In addition heavy terror raids were made on towns in Saxony. Probably it is the turn of Chemnitz this time. One hopes that there will not be a catastrophe here like the recent one in Dresden.

TUESDAY 6 MARCH 1945

(pp. 1–45)
Military Situation.
No operations of special importance in Hungary. In Slovakia the enemy continued his attacks in the Schemnitz–Altsohl area.

In the sector east of Mährisch–Ostrau as far as the region of Oppeln and also between Oppeln and Lauban the enemy continues his offensive preparations, so that an attempt by the Soviets to pierce this front must be reckoned with. On the German side we continued to attack in the Görlitz, Lauban and Löwenberg areas, the purpose being to harass the enemy at widely divergent points, to interfere with his troop concentrations and so prevent a strong concentrated offensive like that in Pomerania. Our attacks in the Görlitz area scored considerable local success. At Guben too German troops improved their positions. At Lebus a regimental-strength attack by the enemy was repulsed apart from a minor penetration to a depth of only 100 yards.

The main weight of fighting was once again in Pomerania; here the enemy concentrated his forces and succeeded in piercing our thinly manned front between the Oder and Königsberg, expanding his break-through considerably. Advancing north of Naugard the enemy reached Cammin and the area of Wollin. In the area of this wide break-through there are German forces everywhere; some, as in Kolberg and Belgard, are semi-surrounded garrisons; others are major formations, concentrated and still fighting well; they will undoubtedly be of great importance when we start major operations to clear the area. These latter forces are in the region between Bad Polzin and Dramburg. Reinforcements, including the "Silesia" Panzer Division, are on the move up. Soviet assaults on Kolberg and Belgard were repulsed. The western boundary of the enemy breakthrough now runs just east of Wollin to north of Naugard, passes just east of Naugard to just west of Stargard and thence to the Oder in the region of Schwedt. The eastern boundary runs from Rügenwalde to Schlawe (which we still hold), midway between Rummelsburg and Bütow and at Heiderode joins the Heiderode–Vistula stop-line. The enemy has not, therefore, been able to extend his breakthrough much farther east; all enemy attacks between Rummelsburg, Heiderode and Hade were repulsed.

Soviet attacks in East Prussia were less violent as a result of the heavy casualties they had suffered on previous days. There was no change in the situation. In Courland enemy attacks at Preekuln were weaker. South of Frauenburg, on the other hand, the enemy went over to the attack in greater strength and with air support; he only achieved some local penetrations which were sealed off at once. All other attacks failed.

In the West Anglo-American attacking forces succeeded in pushing our defence line back to the Rhine between Köln and Xanten. We still hold some bridgeheads on the left bank of the Rhine, however, for instance one of a 15 km radius round Wesel and including Xanten, and others in the bend of the river at Rheinberg, at Orsoy and opposite Hamborn, Duisburg, and Düsseldorf. In violent fighting the enemy suffered heavy losses of men and material everywhere before his superiority enabled him finally to push us back to the Rhine. Our own losses also were heavy. At Köln the enemy is now on the northern, north-western and western edges of the outer suburbs. South of the city fighting is in progress roughly on the line: western edge of Köln–west of Brühl–Brühl-Euskirchen road. Euskirchen fell into enemy hands. Beyond Euskirchen the enemy succeeded in advancing only 2–3 km towards Bonn and about 6–7 km towards Münsted-Eifel. The southern pivot of the Anglo-American offensive lies in the area between Gemünd and Schleiden; the old Eifel front is still intact southwards from this point. It is not thought, however, that this can hold out in the long run. An enemy advance north-west of Prüm has now produced a large westward bulge in the front. The enemy moved forward here to an area 10 km north-west of Gerolstein. From the area north-west of Bitburg the enemy made another trouble-some penetration, some 60 tanks advancing north-east from Kyllburg along the Bitburg–Daun road and reaching Heidenbach about 12 km south-west of Daun. It has so far not been possible to stop the enemy tanks. East of Bit-burg the enemy drove forward about 5–6 km towards Wittlich and is now about 15 km west of that place. Several enemy attacks were repulsed north of Trier; east of Trier the Americans reached the Ruwer valley at several points and crossed the Ruwer–Hermeskeil road.

In the Forbach area violent fighting is taking place among the fortifications. The situation remains unchanged however.

Activity is increasing in Italy. It cannot yet be termed a major offensive but brisk offensive operations are in progress particularly at Vergato in the area north of Poretta; here the enemy extended his front of attack but could only achieve minor local penetrations in face of strong German resistance.

Very heavy enemy air activity in the East was directed primarily against Breslau which was bombed by some 1200 Soviet aircraft attacking in waves. Numerous fires are burning in the city centre. In Courland enemy tactical support aircraft were very active. Our own air activity in the East was of medium strength and directed primarily on the Pomeranian area.

Over the Western Front numerous enemy twin-engined bombers and fighters were active throughout the day with their main effort directed on Münsterland, the Rhineland, Westphalia and the central Rhine area.

Over Reich territory about 800 American four-engined bombers with fighter escort of almost the same strength made daylight raids on north-west and central Germany and also on the Proctectorate [Bohemia]. Places raided included Harburg-Wilhelmsburg, Chemnitz, Plauen, Rauen, Pilsen, Hannover and Nuremberg. Industrial and transport targets were the main objectives. A smaller British four-engined formation attacked industrial and transport targets in the Ruhr, mainly in the Gelsenkirchen area. So far 11 aircraft have been reported shot down.

During the night a formation of 600 British four-engined bombers with Mosquito path-finders and fighter escort attacked Chemnitz. Harassing raids by Mosquitos were made on Berlin, Hannover, Brunswick and Wiesbaden. A smaller British formation from the south made a harassing raid on Graz. Soviet aircraft from the east made continuous harassing raids on the Stettin area. Fifty-nine of our night fighters shot down 20 enemy.

Anglo-American military experts are very downcast at the fact that, as they admit, the German armies have escaped across the Rhine and moreover, as they explicitly add, in good order. They accordingly state that a new amphibious operation will be necessary since the Rhine is as great an obstacle to military operations as the Channel was. They realise, therefore, that their offensive in the West has not been a complete victory. The aim which Eisenhower had set himself, the annihilation of the German armies, has not been achieved. Reference is made to a figure of 45,000 as the number of prisoners; but even this is not enough to give the enemy any greater hope than hitherto of an early end to the war.

The British-American military experts particularly eulogise our rearguards, who did in fact fight with fantastic courage. It is primarily due to them that our withdrawal across the Rhine was covered.

In the West there will probably now be a waiting period, for we all know that the British and Americans are not over-bold in their operations; they will therefore make sure of their supply lines and make careful planning preparations for the Rhine crossing before risking it. And yet on the enemy side time presses as never before. There is fear that the U-boat war will now tear great holes in enemy tonnage and as a result distress in the enemy-occupied areas of the west will increase, quite apart from the supply problems for the Anglo-American divisions. It is characteristic that the British newspapers are stating quite frankly that in recent weeks both Churchill and I have been right in what we have said when we stressed that on the Western side the tonnage problem would be the decisive one for the coming months. There is considerable hope for us here. Our U-boats must get to work hard; above all it may be anticipated that as the new type gets into action, far greater results should be achieved than with our old U-boats, though these are now fitted with schnorkel.

Rundstedt is again getting high marks in the enemy press. The fact that our troops escaped more or less intact across the Rhine is attributed to him. There is definite fear of the Rhine. The British and Americans naturally realise that in the middle of Germany they cannot carry out an amphibious operation like that of last summer. There are far too many handicaps for that.

Churchill is of course once again visiting troops on German soil. He is lazing in the sunshine of his fame. He visited Eisenhower and Montgomery. Montgomery undoubtedly told him of certain jealousies which have arisen between him and Eisenhower.

Sinclair, the British Air Minister, takes a very serious view of our renewed air raids on the British homeland. From the purely military point of view they are not taken over-tragically but by all accounts they are lowering British morale still further, particularly since the black-out, which had been cancelled some time ago, has now had to be reimposed in southern England and in London. It also seems that our V-weapons are still causing considerable destruction in the British capital, enough at least to have a lasting effect on British morale.

Strikes in Britain are mushrooming again. The British

workers are clearly under the impression that by and large the war is already won and that the time has now come for them to press their social demands. In London alone 10,000 dockers are on strike. Troops had to be used to load vital war material.

Bohle* has submitted to me a situation report on foreign policy summarising reports from his representatives abroad; from it I deduce the following: the British people are becoming increasingly imbued with the conviction that all domestic and external difficulties, the economic problem and all the misery of this winter in England are due solely to the fact that the war did not end in autumn 1944 and the government had no alternative plans. By mid-January the winter battle in the Ardennes, the intensified bombardment of London by V-weapons,† the emergence of severe disagreements with the USA and fear of Moscow's uncontrollable policy had produced so widespread a crisis that the demand for an immediate end to the war had become general. Naturally this was based on the firm conviction that the threat of a German victory is over for ever and it only remains for adroit policy to initiate rapid negotiations with Germany and bring the war to a conclusion tantamount to victory. This explains the sudden severe criticism of the government's ineptitude from all those who continue to preach unconditional surrender in public. The British were horrified by the casualties suffered by the Americans in France, for they showed what the British army might still face if the war continues and all these years England has managed to avoid making over-great sacrifices of blood herself. As against this frame of mind and this outlook on the part of the people the government is faced with certain grave facts of life: first that Britain herself, important positions in her Empire and also France are to all intents and purposes occupied by American troops; secondly that Roosevelt refuses to deviate from the demand for un-

* Head of the *Auslandsorganisation* which existed to nazify Germans living abroad.

† "Flying bombs" (V1) and rocket-borne bombs (V2) which were launched against London in the last months of the war.

conditional surrender agreed at Casablanca even under the impact of the bolshevist advance in the Balkans and Britain herself is therefore faced with the acceptance of very heavy sacrifices; thirdly that militarily Soviet Russia is operating even more selfishly and independently of Britain than are the Americans and therefore, should agreed obligations not be adhered to, Britain's aims and desires in Europe become even more problematical. The inordinate intensification of anti-German atrocity propaganda, together with the emphasis placed on prosecution of a brutal war of annihilation with the aim of unconditional surrender, testify to the rigid determination of the government to fly in the face of public opinion. The disappearance of any genuine parliamentary opposition such as appeared in 1940 and 1941 when the composition of the House was similar, the retreat or suppression of all revolutionary elements and movements, and above all the practically irreplaceable leadership of Churchill, make it comparatively easy for the government to ride roughshod over all criticism. Meanwhile the views of Churchill and his adherents concerning the war and their peace aims have crystallised. Britain must be directly involved in complete victory over Germany and only then can she, together with the USA and Soviet Russia, withdraw from the European conflict. The unexpectedly successful break-through achieved by the Russian offensive makes it even more urgent to keep active operations going and reach early agreement with Stalin on the principles governing the occupation and administration of Germany, in fact of Central Europe, in the event of a German collapse. Moscow has given it clearly to be understood that there is no question of introduction of international commissions or Anglo-Saxon participation in the occupation and civil administration of areas occupied by Soviet Russia. Britain's main anxiety is lest Moscow install a Soviet satellite government, at any rate in the Russian-occupied part of Germany (the cry is a Seydlitz government), and so a communistic Germany allied to Moscow should emerge; not only would this form a bridge to the communisation of France and Belgium but it would govern the political and ideological development of all Europe. Enthusiasm for Soviet Russia has already diminished in Britain and in the City; among broad sections of the upper middle class a definitely anti-Russian policy is being advocated but in fact Britain cannot for the present afford to forgo Soviet Russia's friendship and co-operation, cost what it may. This is reinforced by the fact that in no area of foreign policy has America been prepared to support Britain in a firm stand against Moscow. On the contrary Roosevelt has demonstrated at every opportunity that he intends to improve and intensify America's relations with Soviet Russia at Britain's expense. In this connection Japanese politicians publicly express the view that America will only revise her attitude to Soviet Russia when the war against Japan has been victoriously concluded or when it is no longer dependent on the goodwill or possible participation of Soviet Russia. In addition there are numerous indications that on its side the Moscow government places great value on friendship with America and is always ready to play America off against Britain. Britain has one great question to resolve in any negotiations with Stalin: Stalin must be compelled to give an answer whether he regards the Russian-occupied area of Europe as a Soviet sphere of influence for the foreseeable future, an area in which the other Allies would have no voice whether it be Poland, Rumania, Jugoslavia or occupied Germany. If an inter-Allied settlement is refused by Moscow, Britain will demand, with or without American assistance, a similar arrangement for herself in Western Europe and Italy and possibly in a reconquered Norway and Denmark. There are many indications that America intends to withdraw the majority of her fighting troops from Europe as soon as the war ends, if not sooner. It would be entirely in accord with America's present policy to stand aloof from any political dispute between Britain and Western Europe on one side and Soviet Russia on the other. America is not really in the least interested in the fate of Europe except to keep it in a state of military and economic impotence. In the view of leading political economists in London the resultant position for Britain is as follows: (1) Only if Germany is defeated unconditionally can Britain claim her heritage to lead and exploit economically the countries of central and western Europe. (2) This can only be done if she is on good terms with Soviet Russia and a clear delimitation of Russian spheres of influence has been agreed. (3) The Americans are neither capable of nor interested in taking trouble about or dominating European countries. (4) All countries which have become directly dependent on Russia will turn to Britain both from economic necessity and from political fear of Soviet Russia. Even a defeated Germany is expected to act in this way provided it has not fallen into the claws of Soviet Russia in the concluding phase of the war as Britain visualises it. In general, people in London are still convinced that a communist revolution in Western Europe can be prevented by a foreign policy settlement with Moscow and that then the democratic parliamentary system will keep the communists in a permanent minority, always provided that the proposed limits can be set to Soviet influence. Otherwise Britain seems determined to maintain her influence well into the post-war period by means of military occupation.

Admittedly this report was written at the time of the Yalta Conference [from 4 to 12 February 1945]; nevertheless by and large it seems to me to describe the enemy situation correctly. One may deduce from it that at the moment our political prospects are nil. But this can change from day to day, particularly if developments in Soviet-occupied areas proceed at their tempo of the last few days.

Bohle also submits to me a memorandum on the reform of our diplomatic service which he proposes to hand to the Führer. It contains many useful ideas, but there is little object in useful ideas at the moment. Our diplomatic service should have been reformed years ago. We are now paying dearly for the fact that we failed to do so. On the other hand in this, as in many other problems, we no longer have the time to spend on wearisome reforms. We are living, so to speak, from hand to mouth.

Another treatise handed to the Führer by Bohle and dealing with overall war policy merely repeats ideas which have frequently been discussed between the Führer and myself. So Bohle is telling the Führer nothing new. In this connection it is characteristic that Bormann proposes to refuse to submit such exposés to the Führer in future since he does not wish to become involved in foreign policy matters; in any case Ribbentrop is now so susceptible to such ideas that they can be submitted direct to him. I think this is otiose. Ribbentrop has been written off by the enemy to such an extent that he is presumably no longer the appropriate person to make contact with London or Washington.

As far as the enemy-occupied regions of the West are concerned, it can be said that the onset of crisis, though slow, is steady and uninterrupted. The starving rear areas of the British-American front represent a great source of hope for us. A political opposition is forming here apparently leading straight to bolshevism, which naturally the British cannot tolerate in the west of our continent. Food riots are reported from all over Europe. Churchill and Roosevelt have in fact succeeded in plunging this part of the world into frightful chaos. The reports of the food situation coming in from all the Western-occupied areas make one's blood run cold. It cannot be assumed that the British will take any stock of this for humanitarian reasons but they will be compelled to react if there are military repercussions which will probably be the case in the foreseeable future.

It is real naïveté when the British government issues a declaration that henceforth they propose to mediate in Rumania. They may want to, but can they—that is the question. The Soviets will simply refuse to discuss any British involvement in developments there.

According to one report submitted to me dreadful confusion reigns in Croatia. The Ustaše* are conducting a

---

* The pro-German, Catholic militia of the Croatian fascist leader, Ante Pavelić, who was known—in imitation of Hitler and Mussolini —as the Poglavnik, or leader. Pavelić escaped to South America at the end of the war.

regime of terror which defies description. Tito is the one who has the last laugh. In fact he is proving to be a high-grade popular leader. In contrast to him the Poglavnik cuts a truly piteous figure. He is only maintained by German military might. Moreover I have the impression that our men in this area of the south-east are merely defending chaos. Confusion is so great that one can no longer make head or tail of the situation.

Sensational news comes from Helsinki. Mannerheim is sick and has resigned his office as Minister-President in favour of Paasikivi. His illness is quite openly said to be a diplomatic one. He could no longer do his job. In other words the Bolshevists have had enough of fair words in Finland and want to see action. The news of Mannerheim's illness has produced considerable shock in Sweden. The Stockholm newspapers act as if they had never foreseen such a development. They were the people who persuaded the Finns months ago to come to some arrangement with the Soviets and withdraw from the war. Now all the forecasts which we made at the time have come true.

The military situation in Pomerania is still extraordinarily menacing. Apparently our counter-measures have come too late. In certain places the Soviets have crashed into them so that there is no longer any question of an orderly concentration and we have been able to do nothing large or effective. During the Sakharov operation in the Küstrin area General Vlasov's troops fought excellently. But it is humiliating to read in an eye-witness account by officers of these units of their impression that German soldiers were weary and worn out and had no desire to advance on the enemy. Apparently they were forever asking Russian officers and even more Soviet prisoners: "How will German prisoners be treated by the Soviets?" Clearly, therefore, many of them are toying with the idea of going over to the Soviets as prisoners. Here again it is clear that, as far as the front-line situation is concerned, we have greatly overcalled our hand. We no longer possess adequate military strength to score a decisive victory at a decisive point. Vlasov himself opines that, although the Soviets have adequate men and equipment, they face almost insoluble supply problems. They had a mass of tanks in the Oder section but were short of petrol. If we could penetrate deep into their assembly areas, we should undoubtedly score a great operational victory. But again the question is whether we can! Changing the railways from narrow gauge to broad gauge would create considerable difficulties in our occupied eastern territories. In reverse direction it is obviously a great deal easier. Vlasov is of the opinion that the Soviets will not advance direct on Berlin but will first move on Dresden, provided that we do not forestall them with an offensive on our side. The Soviet soldiery too is extraordinarily war-weary but it is inspired with an infernal hatred of everything German, which must be ascribed to sophisticated bolshevist propaganda. When Vlasov says that Stalin is the best-hated man in Russia, he naturally says it *pro domo*. He is right in his contention, however, that the Soviets are suffering from a serious manpower shortage. They have manned all their rear areas with women and this alone explains their astounding numbers of infantry.

Hanke's speech from Breslau has had an enormous effect on the German public. At last a National-Socialist Gauleiter has made a virile speech and has done so from an encircled fortress which he is defending—in sharp contrast to Greiser, who prematurely abandoned a town which was not encircled.

The effect of my last radio speech is now slowly becoming perceptible. I am receiving numbers of radio messages from the front expressing complete solidarity with my statements.

Chemnitz has been very heavily raided three times in the last 24 hours. It is barely possible to communicate with the city. Apparently it has been the same here as in Dresden recently. In their time the Saxon cities were fortunate in not being attacked from the air for so long and now they are paying for it dearly.

The most varied agencies of the Party, the Wehrmacht and the State are now releasing men fit for active service in considerable numbers. The word has gradually got round how serious the situation at the front is and therefore how urgently necessary it is to release men for the front. The Post Office, the Forestry Service and the administration are voluntarily offering me drafts.

At midday I had a conference with the relevant gentlemen from the Wehrmacht Recruiting Service concerning radical simplification of our system of call-up. The officers of the Recruiting Service give me an impression of total inadequacy, weariness and senility. These are the types who have run the call-up system throughout the war. One can imagine what bureaucratic top-hamper there is and what drastic cuts will be required to adapt it to the present military situation. Anyway I am determined to intervene with far-reaching measures and put things right.

In the evening it is reported that the Americans have fought their way through to Köln South railway station. South-east of Neuss they have split our bridgehead in two and so reduced it considerably. They have tried to find a crossing over the Rhine near Krefeld but were driven back. The situation in the Euskirchen area seems somewhat more stable at the moment and in the Schnee-Eifel our troops have in general held firm. German counter-measures are being taken at Trier and promise to produce some temporary or local relief.

Our great offensive with Sepp Dietrich's Army has begun in Hungary. No forecast can be made at the moment. First reports say more or less nothing, merely that our troops met very stiff resistance and have therefore made no great gains of ground on the first day. The enemy is already taking counter-measures, mainly putting very strong air forces into action. In the Lauban area minor gains of ground are again reported. This operation is to be continued, primarily to force the Bolshevists to withdraw forces from the Mährisch–Ostrau area. The two pincers which drove forward at Lauban have not yet been able to close but Schörner hopes that this will succeed. Then we should be able to reckon on capturing some material. So far 136 enemy tanks have been destroyed in this area. The enemy made violent attacks on our bridgehead at Schwedt.

He clearly does not want his flank threatened during his next offensive, whatever direction that may take. In the Pomeranian area he was able to extend his operations. The crisis here is still most serious, whereas in East Prussia and in Courland we held firm everywhere.

This evening I had a visit from Gruppenführer Alvensleben, Senior SS and Police Commander in Dresden. He painted me a horrifying picture of the Dresden catastrophe. This was a real tragedy such as has seldom been seen in the history of mankind and certainly not in the course of this war. Life in Dresden is slowly beginning to emerge from the ruins. Alvensleben had visited Himmler who is sick in Hohenlychen.* He had discussed the whole military and political situation with Himmler and given vent to severe criticism of Göring and Ribbentrop. Himmler had expressed a wish to speak to me as soon as possible. I got in touch with him this evening and we agreed that I should visit him some time tomorrow, Wednesday. I propose to discuss with him not only the war situation but primarily all the outstanding personnel problems in the political and military leadership of the Reich. It seems to me now time to clarify all the decisive measures required in all fields. We have not much more time to lose.

---

* A clinic near Berlin to which Himmler had retired to recuperate from the strain of commanding Army Group Vistula.

WEDNESDAY 7 MARCH 1945

(pp. 1–33)
Military Situation.

In Hungary our local attacks between Lake Balaton and the Drava, made in greater strength, were very successful and in the Kaposvar area our forces pushed some 6–8 km towards Osien. At the same time, attacking from south to north across the Drava from Viroviticar, our forces also moved forward some 6–8 km. Satisfactory initial success was also achieved in attacks southwards and eastwards from the eastern top of Lake Balaton, in the area south of Stuhlweissenburg.

In Slovakia the enemy continued to attack heavily at Schemnitz and Altsohl. No special developments on the neighbouring front as far as Mährisch–Ostrau. Enemy troop concentrations opposite Mährisch–Ostrau and in the Oppeln area have been further reinforced. Nothing fresh around Breslau. Battalion-strength attacks on Zobten and at Goldberg were repulsed and our own local offensive operations between Görlitz and Bunzlau were successful. Small Soviet detachments were surrounded and some of them annihilated. We managed to improve our positions north of Guben. In the Oder sector activity was somewhat greater. The enemy attacked in greater strength at Lebus and also from north, south and east against Küstrin; attacks in regimental strength were made on our bridgehead at Zehden; all were unsuccessful.

The Pomeranian area was once again the main scene of activity. In the Stettin area our line runs from about the Schwedt bridgehead to the west of Stargard and from here north of Gollnow to Siepenitz. The enemy attacked this position at several points, penetrating to a depth of 5–6 km east of Friedrichswalde and north of Gollnow. The bolshevists reached the coast at Bad Dievenow north of Cammin. Our own formations are still fighting their way back and are now west of Belgard, near Greifenberg and south of Regenswalde. On the eastern flank of the break-through a German defensive front exists from Schlawe to south of Bütow; enemy attacks here were not in strength. On the other hand he attacked with great violence from a point north of Heiderode to the Vistula, succeeding in penetrating to an area 20 km south of Berent, as far as the Berent–Schöneck railway and to Stargard (Prussia).

In East Prussia enemy attacks were not in strength and were all repulsed. In Courland too heavy renewed attacks south of Frauenburg were unsuccessful.

On the Western Front the Anglo-Americans concentrated their efforts primarily on reducing the larger and smaller German bridgeheads on the left bank of the Rhine between Köln and Xanten. North of Xanten the enemy was driven off and the bridgehead round Wesel was only slightly reduced. On the other hand the enemy succeeded in crushing our bridgeheads at Rheinsberg and southwards as far as Köln. Rheinsberg is therefore in enemy hands. The enemy increased his pressure in the Köln area. Fighting is going on only 100 yards west of the Cathedral. There is also violent fighting along the Rhine highway from Köln to Bonn. Between Köln and Bonn the enemy made ground westwards* and is now about 12 km north-west and south-west of Bonn. From the Euskirchen area he pressed on along the road to Bonn and also towards Neuenahr. Rheinbach was lost. Our defence line then swings westward south of Rheinbach and runs some 3 km north of Münster-Eifel to the region of Schleiden.

In the Eifel the situation has worsened again. The enemy exploited the fact that the area is only thinly manned and moved along the upper Kyll to the Birgel area some 25 km

* A slip for "eastwards"?

81

north-east of Prüm and into the wood south of Gerolstein. Armoured reconnaissance detachments drove a long way eastwards along the Bitburg–Duan–Cochem road, crossed the Cochem–Adenau road and are now about 10 km north-west of Cochem. Fierce fighting is in progress in the wooded area north of Trier between Bitburg and Wittlich and also south of Trier between the Ruwer and Zerf. At Forbach there were only local actions. The enemy has been reinforced here, however, so that a resumption of major operations must be reckoned with.

No particular operations have been reported from Italy. A small enemy seaborne raid behind our main line in the Adria area was driven off.

Our air forces shot down 20 Soviet aircraft in the East.

In the western zone, owing to unfavourable weather, activity by enemy twin-engined bombers and fighter-bombers was reduced; it was mainly directed on Münster-land, the Rhineland and Westphalia.

In Italy enemy fighter-bombers were very active all along the front. Over Reich territory some 150 British bombers attacked the Rheine area. During the night some 150 British bombers raided Sassnitz. Smaller British bomber formations again made a harassing raid on Berlin.

———

Although our Western enemies remain deeply impressed by the fantastic fighting spirit of our troops in the West, on our side it must be stated that the morale of our men is slowly sinking. This, moreover, is explicable in the light of the fact that they have now been fighting uninterruptedly for weeks and months. Somewhere the physical strength to resist runs out. This also applies to a certain extent to the West German population. Overall some three million people have stayed behind in the region now captured by the British and Americans. They were simply not in a position to evacuate and we put no particular pressure on them since we no longer have enough room on Reich territory to accept such a flood of people.

Eisenhower's orders to the population are very strict. They are not allowed to leave their houses and are tormented by every known form of regulation. But to some extent they seem to be happy that they are now finished with air raids. Wherever one looks at our strategic situation it can be said that the fundamental ailment, which has led to our present miserable situation on all fronts, is the lack of air defence. This lies at the root of all our setbacks.

For the first time Churchill has actually seen the results of his air war. He was in Jülich and, according to Reuters, surveyed the expanse of ruins stretching from Jülich to Aachen with an air of satisfaction—a replica of Nero who sat high above the Eternal City and strummed his lyre while Rome burned. A better symbol of the chaos and ruin into which Anglo-American policy has plunged Europe is hardly conceivable.

During his drive through the occupied areas Churchill addressed the troops. His speech was larded with the old monotonous tirades of hatred of the Huns. This gentleman, who can truly be called the grave-digger of Europe, had nothing new to say on the war situation. He would do better to bother more about the fresh strikes now flaring up all over the British Isles.

The situation in and around Köln has become pretty bleak. As was to be expected, our Volkssturm battalions could not put up adequate resistance. For the first time the British and Americans are now seeing a great city which has been turned into a heap of ruins and it will make a deep impression on them. I do not believe, however, that they will stop their air war as a result; instead they will intensify it, for they undoubtedly think that this is the quickest way of ending the war.

In Köln too the occupation authorities have subjected the population to the strictest regulations. This may be to the good from our point of view since it will reinforce the somewhat sinking moral resistance of our people at home. On the other hand one can understand these people. They are overtired and so worn out that they welcome a night's rest more than anything. But they only need one good sleep and then they will be on the job again.

I cannot understand the fact that hardly any resistance was offered in Köln. The city had been put into such a good state of defence by Grohé that one had to assume that it would offer considerable resistance to the Americans and cause them very great losses in men and material. Apparently this was not the case however. It makes one blush to read reports that the men found in Köln by the Americans were almost all fit for service. Had they been made available to the front at the proper time, things would now be better than unfortunately they actually are.

The situation in the West naturally gives rise to continuous and increasing anxiety, primarily because the Allies now have millions of German people under their thumb. They are trying to govern and administer in some sort of way. Significantly, they have cynically announced that the people best suited for this purpose are the pastors. They have placed themselves at the disposal of the Allied troops in every way. I never expected anything else. The young people, they say, are proving extraordinarily refractory and there is simply nothing to be done with them. One member of the Hitler Youth, who was taken to hospital owing to illness, is said to have complained that he had not been sent to prison.

The severe devastation of German cities wreaked by the enemy air forces has led the British government to make repeated reference to the damage in London. As a result one gets extraordinarily interesting information—that one-third of the British capital has been laid waste, for instance.

Eden has yet again reverted in the Commons to the subject of war criminals. He describes Ribbentrop and me as the leading and greatest war criminals. This is merely a great honour for me and I am quite prepared to put up with this description. Otherwise Eden only trotted out futile reasons for the fact that at the Yalta Conference the British had said that they agreed with the cession of East Prussia to Poland.

The Congress of European Socialists is meeting in

London. It has set out a remarkably more tolerant programme as the condition for German capitulation.

The British Labour Party has realigned itself to a certain extent; clearly it cannot altogether go along with Churchill's rigid war policy. As a result of the wave of radical opinion now noticeable in England, as elsewhere, it has undoubtedly become somewhat suspicious and is afraid that it will lose control of the broad masses.

Reports on the foreign political situation are all couched in the same vein—that the Allies have not the smallest intention of being in any way conciliatory towards us, that militarily they are working in complete agreement with the Soviet Union, that, as an instance, they are now passing large food convoys through the Dardanelles to assist the Soviets in their very tight food situation. It is reported from Japan that a violent conflict has arisen between the moderate and the radical strategists—just as in our case. The moderate strategists are based mainly on the Fleet and the radicals on the Army, which has always been extraordinarily intransigent in Japan.

The Finland crisis is growing all the time. It is creating an enormous stir abroad both among our enemies and even more among the neutrals. The Swedish press expresses extraordinary surprise but it has no reason to do so for the reasons so often set out here.

The escape of the traitor General Roatta has provoked a serious government crisis in Italy. A red rising of considerable dimensions is raging in Rome. The communists have organised gigantic processions and hoisted the Red Flag on the Capitol. Bonomi* is in great difficulties. The rising is markedly communist in nature, as the British explicitly point out. I do not think, however, that they will draw any conclusions from this fact.

Guderian's statement on bolshevist atrocities to the home and foreign press in Berlin has not made the impact that I had hoped for and expected. Guderian's talk was too emotional and flowery and the witnesses who were interro-

---

* Prime Minister of Italy since 1944.

gated were somewhat tired, having had to make statements previously to all sorts of agencies, so that they did
not answer briskly and naturally. This is the reason why
this presentation has not made the impact that I had really
expected in the neutral press. In Stockholm the statements
were derided and held up to ridicule. One can only have
pity for this decadent bourgeois world whose representatives are no more than the proverbial fatted calves choosing
their butcher.

There is no point in saying much more about the air
war. We are bombed uninterruptedly day and night and
damage to our housing and armaments potential is very
severe. We have nothing worth mentioning with which to
oppose the enemy aerial armadas. Last night it was the
turn of Sassnitz. Much damage was done to the remnants
of our high-seas fleet. A report from Chemnitz says that
the situation there is fairly desperate. We must move in
central government assistance to help the city through
the worst.

As commissioned by Himmler, General Gottberg* has
now started a major campaign to comb railway stations for
soldiers travelling around. He has had substantial success
right from the start. The campaign cannot go on in-
definitely, however, because a number of highly important
official journeys will of course be stopped thereby. In addition OKW must screen its senior-level headquarters for
soldiers fit for active service. I am told that Keitel† has
ordered 110 trains to be held ready in Berlin to evacuate
OKW and OKH. These fugitives will never understand. I
would like to know when they will finally make up their
minds to stay where they are and defend themselves, cost
what it may.

New and highly complex problems and troubles are continually arising as regards Berlin. The capital is at present

---

* Curt von Gottberg was a General in the SS (Obergruppenführer). He had been Himmler's Commissioner in White Ruthenia.
† Chief of General Staff of the Wehrmacht (OKW).

in an extraordinarily tense situation from every point of view but I must still make every effort to ensure that it is in good trim to defend itself. One can imagine what that implies. In the afternoon I drive out to Himmler to have a long talk with him. The drive through Berlin shatters me somewhat. It is some time since I have seen the heap of ruins into which the Reich capital has been transformed. Everywhere, however, barricades are to be seen mushrooming. If we had adequate soldiers and weapons Berlin could be defended for as long as anyone likes. On the way we meet one refugee convoy after another, mostly Black Sea Germans.* The type of people entering the Reich calling themselves German is not exactly exhilarating. I think there are more Germanic types entering the Reich from the west by force of arms than there are Germanic types coming in peacefully from the east.

The drive through Mecklenburg is like a tonic. The country is totally undamaged and exudes complete peace. At a casual glance there is nothing to show that there is a war on.

Himmler is in Hohenlychen under medical care. He has had a bad attack of angina but is now on the mend. He gives me a slightly frail impression. Nevertheless we were able to have a long talk about all outstanding questions. In general Himmler's attitude is good. He is one of our strongest personalities. During our two-hour discussion I established that we are in complete agreement in our estimate of the general situation so that I need hardly refer to that. He used strong language about Göring and Ribbentrop, whom he regards as the two main sources of error in our general conduct of the war, and in this he is absolutely right. But he has no more idea than I how to persuade the Führer to cut loose from them both and replace them with fresh strong personalities. I told him of my last interview but one with the Führer, whose attention I had drawn

---

* i.e. "Auslandsdeutsche"—German families long settled in Russia and now forced to flee for safety to Germany.

to the fact that retention of Göring in particular is threatening to lead to a crisis of state, if it has not already done so. Himmler enquired in detail how the Führer had reacted to these remarks. The Führer was indeed much impressed but for the moment he has not drawn the consequences.

As far as the front is concerned Himmler is extremely worried, particularly about developments in Pomerania and the West. At present, however, he is even more worried about the food situation, the outlook for which is pretty gloomy over the next few months. The morale of the troops has undoubtedly been affected. This Himmler admits on the basis of his experience with Army Group Vistula. Another factor is that neither in the military nor the civilian sector have we strong central leadership because everything has to be referred to the Führer and that can only be done in a small number of cases. In every field Göring and Ribbentrop are obstacles to successful conduct of the war. But what can one do? One cannot, after all, actually force the Führer to divorce himself from them. Himmler summarises the situation correctly when he says that his mind tells him that we have little hope of winning the war militarily but instinct tells him that sooner or later some political opening will emerge to swing it in our favour. Himmler thinks this more likely in the West than the East. He thinks that England will come to her senses, which I rather doubt. As his remarks show, Himmler is entirely Western-oriented; from the East he expects nothing whatsoever. I still think that something is more likely to be achieved in the East since Stalin seems to me more realistic than the trigger-happy Anglo-American. We must be clear of course that, if we manage to reach a peace settlement, it will be a small and modest one. The prior condition for this is that we stand firm somewhere, for if we are flat on the floor we can no longer negotiate with the enemy. The entire strength of the Reich must be concentrated to this end.

Himmler agrees that we should locate troops now training in barracks behind the Western and Eastern Fronts as a cushion. So far Jüttner* has resisted this tooth and nail. Himmler will accordingly summon Jüttner and give him a piece of his mind. General Kleiner, Jüttner's closest associate, is the one who is calling the tune and he is in agreement with Colonel-General Fromm's policy.

I discussed the Fromm case with Himmler in detail. That morning Kaltenbrunner† had taken steps to ensure that current proceedings against Fromm are conducted with greater energy than has been the case so far. During the initial stage of his trial Fromm took complete control of the proceedings.

With Himmler the atmosphere is orderly, unpretentious and one hundred percent National-Socialist, which is most refreshing. One can only rejoice that with Himmler the old National-Socialist spirit still prevails.

During the drive home I have an opportunity to think over all that we discussed. The drive through the darkening countryside in the dusk was impressive. Again and again we met columns of refugees on the move; they almost seemed to symbolise this gigantic war.

Barely had I arrived in Berlin than I had to plunge into work again. Mountains of it had piled up during the few hours I was away.

As far as the situation this evening is concerned, it is reported from Hungary that our troops are meeting extraordinarily stiff resistance. They were consequently unable to make any very great gains of ground. In Pomerania the situation has deteriorated further, as it has in west Prussia. There is a danger of our troops being split up into small packets. Our offensive operations at Lauban had some success.

Gauleiter Stöhr‡ telephones me and complains bitterly about the sinking morale of the troops, which unfortunately

* Max Jüttner was chief of the SS operational headquarters (SS—Führungshauptamt).

† Head of the RSHA or Reich Security Main Office of the SS, which controlled Himmler's Secret Police and Secret Intelligence.

‡ Gauleiter of the Saar.

is a fact. To some extent the population is being infected by it and Stöhr proposes to make a public pronouncement over the wired broadcasting system in an attempt to reinforce morale.

The enemy has advanced through Bonn towards Koblenz. In this area the situation as seen on the map is completely confused. An attempt is being made to form a new defensive line west of the Moselle but it is very questionable whether it will succeed.

I commissioned Dr. Naumann to go to the Führer and put to him the question of evacuation from Berlin of the top-level agencies of the Reich and the Wehrmacht. The Führer is of the opinion that at least preparations should be made. I should be glad to see these high-level organisations cleared out of Berlin as soon as possible, since they are no reinforcement to the fighting morale of the capital. They should therefore—and here the Führer is entirely right—be weeded out gradually without causing sensation among the public.

Naumann returned much impressed by his interview with the Führer. The Führer was in his best and most resolute form. Though the situation is extraordinarily serious and menacing, he still represents a firm fixed point round which events revolve. As long as he is at the head of the Reich we have no need to haul down our flag.

THURSDAY 8 MARCH 1945

(pp. 1–39)
Military Situation.

In our offensive across the Drava two bridgeheads were formed despite stiff enemy resistance. Between the Drava and Lake Balaton our offensive continued despite violent enemy counter-attacks. Considerable gains of ground were made in our offensive between Lake Balaton and the Danube south-east and south of Stuhlweissenburg. Two Hungarian towns were recaptured. At the previous scenes of fierce fighting in central Slovakia all enemy attacks failed apart from a few local penetrations. On the whole front as far as Lauban only local actions took place. Fighting continues in the southern sector of the fortress of Breslau. Our own offensive at Lauban is now concluded. The Soviet 3 Guards Tank Army was so mauled that it cannot be in action in the foreseeable future. No change in the situation on the Oder front as far as Küstrin. Küstrin itself was again heavily but unsuccessfully attacked from south-east and north-west.

In Pomerania heavy tank attacks on our position south of Stettin failed but north of Stargard the Soviets succeeded in pushing forward as far as Altdamm. There is therefore danger of the Stettin bridgehead being split open. The enemy captured Gollnow after heavy fighting. He also managed to reduce the Wollin bridgehead. Attacks on the southern edge of Kolberg were defeated. The Soviets also succeeded in extending their break-through north-eastwards capturing Schlawe and Zitzewitz. Soviet attacks from the

Heiderode area also gained ground. Attacks on the eastern defensive ring of Danzig were held at Neukrug. Between Marienburg and Elbing the Soviets attacked in great strength using fresh forces brought up from East Prussia and made a deep penetration reaching the Marienburg–Tiegenhof road.

In the East Prussia area fighting was light.

In Courland fourteen Soviet divisions attacking southeast of Frauenburg achieved some initial success but were brought to a halt by evening as a result of successful counter-attacks.

On the Western Front a complete defensive victory was scored in the Wesel bridgehead; on the other hand the enemy succeeded in pushing our forces back in Köln and either side of Brühl. East of Euskirchen strong enemy armoured forces advanced into the Ahr valley and reached Neuenahr. North of Kochem the enemy gained ground towards Koblenz. His efforts to extend his penetration southwards failed. Fierce fighting continues between Kyllberg and Ehrang and also north-east of Trier as the enemy attacks eastwards. Fluctuating fighting is taking place along the Ruwer. Other operations on the Western Front were of local significance only.

In the main areas of fighting on the Eastern Front enemy air activity was very heavy. Our own close support aircraft were in action mainly in Pomerania. Nine Soviet aircraft were shot down in air battles.

In the West air activity was small owing to unfavourable weather.

Over Reich territory American bombers made daylight attacks on transport and industrial targets in Westphalia and central Germany. During the night a strong British formation, preceded by harassing aircraft, raided primarily Hamburg, Hemmingstedt, Dessau and Leipzig. The capital was raided twice by high-speed aircraft. Night fighters shot down 41 enemy aircraft confirmed and two probables—all bombers. Anti-aircraft results are not yet to hand.

Our Western enemies state on the one hand that our troops are offering heroically tough resistance and that the Anglo-American victory will be a blood-soaked one; on the other hand they say that the population is giving them a sincere welcome and that the hoisting of white flags on houses is now a regular occurrence. I believe these reports to be partly right and partly wrong. In any case it is clear that in no case have our troops surrendered in any large numbers and that they are resisting at all costs—to the extent that the situation and their equipment permit. People are quite clear about this on the enemy side too. Nevertheless an early end to the war is anticipated. The *Exchange Telegraph*, for instance, reports that official British circles are convinced that the war will end shortly, that little account need be taken of the final battles in Germany and that the war can be brought to an end simply by proclamation by the King of England. Little stock is taken of clandestine resistance which the British maintain we are planning. It is thought that the German people are so worn out that they are no longer capable of it. In light of the climate of opinion at home Churchill has clearly been compelled to forecast the date of termination of hostilities more precisely. He now talks of the war lasting another two months. He has no intention, he says, of recognising any German government. The German people will be governed exclusively by the occupation authorities. That is what the future world looks like in the mind of a British plutocrat! Are they incapable of realising in London that a people of 80 million souls will never accept such a solution and that Europe would prefer to go down in chaos, flame and smoke rather than submit to such a prescription for disintegration.

This evening the alarming news comes from Eisenhower's headquarters that the Americans have succeeded in forming a small bridgehead on the right bank of the Rhine. I cannot confirm the accuracy of this information since communications to the west are not working. I regard it as more or less out of the question however. Street fighting is going on in Bonn and Godesberg. The damage which they found in Köln has made the deepest impression on the British and Americans. For the first time they are now seeing the devastating effect of their prolonged air bombardment and I fear that they will merely be encouraged thereby to continue with his barbarous method of warfare, indeed to intensify it considerably.

As far as our people's attitude to the enemy is concerned, accounts differ considerably. On the one hand it is said that there is absolutely nothing to be done with these people since at heart they are still nazified, on the other hand many statements have been made to the effect that their attitude when they encounter the enemy is a submissive one. One cannot clear this question up at the moment. One must wait for the initial confusion of military operations to be over and see what happens when things have settled down. Then the enemy will learn how National-Socialist Germany reacts to his brutalities.

Our sole great hope at present lies in the U-boat war. Our Western enemies are very worried about it. They had not expected a resumption of activity by our U-boats at this of all times. Moreover they are particularly taken aback because, with the extension of the Pacific war, the British and American tonnage situation is so stretched that they have not a ship to spare. It is therefore understandable that repeated declarations are being made, primarily from Washington, that the USA is now more interested than ever in ending the war in Europe as quickly as possible. We, however, are more interested than ever in prolonging it as much as possible and putting a good fat spoke in the wheel of the American War Minister, who made the statement referred to above.

A series of false reports given worldwide publicity primarily by London shows that the enemy now proposes to bring into action his big psychological warfare guns. There is talk of serious unrest in Munich, of a staged anti-government revolt which allegedly took place in the Babelsburg film studio and which gave me a particularly thankless role to play. A spurious speech by the Führer to Gauleiters on 24 February is being peddled round. It is such despicable nonsense as not even to be worth repeating. The Berlin population is being summoned to capitulate before the Soviet assault begins. In short all hell is loose and the enemy is sowing a minefield in order to shake the German people's imperturbability at this extraordinarily critical time. I do not think it necessary, however, to react to all this in our domestic propaganda. Every German knows today precisely what he has to do and he is quite clear what hangs over him should the enemy achieve his purpose. For the benefit of enemy countries I shall issue a short categorical *démenti* of these fake reports.

In all this confusion it is pleasing to note that the political crisis on the enemy side continues to grow. It is still raging round the Yalta communiqué. The American papers are now being more outspoken. They accuse the so-called "Big Three" of trying to turn back the clock of history and say that in this case, as always, their mistakes will come home to roost with a vengeance.

The Japanese too are now slowly beginning to realise the seriousness of the situation. Tokyo newspapers write of the possibility of an American landing on the Japanese mainland and are saying that the Japanese nation would rise against them as one man. It is good that the Japanese are now being dragged somewhat more into the firing line; it will probably lead them to make greater efforts against the enemy than they have done so far.

In Rumania the Legionaries* have been hard at work recently creating difficulties for the Soviets. On our side we are in the process of organising a large-scale partisan organisation in German-occupied eastern territories. It will be a considerable time before such a partisan organisation can actually start activities, but nevertheless it should do us some good.

In Moscow they are now threatening us with a pincer movement on Berlin. I fear that this is in fact their intention now that the Soviets have secured their extended flank by their advance in Pomerania. Preparations in the sector

---

* i.e. the Iron Curtain. See above p. 29.

of the Oder front facing Berlin, however, do not lead to the conclusion that at the moment they are planning a military operation directed on the Reich capital. I do not think that their forces are adequate to do this at the present time. They would have to use at least two fresh armies for an advance on a city like Berlin and at present they are not available.

Rendulic* has now put things in order in East Prussia. From one of his reports I see that when he took over the Army Group, there were no fewer than 16,000 stragglers. He has quickly reduced this figure to 400 using fairly brutal methods. In this respect he is acting just like Schörner and Model. It seems that Rendulic's ambition is to earn a place in the ranks of our leading modern army commanders.

The Duce has made an extraordinarily firm and self-assured speech. Its central theme is that Germany cannot be beaten. If only the Italian people thought, or rather had thought, the same way as the Duce, the war would have taken a very different course. But the Italian people is not worthy of the Duce; it is not worth a row of beans.

During the last 24 hours the air war has again raged over Reich territory with devastating effect. It was the turn of Magdeburg and even more of Dessau. The greater part of Dessau is a sheet of flame and totally destroyed; yet another German city which has been largely flattened. In addition reports coming in from towns recently attacked, Chemnitz in particular, make one's hair grow grey. Yet once more it is frightful that we have no defence worth mentioning with which to oppose the enemy air war.

The Party Chancellery is now planning a special operation to raise the troops' morale. Each Gau is to make available five selected political leaders of officer rank in an attempt to revive the sinking morale of the troops. Evidence of demoralisation is now to be seen primarily

---

* Col.-Gen. Lothar Rendulic—a general trusted by Hitler—had been sent out to command the Army Group "Courland" and shore up the crumbling German position in East Prussia.

in the West, proving that the objection to my recent proposal to denounce the Geneva Convention was quite wrong —that the morale of our troops in the West was holding simply because the soldier felt that he was facing a fair foe. Desertions have reached a considerable level. The population, primarily in the West, is to some degree helping deserters. What else is to be expected of them when they receive the enemy with white flags? In the Neuss bridgehead, for instance, considerable numbers of men slipped away from the battlefield during the course of a single night. This is another proof that in our whole war strategy we have overcalled our hand and the results are now descending on the heads of the people. Again and again one hears that the enemy air bombardment is at the bottom of it all. It is understandable that a people which has been subjected for years to the fire-effect of a weapon against which it has no defence, should gradually lose its courage.

A flaming row has arisen over Dr. Ley's* recent article; in it he said that the air war had made us so poor that people almost took comfort from it and that the recent raids on Dresden had been greeted with a definite sigh of relief by the German people. It is always quite easy to see what Dr. Ley means by his articles, but unfortunately he expresses himself in such a tactically inept way that they arouse the greatest repugnance among the public. He is not the sort of man we want writing in the press.

At midday I drive out to visit Görlitz. The weather is clear and frosty; the whole countryside is bathed in wonderful sunshine. On leaving the ruins of Berlin one enters a region apparently quite untouched by the war. One feels really happy to see open country and breathe fresh air again. Everywhere, not only in Berlin but also along the road, barricades against the advance of Soviet tanks are being built. In this flat country people's lives are comparatively undisturbed. They are to be envied. We drive

---

* Dr. Robert Ley was Leader of the Nazi "German Workers' Front." His loyalty to the cause was fanatical but (since he was seldom sober) indistinctly expressed.

past Dresden and through Bautzen. Bautzen is totally un-damaged and the sight of it is refreshing. Immediately afterwards, however, we enter the operations zone. We drive close behind the front for some way. Occasionally one can see enemy or German gun-flashes in the distance. We have to stop for a short time just outside Görlitz. A group of women come up to the car and give me a rapturous welcome. It is clear that there is still a great store of confidence in us at the grassroots and that our position of authority is still intact. We must make use of the fact. In other words, if National-Socialism could once more present itself to the people as a pure ideology, freed from all manifestations of corruption and time-serving, it could still today turn out to be the great victorious ideology of our century.

We reach Görlitz about 2:00 p.m. The town presents a remarkable sight. There are hardly any women about; they and their children have been evacuated long since. Görlitz has become a town of men only.

Kreisleiter Mahler, formerly a district leader in Berlin, receives me in Görlitz. He has put the town into a splendid state of defence and is firmly determined to hold it under all circumstances alongside the Wehrmacht. Colonel-General Schörner has come from his headquarters specially to be present during my visit to Görlitz. He presents his officers to me and they make a first-class impression. Schörner has obviously done an excellent job in training them. In any case there is not the smallest sign of defeatism here.

I then drive with Schörner to Lauban, which had only been cleared of the enemy by our troops that morning. On the way Schörner briefs me on the situation of his Army Group. He launched his offensive in the Lauban area in order to keep the enemy on the move and in this he has succeeded. During his offensive he destroyed the greater part of an enemy tank Corps without our troops suffering very great casualties. He is of the opinion that, if one hits the Bolshevists hard, they can be beaten under all circum-stances. His infantry is wretched; he is basing his strategy exclusively on his material superiority, particularly in tanks. As far as Breslau is concerned, Schörner believes that he can liberate the city in a few weeks' time. He had intended to do so as a result of his Lauban offensive but unfortunately he had to release his assault divisions to bolster our defence in Pomerania and so could not continue the Lauban offensive. Schörner is very worried about the situation in the Mährisch–Ostrau area. He expects the next major Soviet offensive to come here and so must now take precautions against it. He has therefore arranged a fresh attack in the Ratibor area; it started at dawn this morning and he is hopeful of some result. In general his principle is to harass the enemy, create difficulties for him and force him to make moves which will gradually lead to the disintegration of his front.

Schörner is decidedly a personality as a commander. The details he gave me about the methods he uses to raise morale were first-rate and demonstrate not only his talents as a commander in the field but also his superb political insight. He is using quite novel modern methods. He is no chairborne or map general; most of the day he spends with the fighting troops, with whom he is on terms of confidence, though he is very strict. In particular he has taken a grip of the so-called "professional stragglers," by which he means men who continually manage to absent themselves in critical situations and vanish to the rear on some pretext or other. His procedure with such types is fairly brutal; he hangs them on the nearest tree with a placard announcing: "I am a deserter and have declined to defend German women and children." The deterrent effect on other deserters and men who might have it in mind to follow them is obviously considerable.

In all this work Todenhöfer, a member of my staff, is being a great help to Schörner, who thinks a great deal of him. Todenhöfer had also made the journey and was overjoyed to see me again. Schörner tells me that Todenhöfer is doing him great service in giving the right political slant to all his proclamations and orders.

Meanwhile we arrive in Lauban. The town has been fairly

badly damaged in the fighting of previous days. Naturally a single Anglo-American air raid is more devastating than a whole day's artillery duel. Nevertheless to see so badly damaged a town in Silesia, which is otherwise pretty well untouched by the war, is somewhat horrifying.

Paratroops, who had made a great name for themselves in the Lauban operation, were on parade in the totally ruined marketplace of Lauban. Schörner addressed the troops and his speech included the most complimentary remarks about me and my work. In particular he eulogised my permanent and indefatigable struggle for total war and wished good fortune to my efforts. He said that I was one of the few men who had the ear of the front-line troops to the full. I replied with a very strong appeal to the morale of the troops, referring particularly to the historic duty they now have to perform. A bit of local colour provided an excellent background. In this area there is hardly a town or a village in which Frederick the Great did not win one of his victories or suffer one of his defeats.

As the soldiers marched past I noticed a lieutenant who proved to be Haegert, one of my old associates who had volunteered to return to the front with the "Grossdeutschland" Division. He was deeply moved to see me again. On the flank of the troops as they marched past was a member of the Hitler Youth aged only 16 who had just won the Iron Cross.

Both the market-place at Lauban and the roads into and out of the town were littered with burnt-out enemy tanks. Our anti-tank guns had really done a good job here. Privately one is seized with horror at the sight of these monstrous, robot-like steel colossi with which Stalin wants to subjugate Europe.

Schörner then has to return to his headquarters to direct his new operation at Ratibor. Our leave-taking was extraordinarily friendly. I have really taken Schörner to my heart.

We then drive along immediately behind the front. From a look-out post I can see the Soviet concentration. This was the area in which the battle of Lauban took place. My conducting officers brief me about the enemy's morale. It is not particularly brilliant. They repeatedly assert that, if he is hit hard, he is bound to take to his heels soon. He must be faced with a certain weight of material however. His losses during the Lauban battle were enormous. Having seen the atrocities committed by the Soviets, our men are giving no quarter. They beat Soviet soldiers to death with shovels and rifle butts. The atrocities committed by the Soviets are indescribable. Frightful evidence of them is visible everywhere along the road.

We then pay a short visit to an artillery position and a rolling salvo is fired in my honour. Officers and men are of the best type. It is refreshing to talk to them. It must not be forgotten, however, that they belong to an elite formation, the "Grossdeutschland" Corps, which has always been very selective as regards its personnel. My visit to the frontline troops gives the greatest pleasure. From the men's faces one can see how pleased and happy they are to see me so far forward. The enemy is giving us a little momentary peace. He seems to be licking the wounds he suffered during the Lauban battle. He welcomes us merely with an occasional artillery salvo.

We then drive back to Görlitz. In the hotel, where the impression is one of complete peacetime, I have endless discussions with political leaders and officers, all of whom naturally want to know more about the war. This does not imply that they are in any way depressed. On the contrary the fighting spirit here is like that of the good old days. General Graeser, who has lost a leg during the war, is admittedly rather one of the old school but his attitude is splendid. The young General Mäder, commanding the "Führer" Grenadier Division which played a major part in the Lauban battle, is outstanding. He has his general's tabs at the age of 35. The mood of this circle is truly infectious. No trace of defeatism. I notice this too when I address soldiers and men of the Volkssturm in the overflowing Town Hall. Here is an audience entirely receptive to my views. My speech is entirely concentrated on fighting and tenacity. I give these men the watchwords for the present situation, reinforcing them with a series of historical examples which carry much conviction, particularly in this area. One can imagine the effect of such a speech in an assembly such as this. I feel totally happy and relaxed and am glad that for once I have managed to escape from the atmosphere of Berlin at last.

A full-course dinner is then served in the hotel. The food situation in Görlitz is as good as it can be since large stocks of meat and fat have been evacuated from the Soviet-occupied areas and must now under all circumstances be eaten. Once again I observe that firm faith in victory and in the Führer is prevalent among these men. The behaviour towards me personally of the officers from this operational zone is fabulous. Clearly my work over all these years has given them the greatest confidence. I sit with them until late into the evening. These are fine moments which really do one good.

Then we drive back to Berlin. For 25 miles we have to drive straight behind the Soviet front. One can see Very lights going up at the front and the occasional flash of an artillery salvo. It is naturally difficult to find the right road since the front here is very twisty and makes the most improbable twists and turns. However eventually we succeed in finding our way out of the maze and reaching the autobahn at Cottbus. Then we go at full speed back to Berlin. I am glad to be back in my beloved old Reich capital. At home I find a mountain of work. Magda has again got one of her headaches and is in great pain. We could do without that at the moment. I am dog-tired but only manage a few hours' sleep.

FRIDAY 9 MARCH 1945

(pp. 1–30)

Military Situation.

Our offensive made progress everywhere in the Hungarian area. Its success on the Malom Canal and south-west of Stuhlweissenburg is particularly noteworthy.

In southern Slovakia enemy pressure either side of Schemnitz was as severe as ever. The enemy made one or two penetrations but was then held deep in the battle zone. At Altsohl and Nikolas his attacks were driven off. In the area north of Ratibor German formations made a surprise attack from the west and north-west in a south-easterly direction, fell upon the enemy as he was moving up and spread considerable confusion in the Soviet concentration areas. One or two blocks of houses were recaptured by counter-attacks in the southern quarter of Breslau. The Lauban operation has meanwhile been concluded and German troops are going on the defensive again. An enemy army was severely mauled here and the vital Görlitz–Greifenberg–Hirschberg railway line reopened. At Guben the enemy, who had penetrated into the eastern quarter of the town, was ejected again. In the Lebus bridgehead too the Soviets attacked in strength but were thrown back by a counter-attack and our positions were improved. Very heavy enemy attacks were made on Küstrin from south, south-west and north. The attacks from south and south-west were driven off but from the north the Bolshevists succeeded in penetrating into the town and capturing a row of houses.

In Pomerania the situation has become more acute, our

bridgehead round Stettin having been driven in further. The new line now runs north of Pölitz to Altdamm, which we still hold, and thence to Greifenhagen. The enemy made very heavy attacks at Altdamm and Greifenberg but was either held or driven back. An attempt by the Bolshevists to land on the island of Wollin failed. Moving from Treptow the enemy succeeded in reaching the coast at Bad Horst. In Kolberg the situation is unchanged. A strong German formation is still in the Greifenberg area. It first tried to fight its way through westwards but failed to get through and has now turned northwest. On the eastern flank of the break-through area around Stolp and Bütow no change in the situation. On the other hand the Soviets did succeed in advancing north from Heiderode and reaching the outer ring of the Danzig fortifications. Leading elements were held at Zuckau. Between Marienburg and Elbing the Soviet advance was halted by a counter-attack.

In East Prussia the enemy is regrouping so that resumption of offensive activity must be expected in the very near future.

In the West the enemy renewed his attack in strength on either side of Xanten and south of it. In some places his attacks were repulsed, in others he succeeded in penetrating deeper into the bridgehead. The fighting here is extremely severe. In the southern sector of the Köln bridgehead the enemy penetrated as far as the Köln–Bonn railway. Violent street fighting is going on in Bonn and also in Bad Godesberg. Some enemy armour from the Ahrweiler area reached the east bank of the Rhine across the Remagen bridge. The enemy force consists of an armoured detachment and three infantry battalions. The enemy advance was sealed off and held at Linz. Counter-measures were initiated at once. The bridge was attacked by dive-bombers during the night and damaged; it is possible, however, that it can still be used. South of Remagen the enemy pushed forward to the west bank of the Rhine in the direction of Niederbreisig. In the Eifel break-through area the leading enemy armour reached a point 4 km west of Koblenz. Strong attacks against our switch lines north and south of the breakthrough area were beaten off. A feature, however, is an enemy armoured thrust southwards from Euskirchen; the purpose of this is clearly to cause the collapse of the German front still holding out and so our formations in the Kyll sector have had to fight their way back to a new position 4–5 km farther east. The enemy followed up closely but were beaten off on the new line. Equally our forces in the Hillesheim area have escaped encirclement by withdrawing to the Nürburgring and the area to the west. In their new positions all enemy attacks were repulsed. On the Trier battlefield the enemy attempted to extend his penetration eastwards to the Moselle. He crossed the Ruwer towards Kent but was then held. South of Trier some American forces are still encircled and fighting continues.

No operations of significance took place on the rest of the western front.

No special reports available from the Italian front.

Enemy aircraft were very active in the East yesterday. They attacked primarily localities near the front and our supply lines. 1400 sorties were noted in the central sector alone. Our own air activity was also very considerable. 365 German close support aircraft were in action in the central sector. A total of 26 enemy aircraft were shot down.

On the Western Front enemy air activity was small owing to unfavourable weather.

Over Reich territory three American bomber formations raided Siegen, Frankfurt am Main, Bad Homburg, Giessen, Dortmund, Recklinghausen, Essen, Bochum and Wuppertal. A strong American formation from the south raided Marburg and Kapfenberg. None of our own fighters in action. No reports yet of aircraft shot down by our anti-aircraft. Some 300 British bombers attacked Kassel around 9:00 p.m. A formation of some 200 Mosquitos carried out an attack on Hamburg. 60 Mosquitos diverted to Berlin and another 20 to Osnabrück. A few bombs were dropped on Bremen.

The British press reports that Churchill took malicious pleasure in what he saw during a visit to Aachen. He expressed himself as extraordinarily satisfied with the extent of damage wrought by the air terror. This is completely in character. He is a top-class gangster. We shall not be the only people, however, to bemoan what he has done; rather it will be the British people who have placed themselves in his hands at this fateful moment in their political development. The British now state flatly in their press that five million Germans will probably have to starve after the war since they have no intention of providing food for them. This entirely accords with their mentality. But we shall not be misled. The British have become totally obsessed by their hate complex and in the end they themselves will be its victims. The fact that they now openly admit that terror is the purpose of their air war is particularly characteristic. They no longer take any account of worldwide public opinion. I believe, however, that this will be to our advantage in the long run, for world public opinion is not yet so brutalised as to accept such a cynical attitude without comment.

To read Anglo-American reports on the damage in Köln one would almost think that *we* had been responsible for turning this lovely Hanseatic city into a heap of ruins. The Americans in particular accuse us of being responsible for the damage by prolonging the war. This is a world of contradiction, mendacity and hypocrisy inconceivable even in one's wildest dreams. Yet I suppose that from these fearful misconceptions and misunderstandings a better and more beautiful world will arise.

London is now giving vent to exaggerated optimism about the prospects of peace. From the latest government statement one would think that the war could end any day. Of course the enemy is in a great hurry since the British in particular are slowly realising that the longer the war lasts the more they are forced to take a back seat *vis-à-vis* their powerful allies, especially the Soviet Union. The situation is not of the best on our side of course. Particularly in the West a fairly severe dent has now been made in our fighting morale, which is slowly beginning to sink. Naturally the indications must not be overestimated. When military operations are so bloody it has always been the case that some of our soldiers and some of the civilian population lose their nerve. It is a great exaggeration, however, when it is said that people are trying to stop the soldiers shooting. Some madman may have done something of the sort from time to time but it is far from being the rule. The end-the-war psychosis which had manifested itself here and there is worldwide. The popular masses everywhere would rather end the war today than tomorrow. The only question is how it is to be done.

Developments in the West naturally give rise to the greatest anxiety from the military point of view. They have led the Führer to summon Kesselring to Berlin. After talking to him the Führer will possibly put him in Rundstedt's place.* Rundstedt has become too old and works too much on First World War ideas to master a situation such as is now developing in the West. It is quite devastating that the Americans should have succeeded in capturing the Rhine bridge at Remagen intact and forming a bridgehead on the right bank of the Rhine. Large-scale countermeasures are now being initiated since everyone is naturally clear on the threat which a bridgehead on the right bank poses for us. During the night Ju 88s were in action and partially destroyed the bridge, but it is not yet known whether this has made it unserviceable. On the enemy side of course people are overjoyed at the news. They act as if they already held the whole right bank of the Rhine. In fact it is a raving scandal that the Remagen bridge was not blown in good time. The Americans were able to capture it without a fight.

The Soviet press evinces no interest in the war in the West. It is dismissed in a couple of anodyne lines; instead the greater part of their publicity is devoted to events in Rumania which are of greater importance to them. The Anglo-Americans are forced to accept literally shocking

* i.e. as C-in-C West.

treatment from Moscow. But they have no strong-arm methods available with which to counter it. All they can do is to voice occasional and increasing press criticism of Soviet high-handedness.

The results of Yalta are still being violently attacked—both by the American and the British publics. Criticism is concentrated on the solution to the Polish problem but of course people really mean the handling of the German problem, for there comes the real rub. This criticism is very moderate, however; with the Anglo-Americans fear of Moscow overshadows all other motives.

In the region which was formerly Poland the Soviets are pursuing their bloody reign of terror undeterred by Anglo-American protests. They take not the smallest notice of Churchill and Roosevelt. A new wave of arrests is sweeping across the country, the victims being mainly the Polish nationalists.

In Rumania things are going according to plan, in other words according to the Kremlin's wishes. A spicy bit of news is that Radescu, the former Rumanian Minister-President, has taken refuge in the British Embassy, a fact which Moscow pretends to find most astonishing.

In a recent speech Koiso, the Japanese Minister-President, set out the seriousness of the situation now quite definitely faced by the Japanese. He pleaded for mobilisation of all Japanese forces for war purposes. Japan is now going through a phase similar to ours two years ago. I hope that she will draw different conclusions from it than we did at that time. The German example should have provided an adequate lesson of the results of initiating war measures too late.

The Soviets are complaining loudly of increasing sabotage activity behind their front. They have definitely not got total control of their rear areas, particularly seeing that they have only been able to station a few troops there. They are putting everything in the shop window in preparation for their next offensive against us.

The political repercussions of military victory are now becoming noticeable among the neutrals. The Swedes are indulging in lavish expressions of friendship for the Soviet Union. If the Swedish tycoons think that this is the way to gain the sympathy of the Kremlin, they will find that they are making a fatal error. Nothing that is not definitely bolshevist influences the Kremlin. Bolshevism usually answers any approaches with a kick in the stomach.

Terboven* is once more having a serious row with the Swedish government on the subject of frontier traffic. The Swedes are continually trying to pick a quarrel with us about Norway in order to curry favour with the British and Americans. Terboven has submitted a memorandum to the Führer about the system of command in Norway in emergency. He proposes that he should become deputy Commander-in-Chief to Böhme† to ensure that political affairs would be handled correctly in emergency. I do not think that the Führer can accept this proposal.

It is quite grotesque that the Norwegians should now be hoping that they will be liberated from the German yoke by the Soviets. Their jaws would drop if it actually happened.

The Czechs are now becoming somewhat refractory. This is noticeable in an increase of sabotage activity. The reason is that no one among the Czech people believes in a German victory any more and the opposition elements are trying to provide themselves with an alibi for the future.

Measures now being taken in Hungary to set up a labour service on the German model come plenty late. Little help can now be given the Hungarians. They have missed their moment and can now only be regarded by the major belligerents as pawns in their game.

At midday I receive a large delegation of foreign workers with occupations in the Reich; in their addresses they express their readiness to collaborate. I reply with a very emphatic speech in which I outline our future programme for Europe based on a socialist reorganisation of the continent. I expect this speech to have some effect if it is

* Reich Commissioner for Occupied Norway.
† Commander-in-Chief of German forces in Norway.

published in the foreign workers' newspapers. The majority of these foreign workers have been attracted here by conditions in the Reich. If they go back home after the war they will undoubtedly be our best propagandists.

The series of heavy air raids on our major cities continues. This time it was the turn of Kassel, Hamburg and Bad Homburg. Pure terrorism is the only reason for the Americans to attack Bad Homburg. Reports coming in about the state of Dessau are truly horrifying. The city has been largely destroyed.

Letters I am now receiving show that German fighting morale has reached its nadir. My correspondents bemoan the defeatist attitude to be seen on large sections of the front and also the considerable breakdown in morale among the civil population. Even the optimists are now beginning to waver, a sign that we have now reached the zenith of the crisis. Almost all letters describe Göring as the nigger in the woodpile responsible for the German set-backs on all fronts. For many of the letter-writers the fact that he is still in office is a sign that we are now in the midst of a latent crisis of state.

In the event of emergency OKW and OKH propose to evacuate some 50,000 men from Berlin. Such is the size of our military command organisation! No wonder nothing worth mentioning in the way of useful output emerges from it.

The formation of a manpower cushion behind the Eastern and Western Fronts has now entered a new phase. Jüttner has opposed my plan energetically and partially torpedoed it. Only the replacement units from four Wehrkreis [Military districts] are now to be moved to the rear operational areas. Overall this means about 40,000 men which is of course too few for the purpose envisaged; nevertheless it is better than nothing and I shall continue to batter on in the direction I want in order to achieve my purpose in the end.

Colonel-General Fromm has been sentenced to death for cowardice in face of the enemy. He thoroughly deserves this sentence. Admittedly it could not be proved that he was actually involved in 20 July; but he did not take the measures which were his duty in order to prevent 20 July.

I have a long talk with Marrenbach* about Dr. Ley's leading articles. He has recently indulged in a number of follies entitled "Without baggage" which are simply intolerable. For instance he writes that the destruction of Dresden has been greeted with a sigh of relief by the German people since we have now lost our last city of culture. Of course the air war cannot be treated in this way. The ultimate conclusion to his line of argument is that we had best abandon the entire Reich to the enemy since we should then have no baggage at all to drag around with us.

The evening report from the West unhappily says that it has still not been possible to eliminate the Remagen bridgehead. Improvised counter-measures have been taken but they have not been successful. In the area north of Koblenz isolated groups are still fighting their way back to the Rhine.

The interview between the Führer and Kesselring went well. Probably Kesselring will now take over the Western Front in place of Rundstedt.

Good news comes from Hungary. The Sixth SS Panzer Army has succeeded in penetrating deeply into the enemy defence positions. An effort is now being made to reach the enemy rear areas so as to annihilate his forces and it is thought that a considerable portion of his front must collapse as a result. The Soviets are naturally resisting tooth and nail; it is to be hoped, however, that Sepp Dietrich will succeed in implementing the Führer's plan. Operations at Ratibor have in general gone well, though they are only of a local nature. We have reached Steinau where the Soviet garrison is surrounded. The enemy has penetrated into the northern part of Küstrin. The Altdamm bridgehead was again very heavily attacked; the enemy succeeded in penetrating deeply and further compressing the bridge-

---

* Ley's adjutant. See above p. 97.

head. The situation in West Prussia is definitely bad. The enemy advanced towards Zoppot. Forster's* position in Danzig is therefore highly precarious. The situation in East Prussia is unchanged. The general picture presented by the front is now a fluid one but not solely to our disadvantage, thank God; in fact, to a modest extent, it is to our advantage. It is to be hoped that this favourable trend will have some effect. We need a military victory now as much as our daily bread.

* Albert Forster was Gauleiter of Danzig.

SATURDAY 10 MARCH 1945

(pp. 1–27)

Military Situation.

In Hungary German offensive operations achieved further local gains yesterday. Progress in the area between Lake Balaton and the Danube is especially satisfactory; there our attack is moving forward on a broad front along the Malom Canal.

In Slovakia all enemy attacks at Schemnitz, Altsohl, Briesen and Nikolas failed. There was active enemy reconnaissance activity in the Schwarzwasser area. North of Ratibor violent counter-attacks against our penetration into the enemy bridgehead were defeated. In the northern part of Breslau the enemy attacked in vain; bitter fighting is going on in the southern part. Our local offensive is making good progress at Striegau. At Guben also German troops continued their attacks and improved their positions. North of Forst a small Soviet bridgehead over the Neisse was driven in. Continuing to attack in strength at Küstrin the enemy penetrated farther into the town from north and east so that now we only hold a bridgehead over the Oder in the south-western sector. In a local attack our front advanced from the German bridgehead at Zehden.

The situation in the Stettin area has not changed much. Enemy pressure is still very heavy, particularly just to the west of Stargard where leading enemy troops were able to reach the autobahn. Enemy attacks in the Wollin sector failed. The German formation from the Greifenberg area has fought its way farther north-west and is now moving on Dievenow, the Navy having reinforced it by sea. Heavy attacks on Kolberg from all directions were repulsed but with fairly heavy losses to the garrison. In the Stolp area the situation is unchanged. The new line now runs from Bütow to the northern edge of Berent, from Zuckau turns south-east to just north of Dirschau, crosses the Nogat valley, passes Neuteich and ends on the seat at Tiegenhof. Attacks on our new front line were all driven off. Half of Marienburg is still in our hands.

In East Prussia activity was small.

On the Courland front attacks south-east of Frauenburg were again very heavy. Apart from some minor penetrations, however, all were repulsed.

On the Western Front very bitter fighting continued in the Wesel bridgehead. Despite very heavy artillery preparation of a violence hitherto almost unknown, the Canadians achieved only comparatively small penetrations to a depth of not more than 1½ km. South of the bridgehead all enemy attacks were repulsed, some by counter-attack, with heavy loss to the enemy. Farther south as far as Köln no special operations took place. South of Köln the existing German bridgehead was further reduced. Violent fighting is still going on in Bonn. The enemy bridgehead at Remagen has been sealed off but has still not been eliminated however. The enemy succeeded in expanding it somewhat both to north and south. Southward pressure from the Ahrweiler area continues. In general advancing enemy forces were held on the line Adenau–Nürburgring–Komoenich. All attacks yesterday again failed against the whole front surrounding the break-through area on the south. Attacks westward from Wittlich were either held or defeated on a new position 3 km farther to the rear. In the Trier area and southwards the situation is unchanged.

No special reports from the Italian front.

On the Eastern Front enemy air activity was particularly heavy in East Prussia round Stettin and Küstrin and also in Courland. In the central sector alone 2100 sorties were counted. Very heavy enemy air raids were made on Königsberg and Breslau. Good results were achieved by our own close support aircraft in Hungary and at the main scenes of fighting in the central sector of the eastern front.

In the West air activity was reduced owing to unfavourable weather but on the Italian front it was very heavy. Over Reich territory strong American four-engined bomber formations with fighter escort raided transport and industrial targets in west Germany. Kassel, Frankfurt am Main, Münster, Osnabrück and Rheine were particularly hard hit. There was heavy twin-engined bomber activity directed mainly on the central Rhine region. From the south some 500 American four-engined bombers with fighter escort attacked Graz with a subsidiary attack on Klegenfurt. None of our fighters were in action. Anti-aircraft reports six aircraft shot down so far. In the evening the Reich capital was raided by 60–80 high-speed aircraft.

Naval units carried out a commando raid on the French west coast at Granville. Severe casualties were inflicted on the enemy; German prisoners were liberated and brought back. Five ships of a total of 4800 GRT and 14 lighters were sunk; five locomotives and trucks, 10 motor vehicles, one submarine shelter and a fuel depot were destroyed. The lock gates were again destroyed. The steamer *Esquout* was brought back under its own steam. The town of Granville is in flames.

Churchill's and Roosevelt's report on the U-boat war is couched in somewhat gloomier tones than last time. The two war criminals naturally only refer to a moderate number of enemy ships as having been sunk. Reading between the lines of their statement, however, it is possible to detect increasing anxiety on the enemy side caused by the resumption of activity by our U-boats; they are playing havoc with the enemy's tonnage situation, which is strained anyway.

Otherwise people in the USA and Britain are literally intoxicated with victory. Above all, people think that because the Remagen bridge has been captured the war will now end quickly. In London it is stated, moreover, that the bridge fell into enemy hands as a result of treachery. It had been prepared for demolition, they say, but the officer responsible did not carry it out. I can quite imagine that this may be true.

London also spread the rumour that the Führer proposed to capitulate punctually at midnight Thursday/Friday. This premature optimism has now dissolved into thin air. There is not the smallest sign of surrender in Germany, though today we naturally have to overcome difficulties of far more than normal size.

The morale of our troops and our people in the West has suffered to an extraordinary degree. The Führer has accordingly despatched General Hübner to the West and invested him with the widest plenary powers. Nothing can be achieved in the West now except by brutal methods, otherwise we shall lose control of the situation. The Western Front is now in a similar state to that of the Eastern Front seven to eight weeks ago. An iron hand is now the essential here. The morale both of the civil population and the troops has suffered primarily as a result of enemy air action. We hope, however, that the appearance of General Hübner will quickly put things to rights again.

I am vexed most of all by the behaviour of the people in my home town of Rheydt. The Americans have struck up a real triumphal chorus about it. A certain Herr Vogelsang, known to me from the early days as a downright National-Socialist philistine, has placed himself at the disposal of the American occupation authorities as Oberbürgermeister. In doing so he stated that he had only joined the Party on compulsion from me and otherwise he had nothing to do with it. I am going to draw a bead on this gentleman. I am preparing an operation to liquidate him at the first favourable opportunity. It will be carried out by Party members from Berlin who have been trained for actions of this type. I discussed it in full detail with Schach.* I do not want to

---

* One of Goebbels' officials as Gauleiter of Berlin. For further details of this operation and its outcome, see below pp. 129, 317.

rush the matter but to make careful preparations to ensure that it succeeds whatever happens. I believe that it will not fail to have its effect both on the enemy occupation authorities and also on the population beyond the Rhine.

Naturally, as was to be expected, the Americans have started a so-called free German newspaper in Rheydt as one of the first towns to be occupied. They are trying to humiliate me with it and point out that the fact that such a newspaper should appear in Rheydt of all places is one of the ironies of history. But the triumphal show they are putting on seems to me somewhat premature. I shall find ways and means to put things to rights again at least in Rheydt.

The American and British newspapers report on the attitude of our prisoners in the West, which they describe as excellent. As correspondents report, our prisoners still maintain the view that Germany must definitely win the war. To judge from the answers given by a Berliner to an American correspondent's somewhat impudent questions, I could not have done better myself. All the prisoners, so these reports state, have an almost mystical faith in Hitler. This is the reason why we are still on our feet and fighting.

The *Daily Mail* is acting as spokesman for large-scale opposition in England when it says that the vote of confidence obtained by Churchill at the recent division in the Commons were a mere fraud. In fact, the paper says, criticism of Churchill and his policy is a widespread malady in England. It should not be thought that the vote in the Commons was representative of the British people's real views. This is precisely what we had suspected.

A series of other British newspapers are indulging in sharp criticism of the Kremlin's shirt-sleeve policy and diplomacy. As I have already emphasised so often, however, these outbursts are still kept within tolerable limits and should not be looked upon as promising as far as our future war prospects are concerned.

Roosevelt is said to have declared himself in agreement with the deportation of millions of Germans to the Soviet Union. The Soviet Union, it is said, proposed to demand

800–1000 milliard gold roubles as war reparations from Germany. This astronomical sum should be worked off in labour. One knows that tale. The Soviets are pursuing a systematic long-term policy, but they overstate their demands to such an extent that they will eventually overcall their hand.

There are more unemployed in France today than there were before the war. Despite the fact that work is available in every corner of France, therefore, the de Gaulle regime has not succeeded in mastering this most elementary problem in a people's social life.

The Japanese report that they have taken over in French Indo-China. The French authorities created so many difficulties for them that they have now taken measures to safeguard themselves against openly planned treachery.

The Americans have made very heavy incendiary bomb raids on Tokyo. They are talking very big about it but it does in fact seem that very widespread fires broke out in Tokyo. The Japanese are now beginning to see a side of the air war with which we have long been familiar.

Reports from the Baltic States say that the Baltic peoples are now filled with longing for the return of the Germans. But this yearning comes late indeed; they might have given better expression to it by active participation in the war against the Soviet Union in 1941, '42 and '43. Bourgeois countries invariably take their decisions too late and bolshevism reaps the reward. Anti-Soviet partisan activity is said to be extraordinarily widespread in the Baltic States. The Soviet supply system is increasingly jeopardised thereby.

Under pressure from the Anglo-Americans Switzerland has now banned transit traffic to us. Switzerland is a miserable sort of country whose national sovereignty is comprised only in newspaper articles.

The air war over Reich territory rages on. Reports sound almost monotonous but they tell of so much sorrow and misery that one hardly dares think about them in detail. The Führer has now decided that the 1928 class shall be withdrawn from the Volkssturm. This has implications for us in Berlin since we have 5000 Hitler Youth members of the 1928 class manning our defence positions and we now have to release them for fresh divisions which are to be formed. These new divisions are our great hope for the future, however, so that we cannot evade the problem.

It is significant that, during discussions on total war, the proposal has been made that the entire Luftwaffe should be abolished and such remnants of it as are in any way fit for war be transferred to the other Services. This would be the most sensible solution since in its present state the Luftwaffe is not worth a row of beans. It consists merely of one enormous corruption factory.

For the first time the facts and figures concerning the defences of the Reich capital covering a week were submitted to me. Taken as a whole the situation is extraordinarily satisfactory. According to the figures submitted to me it may be assumed that with the men, weapons, food and coal available Berlin could hold out for some eight weeks if surrounded. Eight weeks is a long time during which a lot can happen. In any case we have made excellent preparations and above all it must be remembered that, if the worst should happen, an enormous number of men with their weapons would flow into the city and we should be in a position to use them to put up a powerful defence.

In the evening comes the news that it has still not been possible to eliminate the Remagen bridgehead. On the contrary the Americans have reinforced it and are trying to extend it. The result is a very unpleasant situation for us. I was told that C-in-C West was due to take large-scale counter-measures this afternoon and tonight, but so far we have invariably had to note that such counter-measures only lead to success in the rarest instances. Here, however, we must succeed, for if the Americans continue to hold out on the right bank of the Rhine, they have a base for a further advance and from the small beginning of a bridgehead such as we now see, a running sore will develop—as so often before—the poison from which will soon spread to the Reich's vitals.

Otherwise there have been no important changes in the

West. Our bridgehead at Xanten has been further reduced. In the East operations in Hungary are developing favourably at the moment. Our penetration was extended farther westwards. One can already talk of a real break-through here. We have torn the enemy front apart to a breadth of 25 km and also a depth of 25 km. The break-in at Lake Balaton has also been widened so that here too we have scored a considerable initial success. In Slovakia the battle swings this way and that. The scope of the major Soviet offensive at Schwarzwasser was not as great as we had originally feared. So far Schörner has dealt with it. The severest street fighting is raging in Breslau. The enemy has attempted to recapture Striegau but these efforts have been defeated. At Frankfurt and Küstrin the Soviets succeeded in making further very troublesome penetrations. Nothing fresh in the Stettin area. The garrison of Kolberg has beaten off all enemy attacks with severe losses. At Danzig the crisis for our troops has become worse. Here is another sensitive spot in the eastern situation.

For weeks now we have had a Mosquito raid on the Reich capital every evening without exception. Recent raids were somewhat heavier than usual. The enemy is apparently dropping larger HE and incendiary bombs. Anyway the Mosquito raids can no more be shrugged off than hitherto. They are not comparable, of course, to the terror raids with which the cities of the west are being hammered. Looking at the air war as a whole we in Berlin have by and large been lucky, though large parts of the city are nothing but a heap of ruins.

SUNDAY 11 MARCH 1945

(pp. 8–56, pp. 1–7 missing)
(Manuscript Note: *pp. 1–7: Military Situation.*)
At the moment the Western Powers treat us simply with
scorn and derision. They feel themselves on top of the
world and act as if they had already won the war. They
think that our morale has been badly affected and allow us
no prospect of victory whatsoever. To listen to them the
Volkssturm is nothing but a Home Guard of tired old men.
The people of the occupied regions, they say, have turned
their backs on National-Socialism and the National-Socialist
leadership; their attitude is so servile and submissive as to
be actually embarrassing. There is no question of an orderly
German administration either in the occupied or non-
occupied regions. That does not matter however, since the
enemy has no intention of allowing any government to take
office in Germany. In short the Reich will be dealt with
like a Negro colony in Africa. In addition the British and
Americans are said to be planning to attack from the north-
west and Zhukov is considering a plan to break through in
Pomerania and join forces with the Anglo-Americans somewhere on the north-west German plain.

This is roughly the picture of future war developments
that is being painted in London, though not quite so much
in Washington. There they are somewhat more realistic. It
is easy to see what the object of these British reports is.
They want to instil a little courage into their tired people
and so they do the bragging while the Soviets and the
Americans win victories for them. The fact that Berlin has
not yet fallen into enemy hands is generously ascribed to

121

the fact that the Soviets have no intention of making a frontal attack on the Reich capital. They are pursuing more important military objectives. In short everything now being published on the enemy side is aimed at our strength of nerve. If they think, however, that they will frighten us as a result they are making a fatal error. Anyway it is completely immaterial to us what the British think or say at the moment. Such panic stories have never paid off unless they have an immediate success. And there is no question of that. I expect their hangover mood to reassert itself in a few days' time.

Our Wesel bridgehead has now been evacuated under very strong British-Canadian pressure. The Remagen bridgehead is still there. Fighting at this point flows back and forth all the time. So far, despite the greatest efforts, we have not succeeded in eliminating it and it is very questionable whether we ever shall succeed.

The enemy side is continually raising the question whether the Soviets will declare war on the Japanese. The Kremlin must make up its mind soon since the Soviet-Japanese non-aggression pact must either be tacitly renewed or abrogated next month. On the Western side people are quite sure that the Soviets intend to attack the Japanese. But I do not think that, whatever happens, Stalin will allow himself to be dragged into the Pacific adventure merely to please the British, still less the Americans.

The bolshevist menace is now clearly recognised in Britain as well. The newspapers make no secret of it. But it is of no importance now what the British think or feel— simply what they are in a position to do and that is nothing at all. The voices of protest in the British press against bolshevist high-handedness in Europe are merely the cries of distress from the heart of a blackmailed people which no longer has a loophole. In fact these voices are not those merely of outsiders; what the outsiders are saying today about the danger of bolshevism is probably the view of the entire British ruling class, which, however, cannot make any use of their opinion.

It is said that the Pope intends to take a hand in the

Polish problem and try to mediate. He will meet his match in Stalin. Stalin is firmly determined—and one can understand this—to negotiate with no one over the Polish question. How rigidly he has already imposed his will is evident from the fact that Mikolajczyk,* the former Polish Minister-in-exile, now proposes to submit to the dictates of the Kremlin. Under protest admittedly, but what value are such protests today? Anyway the only choice for the Poles is either to be exterminated by force or to bow to the Kremlin. Their ruling class has only to look at the nasty example of Bulgaria where 1200 prominent people have so far been executed. A nice round number for the shop-window.

In the East things are developing somewhat more favourably for us. Our offensive in Hungary has got off to a good start. Gains of ground, however, have not been so great that we are altogether over the hump. We must wait a few days before giving a final verdict on this offensive. Schörner has succeeded in beating off the very strong attacks at Schwarzwasser without too serious losses. That is a major victory.

Very serious communist disturbances have again taken place in Rome. The Anglo-American occupation forces are totally powerless since the disturbances are taking place under the wing of the Kremlin. The Bonomi government gives the impression of a lot of old men sitting on the fence and not knowing what to do. It thinks that it can get the better of these disturbances by particularly severe anti-fascist laws. But that is now no good any more. On the contrary it is reported from all quarters that fascism is making a certain come-back in enemy-occupied Italy.

Sundays are generally somewhat quieter. I can spend it doing some reading and catching up on the week's accumulation of work.

---

* Stanislaw Mikolajczyk, leader of the Polish Peasant Party, had succeeded General Sikorski as Prime Minister of Poland in London. Stalin had taken the opportunity of Sikorski's death (and the revelation by the Germans of the Katyn murders) to transfer Russian recognition from the Polish government in London to the "Lublin Committee" in Russia.

In the air war it is the old story. Towns near the Western Front are now being attacked. There is not much left to destroy there.

It must be admitted that the morale both of our troops and of the civil population in the West has been affected. The situation is similar to that in the East seven weeks ago. We must do our utmost to revive the resolution of our troops and civil population in the West.

Heroes' Memorial Day was marked by a wreath-laying ceremony by Göring at the ruined Heroes' Memorial. In addition the Führer issued a proclamation to the troops, repeating once more our old war themes. The proclamation was characterised by virile determination giving an extraordinarily convincing impression.

For this evening we are preparing a broadcast on Silesia containing an account of my visit to Lauban and parts of my speech in Görlitz. The broadcast makes an extraordinarily positive impression for it radiates a strong fighting spirit. My speech in Görlitz has been given excellent coverage in the press. It is my view that such publications cannot fail to have their effect at the present time. We must invariably lead our people back to the fundamental themes of our war strategy and make clear to them that they have no other choice but to fight or to die.

This evening it is reported that the Remagen bridgehead is still there. Our efforts to eliminate it have not succeeded. The Americans have one railway bridge available and have also thrown two pontoon bridges across the Rhine. They have not succeeded in expanding the bridgehead further, however, since we are keeping it under close watch. The American troops in the bridgehead are under heavy artillery fire. The main body of our forces has now reached the lower Moselle. Otherwise there have been no sensational changes in the West during the course of the day.

Our offensive in Hungary is making slow but sure progress. In general developments there may be called satisfactory. Our penetration has been considerably extended. We have also advanced near Lake Velencze, so that we can now talk of a real major offensive.

Schörner has again beaten off all attacks near Schwarzwasser, though the Soviets launched a major first-class
offensive. In the Ratibor area too, where the enemy is
doing his utmost to recapture the ground he has lost, all
attacks were repulsed. Schörner has not yet been able to
finish off the Soviet garrison of Striegau which is surrounded; he hopes, however, to have put matters right by
Monday since we are proposing to send a press delegation
of German and neutral journalists to the town to see the
atrocities committed there. We have slightly improved our
positions at Guben. There has been no deterioration in the
Stettin area. The situation in West Prussia has become
extraordinarily critical however. This is the sensitive point
of the Eastern Front at the moment.

I pay a visit of several hours to the Führer in the evening.
The Führer gives me an extraordinarily assured and resolute
impression and physically he seems in the best of form.
I hand him one of the copies I still possess of Carlyle's
Frederick the Great which gives him great pleasure. He
emphasises that the great prototypes are the men on whom
we must model ourselves today and that Frederick the
Great was the most exceptional personality of them all. It
must be our ambition to set an example today on which
later generations can model themselves in similar crises
and times of stress, just as today we must take our cue
from the heroes of past history.

I give the Führer a detailed account of my visit to
Lauban. He is also of the opinion that Schörner is one of
our most outstanding army commanders. He is the next
army officer whom the Führer wants to promote to Field
Marshal. Schörner has largely succeeded in stabilising the
front in his area of command. It is due to him that the
troops' morale has been kept so outstandingly high.

I tell the Führer of the radical methods employed by
Schörner to achieve this end. Deserters get no mercy from
him. They are hung from the nearest tree with a placard
round their neck saying: "I am a deserter. I have refused
to defend German women and children and therefore I
have been hung." Naturally such methods are effective.

Every man in Schörner's area knows that he may die at the front but will inevitably die in the rear. That is a very good lesson which will assuredly strike home.

The repulse of the Soviet attacks at Schwarzwasser and the retention of Ratibor have so far safeguarded the Mährisch–Ostrau area which is so vital to our war potential. The Führer emphasises yet again that in his view the Soviets never intended to advance straight on Berlin. For a long time he had been telling his generals this over and over again but they refused to listen to him. Had they done so the tragedy in Pomerania would never have taken place. They had concentrated the available forces in front of Berlin instead of locating them in the Pomeranian area to hold the anticipated Soviet advance. The Führer lays much of the blame direct at Himmler's door.* He had repeatedly urged Himmler to concentrate in Pomerania. Himmler had allowed himself to be misled, however, by repeated memoranda from the Intelligence Section, into believing in a drive on Berlin and making his dispositions accordingly. I ask the Führer why he does not simply issue orders on questions so vitally affecting our war strategy. The Führer replies that this would not do him much good, since even if he issued unequivocal orders, they would always be nullified by backstage sabotage. In this connection he reproaches Himmler bitterly. He had given clear orders that a strong anti-tank defence line be constructed in the Pomeranian area; the necessary anti-tank guns, however, had arrived either not at all or too late and so had done no good. At the very beginning of his term as army commander, therefore, Himmler had fallen prey to the General Staff. The Führer accuses him of flat disobedience and intends to give him a piece of his mind on the next available occasion and make clear that, in the event of repetition of such an instance, an irreparable breach would occur between him and Himmler. Himmler will take this to heart and I will speak to him in the same sense as well. Anyway I always thought it was wrong to entrust Himmler with

* i.e. for his failure as commander of Army Group Vistula.

command of an Army Group. That is not his job in the present situation, certainly not if it is liable to lead to a breach between him and the Führer. Himmler has therefore temporarily forfeited his promotion to Commander-in-Chief of the Army.* The Führer is very displeased with him. He is convinced that Pomerania could have been held if his clear and explicit order had been carried out. Now hundreds of thousands of Pomeranians have fallen victim to the fury of the Soviet rabble. Here too the Führer is of the opinion that Himmler must accept the blame for this. He now proposes to stop the increasing indiscipline among the generals by instituting itinerant courts martial under General Hübner; their task will be to investigate forthwith any recalcitrance in the higher levels of the Wehrmacht, to bring those concerned to trial and have the guilty shot. It is simply intolerable that in this critical phase of the war anyone should be able to do just as he likes. I think, however, that the Führer has not yet got to the root of the trouble. He must definitely clean up the top level of the Wehrmacht, for if the top level is not in order, no one can be surprised if lower levels go their own way. The Führer replies that he has no one who could become Commander-in-Chief of the Army for instance. He is right when he says that, had he appointed Himmler to this post, the catastrophe would now be worse than it is anyway. He now wants to promote to officer status young soldiers with front-line experience, no matter whether they know how to use a knife and fork. Recipients of the Knights Cross should be taken from the ranks of the fighting troops and trained as officers. The Führer thinks that this will have a great effect on the rising generation. He points to his experiences in the First World War when it would not have been possible to promote a soldier, however highly decorated, to officer status if he had not the right social upbringing. But what good is social background in this critical time? We must do our utmost to ensure that the right men are in command

---

* It is interesting to note that Himmler had evidently been promised this position.

at the front, no matter whether socially they are of command fibre or not. These measures are all very good and undoubtedly effective. But they come full late, if not too late.

I tell the Führer in detail of the impressions I gathered during my visit to Lauban. I also describe to him in detail the atrocities I saw there. The Führer agrees with me that our propaganda must now highlight vengeance against the Soviets. Our offensive strength must now be switched to the East. The East is decisive. The Soviets must shed rivers of blood; then there may be a possibility of bringing the Kremlin to its senses. Everything now depends on our troops standing where they are and overcoming the bolshevist horror. Developments in Hungary, which the Führer considers very promising, show that if we really concentrate for an offensive, we succeed. It is to be hoped that these operations continue in this fashion.

In any case the Führer is of the opinion that the atrocity propaganda I have initiated is entirely right and should be continued.

As far as the West is concerned the Führer inclines to my view that the whole thing is a complete mess. Rundstedt has not been up to commanding the battle in the West. He is too old, and moreover comes of a school unsuited to modern warfare. The Führer has therefore relieved him and replaced him by Kesselring. He is due to receive Rundstedt this very morning to tell him so. Rundstedt is of course a highly respectable officer who has done us great service, particularly in the liquidation of 20 July. The Führer therefore wants—I impressed this on him forcibly—Rundstedt's relief to be carried out in the most decorous manner.

In general the Führer is pleased with Model. But he has been unable to operate properly under Rundstedt. Had Model been given the entire Western Front, his Army Group would not be in the state in which it actually is.

As far as morale in the West is concerned, we must try to revive it, if necessary by forceful methods. The population will soon recover its poise even in regions occupied by the enemy. It is understandable that they should have lost their nerve somewhat after months of heavy air raids. Experience shows, however, that this changes quickly as soon as the air raids stop and hunger starts to make people think. The fact that white flags were hoisted here and there as the Anglo-Americans arrived should not be taken too tragically. In any case the Führer is firmly convinced that it will be easy for us to get these people back on our side in the next few weeks. I tell the Führer in detail of the situation in my home town of Rheydt, also that I intend to have Vogelsang, the Oberbürgermeister installed by the Americans, liquidated by a terror squad I have assembled in Berlin. The Führer is in full agreement. Moreover we shall now start getting partisan activity under way in the enemy-occupied areas. I intend to make a good start in Rheydt. The pastors have been among the first to place themselves at the disposal of the Anglo-Americans. There will be a good field of activity for our terror groups here. Moreover if we recover this region, the Führer intends to bring these pastors before a court martial which they will never forget.

The Remagen bridgehead causes the Führer much anxiety. On the other hand he is of the opinion that it offers us certain advantages. Had the Americans not found a weak spot enabling them to advance across the Rhine, they would probably have swung forthwith against the Moselle and our stop-lines on the Moselle had not then been constructed; there would therefore have been a danger of the Moselle being crossed on a broad front which the Führer thinks cannot now be done. Nevertheless it must be assumed that the failure to blow the Remagen bridge may well be due to sabotage or at least to serious negligence. The Führer has ordered an enquiry and will impose the death sentence on anyone found guilty. The Führer considers that the bridgehead is a definite thorn in the flesh of the Americans. He has now ringed the bridgehead with heavy weapons whose job it is to cause the severest possible casualties to American forces concentrated in the bridgehead. It may well be, therefore, that the bridgehead will not be all joy for the Americans. The Führer's view is that we must succeed in holding the general line Rhine–Moselle. The situation would then still be tolerable, although we should have had to give up vital German territory. The fact that at Trier the fortifications of the Siegfried Line were abandoned almost without a fight has caused the Führer the greatest anxiety. He tells me that he was in a real fury when given the news. But what can one do? There are certain types of officer who are not up to the demands of war, particularly not morally. Moreover, in this area we have lost much German manpower now under the sway of the enemy. It must be our task to continue to work upon them politically over the radio and we may well succeed in producing very rapid results.

As far as the West is concerned, however, the Führer is still of the opinion that we can be semi-satisfied with developments, although we have had to suffer extraordinarily severe losses. Here too the main thing is to stand firm under all circumstances and halt the enemy on solid stop-lines.

Every effort is being made to destroy the Remagen railway bridge and the two pontoon bridges constructed near it by the enemy; the Luftwaffe and also light naval forces have been in action on a large scale. Moreover in this area on the right bank of the Rhine the enemy is in country extraordinarily unfavourable to him, where he will find it very difficult to deploy for wide-ranging operations.

There is really nothing fresh to add regarding the air war. I tell the Führer that the most recent Mosquito raids on Berlin have been very heavy. This too the Führer had prophesied. During the coming spring and summer these Mosquito raids will undoubtedly be a severe trial since the Mosquito is very difficult, in fact almost impossible, to shoot down. The less said about the enemy air terror the better. The Führer has several times taken Göring severely to task but without result. As a personality he has degenerated totally and is sunk in lethargy. The Führer does not mince words on the subject. But it is impossible to persuade him to make any internal personnel changes in the Luftwaffe; he will not even impose on Göring an efficient State Secretary in the Air Ministry, a move which I am continually proposing. The Führer does not think that this would do much good; in addition he says that he has no one who could undertake the job. I counter this by saying that a good State Secretary would at least put some order into the pandemonium in the Luftwaffe; the Führer opines, however, that even if he were to try this, Göring would eliminate the man at once; Göring will not tolerate a personality of any importance around him, although he has no reason to be afraid, for the Führer will never drop him. What a tragedy this is with our Luftwaffe! It has totally gone to the dogs and one sees no possibility of dragging it up again. It is simply out of its depth.

I am now very forceful in my criticism to the Führer of Göring personally and the Luftwaffe in general. I put the straight question to him whether the German people is ultimately to go under because of the failure of its Luftwaffe, for in the last analysis all our set-backs are due to that failure. The Führer admits all this but, as I have already emphasised, he is not to be persuaded to make any internal personnel change in the Luftwaffe. I ask him at least to clear up the increasing corruption in the Luftwaffe. He thinks that this cannot be done in one fell swoop but that in this case we must work slowly, trying gradually to divest Göring of his position of power and turn him into a mere figurehead. For instance he has commissioned SS-Obergruppenführer Kammler to organise the transport to operational bases of our fighter aircraft. The Luftwaffe is no longer capable of doing even that. What a scandal for an air force and its self-respect as an arm of the service! But what else can one do other than try and attack this disgraceful situation from all angles? In any case I put it quite clearly to the Führer that the Luftwaffe's failure is now gradually leading to the most dire consequences for him himself. The people are reproaching him for failure to take a decision in the dilemma facing us in the air war, for everybody knows that the blame for this dilemma lies at Göring's door. In the present emergency the people will not be convinced by the argument repeatedly adduced by the Führer that in the true German way he must remain loyal to Göring. That does no good, for in the last analysis we cannot allow ourselves to be ruined by this principle.

I describe to the Führer certain details about the Luftwaffe which have come to light as a result of the measures for the introduction of total war. The Führer is largely aware of them; they do not excite him in the least but merely round off the picture he already has of Göring and the Luftwaffe. I am nevertheless of the opinion that I must continue to batter on in this way on the principle of water dropping on a stone.

As far the the political warfare situation is concerned I have the impression that the Führer is slowly beginning to evolve a new concept. He has already discussed the matter with Ribbentrop and reached full agreement with him. I advise the Führer urgently to issue an order stopping the political prattle about the war situation which goes on among prominent people both in the Party and the state. This only weakens people's determination and will to fight. There should only be a few people entitled to speak frankly about the political background to the war. The Führer is also of this opinion. He tells me, for instance, that Göring recently urged the creation of a new atmosphere *vis-à-vis* the enemy. The Führer replied that he would be better employed creating a new atmosphere in the air, which was quite right.

As far as our enemies' situation is concerned the Führer is still convinced that the hostile coalition will break up. He no longer thinks, however, that England will be the instigator of this since, even if England now has a better grasp of the situation, it is of no great importance. The point now is not what England wants but what England can do and that is now nothing at all. Opposition to Churchill's policy is insignificant and, being insignificant, it neither can nor should express itself. Churchill is a gangster who has now got into his head the crazy notion of destroying Germany no matter whether England goes down in the process. So we have no alternative but to look round for other possibilities. Perhaps this is just as well since, if we could come to some arrangement with the East, we should then have an opportunity of giving England the *coup de grâce* and this war would then really have achieved its true purpose.

As far as the United States are concerned they want to eliminate Europe as a competitor and therefore they have no interest whatsoever in continuing to prop up what we call the Western world. Moreover they intend to drag the Soviets into the Pacific war and will make any sacrifice in Europe to this end. Moreover a reversal of war policy is very difficult if not impossible both in Britain and the United States since Roosevelt and even more Churchill have to take too much account of their public opinion. With the Kremlin it is totally different and Stalin is in a position to switch his war policy 180 degrees in a single night. It must therefore be our aim to drive the Soviets back in the east, inflicting on them extraordinarily high casualties both in men and material. Then the Kremlin might show itself more accommodating towards us. A separate peace in the East would naturally alter the war situation fundamentally. In this separate peace we should naturally not achieve our aims of 1941; the Führer hopes, however, for a partition of Poland, retention of Hungary and Croatia under German suzerainty, and freedom of manoeuvre against the West. This would of course be an aim worth expending some sweat to achieve. Elimination of the war in the East and operational freedom in the West —what a splendid idea! The Führer is accordingly of the opinion that one should preach vengeance against the East but hatred of the West. The West, after all, was the cause of the war and has been responsible for its expansion to such fearful dimensions. The West is responsible for the destruction of our cities and reduction of our cultural monuments to dust and ashes. If therefore, with coverage in the East, we could succeed in driving back the Anglo-Americans, we should at once achieve our object of eliminating England for ever as Europe's permanent mischief-maker.

The programme divulged to me by the Führer is grandiose and persuasive. The only objection is that there is no means of achieving it. The opportunity must first be created by our soldiers in the East. We require one or two respectable victories as a start; as things stand at present it might be assumed that these could be achieved. We must stake our all on this. This is what we must work for, fight for and to this end we must, under all circumstances, re-establish the morale of our people.

I tell the Führer certain details of my trip to Lauban, in particular my drive behind the bolshevist front during the evening. The Führer is much taken aback that I should have driven for such a distance behind the front; it would have been unthinkable had I fallen into enemy hands in doing so. Apart from this the Führer shares my view that we should now institute an organised counter-terror against the bolshevist terror. Under all circumstances we must overcome the bolshevist horror and we shall succeed in doing so.

The conversation which I had with the Führer on this Sunday evening was a frank as could be. The Führer no longer holds anything back from me. Admittedly on the really important war problems I have achieved no practical result this time. But I think, as I have already said, that the policy of water dropping on a stone will win. I am very pleased to find the Führer so extraordinarily alert and resilient physically, morally and mentally.

The Führer's generals are waiting in his anteroom. They are a weary-looking crowd making a depressing impression. It is a shame that the Führer has so few respectable military men on his staff. He himself is the only outstanding personality in this circle. Why has no circle of Gneisenaus and Scharnhorsts collected around him! I would make it my first duty to look out such a circle and place it at the Führer's disposal. It is really pitiable to talk to generals of this type and find that General Jodl,* for instance, is making a great song and dance about the trivial matter of the right of entry into air-raid shelters as if it was a question

* Chief of Operations, OKW.

of world-historical importance. So small-minded are the majority of the Führer's military advisers.

I find an enormous quantity of work back at home. Again the regulation Mosquito raid. I am no longer taking these raids as lightly as I did since they are doing us considerable damage.

In the evening the weekly newsreel is run through for me. It includes shots of Lauban and Görlitz which are really moving. The Führer's visit to the front is also included. In short, this newsreel contains pictures of which we can make really good use for propaganda purposes. Unfortunately the weekly newsreel can only appear at irregular intervals since we have neither the necessary raw materials nor facilities for distribution for regular showings. Since it only appears irregularly our efforts to make it effective must be all the greater.

That was an eventful Sunday. I think it is good that I should go to the Führer regularly on Sunday evenings and have a prolonged talk with him, letting other evening visits drop. A weekly conversation with the Führer at such length and in such depth has a more lasting effect in my view than a talk every evening from which nothing much emerges.

MONDAY 12 MARCH 1945

(pp. 1–32)
Military Situation.

In Hungary our offensive made progress, though in some cases it was only small. The Soviets have brought up Bulgarian and Rumanian formations as reinforcements. In Slovakia all enemy attacks in the main centre of activity, the Schemnitz–Altsohl area, were held deep in the battle zone. In the Schwarzwasser area, where the enemy made violent attacks throughout the day, another complete defensive victory was scored yesterday; the same applies to the bridgehead north of Ratibor, where very strong Soviet counter-attacks were repulsed. The garrison of the fortress of Breslau beat off attacks of reduced strength from the north and recaptured a number of housing blocks in the southern part of the city. The Soviet forces surrounded at Striegau have been split into four battle groups of which two have already been annihilated and the remaining two are facing annihilation. No operations of importance on the Niesse front. Between Frankfurt and Küstrin and between Lebus and Görlitz enemy attacks throughout the day by five Rifle Divisions were successfully beaten off. In Küstrin ground lost on the previous day was recovered by counter-attack. In the Stettin area Soviet attacks on our bridgehead south of the city were successfully repulsed. The German formations fighting their way back from Greifenberg gained contact with our own forces in Dievenow. In West Prussia our troops are defending a wide bridgehead round Gotenhafen and Danzig. All enemy attacks were beaten off. In East Prussia enemy attacks in regimental strength were repulsed at Zinten. All along the front there has been lively Soviet reconnaissance activity so that a resumption of major operations must be reckoned with in the next few days.

On the Courland front a complete defensive victory was scored yesterday in the Frauenburg area.

On the Western Front there was heavy artillery fire in the Nijmegen–Emmerich area. In addition very lively enemy reconnaissance activity has been in progress in this area since yesterday, so a fresh enemy offensive is imminent in this area. Apart from isolated artillery duels there have been no special developments along the whole Rhine front as far as Remagen. Strong counter-attacks were made on the enemy bridgehead at Remagen. The enemy was driven out of Honnef and the hills north-east of the town. Counter-attacks are in progress against an enemy advance eastwards. The enemy was also driven out of Hönningen. Counter-attacks are in progress against the Rhine highway south of Linz. Between the Ahr and the Moselle our bridgeheads at Neuwied and Engers were withdrawn, whereas those at Niederbreisig and Niederbrohl are still held. Our bridgeheads over the Moselle at Gondorf and Moselsürch are also holding out. Between the western Eifel and the Moselle front the enemy is moving up to the Moselle. His leading troops are now west of the big loop in the Moselle at Traben-Trarbach.

In other sectors of the Western Front there were only local actions and minor raids.

No special operations took place in Italy.

On the Eastern Front both sides were very active in the air over the main operational areas. Our own air force was in action in considerable strength in Hungary and the central sector of the eastern front. Our fighters shot down a total of 65 enemy aircraft. The bridge at Görlitz was hit and destroyed by close support aircraft.

On the Western Front air activity was small.

Over Reich territory strong American four-engined bomber formations with fighter escort raided port installations in Hamburg, Kiel and Bremen. In the afternoon 500

British aircraft with fighter escort attacked Essen and other places in the Ruhr. Strong twin-engined bomber formations raided the Rhine–Main area, Münsterland and the industrial zone. During the night high-speed aircraft carried out harassing raids on Berlin and Magdeburg.

The morale of the German people, both at home and at the front, is sinking ever lower. The Reich propaganda agencies are complaining very noticeably about this. The people thinks that it is facing a perfectly hopeless situation in this war. Criticism of our war strategy does not now stop short even of the Führer himself. He is being reproached primarily for failure to take decisions on vital war problems, particularly those concerning personnel. The case of Göring is given special mention. The Führer should have changed the top-level personnel in the Luftwaffe long ago. People take the fact that it does not happen as an indication either that he does not know the true state of affairs, which would be very bad, or that he does know but makes no changes, which would be even worse. It must always be pointed out, however, that the present level of morale must not be confused with definite defeatism. The people will continue to do their duty and the front-line soldier will defend himself as far as he has a possibility of doing so. These possibilities are becoming increasingly limited, however, primarily owing to the enemy's air superiority. The air terror which rages uninterruptedly over German home territory makes people thoroughly despondent. One feels so impotent against it that no one can now see a way out of the dilemma. The total paralysis of transport in West Germany also contributes to the mood of increasing pessimism among the German people.

As far as the Eastern Front is concerned people recognise that it has stabilised to a degree but they anticipate an imminent Soviet advance on Berlin and Dresden and think that the war will really be decided in this area. People are hoping, nevertheless, that we have adequate reserves available to hold this advance.

The Führer's recent proclamation of 24 February has made an extraordinarily good impact, principally because the Führer described the overall war situation in such firm assured tones; he held out some hope to the German people when he stressed that the decisive turning-point of the war was to be expected this year.

The only feeling expressed about the war in the East is one of revenge. All our people now give credence to the atrocities committed by the Bolshevists. No one makes light of our warnings any longer. People also know, however, that as a result of the Soviet advance our food situation is very critical and people doubt whether we shall be able to find even a semi-satisfactory solution to this problem.

In general it may be said that, taking into account the extraordinarily critical situation, the people is presenting a comparatively good demeanour, though naturally certain profound cracks in morale are noticeable. To a certain extent, however, they resemble spots which come and go on the face of a person not in good health.

The enemy also confirms that in general German troops in the West are showing an unbroken fighting spirit. Almost all prisoners, they say, are firmly convinced of a German victory. Hitler represents to them a sort of national myth and correspondents fear that, even if Germany is overrun, he will be the embodiment of the German dream to an even greater extent after defeat than he is now.

The enemy still does not know about the change of command in the West* and is still drivelling on about Rundstedt having certain trump cards in his hand which he will now play.

The enemy is issuing pretty severe legislation for the towns and villages he has occupied. That is all to the good

---

* i.e. the replacement of Rundstedt by Kesselring. See above p. 128.

since people in the West were convinced that they would have an easier time with the Americans and British than with the Soviets. People are only allowed out for two hours a day; otherwise they are confined to their houses. We ought to have instituted such measures in the areas we occupied; then things would not have reached the grotesque pass which they did during our occupation of France, for instance.

The crossing of the Rhine at Remagen has led to a fall of thousands of millions of dollars on the New York stock exchange. The enemy stock exchange always reacts sourly to good war news, proof of the fact that the Jews pulling the strings are interested only in prolonging the war as far as possible.

The enemy press agencies, on the other hand, take quite a different view. They think that the war will be at an end in ten to twelve days' time and that a German capitulation is imminent. The enemy is in for a severe disappointment when we do something very different from capitulating.

American war reporters say that very severe fighting is raging in the Remagen bridgehead. The Americans are suffering very heavy losses, which after all is the object of the exercise. In particular they fear that we shall now proceed to take larger-scale measures and that the bridgehead is not tenable in the long run.

At midday I have a telephone call from Gauleiter Simon,* who tells me of his anxiety over this bridgehead. People cannot understand how it came about that the Remagen bridge was not blown at the proper time. The result has been a degree of antagonism between the population and the Wehrmacht. People accuse the Wehrmacht of failing to give them the necessary support at this moment. It is true that in the Eifel villages the farmers want to keep their villages undamaged as far as possible and show no great enthusiasm for war being waged on their own patch of soil.

* Gauleiter of the Moselle.

So-called stragglers are again causing the greatest anxiety in the West. Whenever the enemy breaks through our front they reappear. Marauding deserters get on the road, pretend to be stragglers from units, play on the sympathy of the population and just fish in troubled waters. Simon points out to me most seriously that people in the West are extraordinarily war-weary. This is of course unavoidable in view of the heavy air raids to which they have now been subjected for months and years. He is expecting me to address the West German population. He makes the somewhat naïve request that I should give some real promises for the conduct of the war in the immediate future. It would be very nice if Göring, for instance, who so frequently addressed the people in stentorian tones during the good old days, were now to say something on this subject, since it is he who is mainly to blame for the present war situation.

Balzer* has returned from his trip to the West. He too gives me a fairly depressing report and tells me of the serious antagonisms between the troops and the local population; he stresses, however, that the set-backs in the West have been due primarily to the fact that our lines were too thinly manned, that the troops had been ordered to defend every yard of ground whatever happened, and that once the enemy had broken through it was impossible to hold him. Model is very downcast over this set-back but otherwise is still the dynamic personality which we all know. He is afraid that, unless we succeed in eliminating the Remagen bridgehead, the Anglo-Americans will swing either towards Frankfurt or north towards the Ruhr. Model is therefore demanding a number of reinforcing divisions in order to hold at least the line of the Rhine with some degree of security.

The Anglo-Americans are not setting their sights so high. On the contrary they maintain that there must now be a pause in the fighting owing to their heavy losses. They are full of admiration for the Nazi spirit, still in evidence dur-

* OKW liaison officer with the Ministry of Propaganda.

ing the battles in the West. They are quite clear that the National-Socialist leadership of the Reich will fight on under all circumstances and there is no question whatsoever of capitulation in the true sense of the word.

The situation in France is still very unstable and it is caused primarily by the food problem. The French are cold and starving. The Anglo-Americans take not the smallest account of their allies' domestic situation to say nothing of the Italians. Disease is rampant in enemy-occupied Italy. There is an epidemic of syphilis among the people of Rome, giving rise to considerable anxiety even on the enemy side.

A further factor is the increasing criticism of the Yalta decisions. It has reached a noteworthy level both in London and in Washington. In Washington it is somewhat muted since the Americans are hoping that Stalin will enter the Pacific war. He must make up his mind by 13 April. On that day the Soviet–Japanese non-agression pact must either be revoked or automatically prolonged for five years.

I have sensational news from neutral sources about Chamberlain's timely death. After the Polish campaign Chamberlain had advocated an attempt at a compromise peace with Germany. The real enemy of Europe, he said, and therefore of Britain's position as a world power, was not the Reich but the Soviet Union. If the war were continued, it would certainly turn into a war of attrition. Germany might perhaps go down in this war of attrition but England certainly would. This forecast of Chamberlain's was dismissed by the Churchill clique at the time as the idle talk of a tired and senile man. It has turned out to be true to an astonishing degree. People on the British side even suspect that Churchill commissioned the Secret Service to administer poison to Chamberlain. I do not believe this but is a fact that Churchill was not particularly downcast at Chamberlain's death.

The Japanese are now making *tabula rasa* in French Indo-China. They are dismissing the French military commandants and taking control themselves.

We hear from American sources that Roosevelt intends

to include the Emperor of Japan on the list of war criminals. That is very good. The Emperor is revered as a god in Japan. If he is placed on the war criminals list, no Japanese politician, not even those most inclined to compromise, will dare stop fighting the USA.

Increasing interest in developments in Rumania is being shown in England. Radescu is still in the British Legation and the Soviets cannot get him out. British newspapers complain about the government's policy of silence. They are demanding a frank explanation of developments in Rumania which naturally the Churchill government cannot give.

To appease public opinion the Soviets are spreading the rumour that Mannerheim is back in office. Clearly he is intended to provide a cloak of legality for the electoral campaign now beginning. *Pravda*, however, proclaims most emphatically that the Finnish election is not a domestic Finnish affair. In other words the Soviets intend to interfere using every trick of the trade.

At midday I have a visit from the Berlin Kreisleiters;* I give them a one-and-a-half hour's survey of the present state of the war and the duties now incumbent on leaders in the Reich capital. In this circle one can speak freely and openly. I am happy doing this since I feel I am among people who think as I do.

The evacuation problem has again become extremely acute, mainly as a result of developments in Pomerania. Some 300–400,000 men have fallen into Soviet hands in Pomerania. Military events moved so fast that it was no longer possible to evacuate them from the threatened area in time. The refugee situation in the Danzig–West Prussia area is becoming very difficult. Forster is now encumbered with hundreds of thousands of people from East Prussia and he can no longer get them away.

Hamburg was heavily raided yesterday. The enemy is clearly trying to hit our U-boat yards since here lies a vital chance for us to change the fortunes of war. Recent

* "District leaders" subordinate to the Gauleiter.

Mosquito raids on Berlin have become heavier still. Serious damage is being done to our transport system. The British have now raided the capital every evening for 21 days in a row with these loathsome Mosquitos. There is in effect no defence against them.

The investigation of the Foreign Office by my Total War staff is encountering the greatest difficulties. The gentlemen of the Foreign Office treat this like a major diplomatic manoeuvre. Reading the reports, one can only chuckle. The Foreign Office is manned by a completely desiccated body of civil servants who understand only formalities and show no signs of healthy natural activity.

General Hauenschild will be on the sick list for about three weeks. That is a severe loss for us. He is being replaced by General Reymann whom I do not know. The offices of Fortress Commandant Berlin and Commanding General will henceforth be separated; Hauenschildt will remain Commanding General and Reymann will take over the duties of Fortress Commandant. I must take a closer look at him since I must have a first-class man for these duties which are of overriding importance. Unfortunately General Hoffmeister, the City Commandant, Berlin, is also seriously ill so that at the moment we are very short of high-level military commanders in Berlin. I must put things to rights quickly since a Soviet advance on Berlin may be anticipated any day despite all indications to the contrary.

During the afternoon I write a leading article on the theme "To work and to the guns!" In this article I give a series of stern inexorable slogans for the further prosecution of the struggle.

The evening situation report shows no great change in the West. The situation in the Remagen bridgehead has also remained the same. We are in process of bringing up strong reinforcements at this point. In the Emmerich area the enemy is using smoke and ranging his artillery. So the next offensive must be anticipated here.

As far as the East is concerned developments in Hungary are very satisfactory. We have crossed the River Sio and formed two bridgeheads on the far bank. That is pleasing news. An attempt is now to be made to get the enemy on the run at last. A break-through has also been made higher up, so that we can now probably move on in this area. Developments in the Schwarzwasser area are less satisfactory; there the enemy has penetrated to a depth of 7 km. It is to be hoped Schörner will deal with the situation, for the vital coal-mining and industrial area of Mährisch–Ostrau is at stake here. At Ratibor enemy attacks, though very heavy, were unsuccessful. The last groups of enemy have now been finally annihilated in Striegau. Our home and foreign correspondents can now therefore visit the town. In the Danzig area developments have been unfavourable. The enemy has now reached the sea at certain points. The general situation at the front remains fluid. In some places it is favourable for us, in others unbelievably bad. The vital point now is whether we can achieve a real break-through in Hungary. If that were so, our war prospects would improve considerably and we might possibly be on the threshold of a fresh start.

TUESDAY 13 MARCH 1945

(pp. 1–41)

Military Situation.

In Hungary our offensive south-east of Lake Balaton is making good progress. Two bridgeheads were formed across the River Sio. Equally, south-east of Lake Balaton ground was gained at Aba. East of Stuhlweissenburg our tank attack, led by "Tigers," penetrated some 8 km farther east.

In Slovakia there was violent fighting at Altsohl where the enemy penetrated at certain places. The enemy also made a break-in at the Jablonka Pass. He was then held, however, and in some places thrown back by counter-attacks. Heavy Soviet attacks on the area round Mährisch–Ostrau were again repulsed apart from one break-in to a depth of about 3 km. Striegau was recaptured in a spirited attack. Enemy attacks on Breslau and south of Cosel failed. No special developments on the Neisse front. On the Oder front violent enemy attacks took place between Frankfurt and Küstrin, particularly at Küstrin itself, but the enemy achieved nothing. In this sector 11,000 rounds have been fired from about 100 guns in a space of one and a half hours, showing that the ammunition situation has improved considerably meanwhile. Numerous enemy concentrations were broken up by artillery fire. Enemy attacks east of Stettin failed. Dievenow fell into enemy hands. Attacks on Kolberg were repulsed. In West Prussia the enemy attacked mainly south and north of Neustadt. He made some penetrations south of Neustadt but was driven back to his start lines by counter-attack. Farther north Putzig fell into enemy hands.

The approaches to the Putzig coastal belt, however, are still in our hands. Fighting in East Prussia slackened.

In Courland heavy enemy attacks were again repulsed south of Frauenburg.

On the Western Front there were violent artillery exchanges. Leverkusen in particular and areas to the rear of it were under enemy fire. South of Düsseldorf we pushed our outposts forward to Zons. Violent fighting took place in the Linz bridgehead. The enemy gained a little ground north of Honnef and east of Linz against stiff resistance and counter-attacks. He is now north of Honnef and some 4½ km east of Linz. Only local actions took place on the Moselle between Koblenz and Kochem and in the Trier break-in area. A number of tanks were driven off south of Saarburg. Enemy attempts to advance at Saarlautern and between Saarbrücken and Saargemünd were defeated. There was lively reconnaissance activity by both sides in the Hagenau area.

No special operations took place in Italy.

In the West enemy fighter-bombers and low-flying aircraft were very active. Many sorties were made by twin-engined bomber formations. Our own aircraft scored numerous hits on the railway and pontoon bridges at Remagen.

Some 1100 American four-engined bombers attacked port and transport installations in Swinemünde. Marburg/Lahn, Friedberg, Wetzlar and Frankfurt am Main were also raided. Targets in Dortmund and the Bochum–Gelsenkirchen area were attacked by 600 British four-engined bombers. Some 550 American four-engined bombers from Italy raided Vienna. Smaller formations dropped bombs on Graz and Bruck an der Mur. During the night there was again a harassing raid on Berlin. Bombs were dropped on Magdeburg by 10 Mosquitos.

On the western side the enemy is still not quite sure of himself. Particularly the British are afraid that we may be able to gain enough time to re-form our front beyond the Rhine and of this they are very apprehensive. The state of affairs in the West may be judged from the fact that the British are refusing Soviet reporters access to the front. This may, however, merely be tit for tat for the Soviet refusal to allow Anglo-American correspondents up to the Eastern Front, which has always been the case so far. The British and Americans have been very vexed by this in the past and are no doubt now seeking to take their revenge.

A lively exchange of congratulatory telegrams about the destruction of German cities in the West is in progress between Eisenhower and Harris.* For civilised people this exchange of telegrams is a disgraceful document. I believe that in 50 years' time European mankind will avert its eyes in disgust from this cynicism. These two super-gangsters act as if the destruction of a German cultural city was a deed of heroism. They brag about their barbarities and brutalities, showing thereby that at the height of their triumph they are neither worthy of nor do they deserve the victories they have won. Nevertheless people in Eisenhower's headquarters are clear that they still face a titanic struggle in the West. They declare that on both sides war is being waged without mercy and that there is no question whatsoever of the German Wehrmacht yielding. Above all people in Eisenhower's headquarters are deeply impressed by the fact that all German prisoners of war still have faith in victory and—as they explicitly state—believe in Hitler with well-nigh mystical fanaticism.

Fighting around the bridgehead has become extraordinarily bitter. It is costing us severe losses, but so it is to the enemy. How difficult the situation in the bridgehead is for the Americans is shown by the fact that they are now suddenly saying that it is of no very great significance. Clearly the enemy has been reaching for the sky. Nevertheless this is of course still the most sensitive point in the West.

American reports reveal a cheerless situation in Bonn at

* Air Marshal Sir Arthur Harris, C-in-C RAF Bomber Command.

present. The inhabitants are cold and hungry. Now that the Party and the authorities have gone they have no one to turn to. Some wretched American officer is trying to govern. One can imagine what things are like there.

Over and over again Anglo-American reports emphasise that the population in the West is still sunk in dull apathy. This is entirely understandable after the frightful air bombardments of recent weeks and months. Experience shows, however, that this will quickly disappear. In any case one may be sure that the Americans will have considerable trouble in administering this complex area. Things will not be as easy as they obviously think.

The Jews are re-emerging. Their spokesman is the well-known notorious Leopold Schwarzschild;* he is now arguing in the American press that under no circumstances should Germany be given lenient treatment. Anyone in a position to do so should kill these Jews off like rats. In Germany, thank God, we have already done a fairly complete job. I trust that the world will take its cue from this.

As far as the political situation is concerned opinion in England against Soviet high-handedness in the world is daily becoming more vocal. The *Manchester Guardian* has now joined the chorus of criticism; it is complaining primarily that the Soviets have cut Rumania off from the outside world so completely that no news of internal Rumanian developments can be obtained. These are the old Kremlin tactics; as soon as the Soviets have occupied a country, they let fall an iron curtain† so that they can carry on their fearful bloody work behind it.

The battle about a new so-called Polish government has now flared up in Moscow. The British and Americans are trying to persuade Molotov to accept at least Mikolajczyk on to the Lublin Committee. The Soviets will not allow themselves to be persuaded however. On the contrary they

* Former editor of *Das Tagebuch*, who had emigrated to America.
† It now seems that this phrase must be ascribed to Goebbels (see also below pp. 163, 196, 203). It was also used, at this time, by Schwerin von Krosigk. It was made famous by Churchill in his Fulton speech.

are determined to be the only ones to lay down the law in Poland and for this purpose are making use exclusively of the Lublin Committee which is dependent on them and subservient to them; as is well known it is mere bolshevist camouflage.

In Finland too the bolshevists are making every effort to influence the forthcoming elections. People in England are afraid that the result will be a so-called Baltic election, in other words that the bolshevists will terrorise the electorate as they did in the Baltic States, where in some places they received over 100% of the valid votes.

With the alleged capture of Küstrin Stalin has now issued his 300th victory Order of the Day. These 300 Orders of the Day are for us a unique calendar of misfortune. We ought to have pricked up our ears when the third was issued; but we allowed even the thirtieth to pass unnoticed and drew no conclusions from it; now comes the 300th, which, although not quite factually correct, looms over us like a dark fate. Stalin's Order of the Day, moreover, is not entirely incorrect in saying that with this 300th stage on the road to a bolshevist victory the German military machine has been largely smashed to atoms.

The Duce's socialisation of key industries in northern Italy has produced a certain favourable reaction among the Italian working class. It is not true that this socialisation was an improvised gimmick. On the contrary, from recent reports it is a well-thought-out measure and its psychological effect has been considerable.

At midday I have a prolonged discussion with the Berlin Defence Council. General Reymann, who will be dealing with Berlin's defence problems as long as General Hauenschildt is sick and will probably succeed General Hauenschildt in these duties, paid me his inaugural visit. He did not make any very great impression on me. He is the typical sort of bourgeois general who will do his duty faithfully and honestly but from whom no extraordinary output is to be expected. Examination of the overall state of Berlin's defences revealed a number of gaps. In particular we are very badly off for ammunition. I shall now devote special attention to this problem.

A check on Berlin railway stations revealed an enormous quantity of military equipment—including ammunition—stored away somewhere in sidings. As far as possible I intend to lay hands on these stores for the defence of Berlin.

The pioneers have prepared far more extensive demolition in Berlin than is necessary. The defence lay-out indicates that the pioneers are obviously working on the assumption that they are in enemy territory. In emergency, for instance, they intend to blow all bridges leading into Berlin. If this was in fact done the Reich capital would inevitably starve. I am putting things to rights here and ensuring that the pioneers do not look upon their job purely from the pioneer point of view.

For the moment we are not setting up summary courts martial in Berlin although we have become a front-line city. As long as the Peoples Court is still in Berlin, I think I can manage with that.

General von Knobelsdorf together with Regierungspräsident* Binding has investigated the Army Personnel Section and found arrangements there to be excellent. The Army Personnel Section is the first Wehrmacht organisation where everything is totally in order and of which no criticism can be made. Obviously therefore General Burgdorf† has done a good job here too.

Deputy Gauleiter von Körber‡ reports to me on his investigation of the Luftwaffe. Here the opposite is the case. The Luftwaffe is one great rubbish-heap of corruption and understandably Körber proposes either that it should simply be disbanded or reduced to the essential minimum size, since it is in no way capable of doing its job. When I call to mind that the amount of petrol available to the Luftwaffe

---

* Senior District Government official.
† Head of the Army Personnel Section and Hitler's military Adjutant.
‡ Acting Gauleiter of Mecklenburg.

has fallen from 193,000 tons to 8000, then I realise what can be expected of the Luftwaffe and what cannot. What use is all this mass output of new fighters when we have not even the petrol or the crews to put them into action?

Liese,* a member of my staff, has been busy investigating the Wehrmacht in the Netherlands. There too he found a disgraceful situation. There are in the Netherlands a whole series of headquarters which have simply been withdrawn from France and Belgium and are now leading a comfortable gormandising existence in Dutch villages. I shall put an end to them very quickly.

The air war is still frightful. This time it was the turn of Dortmund and even more of Swinemünde. In Swinemünde the enemy bombed our refugee camps. A number of ships were sunk in Swinemünde harbour including a refugee steamer with 2000 persons on board. There was a sort of mass catastrophe here. In addition late reports are coming from Essen, Dessau and Chemnitz. These places have been reduced to heaps of ruins.

The Führer has now decided that, notwithstanding the extraordinary difficulties, evacuation is to continue in the West. In practice this cannot be done since the people simply refuse to leave their towns and villages. We should have to use force and where can we find men to use force or men who will accept it? The decision taken by the Führer is based on false premises. This I can see from a situation report handed to me by Speer after a trip to the West. Speer studied conditions exhaustively and reached the conclusion that further evacuation is impracticable. Speer grumbles at the measures taken. His viewpoint is that it is no function of war policy to lead a people to a hero's doom and that, referring to the First World War, this was quite explicitly emphasised by the Führer himself in his book *Mein Kampf*. This comment applies above all to German diplomacy which has discovered no way, during the present war crisis, of relieving Germany of war on two fronts which is now gradually hammering us to pieces.

* Kurt Liese, general of infantry.

The evening report shows no major change in the situation in the West, which means that it continues to be unfavourable to us. We have not succeeded in eliminating the Remagen bridgehead. Instead the enemy has reinforced it. It now contains parts of five American divisions. The British, true to form, have withdrawn two divisions from Italy, one for Greece and one for the Middle East. These moves are of a typically anti-Soviet character. They show that antagonisms in the enemy camp have become very pronounced and give us cause for further hope. In Hungary our troops have made only small progress. I have the impression that our offensive has bogged down, the consequences of which would be fateful. Admittedly Sepp Dietrich has succeeded in forming a bridgehead across the Sio but it is questionable whether he can advance out of it. In the Führer's headquarters at least people are beginning to say that things must now really get going. So far one detects no trace of real impulsion about these operations. We must not lose hope however. The enemy launched an extraordinarily powerful attack at Schwarzwasser, but Schörner met it with a counter-attack so that the enemy made no significant gains of ground. In Breslau the situation is somewhat calmer, but we must reckon with further heavy attacks soon. Enemy probes in the Frankfurt–Küstrin area were unsuccessful. In the Stettin sector also no change. It seems, therefore that Soviet forces are fairly well committed and that they cannot carry out any wide-ranging operations at the moment. The situation at Danzig has taken a turn for the worse. Further enemy penetrations are reported and the city is now under artillery fire. In East Prussia a new major offensive has opened and penetrated to a depth of 4 km. It is hoped to deal with it however. In Courland all enemy attacks were repulsed.

In general terms the military situation is still in the balance. No firm estimate of future developments can be made.

In the evening we have the regulation Mosquito raid on Berlin. These Mosquito raids are becoming heavier and more distressing day by day. Above all they are doing great damage to the Berlin transport system.

This evening's Mosquito raid was particularly disastrous for me because our Ministry was hit. The whole lovely building on the Wilhelmstrasse was totally destroyed by a bomb. The throne-room, the Blue Gallery and my newly rebuilt theatre hall are nothing but a heap of ruins. I drove straight to the Ministry to see the devastation for myself. One's heart aches to see so unique a product of the architect's art, such as this building was, totally flattened in a second. What trouble we have taken to reconstruct the theatre hall, the throne-room and the Blue Gallery in the old style! With what care have we chosen every fresco on the walls and every piece of furniture! And now it has all been given over to destruction. In addition fire has now broken out in the ruins, bringing with it an even greater risk since 500 bazooka missiles are stored underneath the burning wreckage. I do my utmost to get the fire brigade to the scene as quickly and in as great strength as possible, so at least to prevent the bazooka missiles exploding.

As I do all this I am overcome with sadness. It is 12 years to the day—13 March—since I entered this Ministry as Minister. It is the worst conceivable omen for the next twelve years.

All my staff are on the spot—Schach, Steeg and Görum —and all of them make the greatest efforts to save whatever can be saved. But from the finest part of the building there is nothing to be saved. But what good is all this lamentation and melancholy. We must turn our back on these things and concentrate on maintaining at least the freedom and territory of our people. That does not prevent one being depressed, however, at so severe a loss, particularly when it affects one personally.

The Führer telephones me immediately after the raid on the Ministry. He too is very sad that it has now hit me. So far we have been lucky even during the heaviest raids on Berlin. Now, however, we have lost not only a possession but an anxiety. In future I need no longer tremble for the Ministry.

All those present at the fire voiced only scorn and hatred for Göring. All were asking repeatedly why the Führer does not at last do something definite about him and the Luftwaffe.

The Führer then asks me over for a short visit. During the interview I have with him he is very impressed by my account of things. I give him a description of the devastation which is being wrought and tell him particularly of the increasing fury of the Mosquito raids which take place every evening. I cannot prevent myself voicing sharp criticism of Göring and the Luftwaffe. But it is always the same story when one talks to the Führer on this subject. He explains the reasons for the decay of the Luftwaffe, but he cannot make up his mind to draw the consequences therefrom. He tells me that after the recent interviews he had with him Göring was a broken man. But what is the good of that! I can have no sympathy with him. If he did lose his nerve somewhat after his recent clash with the Führer, that is but a small punishment for the frightful misery he has brought and is still bringing on the German people.

I beg the Führer yet again to take action at last, since things cannot go on like this. We ought not, after all, to send our people to their doom because we do not possess the strength of decision to root out the cause of our misfortune. The Führer tells me that new fighters and bombers are now under construction, of which he has certain hopes. But we have heard it so often before that we can no longer bring ourselves to place much hope in such statements. In any case it is now plenty late—not to say too late—to anticipate any decisive effect from such measures.

The Führer adds that before the war he had repeatedly demanded the construction of high-speed bombers, primarily of the Mosquito type; he had expected them to be very successful in the bombing of enemy cities. But, like much else, this had not been done and it is no good the Führer saying today that he had wanted the right thing but had not insisted on it. In this too Göring always knew better —just like Himmler during present operations in the East, the Führer adds. Himmler had always reckoned that the enemy would advance on Berlin, whereas according to the Führer's forecast he was more likely to go for Pomerania, as in fact happened. The Führer shows me the shorthand record of the military briefing conferences which took place at that time, from which it was plain that the Führer was absolutely right in his forecast. Here again, however, I can only answer: what good are explanations; the people demand that matters be settled. They are clamouring for measures of a decisive nature to put an end to the jungle of overall military leadership.

The Führer tells me that the itinerant courts martial under General Hübner* have now started work. Their first case was the commanding general responsible for the failure to blow the Honnef bridge; he was condemned to death and shot within two hours. This at least is light on the horizon. Only by such methods can we save the Reich. Colonel-General Fromm too has been shot meanwhile. I request the Führer urgently to continue with measures of this sort so that one day our high-ranking officers will at last be compelled to obey orders. Another general, who refused to permit a National-Socialist Leadership officer to do his job, will now be brought to trial and probably condemned to death.

Before the recent Anglo-American offensive we had a total of 1.5 million men in the West. In fighting troops Rundstedt did not contrive to extract more than 60 full-strength divisions from this number of men. The total war principle has therefore only been followed very superficially in this region, a real scandal when one looks at the results.

Dr. Ley has been in the West and allowed Manteuffel† to pull the wool over his eyes. Manteuffel asked him to make representations to the Führer that commanding generals in the West be given greater plenary powers. But they do not lack plenary powers. All they have to do is to use them. The Führer has never reproached a general for

---

* See above p. 127.
† As C-in-C 5th Panzer Army, Manteuffel had taken part in the Ardennes offensive. He was now moved to the Eastern Front.

failure to make use of his powers to re-establish order and discipline; he has only criticised when generals have failed to use their powers for these purposes. The trouble, therefore, is not that military commanders have not been endowed with sufficient powers of command. On the contrary they go their own way; when it does not suit them they refuse to obey the Führer, either openly or by tacit sabotage, and must now be brutally called to order. The arrogance of the Wehrmacht, which so far has always tended to hold aloof from the Party and the leadership of the State, must now be done away with in every respect. The Führer must insist on stern conduct of the war in all fields if the people is to be saved. He is quite right when he says that this way we shall emerge from this war without a National-Socialist Wehrmacht. But that is not the main problem; in the forefront is the question how and whether we are to emerge from this war at all.

The Führer wishes to make a renewed attempt to stabilise the fronts. He hopes for some success in the U-boat war, particularly if our new U-boats now come into action which for the moment they have not yet done. What a difference between Dönitz and Göring! Both have suffered a severe technical set-back in their arm of the service. Göring resigned himself to it and so has gone to the dogs. Dönitz has overcome it. This shows that set-backs need not be catastrophic if the right conclusions are drawn from them. These conclusions are what matter.

In our Wehrmacht the Army and even more the Luftwaffe are extraordinarily vulnerable. There are few army organisations up to the requirements of modern war. I tell the Führer about the investigation of the Personnel Section.* He is very pleased that General Burgdorf's shop is in order. On the other hand all I can tell about the results of investigation into the Luftwaffe is deprecatory. The Luftwaffe is one great scandal for the Party and the country as a whole.

Once more this conversation ends with me asking the

* See above p. 151.

Führer to act and to do something decisive to put matters in order again. But for the moment there is nothing to be done with him in this respect.

We reminisce together for a long time. The sight of the Führer is increasingly moving. It is touching to see the innate resilience with which, despite his severe physical disabilities he takes a grip of things over and over again and attempts to master the situation.

Outside meanwhile the fire has been extinguished but the beautiful building is totally destroyed. We now make a start with clearing up. Our first thought is to clear the street and then make some arrangement enabling me to work in the Ministry over the next few days, since after all daily work must not suffer because the building is in ruins.

Back at home I pass a somewhat melancholy evening. Slowly one is beginning to realise what this war means for us all. Who would have thought twelve years ago that my twelfth anniversary would be spent in such surroundings and under such circumstances. The whole family shares my melancholy and mourning. We had all taken the Ministry so much to our hearts. Now it belongs to the past. I am firmly determined, however, that when this war is over, not only shall I construct a new monumental ministry—as the Führer says—but restore this old Ministry in all its old glory.

WEDNESDAY 14 MARCH 1945

(pp. 1–38)
Military Situation.
The situation on the Eastern Front underwent no major
change yesterday. The main centres of fighting were in the
Danzig and East Prussian areas.

The bolshevists are now doing their utmost to clear the
Danzig and East Prussian areas. In the course of their
major offensive in East Prussia they were able to make deep
penetrations at Lichtenfeld and north-west of Zinten. The
front maintained its cohesion however. The violence of
the fighting is shown by the fact that in this sector alone
104 Soviet tanks were destroyed yesterday. Contact with
Königsberg has again been temporarily lost. Attacks made
on Danzig and Gotenhafen with armoured support were
repulsed. The Danzig–Gotenhafen bridgehead and the East
Prussian theatre, with which it is closely connected, have
now been combined into an Army Group under command
of Colonel-General Weiss.

In Courland enemy attacks were less violent; in fact all
along the Eastern Front, with the exception of the Danzig–
East Prussia area, Soviet attacks were less sustained than
usual. Only at Kolberg did the enemy attack fairly strongly
yesterday. On the other hand his attacks on the Oder front
between Frankfurt and Küstrin and his probings of our
Stettin bridgehead were in reduced strength. In the battle
round Mährisch–Ostrau Soviet attacks between Bielitz and
Schwarzwasser were repulsed and the previous day's gains
of ground by the enemy were made good. No operations
of special importance took place in Silesia. In Hungary

numerous attacks on our new positions were driven off. In Slovakia the enemy managed to move forward a little closer to Altsohl.

On the Western Front only local actions took place, the main centre of activity being in the Ruwer valley south of Trier. In this area the Americans made some penetrations to a depth of 1–2 km in battalion- and regimental-strength attacks against the upper reaches of the Ruwer.

On the Rhine front the only operations of importance were in the Linz–Honnef bridgehead. In violent attacks the Americans penetrated somewhat farther north-east and east. Their attempts to expand the bridgehead northwards and southwards were defeated. The maximum depth of the bridgehead is now about 8 km.

On the Moselle front the enemy drove our outposts back onto the right bank of the river at several points between Kochem and Bernkastel. The bridge at Traben-Trarbach has been blown.

Fierce street fighting is taking place in Hagenau.

No fighting of importance on the Italian front.

On the Eastern Front there was sustained German air activity in Hungary, where 11 Soviet aircraft were shot down. The main centre of our air activity in the West was the Linz area, where enemy bridges, troop concentrations and movements were bombed.

Throughout the day there was lively enemy fighter-bomber and fighter activity over the Western Front concentrated on Münsterland, the Ruhr and Rhine–Main areas. In addition 300 twin-engined enemy aircraft were in action in the West.

American bomber formations were not in action over Reich territory yesterday. Some 400 British four-engined bombers attacked Wuppertal. About 500 American four-engined bombers from Italy with an escort of 250 fighters made their main attack on Regensburg. A smaller detachment dropped bombs in the Klagenfurt and Landshut areas. Over southern and south-eastern Germany there was much enemy fighter activity throughout the day. During the night some 200 British four-engined bombers raided transport targets in the Recklinghausen, Gelsenkirchen and Dortmund areas. A harassing raid was made on Berlin by 80 Mosquitos. Two Mosquitos were shot down by anti-aircraft.

Both confidential and official reports of planned enemy operations in the West in the immediate future are very contradictory. Some say that Allied troops must now halt and draw breath, others that every effort will be made to force a crossing of the Rhine as soon as possible. In general it is hoped that the latter will lead to a sensational victory since it is maintained that we have no more reserves available. The idea, therefore, is to strike while the iron is hot.

The capture of the Rhine bridge at Remagen by the Americans is said to be due to sabotage and treachery. I also think that these motives played a significant role in all this, since it is barely comprehensible how so important a bridge could fall intact into enemy hands when it had been fully prepared for demolition.

Grigg, the British War Minister, has been making extraordinarily positive statements about England's immediate war prospects. He is good enough to announce that there will be mass starvation in the Reich. The only point of interest in his disquisition is that Britain is still determined to participate in the Pacific war, provided of course (in brackets) that Roosevelt will put up with them. In any case the British now have to introduce further large-scale measures of conscription, which in the present critical state of British war-weariness will certainly not be greeted with enthusiasm. It is stated that British recruits will be trained on German soil for the next 25 years. The British invariably draw-up large-scale plans for the next quarter- or half-century. They have no sort of credibility, however, for the British will probably have very little say in whatever may be happening in Europe in 25 or 50 years' time.

The British Empire admits to losing 1,043,000 men so far. This looks a very high figure at first sight but it must be remembered that it includes wounded and prisoners. Anyway Britain has always been good at allowing her allies and satellite peoples to shed their blood for her.

As far as developments in the West are concerned London is again issuing warnings against exaggerated optimism. People no longer think that the war will be over today or tomorrow. The Americans have calculated that, taking East and West together, one-fifth of the area of the 1939 Reich is now occupied. In itself that would not be so bad, but the regions concerned are so vital for food and armaments production that our percentage loss in potential is far higher.

In England the bishops are coming out increasingly strongly against bolshevist high-handedness in Europe and also against the Yalta decisions. Certain of our informers, who have so far been accurate in their reporting, tell us that Churchill has lost a great deal of popularity in recent weeks primarily because he has proved incapable of directing the war into orderly channels and his policy has resulted in producing total chaos in Europe. For the present this chaos is almost more rampant in the countries occupied by England or allied to her than on the territory of the German Reich. Definite starvation is raging in France. The British quite calmly tell the French that the food shortage will last until about July, in other words until some of the new harvest is available. No food for the French is available from British stocks, it is said, and the Americans too are keeping their pockets shut.

There has been a certain revival of collaboration in France. Large numbers of Frenchmen are now listening to our radio broadcasts, just as they listened to the British broadcasts when we were in occupation. To some extent the tables have been turned therefore. Though one cannot expect much actual military advantage from this, this change of attitude among Western European peoples is highly symptomatic of developments we may anticipate in future.

An almost grotesque impression is created by the news that the Jews of Palestine have called a one-day strike to be spent in prayer and that this strike is an expression of sympathy for the Jews of Europe. The Jews are playing a wicked and thoughtless game. No one can say with certainty which nations will be on the losing side and which on the winning at the end of the war; but there can be no doubt that the Jews will be the losers.

The question whether the Soviet Union will participate in the Pacific war is still much debated. Stalin is said to be increasingly taking the view that the Soviet Union cannot remain uninvolved since she naturally has important interests to defend in East Asia as well. On the other hand it is said that the Americans no longer set much store by Soviet participation in the Pacific war.

Somewhat depressing news comes from Hungary. Our offensive there seems not to be going to work. Our divisions have been halted in front of Soviet defensive positions and are now facing serious counter-attacks. One would think one was dealing with the devil. None of our military operations, however well prepared, have been successful recently. Stalin's marshals have done an outstanding military job and he has good reason to fête them like film stars. Reports from Moscow tell of scenes reminiscent of the days of the Pashas. Göring will undoubtedly be sorry that he cannot arrange for similar celebrations in Germany.

Storm signals are visible over Finland. Having let down their iron curtain the Soviets are now at work bringing the country ruthlessly under their thumb. The Swedish stock exchange has tumbled as a result. The Jews on the Swedish stock exchange are largely to blame for this. Now that the worst is visible they are trying to present themselves as innocent lambs.

In Rumania a definite struggle for power is going on between the West and the Soviet Union. Western countries are trying to regain contact with Rumania by diplomatic means and the Soviets are moving heaven and earth to stop them. The Soviets cannot take too stern measures, however, because they have not enough troops to impose their political will. Everything indicates that, in contrast to us, the Soviets have all their military force in the shop window.

We needed 240,000 men to occupy Rumania whereas the Soviets, it is reliably reported, are making do with four NKVD divisions. Moreover this is quite enough. In occupied countries we Germans always made the mistake of trying to do everything ourselves. On the one hand we used up too many troops for this purpose and on the other we turned opinion in occupied countries against us.

Groza, the new Rumanian Minister-President, is an out-and-out peasant communist. He is merely a willing tool of the Kremlin.

In northern Italy too opinion has now turned very much against us. The Italians are doing another about-turn and starting to flirt with France. Sympathy for the Latin sister has reawakened in Italy. Even some of the fascists are making this about-turn. Mussolini has not yet succeeded in finding a common denominator in fascist policy.

Since it is impossible to work in the Ministry I have to hold all my conferences at home. The Ministry looks like a desert. In the Private Office most of the telephone wires have been cut. The Private Office itself is a heap of ruins. Even doing my utmost to re-establish working facilities in the Ministry as quickly as possible, it will take a few days.

Gauleiter Simon has sent Naumann, his deputy, to Berlin to report to me on the situation in the Moselland Gau. He gives me some information of interest but in general can tell me nothing new. The fact that morale among the troops and the people has sunk very low I know anyway. Naumann, however, protests energetically that no cases have occurred of people trying to stop the troops fighting. The hoisting of white flags was due to people's desire to preserve their own houses undamaged during the fighting. No active opposition to our conduct of the war has been reported. On the other hand it must be realised that the population in the regions now occupied or threatened by the enemy is sunk in lethargy and looks upon the events of the war with apathy. This is primarily due to the months of uninterrupted enemy air bombing.

Dr. Ley also, who has just returned from his trip to the West, can tell me nothing really new. Everything he reports

I have known for a long time. He hands me three memoranda, which he has submitted to the Führer, concerning reorganisation of the Wehrmacht. They do not hold water. As the Führer has already told me, Dr. Ley is proposing that Commanders-in-Chief of Armies and Army Groups should be given greater powers to comb rear Army areas.* They already possess such powers if they wanted to use them. Schörner, for instance, has already combed his rear Army area whereas Manteuffel has not. The trouble is not with the powers but with the gentlemen who do not use the powers available to them.

Ley's estimate of Model is somewhat derogatory. He has become jumpy and nervous, Ley says, and the Gauleiters in the West do not go much by him.

The report Ley gives me about the loss of Köln is shattering. The City Commandant was changed three times in a single night. As one can imagine, with such violent fluctuations in personnel policy, defence of a city of this size was a total impossibility. The people of Köln had fought well, or rather wanted to fight, but had little opportunity of doing so.

After Ley, Speer arrives for an interview. He too has just returned from the West and gives an even gloomier report. Speer's view is that economically the war is more or less lost. At the present rate the German economy can hold out for another four weeks and then it will gradually disintegrate. Speer deplores the fact that he can get no decisions on vital problems from the Führer. He thinks that, owing to his physical disabilities, the Führer has become far less active. Speer is right in his views about maintenance of the German people's basis of existence. He is very much opposed to the scorched-earth idea. He says that if the lifelines of our food supply and our economy are to be snapped it is not for us but for our enemies to do it. He is also opposed, therefore, to the demolition of bridges and viaducts prepared in Berlin. If these are carried out, he says, the Reich capital must quickly starve. I have already

* See above p. 156.

protested energetically against these planned demolitions and have ordered my military staff in Berlin to give me a report on the matter so that I can possibly take steps to remedy the situation.

The reports both of Dr. Ley and of Speer are extremely alarming. I assume, however, that they are much influenced by what they have seen in the West and cannot look at these matters from the necessary distance, otherwise their accounts would probably be different from what they actually are. At times like this it is essential to take an adequately long-distance view of things. Looked at close to, the impression they give is naturally terrible sometimes. War, of course, has its heights and its depths and, when one is in the depths, it is essential to keep a cool head and not to lose one's nerve. This I learn yet again from a study of the Punic War by Professor Frank. This study shows me what must be done in a critical phase of a war and how one must sometimes accept defeat after defeat in order to emerge victorious in the end. People do not talk of the Roman virtues for nothing. They emerged most clearly during the Second Punic War and are still an example to us today. As the Führer has so often emphasised, it must be our ambition that our era goes down in the history of mankind as a period of glory and steadfastness equal to, for instance, the Second Punic War or the Seven Years War. In any case I refuse to be deterred by reports of so-called eyewitnesses. There is no question of any doubt in my mind regarding the possibility of victory for our cause; on the contrary the difficulties which emerge again and again, almost daily and in increasing weight, are there to be overcome if one really has the will to do so. Moreover Dr. Ley looks at things more through the spectacles of the pure Party orator and Speer through those of the pure economist and technician. Neither possesses a statesmanlike view of the present war situation.

The Führer has decided that further evacuation is to take place in the West; this decision will of course have enormous repercussions since we have no idea where in the

Reich we can accommodate people evacuated from the West. In the Führer's view, however, the main thing is not to let men fit for service fall into enemy hands. What the political implications of this are cannot be foreseen at present. In Pomerania, for instance, 400,000 men who should have been evacuated fell into Soviet hands. There is a pretty miserable situation here which we cannot remedy. In Swinemünde in particular masses of men are assembling and we can only feed and clothe them for onward movement to a limited degree. In short we have by no means got the better of the evacuation problem and today it becomes even more acute. Things are somewhat better in East Prussia; overcrowding in the Danzig–Gotenhafen area is becoming that much worse however.

It is interesting, moreover, that although our propaganda has been passing the word round for weeks, departures from Berlin are few. Only some 2500–3000 people leave the capital daily. That is a mere drop in the ocean. The Berliners apparently have such confidence in our military capacity to resist that for the moment, despite the continual enemy air raids, they feel happiest and safest in their own city.

As far as the air war is concerned, so-called suicide attacks are now to be made on enemy bomber formations. The Führer has agreed that some 300 suicide pilots, 95% of whom will certainly sacrifice themselves, should hurl themselves at the enemy bomber formations, so that whatever happens each fighter will bring down one enemy bomber. This plan was proposed months ago but unfortunately did not get past Göring. There is no point even in talking about the organisation and armament of the Luftwaffe; the corruption and disorganisation in this arm of the service cries to high heaven.

A vast number of worrying problems now come before me in reports and memoranda or are laid on my table. Sometimes one wonders where on earth a way out of this terrible war dilemma is to be found. In this critical time it is easy to judge a man's worth. There are only a few who remain steadfast and cling without flinching to our lofty purpose. They are the nation's true leading personalities. This is what separates the wheat from the chaff.

This evening it is reported that the situation in the Remagen bridgehead has worsened from our point of view. The enemy has succeeded in extending the bridgehead, though only to a small degree. Nevertheless there is no longer any word of the necessity or possibility of eliminating the bridgehead. Otherwise there has been no great change in the West. Nevertheless the present period of quiescence there is the calm before the storm.

Kesselring has taken up his command. I place some hope in him. He is expert in the defence of apparently almost hopeless positions.

The Führer has sent me the shorthand records of his briefing conferences during the critical days preceding the Soviet break-through in Pomerania. These records spell out a real tragedy. Again and again during these briefing conferences the Führer pointed out that the Soviets would advance on Pomerania and opposed the opinion of the experts that they would move on Berlin. Unfortunately he failed to follow up his conviction, which was based more on intuition than on knowledge, with clear orders. As a result everyone, including Himmler, did what he wished. These minutes are a shining example of the inefficiency of our military leadership. The Führer perceives the right thing to do and imparts it to his military staff but they draw no conclusions therefrom. What good are these ideas, however, if they are not translated into reality. Ideas become overlaid by the wisdom of the experts and have no practical effect. Instead of making long speeches to his military staff the Führer would do better to issue them with brief orders and then act brutally and energetically to ensure that these orders are carried out. Erroneous methods of command and not erroneous ideas are therefore the main cause of the numerous defeats we have suffered on the various fronts. Our General Staff officers thought that the Soviets would make the same mistake as we made in late autumn 1941 with our planned encirclement of

Moscow, in other words that they would barge on at the enemy capital without looking to right or left and without covering their flanks. That was the costly trap into which we fell. Again and again the Führer emphasised that the Soviets would not make this mistake but his generals would not believe him. Himmler allowed these generals to pull the wool over his eyes and the Führer is not far wrong when he says that Himmler must carry the guilt before history for the fact that Pomerania and much of its population has fallen into Soviet hands.

There is already talk of heavy enemy counter-attacks against our offensive in Hungary. Anyway at the moment no further forward movement is reported. Both sides are regrouping. But one knows what that means. News from the Schwarzwasser, area on the other hand, is satisfactory. Schörner has again succeeded in beating off extraordinarily strong Soviet attacks and in gaining some ground by counter-attack. In Breslau there is relative calm for the first time for weeks—very important for the fighting troops since now at last they can get a little sleep. In the Gotenhafen–East Prussian area the enemy attacked in extraordinary strength but in general he was repulsed.

In the evening we have yet another Mosquito raid on the capital and shall soon be celebrating the Silver Jubilee of these attacks. These Mosquito raids have now become so heavy that they are almost comparable to one by a small force of heavy bombers. In any case they give us a very great deal to do, particularly in the field of transport. We have our hands full to keep the Berlin transport system running even at half speed.

THURSDAY 15 MARCH 1945

(pp. 1–32)
Military Situation.

The main centres of fighting were again in West and East Prussia where the Soviets continued to attack Gotenhafen and Danzig in strength. They reached the Gotenhafen–Zuckau railway line west of Zoppot; farther north the enemy also scored a minor local success, further reducing our position north of Putzig. All other attacks were beaten off. The enemy made particularly sustained efforts to sever our defence line in East Prussia. North-west of Zinten he was able to advance about 3 km and reach the Königsberg–Elbing autobahn. Our front still maintained its cohesion. In all 88 Soviet tanks were destroyed yesterday. In Courland enemy attacks in medium strength south of Frauenburg were repulsed.

On the rest of the Eastern Front strong enemy attacks on the Mährisch–Ostrau area are reported to have been repulsed once more. Otherwise only local actions took place, in the course of which we improved our positions at Striegau and south of Stettin. The Frankfurt–Küstrin area was relatively quiet owing to the enemy's severe losses from our artillery fire.

In Hungary we widened our offensive front advancing between Kaposvar and the western end of Lake Balaton; here we gained 3–4 km on a front of 20–30 km in heavily mined country; we formed a bridgehead over the Sio and destroyed the last enemy bridgehead over that river.

In Slovakia the enemy succeeded in capturing Altsohl.

On the Western Front the Americans continued their heavy attacks in defence of their Linz bridgehead but without success; only at Hönningen were they able to gain a few kilometres of ground; otherwise the situation remained unchanged. The bridgehead is now 15–18 km long and up to 7 km deep.

The main centre of enemy activity was in the Moselle valley. Here the Americans attacked between Alken and Treis towards Boppard. They succeeded in crossing the Moselle at several points and advancing to within 6 km of Boppard. There was also violent fighting between Kochem and Bernkastel. Our forces on the left bank of the Moselle were driven back to the river at several points. The enemy also attacked very heavily in the Ruwer valley where he gained 2–3 km of ground. Our bridgehead on the left bank of the Saar between Saarbrücken and Völklingen was withdrawn. The enemy followed up hard. Enemy pressure also increased north of Saargemünd. Fierce street fighting is taking place in Hagenau.

Only local actions are reported from the Italian front.

On the Eastern Front our air forces were again particularly active over Hungary. A total of 37 enemy aircraft were shot down by fighters and anti-aircraft, including four bombers from Italy.

On the Western Front enemy fighter-bombers were again very active. Some of our fighter formations were in action against low-flying aircraft in the Remagen area.

Some 1100 American four-engined bombers attacked transport targets in the Hannover–Münster–Kassel area and also built-up areas in Hannover, Hildesheim, Osnabrück and Hamelin. Smaller formations raided Rotterdam. Some 150 British four-engined bombers attacked various places in the Ruhr. 300 twin-engined bombers attacked transport targets in the Limburg–Giessen–Siegen area. About 500 American four-engined bombers attacked the Wiener Neustadt–Graz–Klagenfurt area. Harassing raids at night on Berlin and Wiesbaden. A British bomber formation of about 350 four-engined aircraft raided Homburg and

Zweibrücken in der Saarpfalz. Some 200 British bombers raided Leuna and Lützkendorf. Night fighters and AA shot down 19 enemy aircraft.

The Remagen bridgehead is still there and the enemy has even extended it. Our troops are putting up stiff resistance, however, as is reported even from London. The enemy is concentrating very heavily in this area and is clearly planning an attempted break-out. This may well take a few days however. In any case the Americans are proceeding very systematically and are not allowing themselves to be carried away by their impetuosity. As far as the bridgehead itself is concerned, we know all about such developments. We have been through this often enough in the East to have no illusions about it. If a bridgehead is once established and one is not strong enough to eliminate it, it turns into a running sore and the poison spreads to vital parts of the body. Nevertheless the Americans have suffered very severe losses in this bridgehead which will perhaps have a sobering effect on them. Severe manpower shortages are reported on the Western Front as a whole and also in the Pacific theatre so that they have had to institute fresh large-scale measures of conscription.

Churchill is again facing a series of embarrassing questions in the Commons. There were again a number of revoltingly hypocritical expressions of the sympathy allegedly felt for the Dutch population, though Britain is in no position to offer them even the smallest assistance.

The situation in the enemy-occupied regions is becoming increasingly menacing. Here is a great opportunity for us. Most important, the British and Americans are unable to provide any food supplies for the regions they occupy and so there is a large measure of actual starvation impossible to describe in detail. The Americans are no longer in a position to divert supplies even to the British since they need them themselves and are running into serious difficulties even in their own country. It is announced from the White House that food convoys to Britain must be discontinued for the next three months. As a result the British government is compelled further to reduce the ration, the effect of which in London is of course sensational. It is clear that, whereas the military crisis is developing greatly to our disfavour, the political crisis is largely turning out to the disfavour of our enemies. For this reason the British and Americans are doing their utmost to bring the European war to a favourable conclusion from their point of view at the earliest possible moment. They know that otherwise this part of the world will simply be facing starvation and this they admit quite openly.

Part of the political activity directed against us by our Western enemies consists in the spreading of rumours, which recur almost daily, concerning the alleged intention of the Reich to capitulate. It is now being stated that last week Rundstedt offered to lay down arms in the Netherlands which of course met with a generous refusal from the British and Americans. As a result of these rumours the USA is now in a delirium of victory and so the old domestic antagonisms are re-emerging in all their malignancy. The trade unions are presenting the government with their bill. Wage rises are being demanded under threat of a general strike. In short the British and American governments have quickly been given notice that their premature trumpetings of victory have fallen on very fruitful domestic political ground and as a result the domestic opposition cliques are beginning to stir. A general strike is now hanging over the heads of the Anglo-American public like a sword of Damocles. Things are not much better in England and one can understand why the *Daily Mail* states in a melancholy article that the war must be ended this summer or all Europe will sink into chaos. We must take every step, therefore to prolong this war, cost what it may, and we are going the best way about it.

The British Conservative Party is meeting for its Party Conference in London. Nothing special is to be expected from this gathering. Churchill is still absolutely the man of the moment.

Eden is facing embarrassing questions in the Commons about the internal position in Rumania. He has had to admit that the Soviets are stopping all news coming out of Rumania and that Radescu has sought and been given asylum in the British Legation—from fear, allegedly, of his domestic political opponents. Eden ascribes the severance of communications with Rumania to military reasons, which of course was greeted as a joke. Nevertheless developments in Rumania have caused great embarrassment both to the Americans and the British. The course of events is precisely similar to that in Poland or that now gradually getting under way in Finland. In any case the Anglo-Americans are quite clear that it is no good monkeying with the Kremlin and that Stalin is exploiting his momentary advantage. It is really comic to see the British newspapers expressing their disappointment but invariably adding that there is nothing whatsoever to be done against the Kremlin's insolence and presumption.

For the first time the "Free Germany" Committee* has appeared on the scene once more, this time with a call to the people of Berlin. It is having no effect whatsoever since the people are taking not the smallest notice of it. It shows, however, that the Committee's duties are exclusively of a propaganda nature and it is significant that German generals with famous names should make themselves available for this.

A General Staff publication containing *curricula vitae* and photographs of Soviet generals and marshals is submitted to me. From this book it is easy to deduce various matters on which we have been mistaken in previous years. On average these Marshals and Generals are extraordinarily young, hardly any of them over the age of 50. Their background is one of productive political revolutionary activity; they are convinced bolshevists and extraordinarily energetic men; one can see from their faces that they are carved from good popular timber. They are mostly sons of workers, cobblers, small-holders, etc. In short one is forced to the

* i.e. the Seydlitz Committee.

painful conclusion that the Soviet military leaders come of a better background than do our own.

The armistice terms for Italy have been leaked. They prescribe that Italy must bear the whole cost of enemy occupation, must make four million workers available for compulsory deportation to enemy countries, in other words to the Soviet Union. She must renounce all her African possessions and accept considerable cessions of territory at home. In short this is an interim bill which implies the liquidation of Italy as a great power. It must be remembered, moreover, that this is only an armistice agreement. For the moment there is no word of what will be extorted from Italy in a peace treaty.

There have been further heavy air raids, this time on Münster, Hamm and Wuppertal. Every day one wonders fruitlessly where all this will lead. Our armaments potential and transport system are being battered to such an extent that it is easy to calculate when the time will arrive when we shall, so to speak, be standing in a void. It is crippling that—as Gauleiter Hoffmann* points out in a report—we no longer possess any air defence whatsoever. Our fighters do not take off and our anti-aircraft has been largely withdrawn for the front. Not only our military reverses but also the severe drop in the German people's morale, neither of which can now be overlooked, are primarily due to the unrestricted enemy air superiority. Hoffmann thinks that it should be possible to cope with the transport damage in the comparatively short term but that the damage to morale will be very difficult to repair. Above all the morale of the troops has been severely affected. This is evidenced not by any revolutionary symptoms but by the general attitude of lethargy now prevalent among both officers and men. To a certain extent the same must be said of the civil population.

The long-range repercussions of air-raid alerts are noticeable in Berlin. At midday we sat in our air-raid shelters for two hours because Oranienburg and Zossen were being

* Gauleiter of Westphalia South.

bombed. Contrary to what we feared, not much happened over Berlin.

I am getting reports of sinking morale from the Moselle country as well. These also point out that there is no question of active opposition but they say that the people must be given some positive arguments about our prospects of victory if they are to believe in victory at all.

Simon* requests me in a letter to carry on systematic propaganda to the troops. Unfortunately propaganda to the troops has so far been the business of the Press Section [WPR] in OKW; naturally, however, I cannot wait for the corpulent generals and colonels of WPR to bestir themselves. Moreover they understand nothing of this business. I am accordingly appointing General Commissioners for the Eastern and Western Fronts; they will be directly subordinate to me and will go forthwith to the areas concerned with authority to give instructions to Propaganda Companies and Reich Propaganda Offices for propaganda within the Wehrmacht. I hope that this will relieve the situation considerably. In any case I intend to appoint outstandingly qualified persons to both these posts.

At midday I have the propaganda staff of the Ministry and the Reich Propaganda Service in my office—in particular Wächter, Borcke, Draeger and Krämer—and I give them a fairly long lecture about our new propaganda tasks. I emphasise primarily that there must be more low-level work, more improvisation and more system in setting the objectives of our work. Our propaganda agencies rely too much on the official machine, which still provides them with adequate funds and freedom of movement; as a result our propaganda relies too much on posters and is addressed to the masses rather than the individual. This must cease forthwith. Our propaganda must resemble that of the best period of our struggle for power. At that time we had little money and few men with which to carry on propaganda. Nevertheless it was masterly and ultimately led to victory.

* See above p. 140.

In passing it is worth noting that Reich Minister Rosenberg* still refuses to disband the Ministry for the East. Admittedly he no longer calls it the Ministry for the Occupied Eastern Territories since the effect of that would be too ludicrous; it is merely "Ministry for the East." He wants to concentrate all our eastern policy in this Ministry. I might just as well set up a ministry for the West or the South. It is sheer nonsense. Rosenberg is simply clinging on for prestige purposes and refuses to be convinced by me that his Ministry has long become superfluous. A decision will therefore have to be obtained from the Führer on this.

No major change in the West is reported this evening. That is bad in so far as it implies that we have made no progress in the Linz bridgehead; on the contrary the Americans have gained some ground and are now pushing out towards the Frankfurt autobahn. They are still 2 km from it. If they reach it, that will be very dangerous. We are moving up fresh units in this area however. A major enemy offensive has opened in the Moselle–Ruwer area. There are as yet no reports of its success. The Führer's headquarters hopes that we can cope with it. But one knows that tale. So far that has always been said prior to an enemy offensive and afterwards we have had to sing small.

In Hungary unfortunately only local successes can be recorded. There is no longer any question of a headlong advance. On the contrary 6 Panzer Army has now gone on to the defensive. The enemy made no progress at Schwarzwasser despite massive attacks—undoubtedly due to Schörner. Further enemy penetrations are reported from East Prussia; in Breslau savage fighting fluctuates from one quarter of the city to another. In Gotenhafen two enemy attacks were beaten off but, according to information from Army headquarters there, only by using our last reserves.

When returning to the Führer the minutes of the briefing conference on the Pomeranian affair I included in the

---

* The mystical ideologue of the Nazi Party who had been appointed (since he was a Balt, born a Russian subject) Minister for the Occupied Countries in the East.

folder a hand-written note as follows: "It can be seen from these minutes how right the Führer was. But it is shattering to note that not only did the Führer's military advisers fail to understand him but that they systematically contravened his clear categorical orders. How can I still have confidence in such military advisers! In my view here lies the root of all our failures." As a result of this note the Führer telephones me in the evening. We first have a short talk about the air war and then the conversation turns to the minutes he had given me. I give totally frank expression to my dismay on reading them. The Führer gives me certain explanations as to how this situation could have arisen and adds that it was precisely the same in the cases of Moscow and Stalingrad. He had perceived what was right but his military staff had let him down. His intuitive perception had invariably been shouted down by the specialist know-alls and this is largely the cause of our defeats. Now, however, he proposes to act energetically and even brutally. He will not tolerate any more of this behaviour seeing that it has led to such disastrous results. In the Remagen bridge case, for instance, four death sentences have already been pronounced and carried out. Himmler had been with him in the afternoon and he had given him an extraordinarily severe dressing down. I tell the Führer about my perusal of the General Staff publication on Soviet Marshals and Generals and add that I gained the impression that we are totally unable to compete with such a method of selection of commanders. The Führer shares my view entirely. Our generals are too old and worn out and they are complete aliens to our National-Socialist ways of thought and behaviour. Many of our generals do not even want a National-Socialist victory. Soviet generals, on the other hand, are fanatical adherents of bolshevism and so they fight fanatically for its victory, which naturally endows them with vast superiority. The Führer is determined, even while the war goes on, so to reform the Wehrmacht that it will emerge from the war fundamentally National-Socialist in outlook and bearing. I add that although we Germans may learn things very late, we do so that much more thoroughly. It may be assumed that perhaps this will be the case now.

I have received reports from Captain Krüger, National-Socialist Leadership Officer with Ninth Army, concerning the Führer's visit to the Oder front. This visit was a brilliant success. The Führer showed himself vastly superior to the generals not only in knowledge but also in ideas and aroused the greatest admiration. His physical state produced a certain dismay. On this subject the generals said quite frankly that the 20 July putschists were to blame for the Führer's nervous twitch and that they should be dug up out of their graves and torn to pieces.

In the evening we have the usual Mosquito alert. This happens every evening with stereotyped regularity. The millions in the Reich capital are gradually becoming some-what nervous and hysterical. This is understandable too when people have to spend every evening in the air-raid shelters under such primitive conditions. It is a torture which overstrains the nerves in the long run, particularly when people are firmly convinced that for the present no end to these nightly raids is in sight.

FRIDAY 16 MARCH 1945

(pp. 1–34)
Military Situation.
In the East the Soviets have gone over to the attack in strength in the areas of Mährisch–Ostrau, south of Breslau and at Stettin.

In the Mährisch–Ostrau area the offensive front is still between Bielitz and Pawlowitz; the Soviets have also gone over to the attack north of Ratibor. The enemy penetrated to a depth of 5–6 km towards Oderberg. All other attacks were repulsed with very heavy loss to the enemy. In the Mährisch–Ostrau area strong counter-measures are being taken. South of Brieg the enemy moved forward from the Grottkau area towards Neisse. He succeeded in making several deep penetrations in bitter fighting during which he suffered heavy casualties. Here again strong German counter-measures are in progress. Simultaneously violent attacks on Breslau failed apart from one break-in in the south of the city. The garrison of Glogau also beat off heavy attacks from the south.

Only local actions took place on the Neisse and Oder fronts. A minor attack on Fürstenberg was repulsed and the enemy driven back by counter-attack. At Lebus too there was no change in the situation.

The enemy made heavy attacks on our positions on the east bank of the Oder opposite Stettin. He reached the Greifenhagen–Stettin railway and pushed on south-east of Stettin across the autobahn as far as the eastern branch of the Oder. All other attacks, in particular those east of

Stettin, were repulsed. We are putting up a very stern defence at this point. A total of 77 Soviet tanks were destroyed in this sector alone. An enemy attempt to cross the Dievenow was defeated; detachments which had forced their way across the river were thrown back by counter-attack. The enemy has forced his way into Kolberg and fierce street fighting has flared up. By the day before yesterday a total of 40,000 out of the 50,000 refugees assembled in Kolberg had been evacuated.

Owing to a communications break-down there is as yet no news from Army Group North (Danzig–Königsberg area).

Only local actions took place in Courland.

In the West the enemy has now gone over to the attack in the sector between Saarbrücken and Hagenau in addition to the previous flashpoints—the Linz bridgehead and the Kassel and Ruwer fronts. His objective is undoubtedly to drive in our front on the Saar and capture the entire region south of the Moselle and west of the Rhine.

In the Linz bridgehead the enemy succeeded in penetrating eastwards from Honnef as far as Agidienberg and so reaching the autobahn. Our resistance here is very stiff and the enemy has suffered extraordinarily severe casualties. He made no progress at other points in the bridgehead.

On the Moselle between Alten and Treis, where the enemy had crossed the river on the previous day and advanced towards Boppard, he has now swung south and is about 6 km south of the Moselle.

In the upper Ruwer valley the enemy attacked in greater strength and succeeded in advancing 5–6 km farther east. Fighting is now going on some 7–8 km east of the Ruwer valley around Weiskirchen and north thereof. Between Saarbrücken and Hagenau the enemy gained several kilometres of ground north of Saargemünd, as he did between Saargemünd and Bitsch. Bitsch itself is still in our hands. Fighting is taking place in an area some 5 km west and south-west of Bitsch; in the Reichshofen–Hagenau sector the enemy scored only minor local successes.

Nothing special reported from the Italian front.

Our fighters shot down 30 Soviet aircraft over the area of the Eastern Front.

In the Western Front zone there was lively enemy fighter-bomber and twin-engined bomber activity directed mainly on the Rhine–Main area.

Some 1200 American four-engined bombers with strong fighter escort (750 fighters) flew over Reich territory; they attacked mainly industrial and transport targets and railway installations in the neighbourhood of Berlin. Some 300 British bombers with fighter escort attacked industrial and transport targets in Dortmund. Some 600 American four-engined bombers from Italy attacked Schwarzheide, the Senftenberg area, Vienna, Wiener-Neustadt and Moosbierbaum. A total of 7 aircraft were shot down by our fighters and anti-aircraft.

After dark some 200 British four-engined bombers attacked Hagen and another 250 Hannover. During the night harassing raids were made by 30 Mosquitos on Münster and 60 on Berlin. Our anti-aircraft and 50 of our night fighters shot down 16 enemy aircraft.

———

The situation in the enemy-occupied areas on the left of the Rhine seems very miserable. The enemy press, for instance, refers to extraordinarily wretched conditions in Köln. The population is sunk in total apathy. Starvation is already raging in the city and epidemics are following in its wake. I think developments will become even more catastrophic for the British and Americans have no thought in their minds of giving any form of assistance to the Germans who have remained behind. They must now pay dearly for their failure to obey our evacuation instructions.

Churchill, the British Prime Minister, is totally unmoved by all this misery. His speech to the British Conservative Party Conference was one of almost unsurpassed gloom. Churchill has seldom spoken in such tones. He attacked the domestic opposition to his policy which is becoming increasingly noticeable, accused it of being anti-national and proclaimed his determination to pursue the war in Europe whatever happened, even if it should lead to total chaos. He demanded unconditional surrender from the Reich even if it had to go down in chaos and ruin. In itself this demand may do us some good. But we protest energetically that the press should now accuse us of all people of being anarchists who have plunged Europe into this fearful disaster. This is the well-known method of blaming the murdered man rather than the murderer.

Churchill is convinced, moreover, that peace will come soon but that then a long and difficult war with Japan is pending. The Western Allies are in the greatest distress over shortage of transport. It will mean that after the war there will be definite famine in almost all parts of the world lasting several years. But this naturally does not interest Churchill in the least. He will presumably always be able to eat his fill. All that matters to him is victory, or what the British call victory, in Europe and the destruction of the Reich. The effect of this speech on the British public can be imagined. The *Daily Mail* calls it a definite Dunkirk speech, which in fact it is. In the field of war policy Churchill has suffered nothing but defeats. He was forced to admit this quite openly when answering a question in the Commons; he stated that at Yalta a distinction had in fact been made between the great nations and the small ones that the great nations, in other words the victor nations as Churchill called them, had laid claim to all prerogatives, the small nations on the other hand simply had to do their duty devotedly and obsequiously. In terms of the Yalta decisions only a small country will be regarded as an aggressor country in future; the large countries are too moral to be aggressors. In any case they propose to gorge themselves so full during this war that for the time being they will have no appetite for any more. The idea is totally grotesque that the Soviet Union might be attacked by Sweden, for instance, or Britain by Switzerland and that then the Soviet Union, the USA and Britain would have to meet in order to declare that Sweden or Switzerland were aggressor countries. This nonsense has, of course, been thought up by Stalin. It can only be to his advantage since it gives him an alibi for any arbitrary action against small neutral countries. In this question Britain and the USA have had to bow before him. To remonstrances on the subject Churchill replies with a shrug of the shoulders and something on the lines of: "What is one to do? We are, after all, totally powerless."

The entire world is full of armistice rumours. It is stated that Rundstedt sent a flag of truce with an offer to lay down arms. This rumour is complete nonsense. It was denied from Washington 24 hours later, moreover. Nevertheless it resulted in active speculation on a fall on the New York stock exchange. Moreover it has produced a sort of victory delirium in the USA which has already had serious domestic political repercussions.

On the other hand these rumours also originate from the mission of Hesse,* one of Ribbentrop's staff, to Stockholm. The purpose of this mission was simply to gain some form of contact with the opposing party in the West. This approach is now being blown up into something sensational by Stockholm and London. One can imagine how headlines in the entire world press have bounded upon it. The really grotesque feature of this news coverage is that Himmler, not the Führer, is presented as the guarantor of peace for Germany. A powerful German clique is said to have offered the Führer's head as surety. Not a word of this is true, of course. All this has been cooked up by the British themselves. To this they reply that they require many other heads as well as that of the Führer. In London people pretend to be entirely uninterested in all this. The neutral world—primarily the neutral business world—however is very volatile since it thinks that here may lie a loophole to escape from the war and so from the threat of bolshevism. It might be that such a development might lead to some-

* Fritz Hesse was an official of the Foreign Office who, before the war, had been head of the German Information Office (DNB) in London, and had acted as Ribbentrop's confidential agent there. For his own account see his book, *Hitler and England* (1954).

thing if our troops can hold at least the Rhine–Moselle front. At the moment, however, at least as far as the Moselle is concerned, that is not the case. For the present the heavy losses being suffered by the enemy offer us the only military chance. The Americans now estimate theirs at 839,000 men. Admittedly that figure is not particularly large for the present war but it may have a certain significance for the USA.

The British are now slowly beginning to revive the economy in the Allied-occupied zones. They propose to import German coal into England and export British coal abroad in return. They have planned Germany's subjugation with an eye to feathering their own nest and are very put out that the Americans and Soviets should be competing with them in this.

The Soviets no longer take any notice of British public opinion. They are now proceeding to make mass arrests in Poland; they are attacking the Turks over the Dardanelles question and using the prevalent chaos in France to provoke unrest. This chaos is now manifesting itself in food riots, highway robbery and increasing profiteering, in short in symptoms of disease too serious to be disregarded. In addition there are the developments in Rumania where the Soviets are industriously at work arousing the greatest suspicion, but nothing more, in London.

At midday I have a great reception in my house for home journalists, radio announcers and propagandists working in Berlin. I address them for 1½ hours on the present war situation and the conclusions to be drawn therefrom for the conduct of news and propaganda policy. I felt that I was in good form and gave these gentlemen certain pointers for their work. In any case this reception will assuredly have a good effect on the German press and radio.

During the last 24 hours the most savage air raids have taken place on German territory. Among other places OKH [Army HQ] in Zossen was more or less demolished. But we will not take that too much to heart. In Essen the situation is so bad that there is a great bread shortage and violent complaints on the subject are coming from the Gau

Westphalia South. We must move in central government assistance but our stocks of flour are insufficient for action on a large scale. It is bad that we are now getting practically no news from bombed cities. Telephone communications are totally severed and we have to rely solely on radio. But we must keep going nevertheless.

Part of Ellgering's office has been forced to move to central Germany since it was almost impossible for it to work in Berlin. Ellgering himself, however, is to keep his office in Wannsee for the present.

In a memorandum I work out a proposal for a major reduction of the Luftwaffe. The Luftwaffe is now trailing around with it an administrative and personnel organisation far larger than is justified by its present duties and potentialities. We must now start more or less from scratch with the Luftwaffe and screw down its organisation and personnel machine to a size commensurate with its remaining potentialities. Looked at objectively the situation is somewhat as follows:

The Luftwaffe will have a total of 30,000 tons of petrol available by the end of the month. Part of this is kept as an emergency reserve. Major fresh allocations of petrol are not expected before autumn. Until then no petrol-engined aircraft can take off from now on—apart from supply transports. In view of the petrol situation all types of aircraft hitherto in use are being deleted from the armaments programme except for the following: (i) the Me 262 jet fighter equipped with four 3 cm guns: (ii) the HE 162 (still untested): (iii) the Ta 152 single-seater fighter: (iv) the Arado 234: (v) the Ju 88 in night fighter role. In recent weeks losses in fighters shot down by the enemy have reached 60%. Over the next few months the aircraft programme should produce (monthly): (i) 1000 Me 262s with a reserve of 500 and a front-line establishment of 800: (ii) 500 He 162s with a reserved of 1000: (iii) 500 Ta 152s: (iv) 80–100 Arado 234s: (v) 50 Ju 88s. According to a Führer decision production is to be concentrated on the Me 262; this can stay in the air for 70 minutes and uses a sort of diesel oil of which 44,000 tons are available and this level of stock can be maintained. Reich Minister Speer will do his utmost to give all priority to the Me 262. Series production is so far advanced that a major attack on enemy incursions can begin in two to three months' time. Sorties flown so far justify the assumption that the casualty rate will be 5:1 in our favour. In a recent action by 23 Me 262s seven bombers were shot down for certain and four more bombers and four fighters were probables for the loss of only one of our aircraft. A Mosquito will be simply torn apart by a hit from an Me 262. Four hits finish off a bomber. After one month of fighting on these terms Anglo-Saxon losses in the air will inevitably have become so grievous that they will reduce their air raids. To meet the Me 262 programme Reich Minister Speer has ordered concentration of all resources—transport capacity and labour—on the Me 262. The armaments industry can supply parts without difficulty. The design of runways, not using concrete but making use of autobahns, has begun. Aircraft are concealed in woods in dispersal points with earth protection and makeshift head cover so that even area bombing will not affect them on a large scale. Engineer General Mahnke is keeping an eye on the stock potential. It will take the enemy two years to copy the Me 262. Six special commissioners, including Dr. Degenkolb, are employed in supervising the Me 262 programme. The most experienced generals have been given charge of Me 262 operations: (i) General Kammhuber (night fighters): (ii) General Pelz (fighters). The unsolved problem is rapidity of movement of aircraft from dispersal point to runway (10 minutes towed, 1 hour manhandled). The problem is still being worked on. As personnel reserve the Me 262 programme requires all 20,000 trained air force cadets who are now being used as a Rail Transport Defence Brigade.

This holds out some prospect for the immediate future. Too much hope should not be placed in it, however, for reestablishment of a German defence capability in the air has been promised so often and this promise has been broken so often that one would prefer to see some results first before considering the promise a real one.

In investigating individual arms of the service we are continually coming across fresh subterfuges employed by headquarters at home to evade the combing-out process by the Staff for Total War. It is extremely difficult to get men who are fit for service and have been released, actually into barracks or up to the front. We shall have to use fairly rough and ready methods if we are to succeed. The leader in this passive resistance is the Luftwaffe. Various army headquarters are not far behind in this respect, however. On my instructions General von Gottberg is now ruthlessly enrolling on the spot those men who have been released and despatching them in short order to the front where they belong.

Mail received testifies to a deep-seated lethargy throughout the German people degenerating almost into hopelessness. There is very sharp criticism of the Luftwaffe but also of the entire national leadership. The latter is accused of being over-ambitious in its policy and strategy, of having been negligent in its conduct of the war, particularly in the air, and this is given as the main reason for our misfortunes. As far as the accusation of intemperance is concerned, this is applied particularly to our conduct of the eastern campaign and it is not altogether unjustified. Our speakers at meetings are no longer really getting their points home. Arguments relying solely on historical examples are no longer persuasive. My last radio speech has had a mixed reception. In some cases it is given the highest praise but in others it is criticised for failing to provide positive data holding out hope of successful prosecution of the war in future. One has the dull foreboding that even the best arguments can no longer make an impact on a people that is worn out and fought to a standstill.

In a leading article headed "History as Teacher" I seize the opportunity, by citing historical examples in detail, to point out the force of history as leading to conclusions applicable to our present time. I hope that I shall succeed but I realise that at the present time only a victory can be really convincing. Everything else goes in at one ear and out at the other with these people.

This evening it is reported that our front in the Saar region and at Bitsch has held firm by and large. The Moselle front, on the other hand, is slowly giving way. Here the enemy has reached a point north of Saarbrücken so that the town is now in danger of encirclement from the rear. On our side everything possible is being done to counter this threat. Kesselring was with the Führer again and was given precise instructions by him. This is a critical development and it is hoped to master the situation but I am somewhat sceptical about it. I have so often heard hopes expressed and have so often found that these hopes have come to nothing two or three days later that I now prefer to wait for actual happenings before forming a definitive judgement.

Soviet offensive activity has flared up again all along the Eastern Front. West of Lake Valencze the enemy made very strong diversionary attacks which, however, were held by and large. Our bridgehead over the Sio has been extended. It is intended shortly to go over to the offensive again. The enemy succeeded in making some penetrations at Grottkau. This is a first-class major offensive at this point but Schörner is still convinced that he can deal with it. The offensive is aimed at the Mährisch–Ostrau coal-mining and industrial area which we must not lose in any circumstances. Counter-attacks are in progress in this area and one must wait and see whether they succeed. Communications with Küstrin are cut but it is hoped to re-establish them. In Kolberg the final battles are apparently taking place. Our men are no longer in a position to offer co-ordinated resistance to the enemy. The Soviets have attempted to push forward to Zoppot but without success. The situation in East Prussia is that the enemy has made deep penetrations but no break-through. Everywhere the fighting, both offensive and defensive, is extraordinarily severe and everything is again on a knife-edge all along the Eastern Front.

This evening reports of German peace proposals, both from neutral and enemy sources, are even more numerous. They now occupy the headlines in almost every newspaper in the world. London is protesting emphatically that our feelers have not been taken seriously. As soon as Hesse's mission became known the USA and the Soviet Union were informed of the talks forthwith. It is regarded as an obvious attempt to fish in troubled waters and split the enemy coalition. In London the attempt has been met with a flat rejection, whereas the other enemy allies have said nothing. This rejection was, of course, to be expected from the British. Reuters state that the German proposals have been totally ignored. The difficult problem now arises how the Führer is to be told of this; he was always extraordinarily sceptical of this attempt and once again he has been proved right. I too think that the attempt was not made very adroitly or it would certainly have had different and less reverberating reactions. Moreover my view is that the British will very soon stop peddling this news round because they must be afraid that their own people may start taking a more positive interest in it.

My speech to journalists has had a very profound effect. This instance shows yet again that if one talks in the right vein to people who are politically conscious and have an insight into things, one finds the way to their hearts and their minds. I shall now repeat such receptions often.

In the evening we have the regular Mosquito raid on the capital; these raids have now become an almost daily regular occurrence.

SATURDAY 17 MARCH 1945

(pp. 1–24)

Military Situation.

On the Eastern Front the main centre of fighting was the area east and north of Mährisch–Ostrau where the enemy threw very large tank formations into battle. During the fighting between Bielitz and Cosel and north of Neisse 239 Soviet tanks were destroyed during this day alone. In the area between Bielitz, Schwarzheide and Pawlowitz all attacks were repulsed and most minor penetrations eliminated by counter-attack. South of Cosel the enemy succeeded in making minor penetrations to a depth of 3–4 km but these were sealed off at once. Between Glogau and Neisse the bolshevists gained some ground and advanced to a point 10 km north of Neisse. Here too most of the penetrations were immediately dealt with by counter-attack. Attacks in battalion strength on Breslau and Glogau were all repulsed. No special actions took place on the adjoining front as far as Stettin. Enemy attacks on the Stettin bridgehead were somewhat reduced in violence. On the other hand our lines were subjected to heavy Soviet artillery fire which caused not inconsiderable casualties. Several commanders and senior officers were killed. The enemy attacks did not penetrate however. Only at Greifenberg was he able to achieve a small local break-in. South-east of Stettin the bolshevists were driven back a little by counter-attack. In Kolberg the garrison is defending itself in the port area. Again no further news of Army Group North (Danzig–Kolberg) owing to damage to communications. On the previous day the enemy had again been driven back a little in severe fighting near Gotenhafen but the East Prussian bridgehead was further compressed. Severe fighting will have gone on yesterday.

In Courland there was local fighting only.

In Hungary our offensive gained some 2–3 km of ground on a broad front between the western tip of Lake Balaton and Kaposvar; in other sectors of the offensive—particularly in the Stuhlweissenburg area—the enemy put in strong counter-attacks, mainly with infantry. All attacks were repulsed apart from a break-in between Stuhlweissenburg and Felsögalla.

On the Western Front the Americans succeeded in capturing the Moselle heights between Alken and Treis; from here strong armoured forces pushed south through Simmern, Bad Kreuznach and Hochstetten (along the Kreuznach–Kaiserslautern road). Military headquarters ascribe the success of this deep break-through our line to excessive fatigue on the part of the German defensive forces, which are in no great strength, and to the surprise factor.

At the same time the enemy attacked in the upper Ruwer valley east of the river in a westerly direction and achieved a break-through 15–20 km in depth, bringing him to Rheinsfeld and Hermeskeil. Farther south leading enemy troops reached a point about 6 km south-west of Hermeskeil. Enemy attacks between Saarbrücken and the Rhine were in general repulsed apart from minor penetrations. Bitsch fell into enemy hands. The enemy reached the old German frontier 5–6 km north-east of Bitsch.

In the Linz bridgehead the enemy moved north from Honnef and captured the Drachenfels. In the south he succeeded in extending his bridgehead some 2–3 km towards Waldbreitbach.

No special action took place on the Italian front.

German air forces were fairly heavily in action in the East yesterday. They shot down 31 Soviet aircraft and also destroyed numerous tanks, assault guns and columns of troops.

On the Western Front there was again lively enemy fighter-bomber activity centred on the Moselle, Palatinate and central Rhine areas. In the Koblenz–Kochem and Bingen areas 112 German fighters were in action against enemy low-flying aircraft and shot down 4 of them.

American bomber formations were not in action over western Germany yesterday.

Some 350 American four-engined bombers from Italy raided transport installations in Vienna, Korneuburg, Moosbierbaum and Wiener-Neustadt; detached formations attacked Klagenfurt, Graz, Amstetten and St. Valentin. Anti-aircraft shot down 13 enemy.

During the night a strong British aid formation of some 450 bombers attacked Nuremburg with 250 aircraft and Würzburg with 200. The usual harassing raid was made on Berlin in the evening. 42 night fighters were in action against the British four-engined formation and shot down 42 aircraft. Five other bombers were shot down by anti-aircraft.

———————

Herr von Ribbentrop's peace soundings have been a total failure. They have met with an unequivocal rejection from both the Americans and the British. Moreover they were very badly arranged. A man like Hesse is not suited to explain National-Socialist views to the enemy. Even in the friendly disposed neutral press he is described as a German philistine who advocated war with England during our prosperous days and so is regarded as Public Enemy No. 1 by British diplomacy. No wonder, therefore, that in the neutral press his attempt was described as hopeless from the outset. This is therefore simply a mishandled escapade by Ribbentrop; anyone could have foreseen with certainty that this was where it would lead.

On the other hand it is significant that the British have said very little in public about the Hesse mission. Obviously they are afraid that, if there are too many peace rumours at this stage of the war, the effect on public opinion might be very detrimental. Despite the military victories being won by the Anglo-Americans the British people are extraordinarily war-weary and the fact is that, if there is too much peace talk at the height of the war, it will gradually become infectious.

There can be no doubt that Hesse's soundings met with a flat rejection from the entire enemy camp. On the other hand the British realise that hopes of an internal German revolution against National-Socialism or the Führer personally are illusory. In America the widespread rumours of capitulation are described as definite stock exchange manoeuvres. The Jews of New York, therefore, are at present openly speculating on a fall in order to buy war and armaments stocks as cheaply as possible.

Roosevelt too has been compelled to issue a denial of the capitulation rumours connected with the person of von Rundstedt; he was afraid they would lead to undesirable repercussions on American industry.

Military developments in the West are most unfortunate. A pretty miserable situation has arisen in the Moselle area. The Führer had thought that the Moselle could be held as a defence line but the idea has proved invalid. The Americans have succeeded in crossing the Moselle on a broad front and now they are flooding into the region between the Moselle and the Rhine without meeting any resistance worth the name. Naturally our Saar front is most seriously threatened as a result. This has so far held and the Siegfried Line has been defended with the utmost valour but there is now the fear that it will be attacked from the rear. One sometimes wonders despairingly where our troops will at last be prepared to stand. Enemy material and numerical superiority cannot be the reason, for the enemy is not all that superior on this front. On the Western Front there are numerous advocates of the dangerous idea that the Anglo-Americans should be given free passage into the Reich to prevent it falling into Soviet hands. This is, of course, a fatal misconception of the war situation and we must under all circumstances take steps to dissipate it. On the other hand it becomes even more essential to hold out to the troops and the civil population some tangible prospects of victory. But what is one to say to them? At the moment our knees are so weak that efforts to allay people's fears about the military situation bear little fruit. Even the OKW report is couched in a serious gloomy tone. Anyone reading it attentively can see from it that the Western Front has begun to crumble and that at the same time we are not even semi-capable of holding our position in the East.

As far as the West is concerned the Americans are issuing dramatic reports about present conditions in Köln. The inhabitants are in the greatest distress. They have been restricted to one-third of the rations issued in the United States.

The Americans are industriously trying to install their own administration in all the regions they occupy. Even in the Linz bridgehead they have taken steps to this end.

This evening it is officially announced from Washington that even the Reich's unconditional surrender will no longer satisfy the enemy. Whatever happens he intends to occupy the whole area of the Reich. For the present his demands do not go further than that. Perhaps the next one will be that we must all hang ourselves or shoot ourselves beforehand. The enemy's thirst for destruction is taking on the most extraordinary forms. The inordinate thirst for revenge visible in the British and American Jewish press defies description. Moreover the cynicism they evidence is without parallel. They congratulate themselves quite openly on the destruction of German cities and cultural monuments, bearing witness to the present age in a manner which literally brings blushes to the cheeks. Churchill's recent speech illustrates the dark future in store for Europe in the minds of leading British circles. The speech was intended to lay a demolition charge underneath the Conservative Party. Churchill's plan now is to split both the Conservative and Labour Parties in order to form a new party from the splinters of both. Churchill is a factor of destruction. He will surely go down to world history of Europe's Herostratus,* capable of perpetuating his name only by

* Herostratus—a favourite character of Hitler and Goebbels— burnt down the temple of Diana at Ephesus in 356 BC solely in order to immortalise his name.

destroying what many generations have built up over many centuries.

He will shortly be meeting the American Jew Baruch* who then proposes to pay a visit to Stalin. In these conversations the looting of the Reich will be settled in all its detail. Our Western enemies cannot point to a single positive achievement.

Van Acker, the Belgian Minister-President, flatly states in an interview that, when we were in occupation, we imported twenty times as much food into Belgium in five months as the Allies have done. The latter nevertheless present themselves as liberators from want and social misery.

For the moment they are pretending to be extraordinarily surprised by political developments in Rumania. The Soviets have outmanoeuvred them and are pursuing a policy entirely of their own. The iron curtain has descended on the fate of Rumania. An indifferent world no longer knows what is going on behind it.

Beneš† is playing his cards more cautiously than Radescu. He is going off straight away to Moscow to get prior sanction from the Kremlin for the government he plans in Czecho-Slovakia. It will presumably wear a marked communistic appearance.

The Soviets have now begun to get things going again in Upper Silesia. The mines are working at full pressure. The workers get a miserable reduced ration from the Soviet administration but there is as yet no question of any great terrorisation. Stalin's intention is no doubt to extract the maximum possible war potential from Upper Silesia.

A series of major acts of sabotage and assassinations has started in Norway. The Norwegians apparently cannot wait for the time when they come under Soviet control. We are dealing with this wave of sabotage and assassinations with

---

* Bernard Baruch was economic adviser to President Roosevelt and a personal friend of Churchill.

† President of Czechoslovakia at the time of the Munich Agreement. He then went into exile, and was recognised by the Allies as *de jure* President 1940–5.

the utmost severity. Terboven has a proper job on his hands here.

The internal situation in the Reich is governed almost exclusively by the air war. Here is our real weakness in the overall conduct of the war. For the first time for a long time we are again reporting considerable numbers of enemy aircraft shot down at night; this is simply because our night fighters are taking off. Recently enemy casualties have been so deplorably low that they did not even merit a mention in the OKW report.

The evacuation problem still gives rise to the greatest anxiety. Some 600,000 men are said to have passed under the Soviet knout in Pomerania. This is primarily due to the fact that our military leaders refused to listen to the Führer's warnings that the Soviets would drive for Pomerania. The Führer persists in his view that the West should also be evacuated as far as possible. This instruction, however, leads to great difficulties since people show no enthusiasm for leaving the West and moving into precarious conditions in the interior of the Reich.

The fact that in this critical situation Rosenberg still refuses to disband the Ministry for the East is almost comic. I may well take the bull by the horns since reasoning is no good when so-called prominent people are so stupid that they refuse to see plain common sense.

General von Gottberg's* campaign, the object of which is to get as many soldiers as possible to the front as quickly as possible, is being carried on with very radical improvised measures. It is achieving considerable success. Gottberg's procedure is extremely strict; anyway he is at least driving to the front the weaklings who have so far invariably contrived to evade a front-line posting.

The weekly stock-taking of the capital's defences is extraordinarily favourable. In a period of eight days we have succeeded in increasing our stocks of weapons and food remarkably. We could now withstand a siege of the capital for ten to twelve weeks, though we should be in

* See above p. 86.

very straitened circumstances. In various sectors, particularly tanks and assault guns, the figures show a vast increase. Ammunition supply, however, is still a serious bottleneck. But I have already taken the necessary steps to overcome it. A defence line will now be constructed west of Stettin as far as Hoppegarten. By employing 100,000 men this line will be completed in the shortest possible time. Berlin itself has to make a considerable manpower contribution.

I have had to work very hard all day. In the evening we have the customary Mosquito raid on Berlin but, thank God, it did not do so much damage. One now accepts it almost as a daily habit. We do not manage to shoot down many of these Mosquitos. With them the enemy has the upper hand one hundred per cent. When one thinks of this going on long-term one is horror-stricken. But the enemy has his worries too; they may not lie so much in the military field but they are all the more striking in the political. In this struggle, with political crisis on the enemy side and military crisis on ours, all now depends on who gets out of his depth first.

SUNDAY 18 MARCH 1945

(pp. 1–25, 7 omitted in page-numbering)
Military Situation.

In Hungary our offensive made minor gains of ground between Lake Balaton and the Drava. Strong Soviet counter-attacks were repulsed between Lake Balaton and the Serves Canal and we gained a little ground in an attack southwards.

In Slovakia the enemy continued his concentrated attacks in the direction of Neusohl. He made small gains of ground here in woodland fighting.

In the Schwarzwasser area strong Soviet attacks were driven off. Violent enemy attacks from the bridgehead north of [word illegible] and in the Neisse area were met by strong German resistance. The fortresses of Breslau and Glogau repulsed enemy attacks from various directions.

On the whole of the adjacent front as far as Küstrin only local actions took place.

In Pomerania the bolshevists continued their heavy attacks on the Stettin bridgehead. They succeeded in penetrating into Altdamm.

Severe fighting also took place in West Prussia where the enemy attacked the Gotenhafen and Danzig areas with large forces of tanks and very strong air support. In general terms these attacks were repulsed.

The East Prussian bastion also beat off strong Soviet attacks, sealed off penetrations and maintained the cohesion of the front. Numerous enemy tanks were again destroyed.

On the Courland front, in addition to the main centre of activity east of Frauenburg, the enemy went over to the attack south-west of the town after heavy artillery preparation. Apart from certain minor penetrations all Soviet attacks were repulsed yesterday.

On the Western Front an attempted enemy crossing south-west of Duisburg was defeated.

On the central Rhine the day was marked by further bitter fighting round the American bridgehead east of Remagen; the enemy made only small advances in certain sectors.

On the lower Rhine front there was much artillery and reconnaissance activity on both sides.

In the battle area south of the Moselle American armoured forces reached the Nahe valley on a broad front. Three main directions of enemy effort can be detected: towards the Rhine, southwards from Bad Kreuznach in the region of the Nahe valley and westwards in rear of our front on the Saar.

Strong attacks on the Siegfried Line between Saarlautern, Saargemünd and Hagenau were repulsed and penetrations sealed off.

No special news from the Italian front.

In the morning 700 American four-engined bombers flew into Saxony from the west, attacking Bitterfeld, Plauen im Vogtl, Jena and Weimar. Neustadt an der Weinstrasse, Keiserslautern and Frankenberg an der Eder were also attacked.

At midday a larger formation of American four-engined bombers raided Hannover and Münster. Recklinghausen was also attacked. In the evening came the usual harassing raid on the capital by 50–60 Mosquitos. During the night a medium to heavy raid was made on Nuremburg. In addition there was continuous and lively reconnaissance activity over the whole Reich.

A solitary piece of good news has arrived today—that the bridge over the Rhine at Remagen has collapsed as a result of our prolonged artillery fire and attempts to blow it up using naval frogmen. The Americans, of course, say that it is of no significance for supply to the Linz bridgehead since they have adequate pontoons available; in fact, however, they will naturally miss this heavy railway bridge badly. It would be splendid if we could succeed in eliminating the Linz bridgehead. At present, however, the Americans are in such strength there that it is they not us who are making gains of ground. At the moment the bridgehead is one of our greatest worries, apart from the critical situation which has now arisen in the Saar region. Here the Americans are trying to take us in rear and roll up the Siegfried Line from behind, exactly as we did to the Maginot Line during the offensive in the West in 1940. It is clear that we must put in all our forces to stop this attempt, but it is very questionable whether we can succeed.

By the way, five death sentences on officers have been pronounced for failure to blow the Remagen bridge; they have been carried out and announced in the OKW report. Naturally this created some sensation. Officers of OKH fought tooth and nail to prevent this news being given in the OKW report; but the Führer refused to give way, and rightly, since execution of these sentences should be educational. Unless they are announced they cannot have this effect.

Political developments are increasingly governed by the forthcoming conference in San Francisco. A remarkably violent dispute has arisen between the partners in the enemy coalition over the conference's methodology and agenda. United States public opinion demands that firm commitments be entered into at San Francisco for the future world order and the organisation of so-called world peace. The Soviets are fighting this tooth and nail since their main interest, of course, is to keep things as fluid as possible after the war in order to pick up some loot wherever they see an opportunity. Stalin, therefore has no intention of allowing the Americans and British to put handcuffs on him. The British are playing only a sub-ordinate role in this. Shinwell, the MP,* was right when he criticised Churchill in one of his speeches for possessing no programme of any sort; he could not therefore count, Shinwell said, on the existing truce between the working class and the Conservatives being maintained after the war. For this reason alone Churchill has an interest in bringing this war to an end and in the greatest possible chaos since only then can he present himself as the saviour. He has pursued a bankrupt's policy and is now staking his last penny in order to win back England's lost property.

The enemy's situation has so far largely been governed by the increasing food crisis not only in the occupied countries but also among the belligerents. The British are very incensed that the Americans are no longer willing to help them out; the Americans, however, maintain that they cannot afford to make a reduction in their food ration for fear of its effect on the morale of the American people. In a statement to the press Roosevelt attempted to evade making any clear decision. In any case the British now realise that they must make severe reductions in their food ration if they are not to face a catastrophic famine in late spring.

Life in the enemy-occupied areas of the West is pictured as real hell. The French people must now pay dearly for their government's folly in declaring war on us in September 1939. They deserve all they get. Equally the Poles are now going round with tears in their eyes lamenting that they have so far lost ten million men from death, starvation, deportation and liquidation. That is the punishment for Polish arrogance in August 1939. Had the Poles accepted our extraordinarily generous proposals at that time, they would have got off without even a scratch. As they are now, they run the risk of slowly losing their people by a sort of creeping death.

The British and Americans are agreed that the situation

* Emmanuel Shinwell, Labour MP for Seaham Harbour.

in Rumania has reached such a pass that they must take action. They are therefore attempting to consult the Kremlin which, however, is stopping its ears and pretending ignorance of the deplorable state of affairs of which the British and Americans complain. It is clear that, in the present critical war situation, Stalin is doing his utmost to harvest as much as he can. In any case the Anglo-Americans know only a fraction of what is going on in Rumania. Stalin has long since let down the iron curtain and behind it the Rumanian popular tragedy is being played out, as the Rumanian leaders might have foreseen—and as, moreover, they have richly deserved.

This Sunday is anything but a day of rest for us. I had actually put it aside to do a little clearing-up work but the enemy drew a red pencil through that idea. The front-line situation is horrifying, both in the East and the West. For the moment developments in the West cause us the greater anxiety. Here, as I have already stressed, the Remagen bridgehead has been extended further; worse still, however, the Americans have crossed the Moselle on a broad front and now have not only reached but passed the line of the Nahe. Apparently there is at present no method of stopping the enemy armour in this area. In East Prussia too and in the Ratibor area developments have been anything but favourable.

In addition to all this at midday there was a heavy air raid on the capital producing all sorts of trouble. The Americans attacked with 1300 bombers escorted by 700 fighters and we had only 28 new Me 262s with which to oppose them and they can only stay in the air for half to three-quarters of an hour. Already there have been massive air raids on various cities in the Reich during the last 24 hours and now comes this heavy attack on the Reich capital. Berlin was on air-raid alert for two hours. The eastern and northern quarters of the capital, which have so far been comparatively immune, were the main targets. After the raid the capital presents the usual dreadful picture. From my house I can see fires burning all over the government quarter. Opposite us the Blücher Palace, the building housing the Swiss protecting power, is burning. But this is only a fraction of what is going on in this vast city of millions of inhabitants. I drive straight to my command post and am given a provisional survey of the damage by Schach. It is certainly not enlivening.

Schaub* is sent over by the Führer to get the news. For his benefit I add a generous helping of criticism of the Luftwaffe and Göring.

Meanwhile one's ordinary work must be done. At midday the Führer telephones for information about the situation in Berlin. I give him an unvarnished report, primarily on the frame of mind of the capital's population after such an air raid when there has been practically no defence. The Führer thinks that our Me 262s have done something; this is not yet confirmed by figures however. In any case I do not believe that 28 fighters, however fast they may be, can do anything worth mentioning against 1300 enemy bombers escorted by 700 enemy fighters.

The Führer is extraordinarily preoccupied by the military situation in the West. Last night his briefing conference lasted until 6:00 a.m. and he is therefore naturally very overtired. In the long run it is intolerable that he should only have two hours' sleep night after night.

By evening the situation in Berlin is roughly as follows: the majority of fires have not yet been extinguished. The Americans carried out heavy area bombing in Wedding and Niederschönau, causing fearful devastation. At present traffic in the capital is at an almost total standstill. This is largely due to the fact that electricity supply is no longer functioning owing to failure of the transformer stations. We have 60,000 homeless and about 500 dead. In addition there are whole areas where no one knows how many people are buried in the ruins. In extent this raid was at least as heavy as the last terror raid made by the Americans on 28 February. Overall the situation is a fairly crazy one

* Hitler's personal adjutant.

Goebbels addressing the troops in Luban, Lower Silesia, on March 11, 1945, after the recapture of the city.

The Goebbels family in October, 1942. Front row *(left to right)* Helmut, Holde, Magda Goebbels, Heide, Joseph Goebbels and Hedda; back row *(left to right)* Hilda, Harald Quant (Magda Goebbels' son by her first marriage) and Helga.

Goebbels congratulates Generaloberst (later Generalfeldmar-
schall) Schörner on retaking Luban.

A Soviet military policewoman, and a sign in Cyrillic script, show troops of the Red Army the way to Berlin.

A congratulatory handshake for a member of the Einsatzkommando in Luban.

One of the last conferences in the Führerbunker in Berlin, middle of March, 1945. Standing behind Hitler are *(left to right)* Ribbentrop, General Koller, Göring, Keitel and Jodl.

Members of the Volkssturm taking the oath on November 12, 1944, in front of the Reich Propaganda Ministry.

The Reich's Foreign Minister, Joachim von Ribbentrop, visiting troops on the Oder front on April 3, 1945.

Reichsführer-SS Heinrich Himmler inspecting defensive positions on the Oder in March, 1945.

Facing page: A wounded member of the Hitler Jugend acts as a dispatch rider on Berlin's Kurfürstendamnm.

Street scene in Siegburg after a bombing raid.

Winston Churchill is driven through the ruins of Xanten in an American armored car in March, 1945.

British armor in front of the destroyed railway bridge over the Rhine near Wesel on March 24, 1945.

Three of Hitler's final levy, captured by the Americans near Giessen in 1945.

Collecting clothing for the Wehrmacht and the Volkssturm.

In the spring of 1945, goods trucks were called in to keep Berlin's public transport running.

Trenches are dug in the Berlin suburbs in spring of 1945 to defend the capital of the Third Reich.

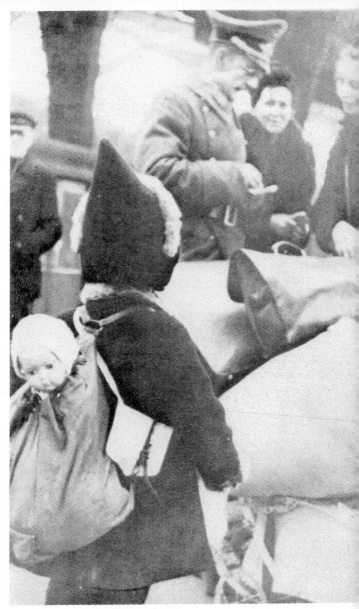

Checking travel permits at the Anhalter station in Berlin.

Field Marshal Montgomery and General Ridgway in consultation with engineer officers on the temporary bridge over the Elbe at Bleckede.

The Soviet Commander in Chief, Grigori Chukov, with his staff in an observation dugout during the battle for Berlin in April, 1945.

One of the last photographs of Adolf Hitler, taken on March 20 in the courtyard of the Reich Chancellery when he decorated members of the Hitler Jugend with the Iron Cross for "gallantry in the field."

In the garden of the Reich Chancellery Rear Admiral Hans-Erich Voss, permanent representative of the Naval High Command to the Führer's headquarters, identifies the remains of Joseph and Magda Goebbels for Soviet soldiers.

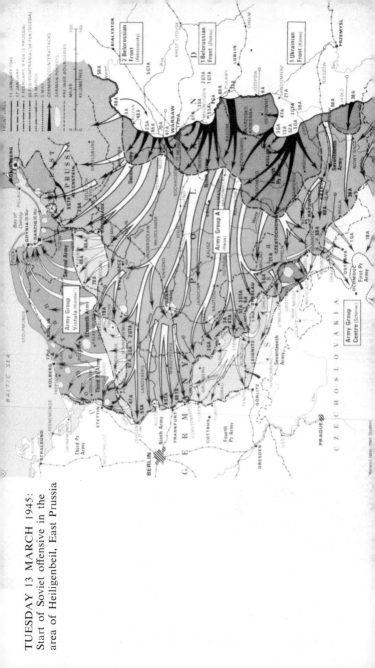

TUESDAY 13 MARCH 1945:
Start of Soviet offensive in the
area of Heiligenbeil, East Prussia

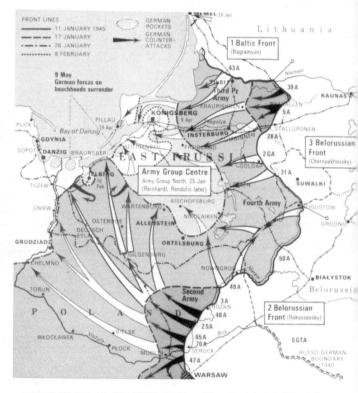

THURSDAY 15 MARCH 1945: The Soviet 1st Ukrainian
Front launches offensive in the area of Ratibor, Upper Silesia;
German advance in Hungary halted

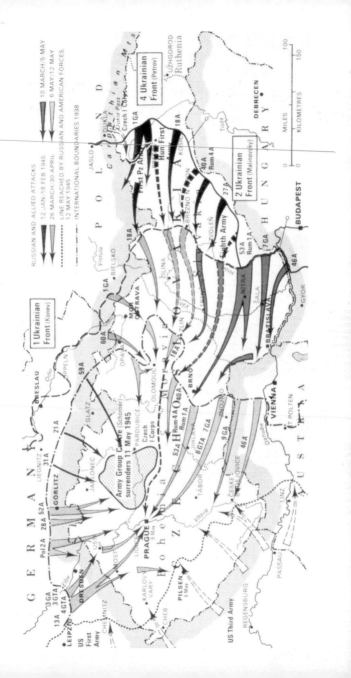

OCCUPIED BY RUSSIAN FORCES

- AUG/DEC 1944
- DEC 1944/APR 1945
- APR/MAY 1945

MILES 200
0
0 KM 300

HELSINKI

TALLINN

LENINGRA

Estonia

PSKOV

Latvia
RIGA

Dvina

MEMEL

Lithuania

KÖNIGSBERG

KAUNAS

E
PRUSSIA

MINSK

BERLIN

Oder

Vistula

BIALYSTOK

WARSAW

Bug

P O L A N D

GERMANY

KIEV

PRAGUE

KRAKOW

LVOV

CZECHOSLOVAKIA

Dniestr

VIENNA

BUDAPEST

HUNGARY

Prut

ODESS

RUMANIA

BUCHAREST

BELGRADE

Danube

YUGOSLAVIA

BULGARIA

ITALY

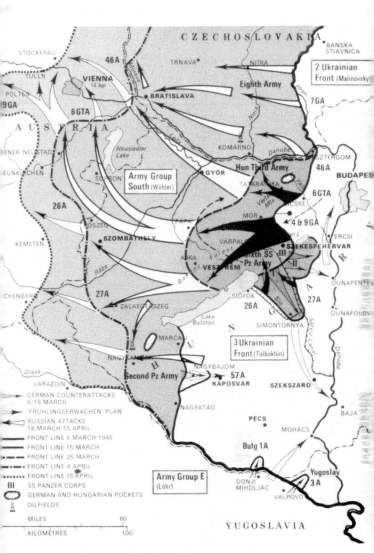

FRIDAY 23 MARCH 1945: Soviet troops break through
German defense positions at Gotenhafen (Gdynia) and Danzig;
British, American and Canadian troops advance across the Rhine
from Venlo and occupy Wesel

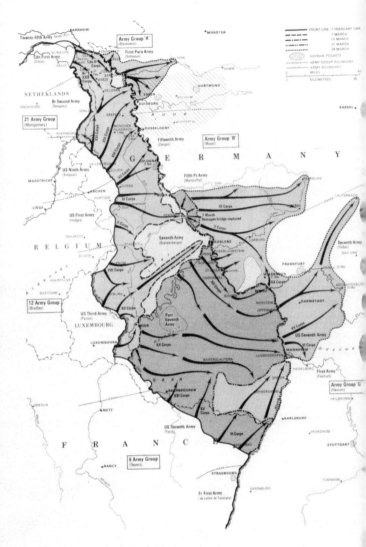

THURSDAY 29 MARCH 1945: German troops withdraw on to the Frische Nehrung; American troops occupy Frankfurt am Main

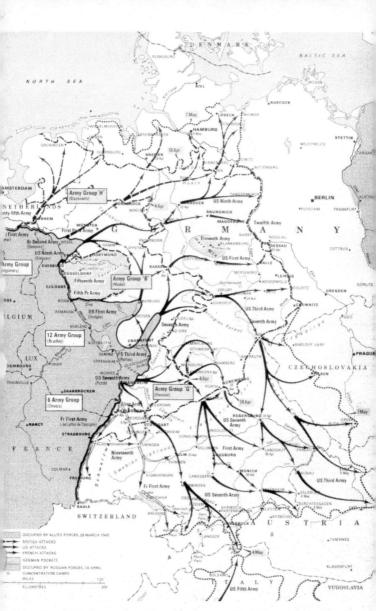

SUNDAY 8 APRIL 1945: Garrison of Konigsberg surrenders; start of major Anglo-American offensive in Upper Italy

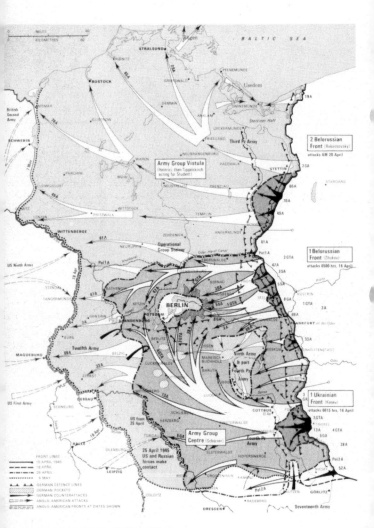

MONDAY 9 APRIL 1945

and we shall have our hands full in the next few days trying to get the Reich capital back to some form of makeshift existence.

On top of this comes the evening military situation report, showing an extraordinarily worrying position. In Remagen the position has been held more or less. The enemy is admittedly still on the autobahn but for the moment he has not yet ventured to move forward from it. Very heavy street fighting is going on in Koblenz. The Moselle can no longer be referred to as a line. The enemy has crossed it on a broad front and during the day was able to widen his break-through considerably. He is now moving towards Bingen and Mainz. In this battle zone we are putting in all reserves available. It is not expected, however, that we can stop the enemy before the Rhine. The greatest danger is on the Saar front which, to judge from the map, can no longer be held. The significance of the loss of the Saar coal for our war potential can be calculated on the fingers of one hand.

In the East small gains of ground are reported south of Lake Balaton; in general terms, however, our great offensive has come to a standstill. A big battle is raging in Upper Silesia. The Soviets attacked at Ratibor and Grottkau and made deep penetrations. There is danger of encirclement here and Schörner is making every effort to prevent it. It is to be hoped that he succeeds. If it is at all possible, Schörner will do it. He still has certain counter-measures in reserve so that one can contemplate future developments with some confidence. After five days of a major Soviet offensive he has at least succeeded in preventing the enemy making a break-through. In the Stettin area and in East Prussia also severe fighting has flared up resulting in some deep enemy penetrations. The same is the case on the Courland front. Nowhere, however, has the enemy made a break-through, thank God. We have now had to evacuate Kolberg. The town, which has been defended with such extraordinary heroism, could no longer be held. I will ensure that the evacuation of Kolberg is not mentioned in the OKW report. In view of the severe psychological repercussions on the Kolberg film* we could do without that for the moment.

In the evening we have the regulation Mosquito raid on Berlin once more. The enemy aircraft flew over a city still burning. One can imagine the jubilation in the Anglo-American press tomorrow.

* For this film see above, Introduction p. x.

MONDAY 19 MARCH 1945

(pp. 1–35)
Military Situation.

In the East enemy attacks in Hungary centred on the area Felsögalla–Stuhlweissenburg, in Silesia on the area Cosel–Leobschütz, on Stettin, on the Danzig–East Prussian area and in Courland.

In Hungary the enemy attacked west and north-west between Stuhlweissenburg and Felsögalla against a front in the Vertes mountains only thinly manned by Hungarian troops; here he made several penetrations to a depth of 15–20 km. Attacks on Mor failed. Between Mor and Stuhlweissenburg the enemy reached the Stuhlweissenburg–Komorn railway. One of our attacks near Marcali south of Lake Balaton gained some ground.

Nothing of significance on the Slovakian front.

The heavy enemy attacks between Stelitz and Schwarzwasser directed on Mährisch–Ostrau have died away and now more resemble holding operations. The bolshevists transferred the main weight of their offensive to the Ratibor–Neisse area. Moving from Cosel the enemy penetrated to the vicinity of Leobschütz. Simultaneously he moved on Neustadt (Silesia) from west and north. He drove south, by-passing Neisse on the east, and joined up at Neustadt (Silesia) with the Soviet forces attacking from the direction of Cosel. Attacks on Neisse failed; our own attacks on the enemy break-in from the area east of Neisse also failed to make progress. North of Neisse he continued to attack both east and west, his object being to extend the flanks of his break-in between Grottkau and Neisse.

Heavier enemy attacks on Breslau also failed.

The front as far as Stettin was relatively quiet. Violent enemy attacks on our line covering Stettin were repulsed apart from some minor penetrations.

Enemy attacks with close air support on Danzig–Gotenhafen and the remainder of East Prussia were very heavy. Those on Danzig and Gotenhafen in general failed with very heavy enemy losses in men and tanks. He managed to capture a hill west of Gotenhafen. The remains of our East Prussian bridgehead now really consist only of the towns of Braunsberg and Heiligenbeil; here heavy enemy attacks were held in our own artillery positions east of Heiligenbeil. Despite a severe shortage of ammunition 102 Soviet tanks were destroyed in the Heiligenbeil sector. At Königsberg and in Samland it was quieter yesterday.

In Courland an enemy penetration south-west of Frauenburg was dealt with by counter-attack. Soviet elements which had broken through were cut off and annihilated. North-west of Frauenburg the enemy made some small penetrations in the course of violent attacks which brought him to the Libau–Mitau railway.

In the West an attempted enemy crossing in greater strength at Rheinhausen opposite Duisburg was defeated. Otherwise there were no actions of importance on the whole Rhine front as far as the Remagen bridgehead. In the bridgehead the enemy, attacking strongly northwards and southwards, made small gains of ground. In the north the enemy is now in the region north of Königswinter; south of the bridgehead fighting is taking place between Hönningen and Waldbreitbach. The maximum depth of the bridgehead is now about 10 km.

In the battle zone between the Moselle and the Nahe the enemy again made ground. He forced his way into Kreuznach and is now south of the town attacking southwards through Hochstetten and south-west towards Sobernheim where he has reached the Nahe. Enemy forces advancing from west and north-west have reached a line Kirn–Idar–Oberstein–Baumholder–Kusel–St. Wendel. Attacking from south to north enemy forces reached the area south of Zweibrücken. The enemy also attacked in the lower Vosges south of Bitsch and between Reichshofen and Hagenau but there was no appreciable change in the situation.

No special reports from Italy.

On the Eastern Front there was sustained enemy air activity in Hungary and in the Königsberg–Danzig area. Merely in the remains of the East Prussian bridgehead, for instance, and at Königsberg 1200 Soviet close support aircraft were in action. Our own air activity was very considerable. 29 enemy aircraft were shot down.

On the Western Front there was very heavy enemy fighter and fighter-bomber activity—about 1200 fighters— directed mainly on the central Rhine and Moselle. In the communications zone there was sustained fighter and fighter-bomber activity directed mainly on the Rhine–Main area and Münsterland.

About 1200 American four-engined bombers with 700 fighters as escort attacked Berlin in three waves. The attack was made from a height of 18,000–20,000 feet, mostly in good visibility. The whole area of the city was affected with the exception of Wilmersdorf, Steglitz, Spandau and Zehlendorf. The raid was concentrated on the city centre and the northern and north-eastern districts. In the afternoon a British formation of 150 four-engined bombers attacked industrial and transport targets in Bochum. Some 300 twin-engined bombers attacked Mannheim, Ludwigshafen, Darmstadt, Giessen, Siegen, Dortmund and Recklinghausen.

38 "Sturmvögel" (jet fighters) were in action against the raid on Berlin and shot down 15 enemy. Anti-aircraft accounted for a further 7.

During the night the usual harassing raid was made on Berlin and another one on Nuremberg. Some 150 British four-engined bombers attacked transport targets in the Dortmund–Bochum area. About 250 British bombers carried out a raid on Hanau with a diversionary raid on

Kassel. Night fighters shot down 5 four-engined bombers. Anti-aircraft results are not yet to hand.

———————————

The situation in the West is becoming ever more complex. To judge from the map we must reckon that we are about to lose the Saar territory for the very good reason that the enemy is getting behind us. Bingen has already fallen into his hands. We shall have to fight very hard to be able to hold the Rhine front at all, for the situation in the Linz bridgehead has become extraordinarily critical. The Americans are exerting the utmost pressure and our forces surrounding the bridgehead cannot contain an assault with such a weight of metal. The result is that the enemy is continually extending his bridgehead, admittedly not by much but by something all the same. Everyone knows that the question whether we can hold him here or whether the running sore will break out again is decisive.

The Americans, however, have their own special worries too, though unconnected with military equipment and manpower. In the areas they occupy they are finding it not so easy to handle matters as they had imagined. Famine is already setting in. The Americans are in no position to guarantee food supplies or to ration properly the stocks still available. They have no sort of administrative experience and the German administrators who have remained behind are not of the highest quality. The population is offering increasing resistance to the enemy occupation authorities, so the American newspapers are now beginning to lament that, taking a long-term view, chaos and famine on the largest scale are unavoidable in the German districts they occupy. So the enemy bubble is now beginning to burst. The Anglo-Americans are extraordinarily unimaginative and inflexible in the pursuit of their war aims. They understand nothing either of war psychology or administration in wartime. They bravely hurled mud at us when we were occupying large areas both in East and West; the fact remains, however, that the German occupying power provided peace, good order and tolerable living conditions and all this has now been completely upset by the Anglo-Americans. They call it all freedom from want and fear. How is it to be expected, however, that the British of all people would possess the strength and intelligence to deal with extraordinarily difficult problems of administration and rationing in the occupied German districts when they cannot even do it in their own country. A definite food crisis has broken out in England; it is a sort of world phenomenon from which our enemies are not exempt. The meat ration has been further reduced and now stands at one-third of the American ration. The British public is very indignant and the British newspapers give vent to this indignation in the most drastic terms. Morally the Americans come out of this very badly.

Parallel with this the political crisis continues and is now affecting domestic affairs in England. In his speech to the Conservative Party Conference Churchill was trying to pour oil on troubled waters, but he succeeded only in pouring oil on the flames. His speech is being challenged on all sides and it is being indicated to him in both Conservative and Labour Party publicity that, although he may still be acceptable as a war leader, as a peacetime leader he would be rejected by practically all circles concerned. There is no doubt, therefore, that shortly after the end of the war Churchill will be despatched to the wilderness. It is, after all, long-established British practice to tolerate men who amass an exaggerated plenitude of power in wartime but in peacetime to cast them off at once.

To make matters worse Churchill is now having a row with the trade unions and his latest speech has put the cat among the pigeons. The trade unions feel that he has defrauded them. They thought that after the war they would regain freedom to agitate and negotiate, but Churchill does not propose to give it them. He is, after all, basically the old obdurate stubborn Tory who understands nothing whatsoever of social problems and so is about as well suited to our century as a dinosaur.

In France also a cabinet crisis has now broken out; the

211

communists are threatening to resign from the cabinet unless the government purges the administration of so-called fascist elements. It is well known that communists always call everything fascist that is not communist and, under the guise of a struggle against fascism, exterminate all forces opposing bolshevisation of a country in which they have any influence. The Soviets are acting far more vigorously in Bulgaria, where their power is absolute. A series of mass death sentences on generals of the Bulgarian army has just been carried out. The politicians having had their shot in the nape of the neck, it is now the turn of the military. No one is being spared even though he may have flirted with bolshevism when we were still in Bulgaria. Equally, in Rumania the Soviets have no thought in their mind of listening to the British and Americans. On the contrary *Pravda* is now heavily attacking the British press because it has supported Radescu. Radescu is described as a super-fascist of the worst sort who has merited death a thousand times over. In this connection the Soviets are giving the Polish government-in-exile in London one or two hard knocks. Arziszewki* is pictured as a depraved wretch. According to *Pravda* the London Poles are a gang of degenerate landowners rejected by the Polish people. In short *Pravda*'s general tone is one hardly customary even between enemies, let alone between allies.

Maniu† has now resigned as leader of the national-zaranist party under pressure from the Soviets. Maniu was the man who prepared and organised the betrayal of Germany. He is now getting the punishment he has long deserved.

Elections have taken place in Finland, the first to be held in a belligerent country during the war. These elec-

---

* Tomasz Arziszewski, leader of the Polish socialist party, had fought against the Germans in the Polish underground movement till July 1944, when he was brought secretly to London. On 29 November he succeeded Mikolajczyk as Prime Minister of Poland.

† President of the Rumanian National Peasant Party. He had opposed the pro-German dictatorship of Antonescu. He would be executed by the communists in 1947.

tions show an unmistakable increase in the communist vote. The percentage of votes cast was small and they came mainly from bourgeois circles. The Soviets obviously conducted a terror campaign outside the polling stations. The communists scored 328,000 votes against 334,000 for the Social-democrats. The communists are therefore able to compete for the leadership of Finland with the Social-democrats who have been omnipotent in Finnish politics. It will be interesting to see how the Anglo-Americans react. The fact remains however, that the Soviets have been unable to implement their full plans as regards the Finnish elections. They have not organised a Baltic election. Obviously they are too apprehensive of the watch kept on them by the Anglo-Americans.

There is much talk in Moscow now of an imminent advance on Berlin. I assume, however, that the object is to lead us down a false trail once more. The Soviet newspapers state that they will soon be in the Reich capital and that will be the end of the war. On the other hand we must be very much on the watch, since the calm on the Oder front is naturally only an ostensible one. There is no doubt at all that the Soviets are bringing up troops and equipment on this front and could move forward any day.

The Czechs are becoming increasingly impudent. They now regard themselves in the role of freedom fighters. They want to join the whole hostile world now raising its head against us. They have not yet plucked up courage, however, to make an open declaration of war; as we all know, the Czechs are too easy-going and too cowardly for that.

The Pope has made a speech to a large crowd in St. Peter's Square. Significantly he said not a word against bolshevism but inveighed against the false doctrines of nationalism, race and blood. Clearly the Pope is shutting his eyes to the rise of bolshevism all over Europe. He is making the best of it and trying to gain some sort of touch with the mighty Kremlin, at least indirectly.

Meczer, the new Hungarian envoy in Berlin, pays me his inaugural visit. Meczer is a markedly fanatical Hungarian nationalist who, so he tells me, has known Horthy for 40 years. He describes Horthy as a complete opportunist understanding little of the conduct either of war or policy but adept in the field of corruption and lining his own pocket. His family was out-and-out corrupt. His wife was a very bad influence on him. His sons were typical lounge lizards who had completely perverted the Budapest gentry. Concerning the Hungarian nationalist movement Meczer tells me that it is doing its utmost to assert itself in western Hungary which it still controls but at the moment this is being extraordinarily difficult. Nothing is to be expected from the Magyars. They were corpses before they were dead. Meczer told me simply horrifying stories of bolshevist atrocities in recaptured Hungarian towns; they were enough to freeze the blood in one's veins. He added that he had passed a report on the subject to the Papal Nuncio in Berlin; the Nuncio had merely shrugged his shoulders. Apparently, therefore, the Nuncio thinks as does the Pope—that one must not provoke the mighty and should try not to antagonise them whatever dirty business they are up to.

At midday we have a long meeting of the Berlin Defence Council. Hahne, Obermeister of Berlin and the first man to win the Knight's Cross to the War Service Cross, has written me an extraordinarily instructive letter on the design of our tank obstacles. In this letter he pleads for simplification of our obstacles which, he says, if his advice were taken, could be made far more solid and secure. I am having this question carefully examined.

The problem of foreign workers in Berlin is creating extraordinary difficulties. We must try to keep these workers here as long as Berlin industry is in a position to function at all. We want to keep at least the arms industry going even if Berlin is surrounded. On the other hand there are some 100,000 workers from the East in the capital. If they fall into Soviet hands, in two or three days they will have turned into bolshevist infantry fighting against us. In extreme emergency we must therefore try to get at least the workers from the East to safety as quickly as possible.

Burgomaster Steeg* wants to move closer to the city all cattle on the Berlin municipal estates which lies to the east of us. This creates difficulties, however, since the people of Brandenburg will naturally draw far-reaching conclusions and that is anything but desirable at present.

As I have already said, during the recent raid on Berlin some 30 of our jet aircraft were in action for the first time. They are making the enemy prick up his ears. The jets shot down a number of enemy planes, a very promising beginning. Nevertheless the raid on Berlin was, of course, frightful. We have registered about 1000 dead and 65,000 homeless. Traffic in the capital is largely at a standstill. Columns of men make their way to factories and offices on foot. I hope, however, that transport can be got going quickly again, at least to some extent, since stoppages are largely due to the failure of the electricity supply. We must set to work on this.

It is reported to me that the recent air-raid on Würzburg destroyed almost the entire centre of this lovely Main city. All buildings of architectural value fell victim to the flames. So the last beautiful German city still intact has now gone. Thus we say a melancholy farewell to a past which will never return. A world is going down but we all retain a firm faith that a new world will arise from its ashes.

Elsewhere the enemy has again raided Kassel, Hanau and the Ruhr, aiming primarily at transport targets which, as we know, do us the greatest damage.

Yet another report confirms that the standard of luxury both in personnel and material enjoyed by the Luftwaffe cries to high heaven. Investigation of Luftwaffe barracks and messes revealed conditions which beggar description. I can only go on repeating that here is the nigger in our woodpile. Here is where our work of reformation must begin.

Supervision of transport of weapons and ammunition is now being carried out from the most diverse angles, so that

* Burgomaster of Berlin.

the danger of quantities of arms and ammunition remaining parked in marshalling yards has been reduced to a minimum.

State Secretary (retd.) Mussehl sends me a detailed memorandum on his investigation of the Foreign Office. This memorandum shows that in addition to the Foreign Service Ribbentrop has organised a propaganda service in the Foreign Office employing more personnel than there are in the Propaganda Ministry itself. Here is an instance of over-bureaucratisation of our Foreign Service. Above all the mere fact that a propaganda service exists in the Foreign Office shows that there is acute danger of our diplomats concerning themselves more with propaganda, of which they understand nothing, and neglecting foreign policy to an extent detrimental to our conduct of the war. I shall make use of State Secretary Mussehl's memorandum to make most categorical demands on Ribbentrop for a streamlining of his office.

On the subject of low-level propaganda activity a whole series of useful suggestions has been made to me. This low-level activity must now be pursued particularly among our troops in the West. Morale among the troops in the West is in a very bad state and to some extent this is aggravated by the fact that the people are now war-weary. The theory that the Anglo-Americans should be allowed into the country so that at least the greater part of Reich territory should not be occupied by the Soviets is a pernicious one. This theory is incredibly naïve and childish. It influences people's frame of mind, however, and therefore we must now counter it. I intend to initiate a large-scale propaganda campaign. Above all, however, it seems to me essential to iron out the serious differences which public opinion thinks have arisen between the Party and the Wehrmacht. It is typically German that Wehrmacht officers should try to lay the blame for our recent set-backs on the Party, and the political leaders lay the blame on the Wehrmacht. The one accuses the other of neglect of duty and of cowardice. In my view, however, this is no time to look for scapegoats, instead it is our duty to work together unanimously and not display our weaknesses to the enemy. Subsequent historical research will establish where blame lies and where merit.

Disagreeable news comes from the Linz bridgehead again this evening. Fighting is very severe there. The Americans have managed to fight their way 5 km beyond Königswinter. In the Moselle–Saar area there is confused fluctuating fighting from which no firm lines have emerged at present. Our troops are trying to set up anti-tank barriers against the advancing American armoured hordes. This will primarily hold up the enemy advance towards Mainz. East of Merzig he has pushed forward to St. Wendel. He is therefore practically in rear of our Saar front. Counter-measures, which have been initiated, are for the moment of a modest nature. Fighting is still going on in Koblenz. In addition one must reckon that the major enemy offensive in the Arnhem–Wesel area will restart in all its fury in the next few days.

In Hungary we are now completely on the defensive. The enemy was able to gain some more ground north of Lake Velencz. There is no more reference to an offensive by our crack army. In Upper Silesia our troops are fighting their way out of an enemy encirclement. Schörner has launched certain counter-attacks. He maintains that they will succeed and states that the situation is better in reality than it looks on the map. In Breslau and in the Stettin bridgehead enemy attacks were repulsed apart from one or two small penetrations. The situation in Danzig and East Prussia is becoming increasingly critical. A major battle is raging here with undiminished fury. We have suffered no major losses of ground here but the whole area we hold is so narrow that we cannot afford any at all.

In the evening I have a call from Forster, who is on a visit to Berlin. He gives me a most dramatic description of the situation in the Danzig–Gotenhafen area. He does not think that we can hold out there much longer. The evacuation problem has become very difficult for him since he has about 700,000 people in Danzig; he can feed them but can no longer arrange to transport them from the city. With its reduced number of vessels the Navy is in no position to do so.

The Führer has received a number of members of the Hitler Youth who have won the Iron Cross during the fighting in the East. He gave them a warm encouraging speech which we are publishing in a press communiqué.

Otherwise the Führer is up to his eyes in work reestablishing firm fronts, primarily in the West.

This evening we thought that for once the British were giving us a night free of Mosquito raids. Instead they arrived at 4:00 a.m. which, of course, is far more unpleasant for a city with millions of inhabitants. If the British intend to repeat this process every night from now on, they will get the three million inhabitants of Berlin into a state of considerable nervousness.

TUESDAY 20 MARCH 1945

(pp. 1–34, 10 omitted in page-numbering)
Yesterday: Military Situation.
The main weight of fighting in the East is still in Silesia, the Danzig area and East Prussia.

The bolshevists who had penetrated into Neustadt in Silesia advanced farther west towards Ziegenhals where they were held by counter-attack. In addition counter-attacks northwards from Leobschütz were successful and drove the enemy back. Some of our detachments are fighting their way back through enemy-occupied country between Oppeln and Cosel and are reinforcing the new security line which runs east of Neisse, north-east of Ziegenhals, south of Neustadt and east of Leobschütz. Meanwhile, however, in the Oppeln–Ziegenhals battle zone the enemy has gained ground to a depth of 30–40 km on a front of 50–60 km. Violent Soviet attacks between Neisse and Strehlen and also on Breslau were repulsed. Soviet attacks were also broken up at Schwarzwasser. The enemy is reinforcing in the Schrau–Rybnik area. He made repeated heavy attacks on Glogau but with no success at all. Local fighting flared up in the sector from Frankfurt on Oder to Küstrin. Heavy attacks were made on our lines on the east bank of the Oder at Stettin; the enemy broke in on the east and south, reaching the Stettin–Altdamm railway. Altdamm itself was occupied by the enemy. Kolberg too fell into enemy hands. The Soviets stepped up their offensive on Gotenhafen and Danzig and particularly on what remains of East Prussia; attacks were made with great violence, numerous tanks and particularly strong close air support. West of Gotenhafen the Soviets penetrated deeper and they made a small local break-in southwest of Danzig. West and north-west of Heiligenbeil the enemy penetrated more deeply, gaining 3–4 km of ground in very severe fighting with headquarters and supply units. Enemy superiority in the air and in artillery is so overwhelming that resistance in this sector cannot be continued much longer. The enemy continued to attack heavily in Courland but was repulsed apart from minor penetrations either side of Frauenburg.

In Hungary our offensive between Lake Balaton and the Drava made some progress in a southerly direction south-east of Marcali. Enemy attacks in the Sio sector failed, as did an attack on the bridgehead at Aba. The enemy bridgehead over the Sarbitz Canal was eliminated. Strong Soviet attacks north-east of Stuhlweissenburg led to a break-in into the town. Continued Soviet attacks between Felsögalla and Stuhlweissenburg compelled us to withdraw our front to a new line.

On the Western Front the Americans attacked northwards and eastwards from their Linz bridgehead. Along the Rhine they reached a point just north of Oberkassel where a strong counter-attack is in progress to cut off their leading armoured units. East of Honnef the enemy gained ground at several points, capturing a number of localities east of the autobahn. He is now 2–3 km beyond the autobahn on a front of 6 km.

In the Kreuznach area the enemy pushed on farther towards Mainz and his leading troops are now some 15 km south-west of the city and have reached the Mainz–Alzey road. South of Kreuznach the Americans were able to make only minor gains of ground southwards. The enemy advanced east from the Kirn and Baumholder areas reaching Meisenheim and Lauterecken. No special developments in the sector between Kusel, St. Wendel and Saarlautern. East of Saarbrücken all enemy attacks were repulsed. In Alsace our troops occupied the Siegfried Line positions between Weissenburg and Lauterburg. Weissenburg fell into enemy hands. Attacks on Lauterburg were repulsed.

No special reports to hand from the Italian front.

Enemy air activity in the East was again extremely heavy especially in the Danzig–Braunsberg area where 2800 Soviet aircraft were in action. Our air force shot down 34 enemy aircraft.

In the West there was sustained activity by enemy fighter-bombers and twin-engined bombers over the zone of the front and areas in rear.

Some 1300 American four-engined bombers escorted by about 700 fighters raided places in central and southern Germany including Jena, Zwickau, Plauen, Schwarzheide and Espenheim. British specialist air formations attacked bridges and viaducts in the area Lage–Arnsberg. About 150 British four-engined bombers attacked transport and industrial targets in the area Bochum–Dortmund–Reckling-hausen. Some 450 twin-engined bombers raided Münster, Unna, Bad Wildungen, Siegen, Marburg, Giessen, Hanau, Darmstadt and Mannheim. Some 600 American four-engined bombers from Italy bombed industrial and trans-port targets in Mühldorf, Passau and Landshut. About 150 British Mosquitos made the usual harassing raid on Berlin. 70 British four-engined bombers raided Bruck an der Mur. During the night 11 enemy aircraft were shot down.

The following figures are available regarding the raid on Berlin on the 18th: dead 227, wounded 849, missing 450, homeless 65,000; HE bombs dropped 6000 (including 650 delayed action), stick-bomb incendiaries 500,000, liquid fuel incendiaries 3000.

———

Gauleiter Stöhr gives me over the telephone an extraor-dinarily tragic account of the present situation in the Saar territory. According to him the people's morale and that of the Wehrmacht has sunk to an extraordinarily low level—as indeed I had assumed. The fighting troops evince little readiness to hold the defence line and this naturally reacts on the people's attitude. There is nothing to be done with the generals commanding on the Saar front. The Party political leaders are the sole strong firm factor at the moment; even they, however, are to some extent infected with the defeatist spirit. To Stöhr's question what fresh arguments he can adduce for the possibility of a German victory I can unfortunately give no satisfactory answer; I can only advise him to continue with the proven lines of propaganda. I comfort him somewhat and in the end he seems quite happy. It must be remembered that at the moment the Saar territory is subject to uninterrupted air attack, that neither the radio nor the wired broadcasting system are functioning and that the political leaders do not even have the necessary paper to print leaflets. In this area the political leadership can only work with improvised methods, the scope for which is extraordinarily limited.

The Remagen bridge, which has given us so much trouble, is now the subject of widespread polemics between our Western enemies and ourselves. The enemy maintain that the bridge did not collapse on its own but was destroyed by the German Luftwaffe. This seems to me also to be the case. It was hit so often that eventually it was not bearing. The Americans, however, explicitly emphasise that the collapse of the Remagen bridge has constituted no obstacle to their military operations in the Linz bridgehead and this may well be right also, since they are attacking on all sides of the bridgehead continuously.

The Anglo-American press is now admitting with truly stupefying candour what we may expect from the British and Americans if we lose the war. A remark such as that Germany will be nothing but a mummy in the museum of history is quite a tame one. The enemy is indulging in an unparalleled orgy of hate and thirst for destruction. If only for this reason no man of honour can draw any conclusion other than that we must fight as long as there is breath in our bodies.

Ten thousand British scientists are now being trained for the destruction of the whole of German industry. This has been officially admitted by the British Ministry of Labour. The British, who are in such a miserable condition them-

selves, can only be described as sons of chaos. They are
destroying a world of which they themselves are part and
on which they are dependent both nationally and individually and they have no conception of the disastrous consequences which will ensue if they do actually succeed in
unhinging this world. These consequences are already to
be seen to a certain extent among the British public. The
British food position has become extraordinarily critical.
The Americans, as they admit, are in no position to provide, for instance, meat for Britain, since they would then
have to reduce their own meat ration which Roosevelt
clearly has no wish to do. He cannot at the moment afford
further damage to the already low American morale
through restrictions in the food supply. The result is a
definite crisis in Britain which is discussed in a challenging
tone by the London press. *The Economist* even forecasts
imminent chaos if the British government is forced to
reduce the meat ration to the level now planned. Various
British newspapers even go so far as to say that for the
rest of the war Britain's main enemy is not Germany but
the threatened food crisis, not to say threatened famine.
Here is something offering us some hope—a considerable
degree of hope. The food crisis not only in Britain but also
in enemy-occupied regions is reaching a height which is
simply intolerable in the long run. This is therefore one
more reason for the German people continuing to hold on,
no matter where or with what.

The Soviets have much simpler ways of dealing with this
problem. In the vilest manner they simply deport whole
sections of people from one part of the Soviet Union or
from some region they occupy to another. They make
short work of certain nationalities in the process. They state
quite callously, for instance, that certain peoples living in
the regions we once occupied are to be deported to eastern
Russia because they are clearly too heavily imbued with
National-Socialist propaganda. How on earth will the
Soviets treat the German people if they lay hands on them?

Stalin is still pursuing his tactics of putting all the
military forces he possesses in his shop window and leaving

the rear areas comparatively undisturbed. From a report which I have received from Bromberg I see that the enemy is keeping comparatively few troops in the town. On the other hand they stream uninterruptedly up to the front.

Hanke sends me an extraordinarily dramatic and instructive report from Breslau. From it one can see that Hanke is absolutely on top of his job. He is representative of today's most energetic National-Socialist leader. The fighting through the city has turned Breslau into a veritable heap of ruins. But the people of Breslau, defending their city like a fortress, have turned this to good account and are defending every pile of stones with dogged fury. The Soviets are shedding an extraordinary amount of blood in the battle for Breslau. Hanke's letter shows that a remarkable aptitude for improvisation is contributing to the defence of Breslau. He writes to me personally to say that the experience he gained in the struggle for Berlin is being of great use to him.

The result of the Finnish elections looks as if it had given the Social-democrats 52 seats and the communists 51. This means that the communists are almost holding the balance. A left-wing government of Social-democrats and Communists is now in the realm of possibility, giving the Soviets a stepping-stone to the assumption of total power inside Finland. They will certainly not hesitate to exert pressure to bring this left-wing cabinet into existence as soon as possible. Paasiviki is already offering himself as head of this left-wing government. His speech on the day before the election had such a depressing effect on bourgeois circles that—extraordinarily typical of them once more—they largely abstained. This explains the great left-wing victory. Paasiviki will not long enjoy his reputation as the Finnish Kerensky, however. A shot in the nape of the neck awaits him in the background.

Switzerland has now broken off almost all economic relations with us and is totally under the domination of the U.S. economy. Economic exchanges with Switzerland had already been reduced more or less to a minimum.

We have had another wild series of air raids on Reich

territory in the last 24 hours. They can no longer be recorded in detail.

A bleak report has arrived from Würzburg. The recent terror raid on the city destroyed all cultural monuments and 85% of the housing. Würzburg was a city which had hitherto remained immune from enemy air raids. So the last centre of German culture goes down in dust and ashes. If ever we are fortunate enough to have this war behind us, we shall have to begin again from the beginning. There will not be much of the old world left.

We have now at least been sufficiently far-sighted in our precautions that we have made makeshift preparations against gas attack. Gas masks so far produced, however, are sufficient to equip only about 35% of the population. Nevertheless that is better than nothing. Moreover, should the enemy initiate gas warfare, the Führer intends to react with drastic counter-measures.

The *Joachimsthaler* newspaper reports that Göring has shot a bison and presented it to refugees on the road.* The newspaper's report abounds in psychological errors and more or less demonstrates the height of degeneracy reached by Göring and his entourage. I pass this report to the Führer with a note reminding him of the Bourbon princess who, as the mob stormed the Tuileries shouting "Bread!" asked the naïve question: "Why don't the people eat cake?" The Führer seizes on this comment and is extraordinarily sharp with Göring during his briefing conference, following it with a long private interview. One can imagine how he reproached Göring during this interview! But what's the good of that? The public hears nothing about it; the public sees only the débâcle of the Luftwaffe and the incompetence of Göring and his staff in dealing with it. The Führer will not bring himself to appoint a new Commander-in-Chief of the Luftwaffe. From many quarters Dönitz is being proposed for the post and I think this proposal is not too wide of the mark. In re-establishing freedom of movement for our U-boats Dönitz has shown

* For a similar story see Semler, p. 176.

that he can cope even with a serious technical crisis. He is a solid honest worker and he would certainly put the Luftwaffe on its feet again, even if on a reduced scale.

Continuing with the Göring problem, I propose to send the Führer a chapter from Carlyle recounting how Frederick the Great dealt with Prince August Wilhelm of Prussia after he had made a complete mess of the Zittau affair. Frederick took his own brother and successor to the throne to court—an exemplary procedure. He took not the smallest account of the fact that they were related. When August Wilhelm threatened to retire to Dresden, Frederick replied tersely in writing that the next convoy for Dresden was leaving that very evening. As we know August Wilhelm died of a broken heart shortly thereafter but Frederick was in no way disconcerted and felt his conscience clear. I call this truly frederician. This is the way we should act in dealing with the obvious failures in the Party, in the administration or in the Wehrmacht. The Führer's procrastination over the matter of Göring has brought the greatest misfortune on the nation.

I now hand the Führer a memorandum on reform of the Luftwaffe. The Luftwaffe now has only a limited radius of action but it is maintaining an organisation of a size bearing no relation to its tasks. The Luftwaffe's potentialities are extraordinarily limited and its organisation must be scaled down accordingly. Today the Luftwaffe still employs 1½ million men. I think an establishment of 3–400,000 would do quite enough, particularly seeing that much of the anti-aircraft has been relinquished to the front and ammunition stocks for the remaining anti-aircraft are small.

I hold prolonged discussions at Gau level on command of the Reich capital, naturally an increasingly difficult problem in this tense situation. In the first place we have by no means overcome the effects of the recent air raids. As far as transport is concerned we are still on our knees. It will require the sternest efforts to get the transport system working again and it is fundamental to any normal existence in the capital.

Müller from Oslo* has come to Berlin on my instructions to be briefed for his new post as propaganda driving force in the West. He is to be attached to Kesselring and he is given full plenary powers for this assignment by me. His task consists of raising the sinking morale of our troops in the West, making use of every propaganda method and every opportunity for the purpose. I regard Müller as the man who can fulfil this task with energy and initiative.

Developments in the West during the day have been much on the same lines as hitherto. The enemy is exerting extraordinarily heavy pressure in the Kaiserslautern direction. North-east of this point we have held firm: elsewhere, however, the Americans are just outside Oppenheim. The situation in the Saar territory is extraordinarily obscure. It is not possible to establish precisely where the lines run; in fact it is all a thorough mess. In general terms the Siegfried Line has held. But what good is that if it is likely to be taken in rear. North of the Saar territory a confused war of movement is raging. The fronts here cannot be delineated at all. In very general terms it may be said that all fighting is moving back towards the Rhine. The situation in the Remagen bridgehead has worsened again. We have again been driven back both on the northern and southern sides.

In Hungary our offensive has now finally come to naught. Not only have we been forced onto the defensive but our defence has become extraordinarily feeble, resulting in considerable penetrations and losses. The enemy has recaptured the town of Stuhlweissenburg. Admittedly we are making counter-attack after counter-attack but they do not penetrate. In Upper Silesia our forces have in general terms escaped from Soviet encirclement. The front has just held. The enemy is regrouping owing to his severe losses; some regrouping is also in progress on our side.

---

* Georg Wilhelm Müller was Goebbels' personal representative. Hitherto he had been attached to the Reich Commissioner for Norway (Terboven).

Glogau was attacked in great strength but it weathered the storm. Very heavy attacks are also reported from Stettin. The Stettin bridgehead is now becoming increasingly constricted. The same may be said of West and East Prussia. The penetrations made in this area by the enemy would not be significant if we had space behind us but he is pressing us ever farther back against the sea. We were forced to throw in our last reserves both in West and East Prussia in order to hold a firm continuous line, and that with difficulty. In Courland too the enemy has launched another major offensive but here he achieved no success. It is noteworthy that the Soviets are now withdrawing two armies from the Pomeranian and East Prussian areas and throwing them in on the Oder front against Berlin. One may assume, therefore, that the assault on the Reich capital will not be long in coming. We shall have to take the utmost precautions, since, having now secured their flank with the capture of Pomerania, the Soviets will now undoubtedly venture to launch the assault on Berlin.

WEDNESDAY 21 MARCH 1945

(pp. 1–62)
Military Situation.
In contrast to the previous day there were no great changes on the Eastern Front.

In Hungary we improved our positions in a large-scale local offensive southwards from the western end of Lake Balaton; an enemy salient jutting west at Marcali was cut off. Strong enemy attacks on our forward positions reaching out southwards from the eastern tip of Lake Balaton to the Malom Canal were unsuccessful. In the area of the enemy break-in between Felsögalla and Stuhlweissenburg the new line now runs south of Stuhlweissenburg westwards to the eastern spur of the Bakony Forest, thence northwards past Kisbar to the west of Hor, then turns east to Tovaros and thence bends south-east to include Felsögalla whence it follows the old line debouching on the Gran east of Dorog. Here the Soviet penetration has gained them 30–40 km of ground on a front of about 30 km. Bolshevist attempts to widen and deepen the area of their penetration remained fruitless.

In Slovakia the bolshevists gain a little ground at Altsohl in the direction of Neusohl.

In Silesia there was very brisk fighting between Leobschütz and Neisse. Our front was continuously reinforced by German troops fighting their way back on orders. All Soviet attacks on our new line were beaten off. Attacks in somewhat reduced strength on Breslau and Glogau were all repulsed. In the Schwarzwasser area too enemy attacks were in reduced strength and were beaten off without difficulty. Nothing of importance on the adjoining front as far as Stettin. Enemy pressure continued on the Oder front opposite Stettin and our forces were withdrawn to the left bank of the Oder at Stettin to save manpower.

The day's fighting again centred on the Gotenhafen–Danzig area and the western sector of the East Prussian Bridgehead. In the Danzig–Gotenhafen sector the enemy made only little progress towards Gotenhafen at the price of very heavy casualties; on the other hand in equally heavy attacks he narrowed the East Prussian bridgehead considerably. Braunsberg fell into enemy hands. The line now runs roughly east between Braunsberg and Heiligenbeil and then south of Heiligenbeil turns north-east. North of Heiligenbeil the enemy made a deep penetration bringing him almost to the Frisches Haff; a concentrated counter-attack recaptured the lost ground. In Courland the enemy made battalion- and regimental-strength attacks along almost the whole front; they were again mainly concentrated north-east of Frauenburg. Some of the leading enemy troops who had advanced across the Libau–Mitau railway were cut off and annihilated in a converging counter-attack.

On the Western Front fighting was again very violent in the Remagen bridgehead. The enemy is attacking in strength and continuously but is meeting considerable German resistance. Nevertheless the Americans succeeded in gaining ground in both the northern and southern parts of the bridgehead. The enemy managed to retain Oberkassel. East of the bridgehead he reached Oberpleis. The autobahn has now been crossed on a front of 8 km to a depth of 4–5 km. In the south the enemy advanced along the Rhine highway as far as Rheinbrohl where one of our combat groups is encircled. Severe street fighting continues in Koblenz; at this point we still retain a bridgehead on the left bank of the Rhine which is now being attacked by the enemy. Niederlahnstein is under heavy artillery fire. Meanwhile the enemy reached the Mainz–Alzey road on a broad front and advanced east through Alzey. From the Kreuznach area the enemy swung north and reached the neighbourhood of Bingen. Three enemy tanks which entered Bingen were destroyed. Moving from Soberrhein and Weisenheim the enemy reached Kaiserslautern. Fighting is going on in Kaiserslautern. West of Kaiserslautern a small tongue, bounded on the south by the Siegfried Line, reaches out to Saarlautern and Saarbrücken. Enemy detachments were encircled south-east of St. Wendel. Enemy attacks on the Siegfried Line between Saarbrücken, Zweibrücken, Weissenburg and Lauterburg were fruitless.

There was somewhat brisker British activity in Italy yesterday.

In the East enemy air activity was concentrated on the Danzig–Gotenhafen and East Prussian areas where numerous Soviet close-support aircraft were in action. 17 Soviet aircraft were shot down.

There were sustained air raids over Reich territory yesterday. Some 400 British four-engined bombers attacked the marshalling yards at Hamm together with industrial and transport targets in the Recklinghausen area. A smaller British specialist formation of 30 aircraft was in action against bridges in the Nienburg area. Hits have not been reported. About 550 American bombers escorted by 500 fighters attacked primarily industrial and transport targets in Hemmingstedt. Throughout the day fighter-bombers, low-flying aircraft and twin-engined bomber formations were very active over the whole western half of the Reich concentrating on Münsterland, the Ruhr, the Rhine–Main area and the general area of Stuttgart. Some 600 four-engined bombers from Italy escorted by about 300 fighters raided Wels, Vienna and its environs. Detached formations raided transport targets in Amstetten, Wiener Neustadt and Klagenfurt. Fighters and anti-aircraft shot down 20 enemy aircraft in all.

During the night 70 Mosquitos made their harassing raid on Berlin. 30 Mosquitos were over Bremen and another 15 over Hemmingstedt. In addition there was much long-range night fighter activity over the whole western half of the Reich. Later in the night 400 British four-engined bombers attacked industrial targets in Böhlen and Espenheim. Bombs were also dropped in the Altenburg and Halle areas. Fighters and anti-aircraft shot down 15 enemy during the night.

Our enemies now look upon the city of Köln as a model example of the difficulties facing them in the west German regions they occupy. A number of highly unfavourable circumstances have arisen giving food for thought regarding future developments. Authoritative British observers, for instance, state that there is now a danger of Germany becoming Europe's fever-spot and preventing peace and quiet returning to this part of the world for decades. We shall do all we can to promote this development since it offers us a considerable opportunity. We must not allow our continent to solidify under Anglo-American leadership. On the contrary, the worse things are for us militarily, the more will the peoples of the continent realise that a new order in Europe is only possible under German leadership.

An extraordinarily hostile attitude is now emerging in the enemy-occupied regions, as I had foreseen and foretold. The people only need a good sleep and release from the scourge of the air war in order to come to themselves again. Once they have realised the ignominy of occupation and rations have fallen below the subsistence level, they will turn rebellious against the occupying powers. In addition there is the total failure of the sanitary arrangements so that a typhus epidemic has already broken out in Köln, over which Anglo-American publicity is positively jubilant. Merely to prevent their own soldiers being infected—so they say—they propose to take certain counter-measures.

At certain points on the Western Front our resistance still remains extraordinarily stiff; the British in particular are very plaintive on the subject. They had thought that they would now have an easy time and charge on into Reich territory across the Rhine. Now they are realising that that is out of the question.

True British and American intentions regarding the Rhine region are clear from their statements that they propose to form an independent Rhineland state. In other words they propose to add one more to the errors of 1918, 1919 and 1920. But just as these attempts failed after the First World War, so they will fail in this Second World War, particularly since the German people are now ruled from Berlin not by a democratic republican Jewish government but by a National-Socialist one.

Disturbing news comes from America to the effect that the Americans have copied our V2 weapons and from 1 April will be in a position to fire them at Germany. That would be the last straw. It would mean that the last German invention produced in this war would be turned against us. One can imagine the effect on the German people if German territory was under fire from V2s.*

A long treatise on present political opinion in America has been submitted to me. It seems to me to contain much that is credible; it explains that in general terms the Americans are uninterested in the continent of Europe; they merely wish to ensure that it does not unite under a single power because they fear that that would result in fierce economic competition. The Americans have no political aspirations in Europe. On the one hand they do not want to see a strong Germany but on the other they do not want too strong a Soviet Union; the moment, therefore, that the Soviet Union sets about trying to bring the whole European continent under its sway, the Americans will oppose them energetically. American friction with Britain is of a secondary nature only. It creates far more of a sensation in the press that it really deserves. The Americans have taken it into their heads to bring about world peace based on American economic imperialism. In addition they harbour strong messianic aspirations, particularly Roosevelt himself who is urged on by his Jews for obvious reasons. Roosevelt's policy has been extraordinarily adroit tactically and he has succeeded in turning himself from a

* See above p. 71.

peace President into a war President without the Americans taking him to task for it. American national pride has increased enormously during the war, primarily because the Americans now have strong military forces in action all over the world and they have achieved considerable operational success. For the moment at least bolshevism presents no threat to the Americans; it would be regarded as un-American and therefore rejected.

England is quite different. In England the Commune is now noticeably beginning to stir. It cannot yet be over-active in public under its real name, but by roundabout means it is trying to bore its way into the British working masses, primarily by infiltrating the trade unions. A whole series of strikes in recent weeks and months were definitely due to communist influence. Churchill's speech to the Conservative Party Conference appeased the Conservatives in so far as he largely came out against all plans for socialisation. Churchill is basically a confirmed Tory, particularly in his economic views. He has been condemned by fate to put bolshevism in the saddle in Europe. In a statement to the Commons Churchill had to defend the present food situation in Britain. He attempted to disarm criticism of the Americans over this question but was nevertheless forced to admit that from April onwards the food position in Britain would be very critical.

I hear from Japan that the air raids so far carried out by the Americans have achieved considerable success. Admittedly the Japanese had made themselves to a certain extent invulnerable as far as war potential is concerned by largely dispersing their arms industry into the country. Nevertheless the damage done to civilian quarters of Japanese cities by the American raids is already very considerable. Japan therefore seems to be facing a development similar to that facing us some two years ago. It is to be hoped that the damage will teach the Japanese something and that they will take the necessary counter-measures.

The Soviets are going quietly on deporting Poles to the interior of Russia. They take not the smallest notice of the

Anglo-Americans. Discussions now going on in Moscow about a reconstruction of the Polish government have so far been unsuccessful. At the Yalta Conference, therefore, as we have long suspected, Stalin merely made a gesture to Churchill and Roosevelt. In fact he has no thought of making any change in the Lublin Committee.

Fake trials of national leaders are now being staged in Bucharest on the Sofia model. Some 250 Rumanians who collaborated with us, including Marshal Antonescu, have been brought before a special tribunal. It is to be hoped that his namesake Mihail Antonescu* is among them since if anyone deserves to be shot it is he.

The Soviets are now demanding more severe judicial procedure in Finland. So far the so-called Finnish war criminals have been dealt with comparatively leniently, but the Kremlin now seems to have had enough of this.

Fresh news comes from Moscow. The Kremlin has revoked its treaty of friendship and non-aggression with Turkey. The reason given is extraordinarily interesting and original. The Kremlin declares that it is interested in retaining a solid relationship of friendship with Turkey; circumstances have changed with the war, however, and so the relationship between the Soviet Union and Turkey must be revised accordingly. Expressed differently this means that Stalin thinks the moment has now come to lay hands on the Dardanelles. Turkey has therefore reaped no advantage from declaring war on us at the Anglo-American behest and consequently appearing as a belligerent power. The Kremlin has not allowed itself to be affected by this at all.

For the moment the situation on the Eastern Front gives an impression of greater solidity. I hear that Himmler wishes to give up his Army Group Vistula and he should do so. Himmler's job, after all, was merely to plug a hole

---

* Mihail Antonescu was Foreign Minister in Marshal Ion Antonescu's government and had made secret approaches to the West. Both Ion and Mihail Antonescu were executed in 1946. In Bulgaria, the Regent, Prince Kyril, and other politicians who had collaborated with the Germans, had already been tried and executed.

in the area of Army Group Vistula as best he could. Unfortunately he allowed himself to be diverted by the quest for military laurels, in which, however, he failed totally. He can only tarnish his good political reputation this way.

The number killed in air raids up to December inclusive is reported as 353,000—a horrifying figure which becomes even more terrible when one adds the 457,000 wounded. This is a war within a war, sometimes more frightful than the war at the front. The homeless are simply innumerable. The air war has turned the Reich into one great heap of ruins. In the last 24 hours a further crazy series of air raids has been reported, particularly on the west of the Reich.

I have before me a shattering report by Gauleiter Hoffmann from Westphalia South. He says that public life is no longer possible in his Gau. Traffic is paralysed and people can no longer move about on the streets. The economy is at a standstill. Coal is neither being produced nor moved. Even the smallest defensive measures are nowhere to be seen. One can imagine the effect on the people's morale. Hoffmann is quite right when he says that people would be happy if at least some trace of defensive activity could be seen. But this is not the case. The memorandum is one long indictment of Göring and the Luftwaffe. It will now be submitted to the Führer.

I have a long talk with Müller from Oslo about his mission in the West.* I give him full plenary powers, in particular authority to give instructions direct to Reich Propaganda Offices throughout the West. I make it clear to him that he cannot expect provision of large-scale additional resources from Berlin. He must try to help himself by improvising; in my view, however, this will be an advantage rather than the reverse for the propaganda which he has to issue. His previous activities have given him so much experience in this field that it will not be difficult for him to make do with makeshifts. Müller is tackling his task with great élan. I think he will get on top of it.

* See above p. 227.

At midday I receive 20 members of the Hitler Youth who have won the Iron Cross during the fighting in the East. They make an excellent impression. A people which has youngsters like this available at a time like this cannot, according to the laws of history, go under.

The latest film statistics from the various Gaus are still very good despite all the difficulties. It is surprising that the German people still wants to go to the cinema at all. Nevertheless in general terms this is the case.

The evening's report on the day's military development shows that, for all practical purposes, we have lost the Saar. Our troops could not be kept there any longer and have now had to be withdrawn. Loss of the Saar territory will of course have the most serious economic consequences. It means the loss of our last intact coalfield. One can imagine what that implies. The situation in the Linz bridgehead has also become definitely critical. Admittedly the Americans have not broken through but they are keeping up pressure on all sides of the bridgehead and there is always the danger that they will break through the front somewhere.

In the East fighting flows back and forth all the time but with no major change in the situation.

In the evening I paid a couple of hours' visit to the Reich Chancellery to have another exhaustive talk with the Führer. I first had an interview with Hewel who briefed me on the Foreign Office's present efforts to start talks with any one of our enemies. As we know, Hesse's attempt in Stockholm failed totally. Hesse 'had anyway behaved thoroughly ineptly. He never negotiated direct with the British, only through certain Swedes whom he knew, though they did pass on his views direct to the British. The British envoy in Stockholm was prepared to discuss direct with Hesse but Hesse could not pluck up courage to do so. In this connection it is interesting that all reference to Hesse's talks ceased in England within 24 hours since Churchill cannot at present do with any peace talk in view of the war-weariness of the whole British people.

At the moment there is a high-ranking man from the Soviet Union in Stockholm and he has expressed a wish to enter into talks with a German. In principle we need not be averse to making use of such an opportunity. Nevertheless the present moment is as bad a choice as it could be. I think, however, that it would be as well at least to talk to the Soviet Union's representative. But the Führer does not wish to. The Führer thinks that for the present it would be a sign of weakness if we were to meet the enemy's wishes on this point. My view is that the enemy knows that we are weak anyway and that readiness to negotiate will not tell him anything he does not know already. But the Führer will not be persuaded. He thinks that talks with a leading Soviet representative would merely encourage the British and Americans to be even more forthcoming to Stalin and negotiations would end in a complete flop. Maybe the Führer is right. He has always had a good feel for these matters and we can entrust ourselves to him completely. It is a pity, however, that in this critical situation we have to go on waiting without knowing whither military developments will lead us in the next two or three weeks.

I make no bones about it to Hewel that it is primarily Ribbentrop's fault that we have been plunged into such a situation. He ought to have made such proposals to the Führer on top priority far sooner than this, at a time when we still had something to throw into the scales in negotiation. Ribbentrop, however, remained rigid and obstinate. He neither sought nor found allies among his colleagues and so got nowhere when he put the question to the Führer; the first time he was turned down he hauled down his flag.

Hewel voiced extraordinarily severe criticism of the conduct of the German Luftwaffe. What he said on this subject is well known and produces nothing new. He is very unhappy, however, that the Führer cannot be persuaded to make some change in the command of the Luftwaffe. This is in fact lamentable, for the psychological effect on the Luftwaffe itself of a personnel change at command level would be colossal.

I then have a two-hour talk with the Führer who makes a very weary and worn-out impression on me after all the exertion and agitation of recent days. His general attitude of mind, however, is still exemplary. He is a shining example of steadfastness of spirit to all his staff. One has the impression that he is only kept going by his iron will. The impression this makes on someone who has been associated with him for years is really moving.

The Führer is somewhat despairing about military developments. In particular he had not thought that we should reach such an extraordinarily calamitous situation in the West. He tells me that the course of events has vexed him very much. Even my historical examples do not make much impression on him this time.

As far as the West is concerned, the Führer admits frankly that in practice the Saar territory can no longer be held and that we must evacuate it. Kesselring was appointed too late and he could not do much to change the course of events. The Führer thinks that, despite 20 July, a certain clique of traitors is still active in the West. This can be the only explanation for the fact that the extremely heavily fortified region of Trier fell into enemy hands without a fight. I dispute this. I think that the Führer is explaining away these events too easily. I think that instead this can be ascribed to the fact that our troops and their commander no longer have the will to fight, that they have lost all courage because they have to submit in so depressing a fashion to enemy air superiority every day and every night, so that they can no longer see any prospect of victory. The Führer, on the other hand, is of the opinion that certain military commanders are still toying with a plan for making common cause with the Western Allies against the Soviets and that they are trying to bring this plan about by giving way. However idiotic and absurd this plan may seem, it is nevertheless possible that it has entered the heads of some of our politically inexperienced military commanders.

Rundstedt's leadership in the West was definitely bad. Rundstedt is too old and too inflexible. The Führer had

239

actually wanted to remove him months ago and replace him
by Kesselring; then, however, Kesselring unfortunately had
a car accident which kept him from active command for
weeks. The Führer did not wish to appoint Model in place
of Rundstedt because he thought him too impetuous and
impulsive, which is in fact the case.

I suggest to the Führer that military developments in the
West can under no circumstances be allowed to proceed on
present lines. If, for instance, the Americans succeed in
breaking out of the Linz bridgehead, we should be plunged
into a tragic situation. The Führer has opposed the enemy's
repeated attempts to break out with everything he has
available. He thinks, moreover, that Model will succeed in
dealing with the situation. In any case no more can be
done than has been done. The Führer himself, however,
has become somewhat doubtful whether the bridgehead
can be contained in the long run. Admittedly the Americans
have suffered extraordinarily severe casualties but they can
afford them at the moment. One shudders to think that
neglect of their duty by one or two officers has led to such
a threat; it is all the more justifiable that they were condemned to death by court martial and shot.

I submit urgently to the Führer that our troops in the
West are no longer fighting properly. Their morale has
suffered badly and as a result they no longer have the urge
to resist so essential in this critical situation. The morale
of the population has also naturally sunk very low, if it
has not already reached zero. Of course it would rise again
the moment we could report any sort of military success
in the West. The people now want to see at least some
glimmer of light on the dark horizon of this war. But at
the moment such a thing is nowhere to be seen.

In the enemy-occupied areas a certain change of mood
is already noticeable and it comes at the moment when stern
cruel facts are making themselves felt. Hunger has made
people think. The Americans are in no position to deal with
the rationing problem as we did because there must be a
system of administration and punishment in the background

and this the Americans cannot impose. As a result a black market is beginning to appear, in sharp contrast to the orderly arrangements which we had hitherto maintained in the food market.

The Führer considers the best piece of recent news to be that at the Yalta Conference Roosevelt conceded to Stalin that German prisoners from the West should be deported to the Soviet Union as slave labour. These and similar reports will undoubtedly contribute to raising the fighting morale of our troops, for we must, after all, stand somewhere in the West. It is quite intolerable that movement in the West should remain fluid. If we now lose the Saar territory, we have no alternative but to seek to defend the Rhine front as a whole. Here again there is this miserable Linz bridgehead which is an obstacle to the attainment of this objective.

Again and again we return to the starting-point of our conversation. Our whole military predicament is due to enemy air superiority. Co-ordinated conduct of the war is no longer in practice possible in the Reich. The necessary transport and communications are no longer available to us. Not only our cities but also our industry have largely been demolished. The result is a deep dent in German war morale. People in the western provinces no longer get any sleep and so become nervous, hysterical and irritable. The results can be calculated on the fingers of one hand. In short the situation has become more or less intolerable and we must do our utmost to score a victory, even if only a modest one, in some military field and so bring the people to heel again.

Then once more my talk with the Führer turns into an exhaustive discussion of the air war. The Führer has just had an interview with Colonel Baumbach who briefed him on our new jet aircraft. The Führer now places extraordinary hopes on these jet aircraft. He even refers to them as instruments of German destiny. He thinks that with these aircraft it should be possible to overcome the enemy's air superiority at least defensively. Even he, however, adds that he hopes they have not come too late. It is shortly before twelve—if the hands of the clock have not already passed midnight.

Everything the Führer says about the Luftwaffe is one long indictment of Göring. Yet he cannot bring himself to take a decision about Göring personally. As a result his complainings are thoroughly unsatisfactory since they lead to no follow-up action. I tell him as much quite frankly. The people do not know what the Führer thinks of the Luftwaffe. Consequently his grievances against the Luftwaffe are of no psychological value. But the Führer remains obdurate in his point of view. I do not succeed in achieving anything whatsoever with him. For the moment he still clings to Göring, although his criticisms of him as a man and as regards his work are sharper than anything I have ever heard him say about any member of his staff. His criticism was voiced in the severest terms but, as I have said, for the present nothing eventuates as a result. I remind the Führer how Frederick the Great acted in such cases, how he dealt with August Wilhelm, his own brother and successor to the Prussian throne, when he brought his army back from Zittau in a wretched state. Even this example, however, fails to impress the Führer. He says that circumstances in the Seven Years War were different from those of today and that in the present phase of the war he cannot afford to make so sweeping a change of personnel. In addition he has no one available who could replace Göring. That is just not true. We have at least a dozen men who would certainly do better than Göring is doing today.

The Führer then refers to the unfortunate affair of the bison shot by Göring for the benefit of evacuees.* This business has stirred up a great deal of mud and caused Göring much embarrassment. Even this, however, has not served to get things on the move. There is no need to emphasise further what the Führer thinks of Göring as a man. He has now just gone off with two special trains to

* See above p. 225.

visit his wife in the Obersalzberg. It is horrifying to think that the man responsible for the German Luftwaffe can now find the time to attend to his personal affairs. The Führer is highly critical of Gritzbach, Göring's personal adviser who, he says, lacks any form of psychological refinement; he is equally critical of Ondarza, Göring's doctor, who is a typical dandy and gigolo and whom I would not tolerate around me for five minutes.

Everything the Führer says is quite right. Yet again, however, it must be emphasised that it produces no effect since no consequences are drawn therefrom.

The Führer was much encouraged by his interview with Colonel Baumbach. He places the greatest hopes on the new jet aircraft. During this month 500 will be produced and next month 1000. Runways are being laid using a very large labour force. All this the Führer has to arrange personally since Göring hardly bothers any more. The Führer's thoughts continually revolve around the question whether these aircraft have not come too late for them to make any impact. The enemy is proving completely inexorable in aerial warfare. He is going all out, disregarding material losses but conserving his manpower. The effects of the air war are obvious not only on the civil population but also on the men of the Luftwaffe. Neglect, for which Göring is to blame, is destroying primarily his own arm of the service.

Everything the Führer says in this connection is already known to me. They are the well-worn complaints invariably ending in the statement that Göring is totally inadequate and incompetent but that no successor for him can be found and, even if he were, no successor can be nominated. I make the proposal that Dönitz be put in his place, but the Führer thinks that Dönitz has so much to do with his U-boats that he could not cope with the Luftwaffe at the same time.

I cite to the Führer certain examples of the exaggerated luxury in which the Luftwaffe lives. As a result of this luxury our fighter pilots have become pampered. They spend more time in the mess than on training and have become timorous and useless as a result of good living. The Führer thinks that the pilots of our new jet aircraft will be more suitable since they will be in action against the enemy more than our fighters. The Führer is confirmed in his opinion by the fact that people like Baumbach, who has hitherto been sharply opposed to the strategy of the Luftwaffe, are now placing their hopes in these jet aircraft. One fortunate feature of the new jet aircraft is that they do not require high-grade fuel but can fly practically on dirty water. As a result we shall soon be on top of the fuel problem. The peculiar logic of air force technical development dictates that the speed of petrol-driven aircraft cannot be increased further but that the new type of jet aircraft can reach a speed 200 km greater.

The Führer is very angry at the fact that our fighters are now using good weather as an excuse for failure to take off. They always have new excuses for failing to go into action against the enemy. The reason is that the whole Service is corrupt and it is corrupt because its Commander-in-Chief is corrupt.

I rage inwardly when I think that, despite all the good reasons and arguments, it is not possible to persuade the Führer to make a change here. But what am I to do? I cannot do more than go on tirelessly urging the Führer and bringing my criticism to his notice. Inwardly I am facing a severe crisis of conscience. I know well that the Luftwaffe can never be revived under Göring. Equally I know well that the Luftwaffe will lead to the loss of the war and the ruin of the German people if it continues to be run as it is at present. I know well that our fronts cannot be defended unless we can sweep the skies clear . . . [11 lines illegible] . . . even Sepp Dietrich is not in the top class. He is a good troop commander but no strategist.

The Führer is extraordinarily pleased with the anti-bolshevist propaganda we are issuing. It has already had the effect of putting our troops in the East back into comparatively good form.

My proposal to bolster the front by stationing replacement units in the rear areas has made a great impact on the Führer. He has now given instructions that all rear areas be furnished with replacement units and they are already on the move. So one of my ideas about the conduct of total war has been implemented one hundred per cent.

I tell the Führer about his visit to Ninth Army and the report made to me on the subject by Captain Krüger.* The Führer is very pleased with this report. I also tell him of the visit I received this morning from Hitler Youth winners of the Iron Cross. These youngsters had made a very deep and gratifying impression on the Führer too.

As far as the political situation is concerned, the Führer remains firm in his view that the turning point of the war will come in some way this year. The enemy coalition will break up whatever happens; the only question is whether it does so before we are flat on the floor or only after we are flat. Under all circumstances, therefore, we must ensure that no military disaster takes place before this moment arrives.

The Soviet pressure on Turkey gives the Führer further hope, since this pressure is undoubtedly most unwelcome to the British, if not to the Americans as well.

People in Britain are at the moment preoccupied with an extraordinary food crisis, an indication that internal conditions in England are much worse than we had generally thought. The British are being taken in, not only by the Soviets but also by the Americans. The Führer has heard, for instance, that Franco proposes to declare war on Japan in order to gain a good mark from America. At heart Franco realises that it is now no good playing the British card and he is relying more on America.

As far as the hoped-for collapse of the enemy coalition is concerned, the Führer thinks that this is more likely to come from Stalin than from Churchill and Roosevelt. Stalin is a marked realist and so from our point of view there is more to be done with him than the others. The Führer is inclined to think that the San Francisco Conference will never take place. The conflict in the enemy

* See above p. 179.

camp will have become so intense by that time that they will not dare parade their differences. I think this view is illusory—I believe that the San Francisco Conference will take place all the same—nevertheless it is possible that it will end in a colossal disaster.

In all these talks about politics we invariably come back to our starting point: that we must hold firm at the front and if possible score a victory in order to start talking to the enemy. The prior condition for this, however, is that we sweep our skies clear. This the Führer admits; the final conclusion, however, is the one he still contests, namely that we can only sweep the sky clear if we have a new Commander-in-Chief of the Luftwaffe.

Towards the end of our talk Speer arrives. He has been in the West and has a fearful story to tell. It is no longer possible to drive along country roads in the West without being attacked by fighter-bombers. Enemy air superiority is such that we cannot even move by car along our own country roads.

While we are talking to the Führer British Mosquitos raid the capital yet again.

When I reach home the house is in total darkness. The electricity supply has been damaged again. A gloomy and fairly melancholy evening. Magda has gone to Dresden to visit Frau von Arent. At such times one can get really depressed, mainly when one mulls over and over the question: What am I to do in order to insist on what I know to be right? I feel a great moral and national obligation towards the German people because I am one of the few who still has the Führer's ear. Every use must be made of such an opportunity. But no one can do more than I am doing.

I spoke to the Führer today in totally frank terms such as I have seldom in my life used to him before. But, as I have said, with no sign of success at the moment.

THURSDAY 22 MARCH 1945

(pp. 1–29, 9 and 17 omitted in page-numbering)
Military Situation.

On the Eastern Front the main centres of activity were in Hungary, the Danzig area, as Heiligenbeil and in Courland.

In Hungary the Bolshevists reinforced the areas where they had penetrated and extended the front of their offensive. At the eastern corner of Lake Balaton they reached the Siofok–Stuhlweissenburg railway. West of Stuhlweissenburg and between that place and Hor in the Bakony Forest the enemy advanced about 10 km. North of Kisber he crossed the Kisber–Komorn railway and north of Tovaros reached the Raab–Budapest road and railway. The Soviets attacked our forward positions south of the Danube capturing Gran. North of the Danube they were able to establish themselves on the west bank of the Gran.

In Slovakia the enemy succeeded in penetrating to a depth of 2 km south of Neusohl.

The new front line was further reinforced between Leobschütz and Neisse. Attacks on the new line were repulsed as were those on Breslau and Glogau.

Soviet reconnoitring patrols advanced on either side of Frankfurt on Oder but achieved nothing.

Enemy attacks on Danzig, Gotenhafen and Heiligenbeil, again with strong close air support, were extraordinarily heavy. Losses on both sides were considerable. Both bridgeheads were further reduced by local break-ins to a depth of 1–1½ kms.

In Courland the enemy reinforced his major offensive on either side of Frauenburg. About 1000 Soviet aircraft were in action in support of his ground troops. In general, however, all attacks were repulsed.

In the West the Americans succeeded in extending their Rhine bridgehead somewhat northwards, southwards and eastwards. In the north the enemy moved through Ober-kassel and reached the vicinity of Siegburg. In the hills east of Remagen they were able to advance to the valley of the Wied. Enemy detachments advancing across the Wied were thrown back at once. In the south of the bridgehead the enemy made a small penetration towards Neuwied; he was held about 6 km north-west of Neuwied. It is suspected that the enemy intends to move north from the bridgehead towards the Ruhr and that, in co-ordination with this, air-borne landings will be made north of the Ruhr. Airborne landings in the Erft area are also considered possible.

Yesterday's fighting centred on the Rheinhesse area, where the enemy made considerable gains of ground. Fight-ing is still going on in Bingen. The enemy has penetrated into the western suburbs of Mainz. Farther south there is still a German bridgehead at Obenheim but it is now under pressure. Nierstein fell into enemy hands. Street fighting is going on in Worms. Moving through Franken-thal the enemy penetrated into Oppau reaching the hydro-genation plant. He is in the western suburbs of Ludwigs-hafen where he is held up by a newly constructed German switch position. House-to-house fighting is also taking place in Neustadt and Bad Dürkheim. Reports, so far unconfirmed, state that leading enemy tanks are in Ann-weiler. Our narrow salient jutting west as far as Saar-lautern and Saarbrücken is being evacuated on orders.

No special operations took place in Italy.

Enemy air activity was very extensive both over the fronts and over Reich territory. Some 1100 American four-engined bombers attacked Plauen and Reichenbach. A smaller British formation raided the Bremen and Münster areas. During the afternoon 250 four-engined bombers attacked targets in the Rheine area and 120 American four-engined bombers raided Mülheim in the Ruhr. About 600 American four-engined bombers from

Italy attacked Vienna, Graz, Bruck an der Mur and Villach. Bombs were also dropped in Bavaria. Throughout the day some [figures illegible] twin-engined bombers and fighters were active over the whole western half of the Reich concentrating mainly on transport targets [nearly 4 lines illegible]. Mosquitos were over Bremen . . . 200 British four-engined bombers raided Hamburg and some 150 British four-engined bombers the Witten–Langendreer area. Thirty-one "Sturmvögel" shot down 11 enemy. Anti-aircraft shot down 20 enemy aircraft. During the night 28 fighters were in action and shot down 6 of the enemy. Anti-aircraft shot down 4 enemy aircraft during the night.

The military situation both in East and West has become extraordinarily critical; during the course of the last 24 hours it has changed noticeably to our disadvantage. Not only are we making no progress in Hungary but the enemy has launched a counter-attack on a broad front and our previous gains of ground have largely become illusory. In places he has passed our starting line. So the Führer's plans to make good the whole line of the Danube have come to nothing and we must now take the greatest care that we do not lose our Rumanian* oilfields as well. That would have the most disastrous consequences for the whole German conduct of the war.

In the Berlin area the Soviets have now launched an admittedly local but nevertheless extraordinarily violent attack in an attempt to cut off our Küstrin bridgehead. As a result I cannot make my planned visit to 51 Corps. General Busse asks for the visit to be postponed until next week since the situation is very obscure at the moment in the area I was to visit and every officer is urgently needed.

As far as the West is concerned, the situation in the bridgehead has become extraordinarily menacing. Despite

* Presumably a slip for Hungarian oilfields. See below p. 300.

our large-scale counter-measures the Americans are continuously extending the bridgehead in all directions. Our
counter-measures could not get under way because our
lines were under uninterrupted attack by enemy fighter-
bombers. So here again the Luftwaffe is to blame for the
extraordinary crisis with which we are faced at the moment.
The threat remains that the Americans may succeed in
breaking out of the bridgehead and one can imagine what
the consequences of that would be for us. A flood of
material concentrated in this running sore would then pour
out over the surrounding countryside. In such an eventual-
ity we should be unable to stop the enemy's armoured
thrusts. Everything depends, therefore, on whether the
Americans, who have so far scored only tactical victories,
can achieve a break-through. Naturally everything is being
done on our side to prevent this but the ratio of forces is
such that the situation is on a knife-edge, to say nothing
of the position in the Rhine–Saar area. Here our troops
are conducting a desperate rear-guard action since otherwise they run the risk of being completely cut off. A fortnight ago towns now being mentioned in the OKW report
would not have been in the news even in one's wildest
dreams, an indication of the extraordinarily severe crisis
which has developed for us in the West. The Anglo-
Americans have good reason to think of themselves at the
height of their triumph. Reuters are already saying that the
war's finale is now being played. Everything takes time,
however, and it is not true to say that the columns of
refugees allegedly hurrying eastwards from the West and
westwards from the East are proving such an obstacle to
military movement that we are no longer in a position to
make any dispositions. The reasons are quite different. The
main one is that the transport system, particularly in the
West, has been smashed so completely that it is practically
impossible to move troops by rail on any even semi-
reliable time-table. Whether the battle of Remagen will
help the Americans—as they say it will—to establish themselves on a broad front on the right bank of the Rhine,
depends—as I have already said—on a number of other

eventualities. In any case it is clear that we are offering extraordinarily stubborn resistance at this point. Model is on the spot himself to direct operations.

Our Western enemies now realise that at present there is no question of a collapse in morale on the part either of the German people or the German front.

My war propaganda is now being eulogised quite openly in London. It is being said that it is the most exemplary of all the war efforts being made anywhere today and that it is primarily responsible for the fact that German resistance is so much in evidence, even though on a reduced and enfeebled scale.

In rear of the Anglo-American front, of course, the outlook is miserable. Not much is to be heard from the German regions at present because the enemy has imposed a news black-out. Reading the news from France, however, one can more or less imagine what things are like. The French people are facing sheer starvation. Processions wend their way through every city protesting against the government but also against Anglo-American occupation. But what is the good of that? If there is no bread available, they can demonstrate as much as they like; they will not be rescued from the consequences of the bread shortage, however.

In England too the food crisis has now reached most serious proportions. Public opinion is furious over the forthcoming reductions in the ration now being promised the British people. Churchill's speech in the Commons could in no way alleviate public discontent. On the contrary he voiced loud complaints particularly against the Americans for their ruthlessness over the question of food shipments from the USA to Britain.

The political situation in the enemy coalition is developing just as we would wish. Eden was forced to admit in the Commons that San Francisco offered the last chance for the enemy coalition. If this chance was not seized, then the world would inevitably sink into chaos. It is interesting that in this speech Eden admitted that the aim of England's policy always has been and still is never to allow any one

Power to dominate Europe. This was the reason, of course, for the British declaration of war in 1939. It is therefore incomprehensible that she should now accept without protest the increase of Soviet domination over large parts of Europe. Eden was also forced to admit that Great Britain no longer possesses the mastery of the seas. She has Churchill to thank for losing it since the rise of American dominance of the oceans is due to this accursed war, into which Churchill has led the British Empire. The results of this war in all countries—including Britain—were described in vivid terms. In any case it is noticeable that a sort of world catastrophe attitude of mind has spread among the British public. There is no pure rejoicing over their military victories in the West.

At a press conference Roosevelt refused to commit himself on any date for victory. Obviously our stiff resistance in the West, now making itself felt at various points, has given him to think.

A strong upsurge of anti-semitism is reported from the USA. The Jews are wailing about it to high heaven. It is even being said that, in certain parts of the United States, no one wants to hear criticism of Axis policy. Isolationism is raising its head again. Moreover Colonel Lindbergh is becoming active in politics again.

The USA and Britain are allegedly exerting pressure on the Kremlin in the matter of negotiations over the Polish government. On this question the Kremlin is showing itself extraordinarily unyielding and is even refusing to accept the Anglo-American proposal that Mikolajczyk be accepted onto the Lublin Committee. Stalin is submitting Roosevelt and Churchill to a very severe test, but in the present war situation he can obviously afford to.

Over the question of the abrogation of the Turkish treaty the Kremlin also acted without giving prior notice to Britain, as London admits. No secret is now made of the fact that, with the abrogation of the Turkish treaty, the Kremlin intends to tackle the Dardanelles problem. The Turkish declaration of war on Germany, therefore, was of no advantage to her. In this question too Stalin is exploiting a favourable moment. He knows very well that things will not be so favourable in the foreseeable future.

The British have now plucked up courage to execute Lord Moyne's murderers.* Jewry is highly indignant. It has suffered a defeat here, for it thought that it could exert pressure to prevent this execution.

As an oddity it is worth noting in passing that at the great staged trials in Sofia two priests declared with tears in their eyes that they were present when the Katyn graves† were opened and were forced to make statements favouring us and blaming the Soviets. That is a cowardly impudent lie but, priest or not, a man will do anything to save his skin.

Graf Krosigk sends me a long letter explaining that we must now pursue a more positive policy towards Russia and one more likely to succeed. We . . . [3 lines illegible] . . . Graf Krosigk is extraordinarily naïve over this question. If only he knew how I have had to struggle over policy towards Russia and how . . . [4 lines illegible] . . . in Zurich turn into a first-class political dispute. Bourgeois Switzerland is torn by this problem. She is slowly beginning to realise that there can be no question of freedom of thought under pressure from the street.

It is hardly worth recording the daily series of air raids which thunders down on the Reich hour by hour. There is hardly any defence to be seen. One can imagine what the effect is on public opinion.

The Führer has again issued a categorical order that

* Lord Moyne, British Minister of State in Cairo, had been murdered by Zionist fanatics (since canonised by the state of Israel) on 6 November 1944.

† The graves in which the Russians buried some 4,500 Polish officers whom they had murdered. The graves were discovered by the Germans in 1943, when they had invaded Russia. Goebbels exploited the fact in his propaganda (see *The Goebbels Diaries*, pp. 245 foll.) but having lost credibility, was not believed even when he spoke truth. The Russians pretended that the Poles had been murdered by the Germans.

western regions threatened by the enemy are to be evacuated. In practice this order simply cannot be carried out because people just will not go and we have no forces available to compel them to do so. There is no one either in the Ministry of the Interior or the Party Chancellery who has the courage to tell the Führer this to his face. So the problem is allowed to slide, in other words one marks time, naturally dealing a severe blow to the prestige of the authorities in the process.

The situation in Danzig has become fairly horrifying. Diewerger gives me a detailed report on the subject. Danzig is accommodating a vast mass of refugees and the available space is naturally becoming smaller all the time. Forster gave early warning against bringing so many East Prussians into Danzig but no other possibility was open to us for their evacuation.

I am working with my staff on a fundamental reorganisation of the Army Medical Service. The allocation of doctors to units has remained totally unchanged despite the shrinkage of the Wehrmacht. As a result the Wehrmacht has a surplus of doctors, whereas in civil life there is the greatest shortage of them. We are therefore working to obtain the release of considerable numbers of doctors from the Wehrmacht. On a proposal from Professor Ratzschow* medical officers in the Wehrmacht must be sent on retraining courses. They consist largely of medical students or doctors' assistants who have naturally not had much practice in medicine.

Since my visit to the Oder front cannot take place owing to the military situation in the Küstrin area, I have a free day in which to catch up on all the reading matter which has piled up and remained unread hitherto.

In the evening General Busse† rings me and tells me that the first day in the Küstrin area has gone off very satisfactorily. He hopes that he can counter Soviet attempts

---

* Professor of Medicine at Halle University.
† In command of 9th Army, on Eastern Front.

at encirclement. But one must wait for the next few days to see how matters develop further.

In the evening we have our usual Mosquito raid on Berlin, which however this time does somewhat less damage than has recently been the case.

FRIDAY 23 MARCH 1945

(pp. 1–32)
Military Situation.

On the Eastern Front fighting again centred on Hungary, Silesia, the Danzig–Gotenhafen area and at Heiligenbeil.

In Hungary the enemy was able to advance between Kisber and Veszprem as far as the eastern spur of Bakony Forest. He is now east of Veszprem. Our counter-attacks between Kisber and Tovaros drove the enemy back some distance. The Soviets made converging attacks on the salient south of the Danube which runs from Tovaros, south of Bannida and Felsögalla to the vicinity of Gran. They captured Bannida and Felsögalla and pressed the salient back a little towards the Danube.

In Slovakia the enemy pursued his concentrated local attacks between Altsohl and Neusohl. The situation remained generally unchanged.

In Silesia the Soviets launched a major offensive in the Bauerwitz–Leobschütz–Neustadt area aimed at the Mährisch–Ostrau region. All attacks were repulsed with extraordinarily severe losses in men and materials to the enemy—in this sector alone 143 Soviet tanks were destroyed; on the first day of the enemy's major offensive, therefore, a complete defensive victory has been scored all along the line. An extension of Soviet attacks from the Schwarzwasser area must be anticipated. So far only attacks in regimental strength have been made here and all were repulsed. Enemy attacks on Breslau and Glogau again failed.

North-west and south-west of Küstrin the bolshevists

moved out of their bridgehead with the intention of cutting off Küstrin and annihilating the garrison. They employed six Rifle Divisions (about 20,000 men) and two tank brigades (about 70 tanks) of which 55 were destroyed. We were able to keep the approaches to Küstrin open.

In the Danzig–Gotenhafen area and at Heiligenbeil the enemy continued his attacks in strength. At Heiligenbeil all attacks remained fruitless but between Gotenhafen and Zoppot the enemy succeeded in reach the Gulf of Danzig. He also penetrated as far as the western edge of Oliva. All other attacks on the Danzig–Gotenhafen enclave were repulsed with bloody losses to the Soviets. In Samland enemy troop concentrations presage an imminent offensive.

In Courland our troops scored a complete defensive victory against the Bolshevists attacking in great strength. One Soviet division was cut off and faces annihilation.

On the Western Front the Americans continued to attack heavily in the Remagen bridgehead but were unable to extend it further. In the north they could only reach a point just south of Siegburg where fighting is in progress on the southern outskirts of the town. On the southern side of the bridgehead the enemy could only make minor local advances near Leutesdorf. The enemy made no progress eastwards.

The Americans have penetrated into the city of Mainz. They are now in control of the whole bank of the Rhine from Koblenz to north of Ludwigshafen. On the western edge of Ludwigshafen ... [8 lines illegible] ... so that the greater part of the Pfalz Forest including Pirmasens is still in our hands. Troops from the Saar territory, who withdrew according to orders have meanwhile reached our lines in the Pfalz Forest area bringing most of their equipment with them. West of Pirmasens the new front runs along the Siegfried Line to Lauterburg. Attacks on the Siegfried Line were all repulsed.

According to various reports from the northern sector of the Western Front Montgomery's airborne divisions are now ready to jump.

No special reports to hand from the Italian front.

Enemy air activity in the Eastern Front zone was very brisk. A total of 33 Soviet aircraft was shot down yesterday.

Over the Western Front zone too there was sustained activity by enemy low-flying aircraft, fighter-bombers and twin-engined bombers.

Over Reich territory 1200 American four-engined bombers escorted by 700 fighters together with several British formations—totalling about 550 four-engined bombers with 400 fighters as escort—attacked Münsterland, the Ruhr and the Siegen area. Among other places Düsseldorf, Duisburg, Gelsenkirchen, Essen, Bochum, Hildesheim, Bremen and Oldenburg were attacked.

About 600 four-engined bombers flew in from Italy in two groups. The first made an attack on Vienna with isolated bombs dropped on Graz. The second group attacked Schwarzheide and Lauterburg. During the night harassing raids were made on Berlin and Paderborn. The enemy mined the German Bight. About 100 British bombers from Italy raided Villach.

During the day fighters shot down 15 enemy and anti-aircraft 23. During the night one enemy aircraft was shot down by fighter and another three by anti-aircraft.

The British have thought up a very naïve explanation for the appointment of Kesselring. They think that he has been commissioned by the Führer to make preparations for German capitulation. Naturally the opposite is the case. Kesselring will need some time, however, and above all troops and equipment if he is to clear up the situation in the West. As things stand at present it is almost a matter of impossibility to re-create an absolutely firm stable front in the West.

The speed with which the enemy works is to be seen from the fact that Anglo-American bomber formations are now taking off from German airfields. Our withdrawal, of course, was so rapid that we could hardly destroy anything. The enemy was able to take over all our airfield installations in working order.

"Exterminate the German people and as quickly as possible including the women and children," is now the cry reaching us from England. The British war agitators have still not yet come to their senses. I believe they would be prepared to set fire to the entire world in order to achieve their aim of annihilating the German people. The fact that the British Empire is creaking at every joint and sooner or later will be in the severest straits is of no interest to these British jingos. The abrogation of the Russo-Turkish treaty ought really to be a first-class alarm signal for British policy; in fact, however, the London press says hardly a word on the subject. Here and there some fringe newspaper points out that the Dardanelles may become a fresh bone of contention between the Soviets and the Anglo-Americans; but Stalin will not be in the least disconcerted by that. The British admit with a sardonic smile that they were not even informed beforehand that the Kremlin intended to revoke the Soviet-Turkish Pact. The people in Ankara have earned little thanks for their adherence to our enemies' camp. It is now realised that sooner or later the Soviets will broach the Dardanelles question in the most fundamental manner; in fact the Soviets are already letting it be known through publicity channels that they intend to revoke or abrogate all treaties concluded with the Soviet Union prior to the year 1925 since they no longer accord with present power relationships or the position in military matters.

At his so-called Wednesday reception Ribbentrop has made a statement on the subject of the revocation of the Turko-Soviet pact. The statement is disarmingly meaningless. It consists merely of four or five sentences which have appeared in every German newspaper for days. The Foreign Office is acting as if this statement had created a sensation, primarily because Ribbentrop added the oracular comment that the Turks should distinguish between Germany and the Reich. The Reich itself will survive given the necessary material. Ribbentrop is behaving as though he were Foreign

Minister of a power transcending the universe. In practice no one is taking the smallest notice of his statement and it has aroused no echo whatsoever in the international press.

Certain views in the commercial British press are of more importance. *The Economist*, for instance, writes that the Dardanelles is a sensitive spot for Berlin, adding elsewhere that the present anti-German hatred and annihilation campaign is without substance. It is not possible, for instance, to sever the Rhineland from the Reich; the Reich must remain united if Europe is ever to be consolidated again.

In passing it is worth noting that a few voices are to be heard in London saying that the gulf between Moscow and the West will become unbridgeable unless Moscow is prepared to give way on the Polish question. The San Francisco Conference, they say, is the final deadline. This conference will either never take place at all or fizzle out. The mere fact that 5000 delegates will be assembling is proof enough that nothing worthwhile can come out of it.

We now propose to reinforce our propaganda against the Seydlitz Committee, particularly among the soldiers on the Eastern Front. This Committee is making itself conspicuous again. It invariably makes its appearance when German resistance at the front becomes stiffer. As soon as the Soviets get on the move, however, the Seydlitz generals are cast aside like squeezed lemon-skins. These generals are typical bourgeois who have not an inkling of what bolshevism means. Just like Paasiviki, the Finnish Minister-President, who explicitly denied in an interview with the British press that the Finnish elections had taken place under Soviet pressure. He maintains that complete peace and prosperity reign in Finland and that the country has a promising future in front of it. There is nothing to be done with the man. He will probably finally learn to understand the true nature of bolshevism only when he gets his bullet.

Roosevelt has despatched Flynn[*] as special envoy to the Pope. Clearly Roosevelt wants to win the Catholic Church

_____
[*] Edward J. Flynn.

over to his side. The Pope is said to have been very displeased with the Anglo-Americans after the Yalta Conference. Other considerations may play a part here however. The Americans are working actively in the background to cheat not only the Soviets but also the British out of the international game. This also seems to have been noticed by Franco, the Spanish Head of State, and he obviously intends to enter the war against Japan on the side of the USA. For this reason he has sent an extraordinarily sharp note of protest to Tokyo about the treatment of Spanish citizens in the Philippines. Franco is trying by every conceivable means to take a hand in the great game and, having failed with Britain—and Britain, moreover, having too little power at present to afford him the necessary protection—he is now making a renewed attempt via the United States.

The Anglo-Americans have again attacked furiously from the air. The series of fearful raids on Reich territory never stops. The beautiful town of Hildesheim has been reduced to one great heap of ruins by a single British terror raid. I am told that there are 40,000 homeless in the town. Probably a fresh catastrophe has taken place there.

Parbel* reports to me on a trip to the West which he undertook together with Stuckart and Klopfer† and during which a series of meetings took place with the western Gauleiters. During these discussions Stuckart established that we have now rehoused about 19 million people. The Gauleiters in the West say emphatically that further evacuation in the West is not possible and that they are quite incapable of carrying out the Führer's order. They are satisfied if they can evacuate soldiers, weapons and the essential armaments. The problem of the foreign workers is extraordinarily disastrous. If they are left in enemy-occupied regions, workers from the West will be formed into infantry regiments forthwith and those from the East

---

* Head of the Film Department in the Ministry of Propaganda.
  † State Secretaries in the Ministry of the Interior and in the Party Chancellery.

placed in armaments factories. We therefore increase the enemy's military and economic war potential to an almost intolerable extent. The food situation in the West has become extraordinarily critical. Many towns have been without bread for days or weeks. One can imagine what the psychological effects of this are. The Reichsbahn is very severely criticised by the western Gauleiters. It has got into such a desperate state that it is no longer in a position to transport even the most essential war equipment. Decentralisation of the arms industry, which was undertaken as a result of the air war, has now become our Achilles' heel since the Reichsbahn is no longer able to move to the right place the components needed for our weapons. The Party is ready to help actively here and protests that Speer is keeping hundreds of thousands of men sitting around in the West doing nothing but wait for enemy air raids so as to repair damage to the transport system. The Party is of the opinion that the local people could do this just as well, if not better and quicker. The state of the Reichsbahn is made worse by the fact that the men at the top are in a mood of resignation. The organisation is too old and inflexible to cope with the frightful new conditions. In the West the air war is the alpha and omega. Again and again it is emphasised that, if only we could put up even a semi-effective defence, the problem of holding a defence line could easily be solved. In many places the population hoisted white flags in areas occupied by the Anglo-Americans, as the Gauleiters freely admit. The reason is, however, that they had no wish to lose what remained of their houses and dwellings. At the moment no one in the West talks of capitulation; but when the war reaches anyone's vicinity, everyone hopes to see it blast its way over him as quickly as possible.

Reich propaganda offices throughout the country report a similar attitude of mind. Among most sections of the German people faith in victory has totally vanished. People wonder whether a counter-offensive in the East is possible at all. They give nothing whatsoever for the prospects of our air defence. Definite hatred of the Reich Marshal is noticeable. Not a shred of his former popularity remains. Criticism is now being directed, however, at the whole conduct of the war and unfortunately even at the Führer personally. Admittedly the people are doing all they can to assist their leaders in further prosecution of the war—no one is failing to work or losing his will to fight; hardly anywhere, however, is there any hope of a happy ending to the war. It is significant, moreover, that refugees from the East put a better face on things than those from the West. Those from the West are too worn out by air raids for their morale still to be totally intact.

Worry about food is overriding throughout the population. Further severe reductions in the ration are expected and in the immediate future.

Enemy propaganda is beginning to have an uncomfortably noticeable effect on the German people. Anglo-American leaflets are now no longer carelessly thrown aside but are read attentively; British broadcasts have a grateful audience. By contrast our propaganda has a difficult time making an impact.

I learn with pleasure that my speech in Görlitz has made a profound impression on wide sections of the population.

I am now increasingly switching our propaganda on to low-level activity. To this end I am holding discussions with my propaganda staff in Party and State. We propose to publish, among other things, a series of slogans which are much in vogue among the people at present. Propaganda by sticker and chain-letter will also be stepped up. What things one does at this critical time to keep people in a good mood!

The letters I receive evince profound apathy and resignation. All refer quite openly to the leadership crisis. All the letter-writers show marked aversion to Göring, Ley and Ribbentrop. Unfortunately even the Führer is now more frequently referred to in critical terms. I get off somewhat more lightly in the letters I receive but that must not be over-estimated. Everything must be looked at relatively. I think that my work too is no longer being totally effective today. A fateful development seems to me to be that now neither the Führer in person nor the National-Socialist concept nor the National-Socialist movement are immune from criticism. Many Party members, moreover, are now beginning to waver. All our set-backs are unanimously ascribed to Anglo-American air superiority. We could soon deal with the Soviets if only we could put things right in the air. The Soviet atrocities we have published have evoked unanimous rage and thirst for revenge. The fact that we are now referring in our press and radio to the potential crisis in the enemy camp is beginning to have its effect. In this the people see at least a small speck of hope on the dark horizon.

I have a long interview with General von Gottberg* on accelerated call-up for the fit men I have released from the Wehrmacht, the armaments industry, the Reichsbahn, etc. General von Gottberg thinks that he can overcome the present disastrous situation by the issue of new regulations. I disagree with this emphatically. We have enough regulations already. What we do not have are energetic men who will do something on the spot. I therefore demand that General von Gottberg delegate to my Total War staff a man who can receive instructions direct from me and can also act as liaison officer to all Gauleiters so that men made available for service by the Gauleiters, particularly men from the Wehrmacht, may be transferred to the front as quickly as possible.

General Reymann† reports that my proposal for bolstering a 50-km zone in rear of the front with replacement units for Berlin has had one unfortunate repercussion in that schools located in Berlin ought now to move east with their equipment. I shall do my best to stop this; Berlin is, after all, a front-line city in the most definite sense of the word and if our higher-level units are now removed, we shall not even be able to train the Volkssturm, let alone have available adequate men and weapons for an emergency.

---

* See above pp. 86, 197.
† See above p. 150.

In a new leading article I set out yet again, in a calm, totally assured and lofty vein the arguments capable of giving the German people hope of victory.

In the evening we have our regulation Mosquito raid again.

I have recently been reading Thomas Carlyle's book on Frederick the Great. This biography is extraordinarily instructive and uplifting. Carlyle is an ardent admirer of Frederick the Great and the picture he draws of his life is that of an heroic epic. From this account one can judge the critical situations in which the great Prussian King was sometimes placed, the lofty relaxed frame of mind in which he met them and the admirable stoicism with which he overcame them. He too sometimes felt that he must doubt his lucky star, but, as generally happens in history, at the darkest hour a bright star arose and Prussia was saved when he had almost given up all hope. Why should not we also hope for a similar wonderful turn of fortune!

SATURDAY 24 MARCH 1945

(pp. 1–30)
Military Situation.

In the East fighting was again concentrated in Hungary, in Silesia, in the Küstrin area and in the West and East Prussian bridgeheads.

North of Lake Balaton the Bolshevists advanced some 10 km farther west through Veszprem. Attacks on our position south of . . . [word illegible] failed. Violent enemy attacks between Dorog and Tovaros narrowed our bridgehead on the south bank of the Danube, while we further reduced the enemy's small bridgehead at Gran.

Fighting flared up in Slovakia. The Bolshevists made small gains of ground west of Neusohl and west of Briesen.

In Silesia the enemy pursued his major offensive in very great strength between Bauerwitz–Leobschütz and the vicinity of Neisse. Our units scored a complete defensive victory; apart from minor penetrations all attacks were repulsed and 112 enemy tanks were destroyed. Attacks on Breslau were in somewhat reduced strength but artillery fire was heavier again. Several fires broke out in the city. In the Küstrin sector the enemy brought up fresh reinforcements, having suffered extraordinarily heavy losses on the first day of fighting. In spite of these reinforcements the weight of his attack was somewhat reduced. In this sector 66 Soviet tanks were destroyed and 116 on the previous day. In the light of the numbers of men and weight of material in action the enemy success was extraordinarily small. He was able to extend his two bridgeheads north-west and south-west of Küstrin only by some 100 yards. The two bridgeheads succeeded in joining up on a front of about 500 yards. OKH reports that access to Küstrin has been re-established.

Enemy attacks on Danzig and Heiligenbeil were again extraordinarily heavy. North of Gotenhafen the enemy reached the northern edge of the town. Zoppot passed to the enemy. All other attacks were beaten off with severe losses to the enemy. All attacks on Heiligenbeil also failed.

In Courland the enemy continued his attempts to break through at Frauenburg and in the sector between Frauenburg and Mitau but without success. He only achieved minor local penetrations, some of which were dealt with by counter-attack.

In the West the Anglo-Americans have launched a general offensive all along the front. After very heavy artillery fire and bombing the enemy crossed the Rhine on either side of Wesel during the night and formed a bridgehead on the right bank. In the Linz bridgehead, which now stretches as far as Neuwied in the south and the lower reaches of the Sieg in the north, heavy attacks continued uninterruptedly without the enemy being able to expand the bridgehead noticeably. The Sieg front is under very heavy enemy artillery fire.

At Freiweinheim—between Mainz and Bingen—the enemy is using smoke. Violent street fighting continues in Mainz.

At Oppenheim the Americans put heavy tanks across the Rhine and pushed forward to the Gross-Gerau area and west of Darmstadt. They occupied Gross-Gerau. Some of our reserves are on the move up.

In Ludwigshafen the enemy penetrated to the city centre and advanced south to Speyer, which he captured. Advancing south from Landau the enemy reached the area east of Bergzabern and so is in rear of the Siegfried Line. Three of our divisions from the Pfalz Forest have already fought their way back through the enemy lines and formed a new front running roughly south from the Speyer–Landau road and then south from Landau to the Siegfried Line. German

forces still in the Pfalz Forest area will probably be able
to get through since the enemy is not yet in great strength
at this point.

No fresh reports to hand from the Italian front.

In the Eastern Front zone there was heavy air activity on
both sides. Many vehicles, tanks, etc., were shot up from
the air and 34 Soviet aircraft shot down.

In the Western Front area enemy fighter-bombers, low-
flying aircraft and twin-engined formations were very active
in support of the ground operations.

Over Reich territory 1100 American four-engined
bombers with fighter escort and two smaller bomber
formations concentrated on Münsterland and the Rhine–
Main area. From Italy 600 American four-engined bombers
attacked the Vienna complex, Schwarzheide and Ruhland.
A smaller formation of about 50 bombers was over the
Innsbruck area. In the morning Soviet close-support aircraft attacked the region of Bernau and Eberswalde. During the day 18 enemy aircraft were shot down.

During the night the usual harassing raid was made on
Berlin, when three Mosquitos were shot down. There was
heavier night harassing activity as a screen for the bombers.
In addition 110 long-distance night fighters were in action.

The daylight raids were directed among other places on
Bremen, the Bocholt area, Münster, Osnabrück, Rheine,
Dinslaken, Hagen and numerous places in the Ruhr.
Specialist formations attacked a bridge over the Weser in
the Nienburg area and damaged it.

The situation in the West has entered an extraordinarily
critical, ostensibly almost deadly, phase. Not only has
Patton forced a fresh Rhine crossing in the direction of
Darmstadt but now the British and Canadians also have
launched a decisive large-scale offensive on the Lower
Rhine and have already scored a surprise victory. They
were able to cross the Rhine on a broad front; they have
also used parachute troops and are attempting to press

forward north of the Ruhr with this concentrated force. It cannot be denied that as a result an extraordinarily critical situation has arisen for us. The statement from Patton's headquarters that his troops met no resistance is not true, no more than that of the Canadians and British who say that they were able to advance across the Rhine north of the Ruhr without resistance; nevertheless the enemy now has three extraordinarily dangerous bridgeheads east of the Rhine and from this position he will undoubtedly do his utmost to surround the Ruhr, in particular from Montgomery's bridgehead and the Remagen bridgehead. In addition there is the dangerous advance towards Darmstadt, putting the whole of that region into an extraordinarily critical situation. The question now arises whether the Rhine will be held. The war in the West has entered its decisive phase. Our ability to win, even partially, this decisive phase of the war in the West now depends on our soldiers' will to resist and their morale and on the speed with which we can reinforce. At the moment the battle on the Lower Rhine seems to me the most important. The British and Canadians have been in reserve and have undoubtedly amassed an enormous quantity of material. Their divisions are in very good shape and they will undoubtedly do their utmost to win a decisive victory here.

In London people are already talking of the last battle of the war having started. Whatever happens they want to bring the war to an end in a few weeks' time primarily because of the critical political war developments which are now giving our Western enemies extraordinarily severe headaches. They are trying to overcome their difficulties by military victories. Kesselring is being compared to Groener at the end of the First World War or Weygand in the decisive phase of the Battle of France in 1940. It is openly admitted that the intention is not to take the Ruhr by frontal attack but to encircle it from both flanks. The use of airborne troops is described as an act of retribution for Arnhem. It would be splendid if we could succeed in smashing this enterprise as we did that of Arnhem.

According to custom Montgomery issues a pompous call

to his troops and one of unparalleled cynicism. In his mind he is already across the Rhine and charging on into the North German plain. He talks of the last round of the war as having started and with incomparable callousness comments that it will be interesting to see how long the German people can hold out against uninterrupted air bombardment. Finally he wishes his troops good hunting in Germany. This Montgomery is a brainless fellow; not only that, he has not the slightest emotion of the human heart. The British have always boasted of their fairness in fight—in this war they are showing that they possess not a trace of it.

In the evening the British announce that they have succeeded in crossing the Rhine on a broad front. The airborne troops, they say, met little resistance. It may be assumed, therefore, that their operation has already succeeded. Churchill is with Montgomery. This old criminal would not miss being present at such a decisive operation and shooting off his mouth.

British bombers have recently raided The Hague, causing fearful devastation and loss of life. The British government is trying to talk its way out of this, saying that it was a mistake. When we had to bomb Rotterdam for definite military reasons, the British shrieked to high heaven and made use of this bombing as justification for beating the German Reich to pieces. When they, on the other hand, bomb a peaceful city, that is merely due to an error.

A most interesting development is noticeable in the United States: a plea is increasingly being voiced that lenient peace terms be imposed on Germany; it is added that Roosevelt is afraid that otherwise the German people might become an abscess on the body of Europe, if not of all mankind. Roosevelt is to some extent forced into this position in that the U.S. Senate is now making very great difficulties for him over his external and world-political relationships. It is now stated flatly in Senate circles that a two-thirds majority for the Yalta foreign policy decisions cannot be mobilised.

Tokyo is denying most energetically that atrocities have

been committed against Spanish citizens in the Philippines as the Spaniards maintain. I do not think there is any truth in it. Franco, having failed with the British, has now seized what he thought was a favourable opportunity to side with the Americans. The Japanese think that American intrigue is at the bottom of Franco's move.

Serious communist disturbances have broken out in Calabria and Apulia. The Bonomi government is in no position to deal with them. It is one of the most incapable and impotent governments to be found in the whole of Europe today. But it is well known that the British and Americans prefer to have the weakest possible governments in the countries they occupy.

There is extraordinary dismay in London over the Dardanelles policy now being inaugurated by the Kremlin. The newspapers declare with all seriousness that the Mediterranean can no longer be regarded as a British lake and that, Italy being out of the running, Britain must now make up her mind to compete with the Soviets for control of the Mediterranean. In Ankara people are naturally extraordinarily nervous. They know that, if the Soviets put pressure on, they have nothing worthwhile with which to oppose them.

At midday I have a visit from Gauleiter Koch* so that he may brief me on the situation in East Prussia. Our divisions there are fighting with incomparable courage, but in the long run they cannot hold out because they are short of equipment and also of food. Ammunition is now so short that each gun is allowed to fire at most only three to four rounds a day. In Samland, on the other hand, the situation is better. More space is available in which to operate. Koch therefore advocates transfer to Samland of the remaining divisions operating in East Prussia so that they can protect Königsberg and there they should be able to hold out much longer.

The Party in Königsberg has taken very comprehensive defence measures which in some cases may serve as a

_____
* Gauleiter of East Prussia.

pattern for us in Berlin. Accordingly I am sending Hartung, a Party member from Gau headquarters, to Königsberg so that he may study these defence arrangements on the spot and draw lessons from them for our defence arrangements in Berlin.

Koch maintains that the Soviets have suffered extraordinarily heavy losses in East Prussia. He even says that they have so far registered one million killed; anyway it is clear that Stalin is having to lose a good few tail-feathers for the conquest of East Prussia. Moreover the general aim of our overall war strategy at the moment must be to inflict the highest possible personnel casualties on the enemy.

The Fortress Commandant of Königsberg is a General Lasch, about whom Koch grumbles very much. His name fits him [in German "lasch" = "flabby"]. Koch himself, however, has been very busy preparing the defence of Königsberg and it may be assumed that, if the battle for the city starts in the near future, the Soviets will face bitter resistance.

We have to record a further crazy series of air raids during the last 24 hours. Again it was mainly the turn of the Ruhr and Bremen.

The report I receive from Hildesheim is frightful. This beautiful old city has been flattened. No end to the air war is foreseeable. Our new fighters have arrived too late and they can only appear in such small numbers that they cannot register much success.

At midday we had another heavy bombing raid on Berlin, hitting mainly Langwitz, Marienfelde and Mariendorf. The main targets were industrial installations, particularly Stock & Co., Askanta and Siemens. The damage done is very considerable, primarily to our arms production in Berlin. We now hardly know where our heavy weapons can be produced. Mariendorf station has been flattened. Many people have been buried alive. Damage to the transport system in this raid, made by 250 American bombers, will undoubtedly keep us busy for a long time. Moreover we were only just in the process of overcoming the damage of the previous Sunday's raid. At the moment the transport sector is the worst off. It has suffered enormously, also from the nightly Mosquito raids. Again and again important thoroughfares are closed and in the long run the capital's entire transport system becomes extraordinarily restricted.

The weekend Berlin defence stocktaking unfortunately shows somewhat reduced figures. Considerable forces of troops have moved out of the capital with their equipment. Moreover figures for heavy weapons completed or under production by the various firms have fallen but this is mainly because they had to make deliveries by the end of the month. I hope that the figures will be better next week.

I am now at work, together with Obergruppenführer Gottberg's organisation, on an acceleration of call-up for men released as fit for service. An investigation of the Todt Organisation and the Reich Labour Service is now to be undertaken. It is hoped that this will produce greater results since both these organisations contain large numbers of men fit for service.

We have carried out a two-day check of leave trains in Berlin, hunting for deserters. The result has been disproportionately small. It is therefore not true that—as is frequently maintained—thousands of deserters are loitering around in Berlin.

The National-Socialist Leadership Organisation* is now being placed under firm control. General Reinecke has proved too old and too inflexible. He will therefore be recalled from the post of leader of the organisation. The organisation is now to be run by the Party Chancellery itself. Under their respective commanders National-Socialist Leadership officers will be given greater powers; they will no longer be subordinate to but on a level with Army Operations officers. So at last the Leadership Organisation has achieved an aim for which it has long been striving. Unfortunately this development comes full late—one sometimes wonders whether it is not too late.

Graf Krosigk writes me another letter about the present

---

* NSFO, an organisation which supplied political commissars to the Army. General Reinecke was its head.

war situation. The things he tells me in this letter have been my bread and butter for months, if not years. When he says, for instance, that we must act quickly to reach a conclusion with one of the enemy camps or the other, this is what I have been saying for ages! He considers that we are hardest pressed by the air war and the threat from the East. He thinks that the best mediator with the West would be Professor Bruckhardt* from Switzerland or Salazar, the Portuguese Minister-President. But at present there is no possibility of mediation to be seen and Graf Krosigk takes too simple a view if he thinks that one has only to express such a wish and one will start talks with the British or Americans at once. At the moment military developments are so much in the forefront that there is hardly any question of a political initiative in this war. As long as we cannot achieve even semi-stabilisation of the fronts, there can be no question of bringing about a political turning-point to the war.

I am now no longer asking for an evening situation report because communications to Berlin are so uncertain that one can get no clear picture in the evening. The news which comes in only confuses one. It is quite enough to be given a comprehensive situation report at midday. Moreover one can more or less sense from the general tone of the foreign press how matters stand. At the moment that is the reverse of good.

In the evening we have the regulation Mosquito raid once more. It is gradually turning into a habit. It is a habit, however, which produces great nervousness, not to say hysteria, among the general public.

* Carl Jacob Burckhardt had been High Commissioner of the League of Nations in the Free City of Danzig before the war. He was now President of the International Red Cross.

SUNDAY 25 MARCH 1945

(pp. 1–21)

Military Situation.

Continuing their major offensive on the Lower Rhine the Anglo-Americans have so far sent two airborne divisions into action; their main body landed in the Dorsten–Dinslaken–Kirchhellen area. Subsidiary landings took place along the Bocholt–Wesel road, at Bocholt-Bingen and south thereof. A special combat group and a Panzer division are moving up against these forces. A further division is on the way. After very heavy artillery preparation the enemy extended his bridgehead on either side of Rees. He has so far succeeded in constructing three temporary bridges at Rees, Wesel and Xanten. Successful counter-attacks drove the enemy back on either side of Wesel. Street fighting is taking place in Wesel. Enemy tanks penetrated into Dinslaken.

In the Remagen bridgehead an enemy attempt to extend the bridgehead eastwards was stopped in fluctuating fighting; on the other hand in attacks carried out partially at night the enemy succeeded in extending the bridgehead south-eastwards as far as Engers east of Neuwied.

In the Oppenheim Bridgehead the enemy succeeded in advancing both eastwards and southwards and has meanwhile thrown four temporary bridges across the river, of which one was damaged by our counter-measures. The enemy entered Gross-Gerau, moved on thence farther south-east and is now at Kesselborn. Dornheim was recaptured by counter-attack. Leading enemy tanks have been held at Griesheim on the Darmstadt road, at Ehrenfelden and Guttlau as they were moving forward to the attack on Schollbrücken.

Bitter house-to-house and street fighting continues in Ludwigshafen. Speyer was lost after severe fighting. Germersheim was attacked by the enemy from two sides, as was our bridgehead covering Karlsruhe.

Continuing his offensive in Hungary the enemy gained ground westwards and southwards, penetrating deeper into Bakony Forest. Soviet attacks northwards towards the Danube east of Komorn were unsuccessful.

In Slovakia the enemy gained some ground south-west of Neusohl. Continuing his major offensive in the Leobschütz–Neisse area the enemy made strong local holding attacks on Sohrau which were contained apart from minor [word illegible]. The enemy penetrated into Sohrau. In the Leobschütz–Neisse area all enemy attacks against our line, which had been withdrawn a little, failed almost without exception with heavy Soviet losses in tanks. As a result of this withdrawal Neisse and Leobschütz fell into enemy hands after severe fighting. Breslau and Glogau beat off heavy attacks.

Attacks on Küstrin from the north were repulsed. The enemy is concentrating along the Oder and in the Königsberg and Zehden areas.

In the West Prussian and East Prussian areas the situation has now deteriorated owing to continued shortage of ammunition. Attacking from the south-west, the enemy succeeded in penetrating the outer defences of Gotenhafen and capturing Oliva. Attacks on Praust were repulsed. In the East Prussian area all attacks were repulsed except for a concentrated attack which enabled the Soviets to penetrate Heiligenbeil. In these two areas 143 Soviet tanks were destroyed.

On the Courland front all attacks were repulsed except for a few penetrations which have been sealed off. Counterattacks are in progress.

No special reports to hand from the Italian front.

During the morning 800 bombers and 3000 fighters were over northern, western and south-western Germany. The

main raids were on transport targets. In addition 1100
American bombers from the west attacked a total of 11
airfields. About 650 bombers flew in from the south, of
which 40 raided Budweis. Berlin was attacked by 250 aircraft; Marienfelde, Tempelhof, Steglitz and Mariendorf
were the main targets. Other places raided were Neuberg an
der Donau, Riem near Munich and Lindau. Garmisch, Innsbruck and places on the Brenner were attacked by 86 twin-
engined bombers. Essen, Bochum, Gelsenkirchen, Duisburg
and Wesel were attacked by 250 British aircraft; 300 British
aircraft attacked transport and industrial targets in the
Bochum, Recklinghausen, Herne and Hattingen areas. In
the afternoon 400 American aircraft attacked transport
installations and airfields in the Kassel area. In the evening
the usual harassing raid was made on Berlin by 40
Mosquitos.

During yesterday's air battles over the fronts and over
Reich territory at least 65 enemy aircraft were shot down
according to reports so far.

In London they now feel on top of the world. Everyone
thinks that, now that the Lower Rhine has been crossed,
the war will soon come to an end. Churchill himself is at
Montgomery's headquarters and the British war reporters
are recounting in triumph that he made a trip along the
Rhine in a motor-boat. This fits Churchill absolutely.
British newspapers report that he gazed at the destruction
in the Wesel area through field glasses. Probably he will
pride himself a great deal on that. One day he will go down
to history as the destroyer of the European continent.

He issues a message to Montgomery's troops. This
message abounds in British hypocrisy and cant. He says that
the Rhine crossing was only possible through the help of
God and promises the British people an early peace. As
can be imagined, the British public is in a real victory
delirium as a result. It thinks that a decision is imminent.
Public opinion in the United States takes the same view as

that of Britain. Montgomery, however, pours a little vinegar into this cup of joy. He warns the British soldiers against the German population. It is up to something nasty, he says, and is not to be trusted.

Although the situation in the West is worse than menacing and at the moment one cannot see how or where we can consolidate, I myself have no doubt that we shall succeed in putting up a barrier somewhere to the Anglo-American advance eastwards. It is perhaps of real advantage to us that the Anglo-American leaders have set their sights on so short-term an aim; disappointment will be all the greater when the war in the West bogs down at some point again.

Under the pressure of military developments neutral public opinion is naturally swinging totally onto the side of the Anglo-Americans. How sure they are of themselves is to be seen from the fact that they are now cynically informing the German people that under their rule 5000 Germans will have to die daily from hunger for the first one to two years.

For the present the situation in the West is totally obscure. Particularly in the area of the Rhine crossing there is much hithering and thithering and our countermeasures have not yet developed sufficiently to enable one to judge whether they will succeed. Somewhere we must bring the enemy to a halt, and it is of course disastrous that, by all indications, we have not succeeded in doing so on the Rhine. This again is due to the enemy's catastrophic air superiority. He lays an area he wishes to conquer so flat by massive air attack that resistance is practically impossible.

It is cheering that we are now recording 40–50 enemy aircraft shot down daily. This is due to our new fighters; but they are only in action in such small numbers that they cannot really register any decisive success.

The fact that they are finding the European continent in such a miserable state is causing the British some worry. Labour Party observers in particular lament that, instead of a blooming continent, a corpse is falling into their hands.

The British public is now slowly beginning to realise that, even if the Anglo-Americans do win a victory over us, it will be a Pyrrhic victory.

The Spaniards have made a further sharp protest in Japan. The British maintain that the Spaniards intend to sever diplomatic relations with Japan. In any case developments have reached a critical stage. The British should not be so pleased about it since the beneficiaries of these developments will undoubtedly be the Americans instead of them.

The final results of the Finnish elections show that the Social-democrats together with the Communists scored 821,000 votes and the bourgeois parties 829,000. The swing to the left, therefore, was not as marked as one had originally suspected; it is nevertheless sufficiently significant for Finnish policy now to be oriented to the left—quite apart from the pressure of Soviet occupation. Any knowledgeable person must realise that Finland will now slide more and more on to the communist side and will be Eastern-oriented. In any case it looks as if she is totally lost to the Western Powers.

Were there no war we should be celebrating the start of spring this Sunday. A wonderfully refreshing sun beams from the firmament; in view of the general situation, however, this is merely provoking, seeing that we have already had an early morning air-raid alert in Berlin. Strong bomber formations were again on the way and it was initially assumed that they were making for Berlin. This time, however, the capital was spared.

The series of air raids during the last 24 hours has again been horrifying. This time the Anglo-Americans concentrated on our airfields; clearly our jet fighters are causing them some anxiety. In addition they attacked transport targets in the west and south. Rail traffic is totally at a standstill. There are districts in which not a single train runs; where trains do run they can only do so at night and at a snail's pace.

All day long I have had a mountain of work to deal with, so that I have hardly been able to realise that this is Sunday and a lovely spring day. Day by day one's worries increase, particularly about the situation at the front. More and more one wonders where things will come to rest in the end.

This evening the situation in the West is no less obscure. Admittedly the British have made no great progress with their attacks east of the Lower Rhine; the Americans, however, have made a most menacing advance in the direction of Dinslaken. In addition they have succeeded in expanding their bridgehead towards Darmstadt to such an extent that they have by-passed the city and almost reached Aschaffenburg. This offensive is a complete surprise. Looking at the map one is to a certain extent horror-struck. The Führer's headquarters is trying to put everything we can lay hands on into action against this advance. Communications are so wretched, however, that our reinforcements are likely to arrive too late.

In Hungary the Soviets have crossed the Gran. The situation there has become precarious. Fighting in Upper Silesia is again very severe as it is in West and East Prussia. Nevertheless the Soviets have not yet been able to score a decisive victory.

Naumann* has paid a two-day visit to Tölz and Munich. He tells me of prevailing opinion there. Everywhere the same questions are asked: When will the Führer at last make the changes of personnel in the Reich leadership which the whole people is demanding? As is generally known criticism is directed mainly against Göring and Ribbentrop. Since the Führer consistently refuses to make changes here, there is gradually developing not only a leadership crisis but a definite Führer crisis. In Augsburg Dr. Naumann heard that 100 of our Me 262s, our most valuable and most expensive new aircraft, were destroyed on the ground by an enemy bombing raid on the place. One can imagine the effect on the work force which has laboured day and night to make their contribution to clearing the German skies of the enemy again. The Luftwaffe is no longer able to guarantee even the most elementary

---

* Acting Gauleiter of the Moselle.

conditions. This is not to be changed by mere reorganisation but only by fundamental reform at the top and in branches.

I have sent the Führer a long letter on organisational reform of the Luftwaffe. The Führer declares that he is in agreement with my ten proposals and gives me the necessary powers. With these powers I have an opportunity of streamlining the whole Luftwaffe organisation so that its hydrocephalic structure will at last really be done away with. I shall try to complete this task with the utmost speed. Nevertheless I am convinced that this alone is not enough. The point is not whether one is doing a job but the spirit in which it is done.

MONDAY 26 MARCH 1945

(pp. 1–31)
Military Situation.

In Hungary the Soviets reached the western edge of the Bakony Forest in the Papa–Cewecser region. Attacks on Komorn and on the Danube were repulsed. On the Slovakian front the enemy also went over to the offensive at Leva and formed three bridgeheads over the Gran. One of these bridgeheads was broken up at once and the second reduced. The Soviets were able to expand the third bridgehead southwards.

In the Mährisch–Ostrau area the enemy penetrated to a depth of 4 km near Sohrau but the break-in was sealed off. In the main area of the offensive between Ratibor and Neisse all Soviet attacks were repulsed, some by counterattack, and 101 out of 200 attacking Soviet tanks were destroyed. A heavy concentrated local attack at Strehlen enabled the enemy to capture this place. At Breslau violent attacks from north-east and south-west were driven off and minor penetrations contained.

In the Küstrin area enemy offensive activity was reduced. Küstrin Old Town is at present under artillery fire. Enemy reconnaissance activity against our bridgeheads at Zehden and Pölitz increased.

In West Prussia the enemy was able to penetrate somewhat deeper into the inner defences of Gotenhafen as a result of severe fighting. Fighting is still going on in Oliva. At Praust the enemy gained some ground towards Danzig. Heavy fighting continues in East Prussia. A defensive victory was again scored at Heiligenbeil. German troops in

282

the Heiligenbeil area are now to be evacuated to the Königsberg–Samland area.

On the Courland front a complete defensive victory was again scored at the main centres of fighting.

No very favourable picture emerges from the second day of the battle on the Lower Rhine, in the course of which two enemy airborne divisions have so far been dropped, concentrated in the Bocholt–Dinslaken area. Enemy forces dropped near Bocholt and south of it were driven westwards and south-westwards towards the Rhine by strong German counter-attacks. Enemy efforts to extend his bridgeheads either side of Rees, at Xanten and at Wesel had only little success. On either side of Wesel the enemy was driven back towards the Rhine; from . . . [2 lines illegible] . . . enemy airborne divisions dropped in the Dinslaken–Kirchkapellen–Castrop area succeeded in gaining contact with forces moving up north-eastwards from Dinslaken. It is suspected that the enemy, who has so far used two of his six available airborne divisions, intends to make airborne landings only in the zone near the front.

No special developments on the entire front from Duisburg to Köln.

In the Remagen bridgehead the enemy did not succeed in crossing the Sieg northwards. He was equally unable to extend his bridgehead north-eastwards or eastwards. Only in the south and south-east did he succeed in making minor gains of ground. In general terms, however, the situation in the bridgehead is unchanged.

Fresh crossings of the Rhine took place in the area between Braubach, Boppard and St. Goarshausen. Near Braubach the enemy moved forward to Oberlahnstein. At Boppard he was held in the bend of the Rhine and at St. Goarshausen driven back across the Rhine by counter-attack. The enemy has not so far extended his crossings northwards or eastwards.

The most critical situation is that at Darmstadt where the enemy crossed the Rhine on the previous day, moving forward to Gross-Gerau and also west of Darmstadt. Strong armoured forces have meanwhile been brought forward across three temporary bridges erected at the crossing points and yesterday they attacked from the bridgehead, breaking through our comparatively weak defensive front. They drove our forces back northwards and southwards where they occupied switch positions. Leading enemy tanks drove on eastwards, reaching Aschaffenburg where they crossed the Main by the undamaged bridge. Other leading enemy tanks crossed the Main at Hanau where the bridge was semi-destroyed. It is suspected that from here the enemy will swing northwards.

Farther south the main feature of the situation is severe fighting in the bridgehead in front of Karlsruhe.

No special reports from the Italian front.

There was sustained air activity by both sides on the Eastern Front yesterday. In air battles 45 Soviet aircraft were shot down.

In the West a limited number of our fighters were in action against low-flying aircraft.

Over Reich territory strong British and American four-engined formations with fighter escort flew in from west and south during the day, attacking industrial and transport targets and built-up areas in Hannover, Münster and Osnabrück. From the south 650 [word illegible] four-engined bombers attacked primarily industrial and transport targets and also the airfield of [word illegible]. Final reports on the air situation, in particular numbers of aircraft shot down, are not yet available.

The critical development in the West is undoubtedly that in the Main area and at Aschaffenburg. Here the Americans have succeeded in making a surprise advance deep into our hinterland, producing an extraordinarily precarious situation for us. We are of course trying to get the better of this situation with all the resources available to us, but these resources are very limited so that the Americans will probably retain considerable freedom of movement. This could lead to the most unpleasant repercussions since such deep penetrations into the hinterland generally descend upon both the population and the few available Wehrmacht units quite unexpectedly with proportionate results. On the other hand the situation of the airborne units, both British and American, is not so good for the enemy. The British in particular have suffered extraordinarily severe losses. So far neither they nor the Americans have succeeded in establishing touch between the airborne troops and their bridgeheads. Here too, however, the situation is most precarious and it must be anticipated that they will succeed in gaining contact sooner or later. Our troops in this area are putting up very stiff resistance. But we are poor folk and have only limited resources and potentialities with which to oppose the enemy. As a result both in the north of the eastern Rhine region and in the south the situation is completely fluid, as of course emerges in today's OKW report, producing a corresponding shock effect throughout the entire population. In view of the explicit terms in which our official reports are couched this shock effect is no longer avoidable. The result is a further deep dent in the war morale both of the troops and of the civil population.

Slesina* gives me a detailed report on the subject. He describes to me the rout on the Saar front which was really terrible. As we know, the Americans succeeded in taking our Saar front in rear. The Army fighting on the Siegfried Line was withdrawn too late and largely fell into enemy hands. The troops' morale was correspondingly low. That of the civil population was even worse; in many places people opposed the troops and placed obstacles in the way of the defence. To a great extent the tank barriers constructed in the hinterland were captured by the enemy without a fight. I tax Slesina with the fact that not a single symbol of resistance has emerged in the West, like Breslau or Königsberg, for instance, in the East. His explanation is that people in the West have been so worn down by the months and years of enemy air raids that they prefer an end to this horror rather than a endless horror. A contributory

* Head of the Propaganda Office in Westmark.

factor, I believe, is that people in the West are not by
nature as tough as those in the East. They are nearer to
France, Europe's most over-civilised country, whereas
people in the East are nearer to Poland and Russia, the
more primitive countries of Europe. In any case it is noteworthy that the situation in the West is developing far
more unfavourably than that in the East. I shall probably
now find less use being made of the argument adduced
against me in recent weeks that our withdrawal from the
Geneva Convention would lead to a collapse of morale
among our troops in the West. I believe that, had we proceeded in more radical fashion in our treatment of prisoners
of war, the number of German soldiers and even officers
surrendering to the British and Americans would have been
smaller than is the case today. At the present moment the
enemy is having an easy time in the West. Neither the
troops nor the civil population are putting up organised
courageous resistance against him so that the Americans
in particular can drive about the countryside at will. In
view of this situation the Führer's continued insistence on
his evacuation order is purely academic. In practice such
evacuations simply cannot be carried out. The people just
will not move and we do not possess adequate force in
this area to compel them to do so. In most of the occupied
areas we have at least succeeded in getting back the men
fit for service, especially the youngsters whose behaviour
in this extraordinarily military dilemma is still exemplary.
I foresee that the Führer's evacuation order will result in
a severe loss of authority, for impracticable orders invariably do damage rather than the reverse to the giver of
them. Nevertheless fundamentally the Führer is right since
any human, material or economic potential which we allow
to fall into enemy hands will be turned against us in a
very short time.

I have already emphasised that the weary impression
given by the western population is due primarily to the
enemy air terror. In the west and south-west of the country
there are now hardly any periods free of air-raid alerts.
People sit day and night in the air-raid shelters which have

increasingly become hotbeds of defeatism. There are no longer any free periods at all when people can move about on the roads. People largely look upon the air war as a sort of natural catastrophe, for the end of which one waits with no idea how the end can be brought about.

In general it may be said that the attitude of the civil population is somewhat better than that of the troops. But bad morale among the troops invariably has lasting repercussions on that of the civil population. Our Gauleiters in the West are not quite up to the situation. Some of them are too old—Murr or Sprenger, for instance—and they have long since resigned themselves. Changes of personnel should have been made here years ago, for men aged between 60 and 70 are no longer capable of meeting the frightful demands now being made on the National-Socialist leadership class.

I am now busy organising the so-called "Werwolf" movement* on a large scale. The purpose of Werwolf is to organise partisan groups in enemy-occupied territories. Not much preparation has been made so far. The reason is that military developments in the West have been so sudden that we have had absolutely no time. In general, however, partisan activity in enemy territories formerly occupied by us has only got going after a certain time but has then gone up by leaps and bounds. I propose to release a transmitter for our Werwolf organisation and also issue a newspaper; this will be done quite openly. We do not intend to hide our light under a bushel and do secret-service work. On the contrary the enemy should know precisely what we are planning and doing.

The enemy naturally feels at the height of his triumph as a result of the military victories won by the Anglo-Americans in the West. The Soviets however, take hardly any notice of them and dismiss them in their newspapers in a couple of lines.

* The Werwolf organisation was intended, and advertised, as a massive guerrilla resistance movement within Germany, comparable with the movements in German-occupied Europe. It was a complete fiasco.

The Americans are at present having most anxious moments about steel. They had made premature readjustments based on an end to the war and must now set their arms production in motion again. I anticipate that the present military crisis in the West will bring us certain advantages *à la longue* in that once again the enemy has made preparations for a very quick end to the war which we must do our utmost to prevent. Meanwhile the political crisis will continue. The Soviets, for instance, have demanded that the Soviet Union have five votes at the San Francisco Conference; in other words they wish to outvote their rivals in the coalition. Negotiations in Moscow over reconstitution of the Polish government are proceeding only very hesitantly. The Soviets are said to have threatened that, if the Anglo-Americans demand fundamental changes in the Lublin Committee, they will quite simply torpedo the San Francisco Conference. In Finland Mannerheim is now doomed. Swedish reports say that he is to be shelved following the recent elections. Paasiviki will be his successor. The Soviets will be able to manage Paasiviki better than Mannerheim. He is the typical drawing-room bolshevist, a craven unprincipled bourgeois whose sole ambition is to play the role of Kerensky for Finland.

In the light of Soviet intrigue in all countries of Europe it is little better than a bad joke that at this of all moments *Pravda* should proclaim the Soviet model man. He is said to be characterised by generosity and simplicity. Millions of tortured people in Europe today could sing a little song about this generosity. But the paper is indulgent and complacently accepts the most repellent Jewish twaddle, as this example proves once more.

At midday I have a long visit from the Croat Minister. I take the greatest trouble to comfort him somewhat. He is naturally very downcast over military developments. Nevertheless he is still a revolutionary character. It would be interesting to know what Oshima, the Japanese Ambassador, is thinking at present since his reports to Tokyo have been completely contradicted by the latest war developments.

In the last 24 hours the Anglo-Americans have raided mainly Osnabrück and Fulda. There is not much left to destroy in these cities; they are little more than heaps of ruins. The enemy air forces are now going primarily for industrial and transport targets where they can still do us considerable damage.

Gauleiter Sauckel* addresses a protest to me against any further crowding of the Thuringian area with evacuees. Thuringia, however, is not as badly crowded as a number of other Gaus. We must now squeeze ourselves closer into those parts of the Reich which remain to us, particularly if the Führer's evacuation order for the West is to be carried out even partially.

Supplies of coal are becoming ever shorter in Berlin. To all intents and purposes Ruhr coal no longer arrives. We are going to try to divert some Central German coal to Berlin since Berlin is carrying some 80% of the emergency armaments programme today. It is therefore essential to keep Berlin's coal supply going. Since we are getting to all intents and purposes no more coal from the Saar or the Ruhr, our coal resources have become extraordinarily restricted. Not much can be done with emergency measures. Fortunately warm spring weather has now arrived so that people do not have to suffer so much from the cold.

A number of training units from Berlin have been released for the Eastern Front. As a result Berlin's defence capacity has been severely reduced, particularly since these units took their weapons with them. I shall try to have further replacement units transferred to the capital from the Reich.

A most serious problem for us is the question what we are to do with the population in front of and behind the main battle line in Berlin should the enemy really break through on the Oder front. We must work out an evacua-

---

* Gauleiter of Thuringia and Plenipotentiary for Forced Labour.

tion plan for all eventualities and in the last resort implement it by improvisation. The Führer has given his approval for use of the East–West Axis as a runway. The Tiergarten* is not to be cut down however. The Führer thinks that the Axis itself must suffice as a runway. The Luftwaffe of course would like to hack down the whole Tiergarten. They take a frightfully simple view of things. It is provoking, when talking to Luftwaffe officers, to hear them referring to the air war as if the Luftwaffe had nothing whatsoever to do with it.

The whole day is filled with the most serious worries. One dramatic report after another is submitted to me and in each of them I am loaded with a host of the trickiest problems. In this atmosphere the wonderful spring weather is simply an irritation. One would like to close the shutters and hide within one's four walls.

In the evening the new *Wochenschau* [Weekly Review] is submitted to me. It includes some really shattering pictures from the West which we cannot possibly publish. Demolition of the Rhine bridges in Köln, for instance, makes one heavy at heart. To see our beautiful cities on the left of the Rhine now being bombarded by our own artillery is truly heart-rending.

Late in the evening I have a call from Müller from Kesselring's headquarters. Müller has had two long talks with Kesselring during the day. Kesselring is now very worried indeed about signs of disintegration at the front, particularly in the Hanau–Frankfurt area. Here people are meeting the Americans with white flags; women are so far demeaning themselves as to welcome and embrace the Americans. In the light of this the troops are no longer willing to fight and are either withdrawing unresistingly or surrendering to the enemy. Kesselring regards this as the real reason for our lack of defensive strength. He says that the situation is now ripe for the Führer to speak at

---

* i.e. the trees in the Tiergarten, the park in central Berlin. The East–West Axis is the main avenue leading into Berlin: it was converted into a runway.

once. I too think this necessary. In so serious a situation the nation cannot remain without a call from the highest quarters. A talk by the Führer over the radio would be as good as a victorious battle today. Late in the evening I get in touch with General Burgdorf and ask him to submit the matter to the Führer on my behalf during the course of the night. I hope that Burgdorf will succeed. In the hour of Britain's war crisis Churchill addressed himself to the nation in a magnificent speech and put it on its feet again. The same was the case with the Soviet people when Stalin successfully appealed to them with the slogan "Better to die standing than live kneeling." Now that we are in a similar, though not much worse situation, we must do the same. Burgdorf was not impervious to my arguments. He will submit the question to the Führer seriously and pressingly. I hope that he will succeed.

TUESDAY 27 MARCH 1945

(pp. 1–68 + 51a)
Military Situation.

In Hungary the severe defensive fighting south of the Danube moved to the Marczal Canal, south-west of Papa and to the lower Raab. All attacks on the Komorn area and on our bridgeheads on the Danube were repulsed. The enemy was able to form two small bridgeheads north of the mouth of the Gran. He extended his bridgehead at Leva somewhat farther eastwards, south-eastwards and southwards.

At Neusohl fighting moved farther into the hills north-east of the town, the town itself beating off all attacks.

In the Mährisch–Ostrau area the enemy is trying to penetrate farther into the industrial zone from Sohrau and Leobschütz. All enemy attacks were repulsed, in some cases on shorter lines; only at Joslau, which fell into enemy hands, did he succeed in making a minor break-in. The main centre of fighting was again in the area south of Neisse where all enemy attacks were repulsed. Very heavy Soviet attacks on Breslau from the south also failed; no more than a few totally destroyed housing blocks had to be abandoned. Soviet troop concentrations have been detected at Forst and Guben indicating the possibility of local offensives, Küstrin is under heavy artillery fire; in addition the town was bombed six times from the air and at the same time heavily but unsuccessfully attacked from north, east and south. Enemy attacks on our bridgeheads at Zehden and Pölitz also failed. In the Danzig–Gotenhafen area the Soviets moved in from west and south-west against the outer defences of Danzig. South-east of Praust the Soviets achieved a small penetration towards Gottswalde. Port installations at Danzig were demolished on orders. In the Heiligenbeil bridgehead, which is under very heavy artillery fire, the troops fought their way through to the ships with the bayonet and were evacuated to Pillau.

All along the Courland front a complete defensive victory was scored, in some cases by counter-attack.

The situation in the battle on the Lower Rhine has not appreciably altered since the previous day. Violent enemy attacks northwards from Rees were driven back on the Wesel–Emmerich railway line. Any further extension of the enemy bridgehead south of Rees was stopped. Detachments of airborne troops who had landed east of Rees attacked northwards and north-westwards from the Hamminkeln area. German defensive forces are on the move up. At Wesel the enemy succeeded in making a deep penetration on either side of the Börsten railway line; here the enemy has gained some 8–9 km of ground since the previous day. The break-in has meanwhile been sealed off. The main body of airborne troops dropped in the wooded areas north and north-east of Dinslaken were able to join up with forces which had crossed the Rhine at Dinslaken. They attacked eastwards but were held and in some cases driven back on a new stop-line running south through Kirchhellen, some 12 km west of Dörstheiden. The enemy has therefore succeeded in expanding his bridgeheads considerably but could make no break-through. As before, the critical point is north and north-east of Dinslaken.

Throughout the day violent fighting took place in the Remagen bridgehead. All enemy attacks on the Sieg and on the German bridgeheads over that river failed. The enemy was able to extend his bridgehead farther eastwards. Leading enemy troops reached the Altkirchen area, where they were held. South-eastwards the enemy reached Hohr-Grenzhausen.

The enemy attempted to expand his bridgeheads and cross the Rhine between Braubach and Kaub. At Braubach enemy troops pushing forward towards Oberlahnstein were contained. At Boppard the enemy is still bottled up in the bend of the Rhine. Enemy attempts to cross at St. Goarshausen and northwards and at Oberwesel failed. On the other hand the enemy succeeded in getting troops across the Rhine at Kaub.

Pushing north from Darmstadt enemy armoured forces broke through our reserve positions. They pushed on farther north-eastwards and entered Offenbach. Severe fighting is in progress on the southern edge of Frankfurt am Main. At Hanau the enemy advanced southwards along the Main and captured Gross-Steinheim. The situation in the Seligenstadt area is obscure. Enemy forces which had crossed the Main at Aschaffenburg were held at Schweinheim. Enemy attempts to expand the bridgehead north of Worms were stopped by counter-attack.

No special reports from the Italian front.

There was heavy enemy air activity on the Eastern Front. In the central sector 885 Soviet aircraft were in action. The fortresses of Breslau and Glogau were resupplied by air. German close-support aircraft again reported good results in the East.

In action against an enemy air attack on a German convoy in Norwegian waters our fighters shot down seven enemy aircraft and dispersed the enemy formation.

Enemy air activity in the West was reduced for reasons of weather. 450 American four-engined bombers made their main attack on Plauen; from the south 800 four-engined bombers with strong fighter escort raided south-west Germany; 20 Soviet aircraft were in the general area of Berlin during the day and dropped several HE bombs on Fredersdorf station. They also machine-gunned Kaulsdorf. 600 bombers made their main target Wiener Neustadt. Most of the bombs dropped north of Vienna fell in the open. During the night a harassing raid was made on Berlin by 70 Mosquitos.

Three aircraft were shot down by AA. One Mosquito was shot down over Berlin during the night.

The British and especially the Americans are at present
pursuing really wide-ranging plans on the Western Front;
this applies particularly to General Patton who has been
conspicuous for his series of audacious advances ever since
the start of the offensive and who is now well under way.
He is letting it be known that practically nowhere is he
meeting any firm resistance and consequently can drive
around in our country unimpeded. This is in fact the case.
The American advance in the Main region in particular has
thrown us into the most vexatious confusion. We hardly
even have replacement units available in this area. We are
now having to have recourse to the Cadet School in Tölz
in order to plug at least the worst holes as best we may.
Patton too, however, cannot do just what he likes. He must
wait for supplies since gains of ground as large as those
he has made in the last week eat up material in the long
run and this seems to a certain extent to be the case with
him today. In any case the American advance in the
southern sector of the Western Front and the British crossing of the Lower Rhine have produced a sort of frenzy of
victory in London. Every Englishman is now convinced
that the war will be over in a few weeks, perhaps in a few
days. People are counting on mid-April at latest. Montgomery has contributed to this mood with his continuous
attacks on the publicity media. It may be of great advantage to us in the coming weeks. Even Eisenhower, however,
who is otherwise invariably most cautious in his estimates,
is allowing himself to be carried away by the general
hypnosis and is saying that there will now be no further
hold-up until Berlin. We shall have a word to say about
that, however.

I am now in process of initiating a very highly coloured
anti-Anglo-American propaganda campaign in the German
press and radio. So far we have treated the Anglo-
Americans far too leniently in our propaganda and have
based ourselves solely on the information issued by them.
As a result morale in the West has not become better but
worse. With our anti-bolshevist atrocity campaign we
succeeded in reconsolidating our front in the East and

making the civil population completely ready to defend themselves. That this has not happened in the West is primarily due to the fact that large sections of the German people and also of our troops think that the Anglo-Americans will treat them more leniently. As far as day-to-day procedures are concerned this may be true; fundamentally, however, the Western camp is far more hostile to us than the Eastern. We must now institute a new propaganda system, going more into the particulars, describing more details and thereby attacking the enemy once more. As the facts prove, our propaganda hitherto has failed to make its impact on the German people.

The British newspapers too are now rejoicing that German morale should be sinking so rapidly. The *Daily Mail* is extraordinarily surprised. It had thought the German attitude to be firmer than it is proving to be.

The British maintain that since 1 March the Anglo-Americans have taken 300,000 prisoners. This figure seems to me highly exaggerated; in fact, however, many of our units have given themselves up when there was no pressing necessity to do so. It would have been better if we had withdrawn from the Geneva Convention at the time of the bombing raid on Dresden. All the foxy fellows in the government opposed the idea. Now my point of view has once more been proved right.

The Anglo-Americans look upon the numerous Rhine crossings almost as an unexpected miracle. They had thought that they would meet much stiffer resistance here. Our severe losses on the left bank of the Rhine of course left large gaps in the ranks of our divisions.

In the evening Eisenhower declares that our main defence line has been broken and that they will now move direct on Berlin. I do not think, however, that the Anglo-Americans will try this. This will undoubtedly first make for other less distant objectives. This is also stated in various quarters on the other side. They are said to be thinking of Leipzig or Kassel, for instance. In short the enemy information policy is not co-ordinated and we can hardly make any worthwhile deductions from it as regards our own strategy.

The political worries facing the Anglo-Americans in the event of a German collapse for which they have longed, and which they now expect soon, are gradually and increasingly beginning to emerge. It is feared that the consequences of this collapse will be devastating, not only for the Reich but for the whole of Europe and for our Western enemies. Europe, they say, has been turned into one great heap of ruins; it is facing complete catastrophe. Nevertheless in the Western camp people are still insisting that Germany must surrender unconditionally. A number of influential Englishmen are drawing up a melancholy political and economic balance sheet for this war. They frankly admit that Britain has lost almost everything, that she is no longer a great power and that this war can be described as the most unfortunate occurrence in British history.

For this Churchill is responsible. He was challenged in the Commons and questioned about possibilities of peace with the Reich. He answered evasively or at least with great reserve.

There is a definite and widespread feeling in London that victory and peace are round the corner. I believe that, if we succeed—and we must succeed—in re-establishing a firm defence line, no matter where, the British barometer will quickly fall below zero again. Churchill is already in such a victory mood that he is now cynically snubbing the workers and trades unions. He does not even receive their representatives. He thinks that is no longer necessary and is ruthlessly throwing overboard all the promises he made to the workers during this war, particularly in Britain's most critical periods.

Lloyd George has died at the age of 82. He was no longer taking any part whatsover in British politics. If he survives the war, Churchill will suffer a similar fate. The British do not treat their war leaders with much gratitude.

Great unease is noticeable in Turkey. People in Ankara are uncertain of Moscow's real purpose in denouncing the

Soviet-Turkish Pact. The Soviet press has launched an extraordinarily violent campaign against Turkey. In Turkish circles it is suspected that these attacks are aimed more at Britain than at Turkey. Soviet policy *vis-à-vis* Turkey bears a typical anti-British stamp. The decision on the Dardanelles question is to be taken in San Francisco. What a lot of things are to be done in San Francisco! And it is not even certain that this conference will take place at all or whether a Soviet representative will participate.

I am receiving frightful reports from Stuhlweissenburg of the Soviet atrocities committed there. They put in the shade those committed in the east German regions. Diaries found on dead Soviet soldiers at Stuhlweissenburg show, however, that the Soviet troops are extraordinarily warweary. There too people would prefer to see the guns silenced today rather than tomorrow. Moreover the naïveté of the Soviet soldiery is really grotesque. They picture themselves as the great world saviours and it is obvious that bolshevist propaganda has inoculated them with a superiority complex producing the most improbable results. Moreover it has been dinned into every Soviet soldier that he should take his revenge on Germany. And indeed he does so to the fullest extent. There are many complaints in the diaries about the partisan nuisance in the Soviet hinterland which in fact is keeping the Red Army extraordinarily busy.

Conti* has now issued a decree to German doctors giving them permission to carry out abortions on German women who have been raped by Bolshevists. This problem will play a considerable role in the future, particularly seeing that vast numbers of German women have been infected with venereal disease by Soviet soldiers.

Plauen has been very heavily attacked from the air. The town centre has been almost totally destroyed. Elsewhere we have again suffered much misery from the air. The British are no longer operating at night, however, probably because of the extraordinarily bright moonlight.

* "Reich Health Leader."

At midday I hold a roll-call in the Ministry. It takes place in the theatre hall which now consists of little more than the outer walls. I impress upon my staff that in the present critical situation they must show themselves models of manly loyalty.

Dr. Ley, who has just returned from a trip to Vienna and the Lower Danube, pays me a visit to report. He is pretty well knocked out and is thoroughly rattled by recent developments particularly in the West. Four days ago he was writing in *Angriff* that the crisis in the West was acting as a healthy restorative. The remark created a considerable public sensation. I reproach him with it. Now he pretends to know nothing about it. He wants to go to the Führer and ask his permission to form a Free Corps of courageous Party members. This Free Corps would undoubtedly be an undisciplined horde and I know in advance that the Führer will refuse permission if only for this reason. In other respects Ley's proposals for dealing with our present emergency are extraordinarily naïve, though they are evidence of goodwill. Ley has become somewhat hysterical under the impact of recent developments. It shows that he is not a naturally strong personality. He is only strong when there is some external cause to be so. Moreover he oscillates like a windsock when times are serious and critical.

The Führer is insisting on his order for total evacuation of western regions threatened by the enemy and total destruction of our industry. In the unanimous opinion of all western Gauleiters this order cannot in practice be carried out. How, for instance, is this now to be done in the Würzburg area, into which the Americans have suddenly and unexpectedly advanced? Who is to take charge of the people on the move and how are they to be moved? Who is to destroy industry and how is it to be done? In many respects today we are moving in a vacuum in our conduct of the war. We issue orders in Berlin which in practice never reach the lower level, let alone being capable of implementation. I see here the danger of an extraordinary loss of authority.

Our rationing system is now being made somewhat more flexible for the first time, in other words people get ration cards on which the various articles of food are not set out in detail. Only the basic foodstuffs such as fat, meat and bread remain in general unchanged.

Krosigk has now completed his draft on tax reform. For me the draft is too anti-social. It is based primarily on taxation of consumption; income tax, on the other hand, is not taken into consideration. Consumption taxation, however, hits almost solely the broad masses and is therefore extraordinarily unpopular with them. It would produce much injustice which at the present time we cannot afford to have. There will therefore be very strong resistance to Krosigk's draft.

At midday the Führer calls me over to the Reich Chancellery for a long talk. I am able to have a few words with General Burgdorf shortly beforehand. Even General Burgdorf is pretty depressed. He sees no way at the moment of opposing the Anglo-Americans in the Main area. People are now screaming from all sides for political salvation. This is a feeble excuse since of course we can do nothing politically when we are in such a miserable situation militarily. The fact that the Americans have been able to advance to Würzburg is of course an absolute scandal but it is primarily due to the facts that the troops are no longer fighting and that the civil population has far too often failed to take the necessary measures to prepare to defend itself. This Ley explicitly emphasised to me. He thinks that, if all the Gaus were as determined to defend themselves as, for instance the Berlin Gau, developments such as those in the Main area could not have taken place.

As far as the situation in the Main area is concerned attempts will be made to salvage something by makeshift measures. The situation is critical, however, not only there but also in Hungary. There we are possibly running the risk of losing our vital oilfield.* Our SS formations have put

* See above p. 249.

up a wretched show in this area. Even the Leibstandarte*
is no longer the old Leibstandarte since its officer material
and men have been killed off. The Leibstandarte bears its
honorary title in name only. The Führer has nevertheless
decided to make an example of the SS formations. He has
commissioned Himmler to fly to Hungary to remove their
armbands. This will, of course, be the greatest imaginable
disgrace for Sepp Dietrich. The army generals are rubbing
their hands at the blow dealt to their rivals. The SS formations in Hungary not only failed to carry their offensive
through but withdrew and in some cases pulled out. Inferior
human material left its mark in most unpleasant fashion.
Sepp Dietrich is to be pitied, Himmler too however, since
he, the Head of the SS with no war decorations, now has
to carry out this severe punishment in face of Sepp Dietrich
who wears the Diamonds. What is far worse, however, is
that our oilfield is now in most serious danger. Everything
must be done to preserve at least this basis for our strategy.

The scene in the Reich Chancellery garden is a desolate
one—just heap upon heap of rubble. The Führer's bunker
is being reinforced at this moment. The Führer is at
present determined to remain in Berlin even if the position
becomes critical. There is a sort of presentiment of doom
among the Führer's military entourage, proof of the fact
that the Führer has assembled around him only feeble
characters upon whom he cannot rely in emergency. The
attitude of the SS officers is good. Günsche reports to me
as Defence Commandant for the government quarter. I
think I can rely on him.

In Berlin we are of course working feverishly to increase
our defence preparedness. But these efforts are being put
to increasingly severe tests. Not only have the replacement
units been removed from Berlin but we now have to
relinquish major portions of the Berlin anti-aircraft—15
heavy batteries in all which are now destined for the Oder
front. I shall try to save at least some of them for the
Reich capital.

* *lit.* Life Guard Battalion—the most élite SS unit.

Then I have the exhaustive discussion with the Führer that he wanted. We talked walking up and down in the Chancellery garden. The Führer, thank God, is in good shape physically, as is always the case with him when things are critical. In this respect he is really admirable. Sadly, however, I note that he stoops even more as he walks; outwardly he is completely relaxed, however, as is only right in the present situation. Nevertheless I notice that he is extraordinarily tense. Recent events at the front have put him under great pressure. We walk up and down the terrace outside his study for an hour and I take the opportunity of expounding my view of the situation. I tell him that, in view of the extraordinarily critical situation at the front, morale both at home and among the troops has sunk to an extraordinarily low level. We must succeed in calling a halt somewhere since otherwise there is a danger of the whole Western Front crumbling. I regard this as the right moment for the Führer to address the nation, both the home front and the troops, over the radio—the speech need be no more than ten to fifteen minutes in length. I cite the examples of Churchill during the British crisis and Stalin during the Russian. They then found the right words to inspire their people again. In the early days of the Party struggle we always did this. The Party never experienced a severe crisis without the Führer addressing them personally and putting them on their feet again. Now the moment has come when the Führer must give the people a signal. I am prepared and determined to develop a great propaganda campaign from it. But the watchword must be given by the Führer. I outline to the Führer the rough content of his speech as I conceive it. The decisive consideration in all his arguments must be that the people should get a word from him on which they can pin their hopes. Moreover the Führer can [half line illegible] no exaggerated hopes [half line illegible] nevertheless some [half line illegible] which in the present emergency [half line illegible] could be mentioned.

Basically the Führer is in agreement with my proposals. He thinks that in itself morale at home is not bad but it has been infected by the bad morale at the front. In general the home front had suffered very severe blows without flinching, but the moment it came in contact with the front its morale sank. The Führer is still of the opinion that the critical developments in the West are the result of treachery from on high. The same Army failed at Trier as had already failed at Avranches. Admittedly changes have been made at command level but the old spirit is still there. In no other way can it be explained how so solid a bunker system as that surrounding Trier should be abandoned without a fight. This bunker zone was abandoned for reasons which sound perfectly childish today— that it was preferable to fight in the open since one could deploy better there and such like. These reasons were advanced in all seriousness. Today one can see how misleading they were. The Führer is furious over this treachery. But at the moment he does not know the quarter from which it comes. He believes it comes from the headquarters of Commander-in-Chief West. Here again, however, it is noticeable that, though the Führer correctly perceives what has happened, he seldom draws the right conclusions. It is a fact that the critical developments began with the loss of the Trier bunker zone. From this flowed the crossing of the Rhine at Remagen. The crossing at Remagen resulted either from treachery or a disgraceful neglect of duty. Operationally only the bridgehead over the Lower Rhine is adequately manned, proof of the fact that, where our troops resist, the Anglo-Americans definitely cannot march about as they please. In most cases the other bridgeheads are no longer under our control. Whether the reason is lack of morale or actual treachery, this is no moment to enquire into the reasons but to register the facts, since the country is in a position of the greatest danger and we must act accordingly. The Führer finds the fact that the enemy was able to advance to Würzburg quite inexplicable. He now proposes to bring up large numbers of units still available in barracks and put as much of the Luftwaffe into action as is possible. But naturally it will take time before these measures can take effect.

Meanwhile we are suffering frightful losses of territory with the corresponding loss of human and war potential. It is questionable whether this can be made good during the future course of the war. I have the impression that at the moment the Führer is taking this too lightly. At least he does so to me, though undoubtedly he thinks differently at heart.

Kesselring's appointment came too late. He should have been put in Rundstedt's place some months ago. Model is of course an excellent commander but somewhat too intellectual. Nevertheless he is a fanatical adherent of the Führer and a true National-Socialist.

Once more I emphasise to the Führer that we must call a halt somewhere if we are ever to get the better of this war. I am sceptical whether we shall succeed in doing so in the next few days. The Führer is right when he says that the morale of the troops and the morale at home react on each other. It is also true that in many cases the troops have infected the home front with their bad morale because they have not been brought up as National-Socialists.

I am very pleased that the Führer should stress that I was the only one to be right over the question of withdrawal from the Geneva Convention. All the others had opposed it, he says. But they are after all only bourgeois people gone to seed; they have no conception of revolutionary conduct of war and so could not be expected to support it. It is really tragic to see the Führer, who is a revolutionary of the highest order, surrounded by such mediocre people. He has selected a military entourage which is beneath contempt. He himself now describes Keitel and Jodl as fuddy-duddies who are weary and worn out and can make no suggestions for really great decisions in the present emergency. The only commanders who are abreast of modern popular war are Model and Schörner. Model, as has been said, is an intellectual type; Schörner puts his heart and soul into the battle. He has undoubtedly achieved the greatest successes operationally. But that is the end of the list of great army commanders. The SS too has failed to throw up any specially notable strategists. Even Himmler has not succeeded in finding one in his ranks. They are good go-getters but not of really high class.

I point out to the Führer at length that in 1934 we unfortunately failed to reform the Wehrmacht when we had an opportunity of doing so. What Röhm wanted was, of course, right in itself but in practice it could not be carried through by a homosexual and an anarchist. Had Röhm been an upright solid personality, in all probability some hundred generals rather than some hundred SA leaders would have been shot on 30 June. The whole course of events was profoundly tragic and today we are feeling its effects. In that year the time was ripe to revolutionise the Reichswehr. As things were the Führer was unable to seize the opportunity. It is questionable whether today we can ever make good what we missed doing at that time. I am very doubtful of it. Nevertheless the attempt must be made. Now, however, we cannot initiate long-term measures but must do what the moment demands and it seems to me that that is the speech by the Führer for which I have asked. At first the Führer is reluctant to do this because at the moment he can say nothing positive. I put such pressure on him, however, that in the end he says that he agrees with my proposal. I must not give way on this point. It is my national duty to press the Führer to give the people a watchword for their life and death struggle. I emphasise to the Führer that 15 minutes over the radio would be quite enough. I know that this speech will be very difficult. But it should be possible for the Führer to cite a whole series of positive factors, in particular as regards the probable future development of the air war. Here the Führer has great hope, particularly in our new fighters. He tells me yet again the whole story of the Luftwaffe's development, which I know since he has frequently explained it to me already. The Luftwaffe's crisis is definitely of a technical nature and Göring is to blame. The Führer is now somewhat more inclined to excuse Göring, however, since, as he says, Göring had insufficient technical background to foresee this development in time. He has also been led by the nose by his General Staff. This same Luftwaffe General Staff is now trying to deceive the Führer, particularly as regards the speed of the new fighter on which he has been given totally false figures. The Führer, however, intends to punish most severely any falsehood on important military matters. He is now taking brutal measures as regards the Luftwaffe's organisation.

On the Führer's behalf Kammler* has now taken charge of the movement of the new fighters from factory to airfield and construction of the new airfields. The Führer has given him the widest plenary powers. Göring, though grumbling, has given his agreement. What else can he do? Airfields, aircraft and oil are now the overriding problems. The results achieved by our new fighters have been most gratifying so far. If these fighters could appear in great numbers it is possible that we could sweep our skies clear again. But, as the Führer explicitly states, it is two seconds to twelve. The best we can achieve is a last-second turn of fortune. Here lies the real decision. The reason for our military decay is to be found in the air terror. So, in our new military measures, we must make a beginning with the Luftwaffe.

As I have already emphasised, the Führer is now inclined to allow Göring some freedom from blame. I regard this as absolutely impossible. It is simply ridiculous now to show any sympathy for a man who has brought the Reich into such a mortal crisis. He carries the blame for our ruin and, if only for historical reasons, he must bear the consequences. The fact that he did not know what he was doing is immaterial. It would be the last straw if he had consciously led the Reich into this mortal danger.

Our new fighters are now being manned by close support pilots instead of fighter pilots. They are more honest, decent and not so mollycoddled. The Führer pins all his hopes on the use of these new jet aircraft. The enemy has no effective answer since jet aircraft cannot operate over Germany from England owing to the fuel problem. More-

---

* Officer in charge of V-weapons.

over the Führer is determined to reform the Luftwaffe from
the bottom up. He is thoroughly in agreement with my
reform programme. He thinks that the Luftwaffe's morale
is not so bad as to be irreparable. The morale of our
fighter pilots has sunk so low merely because they were
forced to fly inconceivably bad aircraft in which they were
miles inferior to the enemy. Speer too carries some of the
blame for the continued production of these old useless
machines, technically no match for the enemy and which
could do us no good. The Führer thinks Saur* a stronger
personality than Speer. Saur is a tough stayer who, when
given a job, will carry it through, if necessary by force.
To some extent he is the opposite of Speer. Speer is more
of an artist by nature. Admittedly he has great organisational talent but politically he is too inexperienced to be
totally reliable in this critical time. The Führer is very
angry about recent statements made to him by Speer. Speer
has allowed himself to be influenced by his industrialists
and is continually saying that he does not intend to lift a
finger to cut the German people's lifeline; this is for our
enemies to do; he does not intend to take responsibility
for it. The Führer counters this by saying that we have to
carry the responsibility anyway, that the point now is to
bring the struggle for our people's existence to a successful
conclusion and that tactical questions play only a subordinate role. The Führer intends to summon Speer during
the afternoon and face him with a stern alternative: either
he must conform to the principles of present-day conduct
of the war or the Führer will dispense with his assistance.
He says with much bitterness that he would prefer to live
in a prefab or creep underground than have palaces built
by a member of his staff who had proved a failure at the
moment of crisis. The Führer uses extraordinarily hard
words about Speer. I do not think that Speer will have an
easy time with him in the next few days. Above all the

* Saur was Head of the Technical Office in Speer's Ministry of
Munitions. In his memoirs, Speer describes how Hitler sought to
build up Saur at his expense in the last months. In his Testament,
Hitler nominated Saur as Minister of Munitions instead of Speer.

Führer intends to put an end to Speer's speechifying which is definitely of a defeatist nature. Speer is another of those who opposed our withdrawal from the Geneva Convention. Moreover Bormann was one of them too. Bormann is not doing very well at the moment. His ideas, particularly on the question of radicalisation of the war, are not what I would have expected of him. As I have already said, these people are semi-bourgeois. Their thinking may be revolutionary but they do not act that way. Now, however, the revolutionaries must be brought to the top. I emphasise this to the Führer but the Führer replies that he has only a few of such people available. Many of our Gauleiters in the West also have shown themselves complete weaklings. I am very downcast over our lack of fighting spirit in the West. That Köln, for instance, should surrender within an hour is really shameful. The Führer places the blame for this on the Wehrmacht but of course the political leadership too must carry a large share of the blame. What a different picture is presented by Hanke in Breslau! The Führer refers to him as the Nettelbeck* of this war and he in fact deserves it. The decline of the Luftwaffe is also due to the bourgeois elements in it. Göring, after all, is more a bourgeois than a revolutionary.

But these questions are only marginal. One cannot broach these fundamental questions today; one must simply be glad if one can muddle along from one day to the next. It is nevertheless right that the Führer should ensure that Speer is extracted from the toils of industry, under whose influence he is. He must no longer be the tool of the economic circles around him. The Führer's decision that we should leave no war potential behind to the enemy is also right; otherwise it would very quickly be used against us. It is simple nonsense to say that we should not assume responsibility for the destruction of our war potential. History will acquit us if we win the war. It will not acquit us if we lose it, no matter the reasons for which this or

* Joachim Nettelbeck was a hero of the Napoleonic war, who defended Kolberg against the French. Goebbels is presumably thinking of his film *Kolberg*.

that happens. We have to carry the responsibility and we must show ourselves worthy of it.

The Führer is already talking of the possible replacement of Speer by Saur, which in my view is extraordinarily significant. As a result the situation is highly critical for Speer. In any case I propose to draw his attention to it. It would be a good thing if the Führer would apply to the Luftwaffe the severe measures he has in mind for Speer or the SS troops, for example. This is where they are most necessary. It is to be hoped that the Führer will not only grasp the facts correctly and say as much but also draw the correct conclusions. Here in my view lies the great difference between him and Frederick II; Frederick after all was so ruthless in his measures both against high and low that he frequently aroused hatred and disgust even among his troops and his generals. After this talk with the Führer one could say yet again: "Yes, you are right. Everything you say is right. But what are you doing about it?"

The way in which the Führer, even in this crisis at the front, invariably and unswervingly believes in his lucky star, is truly admirable. One sometimes has the impression that he is living in the clouds. But he has so often come down from the clouds like a *deus ex machina*. He is still convinced that the political crisis in the enemy camp justifies our having great hopes, however little we can talk about it at the moment. It grieves me very much that at present he cannot be persuaded to do something to ensure the growth of this political crisis. He is making no personnel changes either in the Reich government or the diplomatic service. Göring is still there; Ribbentrop is still there. All the failures—apart from the second level—are being retained and in my view it would be of decisive importance for our people's morale to make a change of personnel in these places. I urge and urge; but I cannot convince the Führer of the necessity of the measures I propose. So I must put off my intentions to next time.

As far as the East is concerned, the Führer is pleased with developments except in Hungary. Schörner is holding firm. He has scored outstanding defensive victories justifying great hopes. On the other hand the situation in Hungary is terrible. Here we are faced with a serious crisis which—as already mentioned—raises the spectre of the loss of the Hungarian oilfields. The Führer is very angry that Sepp Dietrich should have hoodwinked him. He left major units of his Sixth Army at home in order to have them available as replacement units on his return and so went into action with 40,000 men instead of 70,000. Naturally this was noticeable as soon as the offensive began. The Führer proposes to call Dietrich to account most severely. According to the Führer Sepp Dietrich has quickly acquired the Wehrmacht's habit of juggling with figures. The Führer has despatched Himmler to Hungary to put things right there and institute the necessary punitive measures. Nevertheless it is established that the offensive by our SS formations met an enemy offensive and, had it not been made, we should have lost the oilfields long ago. In Hungary too everything now hangs by a thread. The Führer thinks that we must stand firm here if we are not to have the ground cut from under our feet. But military developments are such that today's hopes frequently turn into tomorrow's theories. As I have already stressed, the Führer perceives everything correctly but he draws no conclusions. It is a real calamity that he has no staff capable of putting his ideas into practice. Today it is plenty late to put ideas into practice but there would still be much to be done if the right men were in the right place. I am determined not to admit that it is too late and I am firmly convinced that a way out will be found at the most critical moment. In any case the Führer is doing all that he can. Fate must then decide. Nevertheless it must be added that the Führer is taking action on material matters rather than personnel. The result is that he is increasingly in conflict with his staff. For instance Himmler and Sepp Dietrich are now in high disfavour. Where will all this lead? What will be left at the end of it all? When I picture to myself Himmler tearing the armbands off the SS formations, I feel weak at the knees. It will give the SS a real shock. I am also seriously worried about Sepp Dietrich for he is not the sort of man to take such a humiliation lying down.

I press the Führer yet again for an early speech. I do not give way in face of his objections. I tell him of my roll-call in the Ministry this morning and how it produced throughout the office a greater revival of morale and determination than I had expected myself. I refer yet again to what Churchill and Stalin did when their countries were in extreme crisis. The Führer realises this fully and is now firmly determined to make his speech as soon as possible. I ask his staff to press him further to ensure that he actually does it.

During this talk the Führer poured out his heart to me to an unaccustomed extent. I am most happy that I should have his complete unrestricted confidence. I would so much like to help him in all this worry and distress but my possibilities are limited. In any case I shall do my utmost to ensure that I cause him no particular worry from my side. The essential now is that our leaders and our adherents should fight, hold on and stand firm. We must think and above all act in a revolutionary way. The moment has now come to shake off the last bourgeois egg-shells. Half-measures can do no good now. This is the hour for all-out men and all-out action. Though the situation may be frightful, we can get the better of it by exerting all our strength.

Meanwhile the military briefing conference awaits the Führer. Guderian keeps looking out through the window. He gives an impression of weariness and agitation. The other flabby-looking figures are not calculated to reinforce the Führer's steadfastness. Thank God, however, he possesses enough of that naturally and has no need of reinforcement from others.

I commission Schaub and Albrecht* once more to keep working on the Führer to ensure that the speech is dictated, if possible within the next 24 hours. They all promise me to do their best, for they are all convinced that a speech by the Führer now will work like balm on a wound. So I

---

* Hitler's naval adjutant.

shall hope for the best—that my visit has achieved this result. On the other problems I shall go on hammering away in so far as I can. After all I shall succeed in the end.

Back at home I find a mountain of work. But these days a mountain of work is invariably a mountain of worries. One hardly gets good news any more. And outside there is still this lovely spring weather. Volkssturm battalions pass my window singing. In Berlin at least we are still organising our defence and I am firmly determined that, if it comes to the crunch here, I will face the enemy with a battle unique in this history of this war. How strong are the conflicting influences to which any unstable character is subjected daily at the present time! Sometimes one thinks that one has mastered the impressions of the day; nevertheless sometimes one wonders where all this will lead.

Magda has gone to Schwanenwerder to make preparations for the move of our children there. But she has again somewhat overdone it and is now ill in bed. That is the last straw.

In the evening, after the Mosquito raid, I thumb through various papers still remaining in the safe from the time of our struggle period. Reading them produces a flood of melancholy memories. Their effect is almost that of a salute from the good old days which will never return.

WEDNESDAY 28 MARCH 1945

(pp. 1–33, 9 and 10 omitted in page-numbering)
Military Situation.
In Hungary the Soviets, attacking westwards on a broad front, reached the Raab valley. Farther south they reached the railway line to Lake Balaton. Apart from a minor break-in all attacks on the Komorn bridgehead were contained. Our own strong bridgehead farther east was withdrawn to the north bank of the Danube. Soviet attacks on the lower Gran were repulsed. At Leva the bolshevists extended their penetration of the previous day by about 10 km; their leading troops reached the railway leading south to Komorn via Neuhäusel.

There was very severe fighting in the Mährisch–Ostrau area but the enemy only succeeded in penetrating at Joslau. All attacks in the Loebschütz and Neisse area were repulsed with a loss to the Soviets of 85 tanks. All attacks at Strehlen also failed.

In the Küstrin sector an offensive is in progress to clear the approach to Küstrin and it has already had some initial success. This offensive will be continued. Strong enemy attacks on our bridgehead at Zehden failed apart from a minor break-in. Attacks on the Pölitz bridgehead were all repulsed.

In the Danzig area the enemy continued his attacks, penetrating deeper into the city's inner defence ring. The country east of Danzig was flooded by us. According to hitherto unconfirmed reports German forces on the Belga spit are being transferred to Pillau.

On the Courland front the situation remained unchanged. The Anglo-Americans were able to make no great progress anywhere in the Lower Rhine battle zone; in some cases German counter-attacks were a feature of the situation.

In detail: the enemy captured Millingen and Brünen. South-east of Brünen the enemy was driven back by counter-attack on either side of Wesel Forest. Between Gahlen and Kirchhellen the enemy crossed the Sterkrade road and also late in the evening the road south of Kirchhellen. At Dinslaken the enemy attacked south-eastwards in strength and reached the autobahn at Hausterbruch. Two Panzer divisions are being brought up from Holland and, provided they are not too much delayed by the enemy air forces, will constitute a considerable reinforcement of our line. Should this move not be possible owing to heavy enemy air interdiction, the previous line will not be able to be held in the long run.

In the sector between the Sieg and the Lahn the enemy extended his penetration at Limburg as far as Arnstein and eastwards towards Bad Nauheim and Hesselbach.

The enemy moved out of his bridgeheads at St. Goar and Kaub reaching Miehlen, Nastätten and Grebenroth.

The enemy advance from Limburg southwards to the autobahn, by-passing Wiesbaden on the east, is clearly intended to join up with the advance westwards across the Main from Frankfurt am Main, thus cutting off Wiesbaden and parts of the Central Taunus.

Fighting is taking place at Frankfurt main station and the enemy has crossed the Main west of the city. Counter-attacks by us are in progress at Hanau. The enemy also crossed the Main at Krotzenburg, near Alzenau and at Hörstein. Fluctuating fighting developed at Aschaffenburg and Schweinheim, but here the enemy was unable to advance further. He advanced through Lohr as far as Gemünden, then swung north and thence attacked eastwards again.

Nothing fresh from the Italian front.

Around midday three air formations of medium strength attacked north-west Germany. Bombs were dropped on Bremen and Bremen-Farge. West Germany was attacked by 300 close-support aircraft. Bombs were dropped on Münster, Unna, Hamm and Kamen. In the afternoon 200 bombers with fighter escort raided the Paderborn and Bielefeld area. The evening's harassing raid on Berlin was made by 60 Mosquitos.

———

This morning a report arrives from Würzburg which sounds more hopeful. Gau headquarters says that the situation is completely under control there and that Aschaffenburg has been cleared of the enemy again. Dr. Fischer, head of our Reich Propaganda Office, has taken proper care of those who hoisted white flags on the enemy's approach. In the Mainfranken Gau they will get very rough treatment, which moreover they deserve. On this subject we must proceed with much greater severity than unhappily we did in the Rhineland or this sort of defeatism will spread like a disease.

Tank-destroyer detachments are now in action in the areas over-run by the Americans and they have already done good work. Nevertheless they have not been able to prevent the enemy making extraordinarily large gains of ground in the last 24 hours. There is no question, therefore, of the hyper-optimism prevalent in Britain and the USA diminishing at the moment. On the contrary they are acting as if the war was already won, as if they were meeting absolutely no further resistance on German soil and as if the German people was near to collapse.

The report by the American Press Agency that the capture of the Main bridges was due to treachery may well be true. In fact there are leading elements on the Western Front who would like to put an end to things in the West as quickly as possible and so, directly or indirectly, are playing into Eisenhower's hands.

Eisenhower's public relations policy is at present extraordinarily adroit and it is causing us considerable difficulties. In his headquarters bulletin he changes the probable direction of his advance every day, so that we can gather nothing worthwhile from the official enemy announcements. In addition the Americans have now taken over our Frankfurt wave-length and are trying to play the same game with the German people as we played with the French during our western offensive in the summer of 1940. Almost hourly they put out false reports of the capture of towns and villages, thus creating the greatest confusion among the German public. I have now ordered a military transmitter to use our abandoned Frankfurt wave-length; it will issue concrete reports and contradict the enemy's false announcements. I expect it to have a beneficial effect. I am also having the American false reports contradicted by announcements over the official German radio; they will be made at the same time as the reports on the air situation.

Eisenhower is somewhat more cautious in his forecasts than his war reporters. He says that the war in the West can by no means be written off, that our Western enemies insist on unconditional surrender and that consequently stiff German resistance must be reckoned with. His war reporters maintain that his purpose is to divide North and South Germany from each other. If he succeeds in that, so they say, he will practically have won the war. However he is letting the British and American public know that he has to surmount extraordinarily difficult supply problems, which is certainly true, and that his advance is not directed straight on Berlin.

So far, as Eisenhower states, the Anglo-Americans have taken 250,000 prisoners on the Western Front—a shameful figure which makes one blush. Had my proposal been accepted and had we withdrawn from the Geneva Convention, things would undoubtedly have been quite different. The reception given to the Anglo-Americans by the people would also be much different from that which is unhappily the case today. They have been able to report, for instance, that the people of Limburg welcomed the Americans with demonstrations of joy and flowers. I think that these reports are much exaggerated, as indeed are all reports from the

West—including our own; nevertheless it does seem that the Limburgers did not throw stones at the Americans. Experience shows that opposition to the enemy occupation authorities only begins when the people have to some extent recovered their composure.

It is good news that Oppenhoff, who was installed as Burgomaster in Aachen by the Anglo-Americans, was shot during the night Tuesday/Wednesday by three German partisans. I think that Vogelsang, the Burgomaster of Rheydt, will suffer the same fate in the next few days. Nevertheless I am not satisfied with the work of our Werwolf organisation. It is starting very slowly and it does not seem that there is adequate pressure behind it. At my next interview with the Führer I may well try to annex this organisation myself. I would impart more drive to it than it has at present.

British and American official quarters see no reason at present to campaign against the hyper-optimism which is the order of the day. Not only are they joining in this victory psychosis but they are fuelling it officially. Reuters, for instance, report that the British War Cabinet has been ordered to hold itself in readiness for a German surrender over Easter and not to go on holiday. The same is reported from the USA. Roosevelt has put his ministers on alert for victory. But the cloven hoof is in evidence when he adds that preparations for San Francisco are to be discontinued. That is in fact the crux of the matter. The San Francisco Conference is due to open on 25 April and it will face insoluble problems all along the line. The Anglo-Americans would naturally prefer, even at the risk of cancelling the conference, to await a full-scale German surrender, since they would then be able to exert much greater pressure on the Kremlin. Here may be a great political opportunity for us. In any case we must now do our utmost to neutralise the enemy's panic propaganda now being distributed not only over enemy stations but by every propaganda method. During the course of the day my counter-measures are already beginning to take effect. At least there is now no question of the Radio Frankfurt* reports being widely listened to. It is alarming to see how the enemy is turning our own weapons against us. The only reason, however, is that he has greater potential and uses it more ruthlessly than we do.

Reconstruction of a new front in the West is, of course, beset by the great difficulties since our troop resources are extraordinarily low owing to casualties in killed, wounded and, above all, prisoners. As we did a few weeks ago in the East, we must now try and make do with makeshift units.

As I have already said, a debate on the peace has taken place in the Commons. One MP from the Independent Labour Party challenged Churchill to bring the shooting to an end as soon as possible. Churchill merely replied: "That sounds very good and pleases me"—a truly sibylline remark from which no conclusion can be drawn in any direction.

The Catholic press in Britain, mainly the *Catholic Herald*, is now using fairly strong language against bolshevism. The *Catholic Herald* in general supports our theories. The paper says that National-Socialism is better and more tolerable than bolshevism and, had it not been for the war, would have got over its teething troubles. In any case it must be regarded as the lesser of two evils. One can see in these statements the guiding hand of the Vatican.

The American press too, led moreover by the Jewish journalist Lippman, is now saying that in practice Germany cannot be destroyed, that even after defeat the German people must be accorded a certain standard of living, in short that the Morgenthau plans are no more than out-of-date theory.

The Americans are now giving the world notice of their extraordinarily difficult food situation. They are trying to justify the awful fact that they are simply allowing the peoples they have allegedly liberated to starve. In a cynical phrase it is added that about one hundred million people will be brought to the verge of starvation as a result of the

* The Allied-controlled broadcasting station.

war. Hunger is the Allies' daily dish for Europe. It is small comfort to us to learn from enemy sources that German occupation policy in Western countries was considerably better than that now being pursued by the Allies.

The British are making a battleship available to the Soviets and the Americans a cruiser. The great traditional maritime powers have therefore sunk so low that they are providing from their own resources a complement to the naval power of their present sworn enemy.

The only news from the East is that the crisis in Hungary has become even more acute. Our SS divisions fighting there seem unable to regain their foothold. The oilfield* is now seriously threatened—something that the Führer wished to avoid in all circumstances.

Roosevelt has now succeeded in dragging the Argentine into the war—the last South American country. The reason for the Argentine declaration of war is more than threadbare. Japan is attacked as South America's main enemy and it is added that war must be declared on Germany too since Germany is allied to Japan.

An interesting report has reached us from the Duce's headquarters to the effect that the Pope sets the greatest store on learning the German peace conditions for possible negotiation with the Western Allies. The Führer refuses to meet his request. He describes the report as absolute nonsense, saying that at the moment and with the present situation at the front there can be no question of peace negotiations. In this the Führer is absolutely right. Though I have invariably advocated not letting things go too far and seeing whether we could extract ourselves from the war in some way, now we must first bring the Western Front to a halt again.

In the last 24 hours the air war has not been so bad as in previous days and weeks. The British have bombed our "Valentin" submarine yard at Bremen and their new heavy bombs have even penetrated 4½ metres of concrete overhead cover. Clearly the revival of our U-boat war has made

* See above p. 300.

a great impression on the West. American bombers have not taken off in the last 24 hours, only British. In addition they attacked transport installations, at present the most essential target for the Western Powers. At midday we have another air raid on Berlin, though only by 600 American bombers. They bombed primarily industrial targets in Siemensstadt and Marienfelde. Here we were treated to saturation bombing which is very bad for industrial installations. Daimler-Benz will be out of action for three to four weeks—a grievous loss. But the raid on the Reich capital was not as bad as I had initially supposed. We are listing only 80 killed. The number of homeless is very small since housing areas were not hard hit.

It is deplorable that Berlin should continually be losing its defence capability. The replacement units having already been taken for the front, even more anti-aircraft units, 14 heavy batteries this time, are being removed from Berlin and sent to the front. If this goes on, all my measures for raising the defence preparedness of the Reich capital serve little purpose, since Berlin cannot be held with the Volkssturm alone. I shall nevertheless try to maintain at least a certain degree of purely military defence capability since I am still counting on a serious threat to the capital in the near or very near future.

As was to be expected, no agreement has been reached over the question of the new taxation programme. The Ministry of Finance insists on its consumption tax. This anti-social tax cannot and must not be accepted. We must turn to an increase of income tax and then will undoubtedly achieve the desired result. In any case we must not allow ourselves to be diverted on to a false trail by pressure from industrial and business circles.

At midday I have a prolonged visit from Gauleiter Hildebrandt from Mecklenburg. He lays before me the well-known worries about the front-line situation, the domestic situation, morale and so forth. I can only say to him what I have said to so many Gauleiters recently. At least I manage to send him back to his work considerably reinvigorated and encouraged. His statement that, seen from Mecklenburg, the food situation is considerably better than we had hitherto supposed, is encouraging. Mecklenburg still has ample reserve stocks available. They have been reduced to some extent owing to the gigantic refugee convoys which have moved through the Gau—estimated at over four million. In addition to its 900,000 inhabitants Mecklenburg now has 1,700,000 evacuees, in other words nearly 100% overcrowding. One can imagine the result in this sparsely built-up country. But after all these are minor worries. An agricultural Gau like Mecklenburg will soon cope with them. What are they compared to the problems now faced by our Gauleiters in the West?

Dr. Ley has been to the Führer and submitted to him the question of formation of a Free Corps. It is to be named the "Adolf Hitler Free Corps" and be composed of activists formed into tank-destroyer units equipped with bazookas, assault guns and bicycles. In itself the idea is good but I would not expect the Führer to entrust the command of such a Corps to Dr. Ley. By his last published articles he has forfeited all credibility.* In it he referred to the front and the air war in terms of such total cynicism that one could only shudder. Ley wants to talk to me on the question of formation of the Free Corps. I shall give him my opinion quite frankly. In any case the Free Corps idea must be given better and more solid publicity support than can be done by Dr. Ley.

As the day goes on the enemy's panic announcements increase. I urge the Führer to make his speech over the radio as soon as possible. It is now as essential as daily bread. Only a speech by the Führer can bring the people back to order. Moreover I believe that this is entirely possible by means of such a speech. At the moment the people has somewhat lost its nerve. But that is not the worst of all evils. As soon as the home front is in order again the front-line situation will quickly be reconsolidated.

* See above p. 111.

In the evening I again take out some old papers and find there a mass of reminiscences from the movement's struggle period which make me very hopeful. Then too we were sometimes facing ruin but we always succeeded in the end in snatching victory from the most awkward situations. This will be so again even in the present case.

THURSDAY 29 MARCH 1945

(pp. 1–37)

Military Situation.

In Hungary the Bolshevists continued their attack westwards in strength. They crossed the Raab at several points and penetrated into the southern quarter of the town of that name. Leading enemy troops are at Csorna and Sarvar. Enemy attacks between the Raab valley and Lake Balaton were held on a stop-line running south-east to the western tip of Lake Balaton. Continuing his attacks all along the Gran sector the enemy drove German troops back to a line running northwards to the north-east of Neuhäusel. Further attacks on this line were in some cases repulsed and in others achieved local penetrations. The enemy penetrated somewhat deeper into our Komorn bridgehead. In addition he extended the front of his offensive on the Gran into Slovakia. An attack on either side of Königsburg made two minor break-ins. The situation at Neusohl is in general unchanged. A new development is a concentrated attack north of the High Tatra, where the enemy used four to five divisions and penetrated to some depth. Soviet attacks in battalion strength between Bielitz and Ratibor were repulsed. A complete defensive victory was scored at the sensitive points of the defensive battle in Silesia–Ratibor, Leobschütz, Ziegenhals and Neisse. Breslau successfully beat off enemy attacks.

Küstrin was extraordinarily heavily attacked from north, east and south. The enemy penetrated into the Old Town. The garrison has lost 70% of its officers, large numbers of men and its heavy weapons. Fighting continues, however, in the Old Town. Our atack on Küstrin from the west led to further improvement of our positions. There was increased enemy reconnaissance activity from the Zehden bridgehead to Stettin. Strong Soviet attacks on the Pölitz bridgehead necessitated evacuation of the Pölitz factory.

The enemy penetrated into Gotenhafen and Danzig. Remnants of the garrisons are holding out in the eastern parts of both places. The remainder of Fourth Army, which has been involved in heavy fighting for weeks, has now been transferred to Pillau with its commander after heroic resistance.

Our troops again scored a complete defensive victory on the Courland front. The enemy did succeed in making a break-in immediately east of Frauenburg, but it was held deep in the battle zone.

In the Dutch zone of the Western Front the enemy captured Mechelen. Whether this is the beginning of 1 Canadian Army's offensive is not yet clear.

In the battle on the Lower Rhine the enemy advanced south from Rees and reached Anholt. Leading enemy troops advancing north from the Dingden area reached the southern outskirts of Bocholt. In severe fighting farther east the enemy captured Raesfeld and then, advancing north, took Borken. Dorsten too fell into enemy hands. In violent fighting the enemy advanced from Munx Wood to Gladbeck. Advancing south he captured Hamborn.

Our switch position between the Sieg and the Lahn was moved north to Betzdorf. On the Dill the main line runs through Butzbach and Herborn. The enemy's main offensive was directed eastwards between Herborn and Wetzlar. Here he passed through Giessen and his leading troops are moving on Marburg. After capturing Giessen the enemy is trying to fan out northwards, north-eastwards, eastwards, south-eastwards and southwards.

Fierce street fighting continues in the battle for Frankfurt am Main. Enemy tanks advancing north from Hanau reached Kilianstetten; their object is clearly to gain contact with the formations moving south from Giessen. South of Hanau enemy forces moving out of the Kahlwies–Altenau bridgehead were driven back by counter-attack. Enemy detachments which had advanced through the Lohr area were annihilated.

From the bridgehead north of Mannheim the enemy advanced farther towards the mountain highway, reaching Weinheim from the north and Heddesheim and Wallstadt east of Mannheim. We are in process of forming a line along the Weinheim–Ladenburg railway. In this area enemy attacks on the western slope of the Odenwald were in general held.

No fresh news from the Italian front.

There was sustained enemy air activity on the Eastern Front. In the central sector, for instance, 1300 Soviet aircraft were in action. Our own close-support aircraft again carried out successful attacks on enemy tanks in the south and centre. Eleven Soviet aircraft were shot down.

On the Western Front air activity was reduced owing to unfavourable weather.

Over Reich territory 900 American four-engined bombers with fighter escort made daylight raids in two groups, attacking industrial targets and built-up areas in Berlin and Hannover. Both raids were described as medium to heavy. Reports of aircraft shot down by our fighters are not yet available. Four aircraft were shot down by anti-aircraft. Some 40 Flying Fortresses dropped numerous HE bombs on Minden. HE bombs were also dropped on Stendal air base. There were no night raids over Reich territory. Even the series of Mosquito raids on Berlin was interrupted for the first time.

The military situation in the West is characterised mainly by sinking morale both among the civil population and among the troops. This loss of morale implies great danger for us since a people and an army no longer prepared to fight cannot be saved, however great the reinforcements in men and weapons. In Siegburg, for instance, a women's demonstration took place outside the Town Hall demanding the laying down of arms and capitulation. In a radio message Grohé denies that this women's demonstration was of any great size and maintains that it has been artificially exaggerated by Commander-in-Chief West. Nevertheless the fact remains that, even though they may be on a smaller scale than described, such incidents did take place. The same general trend emerges from the report on the situation there given me by Lieutenant-Colonel Balzer on his return from the West. The report starts by saying that large-scale demoralisation has set in in the West, that a vast army of stragglers is on the move eastwards, that east-bound trains are crammed with armed men, that there is no longer any question of firm cohesion anywhere, and that in places detachments of Volkssturm can be seen marching westwards while the regular troops set off towards the east. This is, of course, extraordinarily menacing and gives rise to the greatest anxiety. I am convinced that we shall succeed in re-establishing some sort of order in this wildly milling mob. But, the war having moved so far onto German territory, we can no longer afford to abandon large areas as is usually associated with such proceedings. The Americans are already saying that they are only 150 miles from Berlin. This is not true but I believe that they are trying to divert our attention in a false direction by such announcements. This is also obvious from the fact that Montgomery, in his statement, says that he is going to advance as far as the Reich capital if possible. In actual fact it is my impression that the enemy's objective is Prague. We shall be able to offer him a great deal of resistance before he reaches that point; nevertheless it seems to me certain that the Anglo-Americans intend to reach the Protectorate before the Soviets.

Our parachute troops are putting up particularly tough resistance in the Wesel area. Here one can still refer to a firm line of resistance.

The exaggerated reports of military victories in the West have led to a real frenzy of rejoicing in the enemy camp. In the United States, in fact, it has produced real chaos. A stock-exchange boom in German securities has started.

Wall Street circles are promising themselves gigantic deals with the defeated and devastated European continent.

The surrender and peace talks have now been launched into international publicity via Stockholm. I have nothing much against this since, if we succeed in re-establishing a firm defence line, the reawakening on the Western side will be all the ruder. As my experiences with the German people show, psychological set-backs of this nature have most disagreeable repercussions. It is also to the good that the enemy should continue to insist that Eisenhower has already signed the act of surrender with the Führer in Berchtesgaden. We are hardly troubling to deny such rumours since they are disproved by the facts themselves.

As far as the Wesel area is concerned, our parachute troops are defending themselves like fighting madmen, in the words of the enemy press. The parachute divisions' morale is excellent. They represent the sole useful achievement of Luftwaffe headquarters.

In London people are somewhat more circumspect in the dissemination of military victory reports than in the United States, though even here they far overshoot the mark. It is being stated, for instance, that the enemy is already in Nuremberg or Leipzig and is marching straight on Dresden.

A report that the Burgomaster of Mannheim offered the city's surrender to the Americans over the telephone is really mortifying. This is a totally new way of conducting a war and one to which we are not accustomed. It is in fact true that morale in the West is still worse than it ever was in the East. I believe the reason to be that both our soldiers and the civil population expect to be treated more humanely by the Anglo-Americans than by the Bolshevists. Had we withdrawn from the Geneva Convention in good time, as I proposed, things would probably be very different.

In the evening I get the news from Gerland* that 400 enemy vehicles, most of them armoured, have reached Korbach. In this area, therefore, there is absolutely no question of active resistance. We shall probably have to

* Gauleiter of Kurhessen.

wait a week or a fortnight before it effectively makes its appearance.

Now, of course, the great moment has arrived for the war-monger on the enemy side. Vansittart* declares flatly that the problem of war criminals is simply one of the location of the gallows and the length of rope. This crazy gangster can still shoot off his mouth in England without anyone more sensible calling him to order.

I have had submitted to me an essay by Churchill written about the Führer in 1935.† The essay is extraordinarily characteristic of Churchill. He evinces great admiration for the Führer's personality and achievements but forecasts that whether he can retain his fame in history will depend on his further measures (from 1935 onwards).

Public opinion in England as a whole is certainly not basking in the sunshine. On the contrary, our foreign political situation report invariably stresses that scepticism about present war developments is now slowly spreading from the aristocracy, the church and leading military circles to the middle class. The future of the British Empire is regarded as being extremely perilous, although against this it must be said that Churchill is still master of the situation. There is general agreement with him that the German threat must first be eliminated before addressing oneself to the bolshevist threat. This seems to me to be the idea of the American war leaders also at present. In any case we cannot at present hope to profit much from the signs of disintegration in the enemy camp.

The Japanese in Berlin, even including those in the Embassy, have become very defeatist. Nevertheless they are urging us to continued resistance, following the old rule that any enemy whom we kill will not have to be killed by the Japanese.

The chaos developing in the remaining parts of Europe is increasing with giant strides. News of starvation and

* Lord Vansittart, former Permanent Under-Secretary of State at the British Foreign Office, was particularly hated by the Nazis for his strong anti-German views, expressed in his pamphlet *Black Record*.
† Published in his book *Great Contemporaries* (1937).

epidemics comes from every quarter; the British, in fact, are good enough to prophesy the Black Death and the plague for the European quarter of the globe in the immediate and more distant future.

Greenwood, the British Labour MP,* gives an extremely gloomy picture of coming developments in individual European countries. Their outlines are already clearly visible. A hunger demonstration by 100,000 men has taken place in Lyons, directed specifically against de Gaulle. De Gaulle is being violently attacked because of his food policy. His regime seems to be in serious danger. Bidault, the present Foreign Minister, is already being talked of as his probable successor. Bidault is a committed Anglophile and I assume that the British will have a decisive word to say in present developments in France.

Comment on the Rumanian problem is now taking on a sharper tone in America. At the moment, however, the Soviets are not reacting at all. The Americans, however, clearly think that, in view of their military successes in the West, they can afford to put pressure on the Soviets at present.

Mikolajczyk is laying down terms for his return to Poland. They are naturally totally unacceptable to the Kremlin. He is demanding that deportations be stopped at once, that the NKVD† be withdrawn from Poland and that free elections be held under the supervision of the Allied Powers—in short that everything that the Kremlin has initiated or planned in Poland be cancelled. Stalin's answer to these demands will undoubtedly be a simple sneer.

The Seydlitz Committee is now at work on the Kremlin's behalf even in neutral countries. I have in front of me propaganda material distributed in Sweden, for instance, by this traitor general. The argumentation put forward in these disquisitions is extraordinarily naïve. One could tear one's

---

* Arthur Greenwood, MP for Wakefield and Deputy Leader of the Labour Party.

† The Soviet Security Service, now KGB.

hair out at the political stupidity evinced here. I think, however, that this is a case of stupidity rather than treachery.

Following the outcome of the recent election the bolshevisation of Finland is proceeding at a somewhat faster tempo. Mannerheim is admittedly still in office but he has apparently little voice in affairs and the Soviets will undoubtedly remove him shortly.

Anfuso, hitherto Italian Ambassador in Berlin, has been nominated State Secretary for Foreign Affairs. He is a somewhat kaleidoscopic personality. He is described by proper fascists as one of Badoglio's second-level hangers-on. In any case we do not have to worry about him very much. Fascism and the social-fascist republic are so impotent that it is fairly immaterial who occupies the various ministerial posts in Mussolini's cabinet.

Hannover was raided yesterday in addition to Berlin. The two raids were described as medium to heavy. Reich territory was clear of enemy aircraft during the night. For the first time for 35 days Berlin was not given the compliment of its Mosquito raid. Among the inhabitants of the Reich capital this produced a sort of definite disappointment. When the Mosquitos did not arrive in the evening, everyone naturally expected that they would come during the night. They probably stayed away for reasons of weather.

I am now very busy with the so-called Werwolf organisation. Werwolf is intended to activate partisan activity in enemy-occupied districts. This partisan activity has by no means got off to a good start. Here and there certain noticeable actions have been reported such as, for example, the shooting of the Burgomaster installed by the Americans in Aachen; for the moment, however, no systematic activity is visible. I would like to take over direction of this partisan activity myself and I shall possibly ask the Führer to give me the necessary powers. I shall set up a newspaper for Werwolf and also make available a radio transmitter with powerful beam facilities; both will carry the same name.

Announcements both in the newspaper and over the radio will be in definitely revolutionary terms without any external or internal political restraints. In the present war situation Werwolf should be what the *Angriff* was during our struggle period when we were fighting not only for Berlin but for the Reich; in fact it should be a rallying point for all activists who are not prepared to adopt the course of compromise.

At midday Dr. Ley pays me a visit in order to tell me in detail of the plans for the "Adolf Hitler Free Corps." I have a considerable rumpus with him on the subject. The way in which Dr. Ley visualises formation of the Free Corps is impracticable. He has got the Führer to sign a decree prescribing that all activists from the Party and the Volkssturm should join this Free Corps. Were that actually to happen, the Volkssturm in Berlin, for instance, and in many other Gaus would lose its backbone and be of no further military value. In addition the organisation of the Free Corps as planned by Dr. Ley seems to me to be on a shaky foundation. Dr. Ley is setting to work with great enthusiasm; but one knows how shallow such enthusiasm is with him and how quickly it can ebb away. He is a man of short-lived passions and, whatever happens, we must ensure that the assembly of activists planned by him is presented in serious, responsible fashion. I also fear that he personally has not the reputation to cause the activists to stake their all. I give him all this quite openly as food for thought. Reichsleiter Bormann also shares my apprehensions. Dr. Ley promises to revise the decrees which he is proposing to issue and we have a further discussion in the evening. The revised decrees which he submits to me are approximately in line with what I had imagined such a Free Corps would be. The proclamation of the Free Corps is not to be made over the radio and aimed at the general public; I will include it in my daily circular to Gauleiters. The Gauleiters themselves are in a position to provide the 10,000 activists, the number required for the Free Corps from the Reich as a whole.

I am sending about 30 of the best speakers in the Party to the West so that they can help re-establish the morale of the troops and the civil population. I assemble them before their departure in order to give them directives and guide-lines for their oratorical activity. The overriding necessity is that we should learn to work with improvised methods. The large-scale technical propaganda media which we have had so far—the radio, wired broadcasting, the press, etc.—are now largely non-existent in the West. To achieve success man-to-man talking is necessary.

I discuss with Staatsrat [Privy Councillor] Tietjen of the Berlin State Opera certain people connected with the theatre. The artists of the Berlin State Opera have largely vanished from Berlin and are leading a drone-like parasitical existence in Upper Bavaria or the Tyrol, drawing their high salaries through the post. In general I am very dissatisfied with the political attitude of our artists. But one cannot expect them to be very courageous. They are merely artists, in other words in political matters totally indifferent, not to say characterless.

Some voluminous material has been submitted to me intended to initiate astrological or spiritualistic propaganda; it includes the so-called horoscope of the German Republic of 9 November 1918 and also the Führer's horoscope. The two horoscopes are in striking agreement. I can understand why the Führer has forbidden people to concern themselves with such uncontrollable matters. Nevertheless it is interesting that both the Republic's horoscope and that of the Führer predict some relief of our military situation for the second half of April; on the other hand the position will deteriorate in May, June and July, whereas apparently hostilities should cease by mid-August. May God grant that this is so. Admittedly we should be facing some difficult months; nevertheless if one knew that the worst period of the war would be over this year, these months would be considerably more tolerable than they will be in fact. For me these astrological prophecies are of no significance whatever. I intend, however, to use them in anonymous

332

camouflaged public propaganda since, in these critical times, most people will snatch at any straw.*

Once again there is alarming news from the West this evening. The enemy has advanced north of Marburg as far as Winterberg; he is near Fulda. He has widened his break-through at Giessen considerably. At the moment we have no regular troops available with which to oppose him. We are at present relying exclusively on part-time units. But we did this in the East a few weeks ago with great success. Our parachute divisions in the Wesel area are doing well. There one can still talk of an evenly matched war.

In the East developments in Hungary are extraordinarily critical and disagreeable. On the other hand Schörner has succeeded in beating off even the heaviest Soviet attacks in Upper Silesia. In Courland our brave divisions have once more succeeded in defeating all enemy attempts to break through. In Küstrin the garrison is fighting on the outskirts of the town, also in Danzig and Gotenhafen. Overall, of course, this situation is terrible; taking only the military situation into account and looking at the map, one could almost lose one's nerve. But war is not only a military but also a political phenomenon and its development depends on so many imponderables that at critical stages it is impossible to forecast even with semi-accuracy. Above all the lessons of history, which are unmistakable and entirely justify our present-day standpoint, give us firm support in the present phase of the war.

I am forcibly reminded of this when I suddenly get a telephone call from Breslau in the evening. By some method which he cannot describe in detail Hanke has succeeded in getting a telephone line to Berlin. During our telephone conversation he expresses himself as full of hope, is in good shape and emphasises that he can hold Breslau for an unpredictable time. As far as political attitude and character are concerned Hanke is undoubtedly our best

---

* Goebbels was soon to make use of these horoscopes. See *The Last Days of Hitler*, p. 110.

Gauleiter. Had our Gauleiters in the West acted as he has, the situation there would probably be very different from what it in fact is.

This time the British Mosquitos arrive in the middle of the night and tear the millions of inhabitants of the Reich capital away from their well-earned rest. It would be very unfortunate if the British persist in this procedure of Mosquito raids by night in future. It would mean that temporarily there would be no question of any regular nightly rest in Berlin.

FRIDAY 30 MARCH 1945

(pp. 1–46)

Military Situation.

In the East the main centres of fighting were in Hungary and the Mährisch–Ostrau area.

In Hungary the Soviets attacked our forward positions west of Kaposvar and penetrated in some places. At the north-west corner of Lake Balaton the enemy was held at Keszthely. Between Keszthely and Steinamanger the Bolshevists broke through our stop-line and reached Zalaegerszeg. These co-ordinated attacks are directed on the Nagy Kanizsa oilfield. On the German-Hungarian frontier the enemy penetrated into Steinamanger and Güns and reached Kaposvar, moving along the Raab–Wiener Neustadt railway. His attacks on Raab failed. North-east of Raab the enemy succeeded in crossing the river and moving some kilometres up the Danube. The enemy also made violent attacks on our positions on the Neutra between Komorn, Neuhäusel and Neutra. He was able to make some deep penetrations north of Neuhäusel. The bolshevists also made violent attacks and achieved penetrations in the Slovakian mountain country between Neutra and Neusohl. The cohesion of our front was maintained however.

In the fighting around Mährisch–Ostrau the Bolshevists continued their attacks uninterruptedly but fruitlessly. Only between Ratibor and Jägerndorf did they make certain penetrations, some of which were dealt with by counter-attack. Our operations improved our positions south of Breslau. The garrison of Küstrin was pressed back further. Radio communications have been interrupted at present.

On the Oder front as far as Stettin the enemy renewed his efforts to cross the river. Some battle groups are still resisting in Danzig. The Soviets again attacked heavily in Courland and achieved local penetrations along the Mitau–Frauenburg road. The loss of the Baltic ports is considerably hampering the supply of Courland.

On the Lower Rhine the British and Canadian forces made further progress, advancing northwards through Bocholt towards the Dutch frontier and through Borken to a point midway between Borken and Coesfeld. Moving along the Dorsten–Coesfeld railway they reached Gross-Reken, some 15 km south-west of Coesfeld. Leading enemy tanks moving along the Wesel–Münster road penetrated into Dülmen and then, advancing east through Haltern, approached Lüdenhausen. Moving forward from Dorsten and Gladbeck enemy forces captured the area north-west and south-west of Recklinghausen. No change on the Rhine–Sieg front. The strong American battle group in the Marburg–Biedenkopf area is now bringing up reinforcements and swinging mainly northwards. Its leading troops have reached Winterberg, Brilon and Audorf. They moved through Korbach towards Arolson and through Sachsenhausen north-eastwards. Enemy forces from Frankenberg reached the Bad Wildungen area. The autobahn viaduct over the Werra at Hannoversch–Münden was blown up. From the Marburg area the enemy reached Kirchhain and from the Giessen area he reached Lauterbach via Grünberg and Ulrichstein. This advance is directed on Fulda. From Hanau enemy forces advanced north-eastwards to the Nidda area and from Osten they reached a point west of Gelnhausen. The enemy moved south from Aschaffenburg and reached the Klingenberg area. A switch line was established here running roughly from Klingenberg east of Michelstadt, Oberbach, Neckarsteinach and Schriesheim, north of Heidelberg to Altrip on the Rhine. The enemy broke through our switch line between Heidelberg and Mannheim and crossed the Neckar.

No special reports from the Italian front.

Enemy air activity both over the front and over Reich

territory was small owing to weather conditions. About 150 British bombers raided the Salzgitter area. There was a harassing raid on Berlin during the night.

Our Western enemies now think that the slight revival of our resistance represents Kesselring's last attempt to ward off a German catastrophe. They say, however, that the Anglo-American advance has been beyond all expectation, so that Kesselring's efforts can have no success; there is no organised resistance to be found any longer; the Anglo-American tanks can drive about as they like. In general terms this is true apart from the Lower Rhine area where our parachute troops are still putting up fanatical resistance with which Montgomery has so far been quite unable to deal.

In the light of this situation in the West it is clear that anxiety about the U-boat war in Britain and America is slowly disappearing. There had recently been much beating of breasts about the reappearance of our U-boats on the high seas but now the view is that this threat is of little importance.

Spaak, the Belgian Foreign Minister, has addressed the country's socialist congress and declared that Belgium is not interested in dismemberment of the Reich. Spaak has clearly got cold feet since he adds that any intention to sever the Rhineland from the Reich, for instance, would be the cause of the next (third) world war.

The dispute in the enemy camp about the forthcoming San Francisco Conference has now assumed considerable proportions, primarily on the question of numbers of votes. The Kremlin is demanding three votes for the Soviet Union —for various parts of the Soviet empire. The Soviets clearly intend to manoeuvre the Anglo-Americans into a corner. They are not particularly keen on the San Francisco Conference anyway. They know that decisions will have to be taken there—and on questions which were shelved at Yalta. No decision has yet been taken in Moscow on reconstruction of the Polish government. The Kremlin is allowing the problem to drag on inordinately and the question now arises how the Polish government is to be represented in San Francisco at all. The most grotesque of all would be if Poland, which began this war anyway, had neither a seat nor a vote in San Francisco. Moscow's interest naturally is to let the matter drag on without allowing it to lead to open conflict with Roosevelt and Churchill. But the Americans are not going to allow themselves to be led up the garden path. They say that there must be clarity on the Polish question by the time the San Francisco Conference opens and that, whatever happens, the Poles must be represented there. If no solution has been found by that time, this could be a *cause célèbre* for our enemies' relationships within the coalition.

The Catholic press in England, led by the *Catholic Herald*, continues to attack bolshevism sharply. Its language could not be bettered by the German press. I assume that this violent attack is being made on instructions from the Vatican.

This is the most horrible Good Friday I have ever had in my life. There is not the smallest sign of a holiday mood anywhere. The only ray of light is that the enemy air war has eased off somewhat in the last 24 hours. But we can pin no hopes on that. The reason is simply the bad weather conditions in Britain.

Developments in the West naturally give rise to the greatest anxiety. Kesselring has not yet succeeded in forming even the beginnings of a defence line. Looking at the map, one could well gain the impression that this is the beginning of catastrophe in the West; the most lamentable feature is that neither the civil population nor the troops possess the necessary morale to continue the fight.

Developments in Hungary are an equal source of anxiety. We shall soon be seriously faced with the question whether we can hold the oilfield. The Soviets are anyway already across the German frontier. Sepp Dietrich's Sixth Army has simply allowed itself to be swept away by them.

Speer has been to the Führer to discuss an emergency armaments programme with him. This led to a most dramatic showdown about Speer's political attitude. The Führer criticised him severely for being too closely harnessed to industry and representing trends which cannot be brought into consonance with the National-Socialist concept of war. Speer ate humble pie; nevertheless he persuaded the Führer to water down the recent decree concerning destruction of industrial installations in districts occupied by the Anglo-Americans; paralysis is now permitted if it achieves the desired object and neither paralysis nor destruction of industry and armaments installations is required if arms production can be continued even though severely threatened.

The Führer calls me over at midday in order to discuss with me once more the question of his speech to the German people. I have the impression that at the moment he has no great inclination to make it. He tells me that he has initiated extraordinarily large-scale measures of a military nature in the West. These military measures must first have some visible effect before he can appear before the people. There is no question of this at the moment. The fighting morale of the troops cannot be stimulated as long as they are unsupported by new formations and new weapons. Overall he has reinforced the western zone with about 150 battalions impeccably equipped. They are on the move up but it will be a day or two before they can be in action. The map shows a number of deep holes in the front which must be plugged as best we may. He is making truly titanic efforts to carry out this job but unfortunately gets only limited support from his military staff. I have the impression that the Führer has been greatly overworked in the last few days. During the last 24 hours, for instance, he has only had two hours' sleep. The reason is that he has no military staff capable of taking much of the detail from him. For example he has had to send Guderian on leave because he had become completely hysterical and nervy and so was a cause of disturbance instead of good order. General Krebs, who has long been Chief-of-Staff to Model, is coming in place of Guderian.* Krebs is an outstanding personality. For a time he was Military Attaché in Moscow but has not been spoiled by diplomatic activity. A particularly talented member of Guderian's staff is General Wenck† who has briefed me on several occasions. Unfortunately when he last drove to Army Group Vistula to deal with military operations in Pomerania, he was badly hurt in a car accident and is still in hospital. Model, of course, would be another person on whom one can rely; at the moment, however, he is facing almost insoluble problems since he does not have available the troops needed to deal with the situation in the West. He cannot, therefore, hold out in the long run unless reserves can be provided. Kesselring—as the Führer re-emphasises —arrived in the West too late and he cannot therefore form a firm front in the West as he did in Italy.

The Führer stresses yet again that the morale of the troops and that of the civil population are interdependent. He is firmly convinced, he says, that the troops have infected the civilians with their bad morale, not the civilians the troops. The disaster in the West originated from the troops, not from the other ranks but from the staffs and officers. Nevertheless we must now make every effort to re-establish a fresh front and suitable measures have already been initiated even though they are of an improvised nature. Our economic losses are, of course, fearful, particularly in coal and steel. We first lost the Upper Silesian industrial zone; then the Saar was wrested from us and now half the Ruhr area has already gone.

The Führer is now busy with Speer reorganising our weaponry. We must now embark on an arms production programme requiring less steel and therefore less coal. The Führer is very angry at the fact that he has to do most of this work himself. He does not get the necessary support

* i.e. as Chief of Army General Staff.
† A young General who rose to influence after 20 July 1944. Hitler would rely on him, in the last days of the war, to relieve Berlin.

in the Armaments Ministry either. Speer, he says, is not the strong personality that he had always made himself out to be; Saur outstrips him both in energy and capacity for improvisation.

The Wehrmacht generals are now real obstacles to the revival of our fortunes in the West. Our Wehrmacht generals, particularly those on the Führer's staff, bend before every breeze that blows. The Führer has to expend much of his time and energy laboriously propping them up daily and putting a bit of whalebone into their jackets. As he emphasises to me, it is a real labour of Hercules. I notice how severely he has been affected by this labour. I have never seen his hand so shaky as during this conversation.

I then brief the Führer in detail about the propaganda measures I have initiated for the West. He is very pleased with the information we have published about Anglo-American despotic measures. He is also very pleased with my exposé concerning the Werwolf organisation and propaganda for it. It is essential that we now refer to the Anglo-Americans in harsher terms. The fact that we have been over-reticent on this point is the reason why the Anglo-Americans are considered more humane than the Soviets by the German people.

I cannot conceal from the Führer that Dr. Dietrich* is making just as great difficulties about this propaganda as he previously did about the anti-bolshevist atrocity propaganda. I quote certain examples to the Führer which make him very angry. He makes up his mind on the spot to give Dr. Dietrich leave of absence from his office at once and appoint Lorenz to deputise for him. Lorenz, however, will not be appointed to the office of Reich Press Officer but will be Press Officer attached to the Führer himself. This will be a great relief for me. Dr. Dietrich is an inveterate weakling who is not up to the present crisis. At this time only strong men are of use, above all men who will unquestioningly carry out their assignments. This is not the

* Otto Dietrich, State Secretary in the Ministry of Propaganda and Reich Press Chief of the Nazi Party.

case with Dr. Dietrich. He wears me out just as the Führer is worn out by his generals. With men like Dr. Dietrich how am I supposed to conduct propaganda, such as that for the Werwolf movement at present, which must be of an extraordinarily radical nature.

The Führer has had a letter from Streicher asking for some assignment in the Fatherland's extreme emergency and saying that he can no longer endure just to remain in his own house in the country. The Führer asks whether perhaps I can give him something to do. It is possible that I could use Streicher in the Werwolf, for after all he is a man of great energy. He could make five-minute speeches which, however, I would have to revise thoroughly beforehand. I will get in touch with Streicher. In any case the Führer would be happy if I could give Streicher some employment. At heart the Führer is somewhat uncomfortable about Streicher since he was a man of stature who only once went off the rails. In any case the Führer emphasises that Streicher's* articles would certainly be better than those of Dr. Ley.

In this connection I refer to Dr. Ley's articles in fairly sharp terms. Above all I stress to the Führer that Dr. Ley invariably maintains that the Führer approves his articles and considers them the *non plus ultra* of journalistic persuasive power. The Führer says with a chuckle that he has never read any of Dr. Ley's articles, still less told him that he thought them good. I describe to the Führer the content of the last two articles, that about Dresden and that about the situation in the West, the effect of which on public opinion was catastrophic. The Führer commissions me to censor these articles severely in future and to ensure that idiocies such as have recently appeared in Ley's articles are no longer published. Otherwise, however, the

---

* Julius Streicher was the most notorious of early Nazi propagandists. He published a paper, *Der Stürmer*, which combined obscenity and antisemitism in pathological form. He was Gauleiter of Franconia till 1940, when even Hitler was obliged to drop him; but he continued to edit *Der Stürmer* to the end.

Führer's view is that Dr. Ley is a real fanatic and that, within certain limitations, he can be useful for tasks requiring fanaticism. This was why he had entrusted him with formation of the "Adolf Hitler Free Corps." In any case, as a result of all our various measures, we shall slowly regain the West.

As far as morale is concerned, I am firmly convinced that, now that the Führer has removed from me the impediment of the Reich Press Officer, I can get going again. I shall very quickly purge the Press Section of refractory and defeatist elements and can now carry on propaganda against the West which will be in no way inferior to that against the East. Anti-Anglo-American propaganda is now the order of the day. Only if we can demonstrate to our people that Anglo-American intentions towards them are no different from those of the Bolshevists will they adopt a different attitude to the enemy in the West. If we succeeded in stiffening the German people against the bolshevists and instilling hatred into them, why should we not succeed in doing so against the Anglo-Americans! Against my advice we unfortunately committed the error of not withdrawing from the Geneva Convention. Had this been done, so many German soldiers would certainly have not handed themselves over as prisoners of war to the Anglo-Americans during the present battles in the West as has unhappily been the case. The Führer agrees with me absolutely. He allowed himself to be talked round by Keitel, Bormann and Himmler and neither did nor ordered what was necessary and expedient. I am the only one to have been right on this point, as the Führer frankly admits.

Otherwise the Führer is convinced that in eight to ten days' time the holes in the West will have been plugged in some way. The "Adolf Hitler Free Corps" can then slowly make its appearance. I promise him to get partisan activity in the occupied western districts to a peak in a very short time. Now that the Burgomaster of Aachen has been liquidated it is now the turn of the Jewish Police President in Köln and the Burgomaster of Rheydt. In any case I am convinced that in the not too distant future we shall succeed in laying low every German traitor among our enemies in the West.

As far as the Luftwaffe is concerned, the Führer has now given SS-Obergruppenführer Kammler* extraordinarily wide plenary powers. In the matter of air armaments the Führer wishes to carry through quite a small programme which, however, must be pursued with the utmost energy. Whatever happens it must be completed. As a result of the powers given to Kammler Göring feels that he is being by-passed but there is nothing to be done about that. The Führer refuses any blame for failure to appoint Kammler earlier. Kammler only came to his notice in the organisation for employment of our V-weapons. He is the right man to activate the Luftwaffe at its reduced level. We must now act on the principle followed by the Soviets during their great war crisis, in other words be as basic as possible and make a virtue of necessity. Should the Luftwaffe generals object to Kammler's orders, the Führer will react with courts martial and shootings. In any case he is determined to put some order into the Luftwaffe now. I think that he will succeed, for the Luftwaffe generals, after all, are cowards just like the army generals and, as soon as they realise that they have a master over them, they will do what they are told.

The Führer promises me to make his speech to the German people very soon. But, as I have said, he is first awaiting the success of his measures in the West. I am somewhat sceptical whether he will in fact speak in the foreseeable future. The Führer now has an aversion to the microphone which is quite incomprehensible to me. He knows too that it is not right to leave the people without a word from him now; unfortunately, however, after his last speech the SD told him that he had been criticised for having nothing new to say. And in fact at this moment he can tell the people nothing new. There is much in what the Führer says—that in a speech he must be able to put for-

---

* See above p. 306.

ward something at least, and at the moment there is nothing available. I reply, however, that the people are at least expecting a watchword. In the present emergency one could give them a watchword. In short the result of the argument is that I cannot persuade the Führer to start drafting his speech at once. But he promises me to do it in the next few days. At least, however, as a result of this talk I have got rid of Dr. Dietrich, which is a considerable relief for my work. The Führer was most of all displeased that Dr. Dietrich should have amended the announcement I had drafted concerning the shooting of the Burgomaster of Aachen. I had referred to a national tribunal which had condemned the Burgomaster to death; on his own initiative Dr. Dietrich deleted this passage, observing that there was no such national tribunal. *O sancta simplicitas*!

The Führer is happy that I am going to try to find some opportunity for Streicher to work. He has Streicher very much at heart and Streicher deserves to be brought somewhat more into the limelight at the present time. In any case he is more loyal than many people working in influential positions in the Party and State today.

The situation in the East, of course, causes the Führer great anxiety. His view is that it has been largely messed up by Guderian. Guderian has not a firm solid temperament. He loses his nerve. He showed this when commanding troops both in the West and the East. During the critical winter of 1941/42 in the East he simply began to withdraw on his own initiative and so started the entire front giving way. Only when Guderian withdrew did Küchler and Hoepner do the same. Consequently the great crisis in the East in the winter of 1941/42 is a black mark against Guderian. At that time the army generals totally lost their nerve. They were facing a crisis for the first time, whereas previously they had only been winning victories; now they were equally determined to retreat to the Reich frontier. The Führer recounts to me yet again the dramatic conversation he had at that time with Küchler. Küchler proposed to him that the troops be withdrawn, leaving behind all their heavy equipment, if necessary as far as the Reich frontier. Had that been done, the war would probably have ended in the winter 1941/42.

A real tragedy is now being staged in Hungary. As I emphasised last time, Sepp Dietrich only put a portion of his troops into action in Hungary and told the Führer a direct lie about his manpower. He wanted to leave reserves behind in the Reich for his next operation on the Oder front. As a result he was short of replacements in Hungary. The Führer is most hurt by Sepp Dietrich's behaviour. He has also reproached Himmler severely on the subject. The result is, as I have said, that Himmler has taken away their armbands from the SS formations in Hungary. But that does not do much good. The harm done cannot be made good that way.

The Führer now takes the view that Himmler has no operational capability. He is a punctilious person but no commander. He totally lacks the divine spark. This he showed during the operations in Pomerania of which he made a complete mess owing to his narrow-minded operational thinking. In general the Führer is of the opinion that no high-class commander has emerged from the SS. Neither Sepp Dietrich nor Hausser have great operational talent. Huber and Dietl were the only real stayers among the generals but unfortunately the Führer has been deprived of them both through aircraft accidents. Who is then left? Schörner who has great talent and is outstanding. He prepares his operations with care and is always driving the enemy back with meagre resources. He is a devil of a fellow and can always be relied on. Above all he tells the Führer the truth. The fact that in the case of Hungary Sepp Dietrich did not do so has greatly embittered the Führer. He even talks of guilt before history that must be laid at Dietrich's door. In any case we must now reckon that we may lose the Hungarian oilfield. It has not got to that yet but it may come. Taking into account the débâcle in Pomerania the SS has a good deal to account for recently. Himmler's standing with the Führer has accordingly sunk noticeably. On the other hand, of course, it must be recognised that at the moment we are pursued by a chain of misfortune. These misfortunes are not due solely to the inadequacy of the Führer's associates but also to the inadequacy of the resources available to us.

As the Führer emphasises to me, he would very much like to appoint better men to his staff if he could find them. But, as I must admit, they are just not available. For instance he says to me that he would, of course, gladly have installed me as Head of Propaganda in the Party in 1922 if he had known me; at that time, however, he had no notion that I existed. It is therefore fruitless to ask why I was not in charge of the Party's propaganda in 1922. Only by association with people can one make their acquaintance. Undoubtedly there are a number of men of operational talent within the Wehrmacht, but it is also very hard to find them.

It is truly saddening to me to see the Führer in such a bad physical state. He tells me that he is hardly sleeping at all, is continually plunged in his work and that he is being totally worn down in the long run by continually having to prop up his feeble characterless staff. I can imagine that this must be a worrying laborious process. I am really sorry for the Führer when I see him in his present physical and mental state. Nevertheless I cannot abandon my demand that he speak to the people as soon as possible. He must call off one or two conferences for a day or two. The most important thing is that he should reconsolidate the people; I can do the rest. Now that I am free of Dr. Dietrich I believe that I shall succeed in taking a grip of the press again in a very short time. The first essential, however, is that the Führer should give press and people some watchword.

The Führer was extraordinarily nice and forthcoming to me during this conversation. One can see that he is pleased sometimes to talk to someone who does not give way at every crisis.

Dr. Naumann's pleasure at the removal of Dr. Dietrich is indescribable. Dr. Dietrich was a foreign body in our

Ministry. The Ministry will now once more be under centralised leadership. I commission Dr. Naumann to create the necessary conditions.

I have had to toil away at home throughout Good Friday. I do not even notice that it is a holiday. The general tone of today's OKW report is terrible. In view of these jeremiads one can see why the German people are slowly losing courage.

On the ground there has been little change in the West this evening. Leading enemy troops have advanced to the Brilon–Paderborn area and will probably move on the Weser. Otherwise, however, the enemy is occupied in bringing up reinforcements. Our counter-measures should slowly begin to take effect during the course of the evening. At the moment, however, one cannot expect much from them. As far as the East is concerned, pressure on the German frontier in Hungary has become heavier. The enemy has crossed the frontier at one point and captured two Austrian villages. We are still holding on south of Lake Balaton in an effort to retain the oilfield. Soviet attacks in Upper Silesia were again extraordinarily heavy. The enemy made some penetrations but all were dealt with. The situation in Glogau has become somewhat critical owing to heavy enemy air activity. One thousand men under von Reinefarth from the garrison of Küstrin have fought their way back to our lines. The situation in the Gotenhafen and Danzig areas is extraordinarily critical. I fear that the end will come soon here.

I work late into the night creating the conditions for a reform of our press section. I hear from Reichsleiter Bormann that the Führer had a three-minute interview with Dr. Dietrich at which Dietrich himself and Sündermann* were sent packing in short order. So at last the path for my work is free. I shall take full advantage of the opportunity and create *faits accomplis* in the press which it will be impossible to countermand later.

* Dietrich's deputy.

SATURDAY 31 MARCH 1945

(pp. 1–38)

Military Situation.

The main fighting on the Eastern Front was in Hungary. Between the Drau and the western end of Lake Balaton the enemy attacked frontally towards Nagy Kanizsa and made a deep penetration bringing him to within 20 km of the oilfield. Simultaneously the Soviets advanced south and south-west from Zalaegerszeg with the intention of encircling the oilfield. The enemy swung north-west from Steinamanger and Güns, reached the German frontier west of Steinamanger and crossed it north-west of Güns. Leading enemy tanks reached Kirchschlag. At the same time the enemy advanced farther along the Raab–Odenburg–Wiener Neustadt railway; here he is some 20 km east of Odenburg. Advancing through Raab, which fell into enemy hands, the Soviets gained some 10 km of ground towards Bratislava. The enemy succeeded in breaking into our rearguard position on the Neutra at several points and advancing as far as the Waag where he formed bridgeheads on the west bank.

A further centre of fighting is the Mährisch–Ostrau area where the enemy again launched a strong attack with tank support and made local penetrations between Freistadt, Ratibor and Katscher. Ratibor and Katscher fell into enemy hands. The enemy was contained immediately south of these two towns.

On the adjoining front as far as Neisse the enemy made violent attacks but all were driven off. Some improvements

349

to our positions were made in the Breslau area. In Glogau
the enemy penetrated to the city centre after severe fighting.
No particular operations all along the Oder front. Equally
no special developments reported from the Danzig and
Königsberg areas. Heavy Soviet attacks continued in Courland without appreciable change in the situation.

On the Lower Rhine, in the British-Canadian sector of
the Western Front, our troops are involved in severe fighting with the advancing enemy. The British penetrated into
Emmerich from north and east and thence attacked towards
the Dutch frontier. No appreciable change in the situation
in the Bocholt area. The battle group advancing from
Borken penetrated farther north into the Stadtlohn area.
Another battle group captured Coesfeld. Counter-attacks
are in progress to confine the penetration area between
Coesfeld and Dülmen. From Dülmen the enemy advanced
some 5 km farther towards Münster; he is now some 25
km south-west of Münster. At Lüdinghausen between
Münster and Recklinghausen the British advanced across
the Dortmund–Ems Canal. The enemy attacked towards
Buer–Recklinghausen from the Dorsten–Gladbeck area but
was repulsed; some localities were recaptured by counter-
attack. Our line now runs along the northern edge of the
Ruhr, then south along the Rhine to Beuel and then turns
along the Sieg to Siegen.

In the American break-through area, where they have
advanced from the Westerwald to the region Wetzlar–
Giessen–Marburg, two operations are now developing. One
enemy thrust is directed northwards in order to join up
with the British–Canadian forces somewhere in the area
between Hamm and Paderborn; a second group is swinging
east and advancing towards Hersfeld and Fulda. Some of
the enemy forces moving north have swung west at Brilon;
the rest are advancing farther north and north-east. Between Brilon and Kassel the enemy is roughly in the area
Arolsen–Bad Wildungen. According to hitherto unconfirmed reports the enemy advancing east from the Marburg
area has reached Hersfeld. Strong enemy troop concentrations have been detected on the autobahn at Alsfeld. The

enemy advancing towards Fulda through Lauterbach is now just west of Fulda.

No major change in the Hanau area. Stiffer German resistance is reported here. At present the enemy is in the Gelnhausen area. At Aschaffenburg too the enemy was unable to make progress. Schweinheim was recaptured by counter-attack. A defence line has been formed traversing the eastern spurs of the Odenwald; it runs from Klingenberg am Main through Miltenberg, Amorbach and Oberbach to Neckarsteinach. The enemy succeeded in breaking through this line at Amorbach and reaching Walldürn and Buchen. Attacking from north to south he penetrated into Heidelberg. He crossed the Neckar between Heidelberg and Mannheim and penetrated into Schwetzingen.

No special reports from the Italian front.

Over Reich territory 1300 American four-engined bombers attacked port and transport installations in Hamburg, Bremen and Wilhelmshaven. Some 500 American four-engined bombers from Italy raided Vienna, Wiener Neustadt, Klagenfurt and Graz. Our "Sturmvögel" shot down eight enemy aircraft. A harassing raid on Berlin after dark was made by 60 Mosquitos. Four "Sturmvögel" shot down four Mosquitos without loss. There was sustained long-range night fighter activity over the western half of the Reich throughout the night.

London is continuing its purposeful scare propaganda aimed at the German people. Its consistent line is that the Reich has to all intents and purposes ceased to exist, that there is no longer any question of internal organisation in Germany and that the government has lost all authority. These tactics are too transparent to be successful in the long run. Both the British and Americans are now doing their utmost to finish matters in some way by 25 April when the San Francisco Conference is due to begin; both London and Washington are clear that the great political crisis problems will first be broached in San Francisco and they have no wish to have us rubbing our hands in the background.

In fact developments in the West are calculated to reinforce the enemy's hope that he will soon be able to overwhelm us militarily. Gauleiter Wagner* from Karlsruhe gives me a full report on the situation in his Gau. He too complains bitterly that the morale both of the population and of the troops has sunk extraordinarily low. People no longer shrink from sharp criticism of the Führer. The Luftwaffe is really to blame for the ruin of Germany but the Führer is accused of failure to make personnel changes there in good time. It is true, Wagner says, that the enemy is afraid of severe casualties but, as soon as he meets resistance, he calls in his air force which then simply turns the area of resistance into a desert. In contrast to the Soviets the Anglo-Americans are not feared by the people— as we have long known; on the contrary, large sections of the people are glad to see them come so that they may be protected from the Soviets. The political attitude of people west of the Rhine was in fact very bad. They had been demoralised by the continuous enemy air-raids and are now throwing themselves into the arms of the Anglo-Americans, in some cases enthusiastically, in others at least without genuine resistance. In some cases—at least at some points—the people have even taken active steps against troops willing to resist which naturally has had an extraordinarily depressing effect on them. In reality there is today no question of any resistance worth mentioning west of the Rhine. Here and there small isolated groups are holding out but these are, of course, of no significance for the future progress of military operations.

On behalf of Commander-in-Chief West Müller also sends me a report on the morale of the civil population which is extraordinarily alarming. Nevertheless I think that Müller has allowed himself to be over-influenced by the General Staff officers in C-in-C West's headquarters. In fact he lays all the blame for the disaster on the civil

* Gauleiter of Baden-Alsace.

population, which is General Staff tactics; they and the army are trying to exonerate themselves for events in the West. Müller's report also emphasises that people are receiving the Anglo-Americans with white flags and that in some towns and villages they have even been given a frenzied welcome. The Party evacuated these towns and villages prematurely and the population has now turned to looting. They have been left defenceless against the tank terror. In the Main district there has even been talk of the Main French coming to displace the Germans. In short it is obvious from this report that C-in-C West's staff is doing its utmost to shuffle the blame onto the population and to whitewash the army and above all the generals. In answer to Müller's report I make a sharp retort which he is to submit to General Kesselring. In this answer I stress that the people's morale has always been first-class so long as the enemy did not appear. The people have endured all the air-raids with great bravery. No one can be surprised, however, at the people losing their courage when all they see are miserable collections of soldiery making their way to the rear, throwing away their weapons and offering no resistance. How little the troops are prepared to fight is clear from the fact that, since the start of his offensive, Patton alone has taken 140,000 prisoners, a fearful indictment of those who, against my advice, prevented us withdrawing from the Geneva Convention. Patton talks of 90,000 killed. This figure is not right; it is greatly exaggerated. The number of prisoners, however, may be correct. Patton is also being entirely inaccurate when he talks of the greatest military achievement in history. How can anyone use the words "military achievement" in view of the enemy's vast material superiority and after such frightful air bombardments which have turned the battlefield into a desert and towns and villages into heaps of ruins.

I am nevertheless of the opinion that slowly the partisan war will start in West Germany. There are already a number of signs of it. Even the British are very worried that they will now be threatened in their rear areas by our freedom fighters. Moreover they are now totally counting on an imminent German collapse. They have even decided to proclaim a fixed date for victory whether we are still resisting or not. They want simply to declare the war at an end by Order of the Day. But things are not as simple as that and the British will be deceiving themselves if they think that such an Order of the Day will make the slightest impression on us. This project illustrates, however, in how great a hurry the Anglo-Americans are to bring the war in Europe to an end. Reports that victory celebrations are already being prepared in London are naturally exclusively intended to influence our mentality.

In passing it is worth noting that London is continually emphasising that only harsh peace terms are under consideration for Germany.

Here and there fears are expressed in London that our withdrawal in the West is part of a high-level plan to combine our resources in troops in the West with those in the East in order to make common cause with bolshevists against the Anglo-Americans. This could produce a real possibility of conflict especially when one considers that the ingredients of political crisis within the enemy coalition are beginning to assume extraordinarily menacing proportions. This morning's *Manchester Guardian* firmly states that there is not the smallest measure of agreement about the San Francisco Conference. Under pressure of public opinion Stettinius has had to admit that a secret agreement was concluded in Yalta under which Stalin was initially granted three votes for the Soviet Union. This secret agreement is very sharply criticised in the U.S. press. At midday comes the sensational news that the San Francisco Conference is possibly to be postponed. Stalin clearly has no wish to enter into prolonged debate with the Anglo-Americans now. He gives as his reason that Molotov cannot be sent to San Francisco since he must participate in Soviet budgetary discussions at this time—a somewhat cynical statement which will undoubtedly have a commensurate effect in London and Washington. London is attempting to explain away the dilemma that has arisen by maintaining that German capitulation is imminent and that therefore a conference cannot take place in San Francisco at this time. In fact, of course, the political crises in the enemy camp are the reason for the probable postponement of the San Francisco Conference. It is suspected that Stalin intends to demand 16 votes at San Francisco which of course would entirely upset all Anglo-American calculations. In addition we have received an official report from Moscow to the effect that the Kremlin is demanding that the Lublin Committee be invited to San Francisco as the official Polish government even if it has not been reconstituted. It cannot be reconstituted at all since the Soviets are dragging out the negotiations in Moscow. This declaration by the Kremlin has given Anglo-American public opinion a real shock. It is couched in harsh terms, ending with the sentence that the Kremlin expects a rapid solution of this problem. In other words Stalin thinks the moment has come to start using sharper language to the Anglo-Americans and to bring the crisis in the enemy coalition to a head.

Bohle tells me of the fiasco of the Hesse mission to Stockholm. Hesse was definitely a Ribbentrop man and British political circles had not the smallest confidence in him. The British had no wish to negotiate with Germans at all and definitely not with Ribbentrop. As a result the despatch of Hesse to Stockholm was undoubtedly a diplomatic *faux pas*.

In the East the course of events in Hungary and on the Austro-Hungarian frontier gives rise to the greatest anxiety at the moment. Cerff, who has just returned from the Hungarian front, gives me an account of events there. He says that the offensive bogged down because the weather was unbelievably bad. The offensive necessarily took place in very marshy ground so that our tanks simply could not move. Sepp Dietrich did his utmost to keep the offensive going but he is no army commander. He is capable of commanding no more than a dvision. In any case our casualties were extraordinarily high and Sixth Army can hardly be scheduled for future operations. This is a fearful thing for Sepp Dietrich of course. One can imagine how unhappy he is over this development.

In the air we once more have to bemoan heavy raids on Graz, Hamburg, Bremen and Wilhelmshaven. The enemy bomber squadrons are now in the air uninterruptedly and they are inflicting the most serious damage on us. Obsolete German aircraft are now to be used as ram fighters against these bomber squadrons. These ram fighters are now to make suicide attacks on the enemy bombers, 90% casualties being reckoned with. The ram fighters should be in action in eight to ten days' time. Extraordinary success is expected from them. Of our fighter pilots 50–90% have volunteered, proof that morale among our fighter pilots is extraordinarily high, even though Göring, for transparent reasons, invariably states the contrary.

Gerhart Hauptmann has made available to us an extraordinarily [one word illegible] statement about the Anglo-American [terror] raid on Dresden. He was himself present during the raid and tells of it in language worthy of the Reich's leading poet.

I am now busy organising the Werwolf radio station. Slesina is to be placed in charge of it; he has considerable experience in this field from the Saar struggle. Prützmann* has not got very far with his preparations for the Werwolf organisation. It seems to me that he is proceeding far too hesitantly over this work. He complains that people in the West German enemy-occupied districts are at present apathetic and are anti-Party. But this is no reason for the work to proceed so slowly. One must now go into it with the utmost energy. I think that a powerful impulse will be given to it by the propaganda to be distributed over the new Werwolf station.

The reports from the Reich Propaganda Offices and the letters I receive are naturally couched in most despairing terms. Their general trend is that people are now convinced that the war is lost. As a result of losing so much territory there is no basis for arms production so that there is no longer any chance for us. Many people are simply asking

* SS Obergruppenführer Prützmann was put in charge of the *Werwolf* organisation by Himmler. For Slesina see above p. 285.

themselves what is the best and most honourable way to escape from this frightful existence. Occasionally radical measures are demanded such as withdrawal from the Geneva Convention for instance—a matter continually being stressed; but people do not expect even that to produce very much. In general the better people are in many cases concerned with the question how to die decently.

A report from Rodde, head of the Reich Propaganda Office in Hamburg, dealing with criticism of the Luftwaffe is thoroughly typical of the present attitude of the German people towards the Luftwaffe and Göring. In particular both in this report and in very many letters the question is raised why draconian sentences were pronounced and executed for the failure to demolish the Rhine bridge at Remagen whereas those responsible for the air war catastrophe have not been called to account in a similar manner. People are demanding a court martial and death sentence on Göring, for instance. The letter-writers make no bones about their views and do not even shrink from putting their names and full addresses at the bottom of their letters.

As far as developments in the West are concerned, the general public is convinced that something is amiss here. It is suspected that treachery plays some part. The Führer is also of the opinion that the course of events in the Trier area, which in effect led to the collapse of the Western Front, cannot be explained in any other way.

The people have reacted with extraordinary repugnance to the instances of bad example set by the Party. The Party's reputation has suffered greatly as a result. On the other hand the people places such hope as it still has solely on the Führer. In general people are conscientiously doing their duty; admittedly there is much criticism of State and Party leadership but developments in the West are thought terrible; some hope is still placed on our resistance in the East; otherwise people are still prepared to do everything asked of them by their leaders.

Food supply is slowly beginning to become extraordinarily difficult. With the recent reductions our rations are now so low that they barely reach the minimum subsistence level. As can be imagined, with all these severe blows descending on the people, a sort of widespread fatalism is emerging. Men look upon their approaching fate as an inexorable natural phenomenon.

The defence stock-taking for Berlin this week has turned out to be fairly well on the credit side. Admittedly considerable detachments of troops have been taken away but the stocks of weapons are that much better. Above all the number of heavy weapons has risen considerably. The level of coal stocks constitutes a very serious threat. We are getting practically no coal from the Ruhr now. There are no other sources of supply for us and so we must make radical reductions in our coal consumption. In particular the traffic must be cut down. In future public transport should only be used by people employed on war work.

I am now busy with a fundamental reform of the radio. It must become more flexible and be better adapted to the present war situation. In particular the news service is to be radicalised. The same applies to news in the press. I am again seizing the opportunity to mount a sharp attack on the bourgeois newspapers in Berlin, in particular the *Deutsche Allgemeine Zeitung*; they talk as if we were at a beer-drinking party.

Dr. Dietrich has now told his staff that he is to go on leave for a few weeks on orders from the Führer. I am not prepared to be satisfied with this. I shall have a new statute drawn up for guidance to the press and there will be no place in it for the Reich Press Officer.

During the course of the day the situation in the West has become more dramatic. The Führer has been in military conferences for over four hours. The Führer is extremely vexed that the measures he ordered have still brought no relief. He has been making long personal telephone calls to individual Army Commanders in the West, imploring them to do their utmost to put up resistance somewhere and pointing out to them what is at stake in major operations.

The deterioration reported is very considerable. The

enemy has almost reached Rheine, almost reached Ahlen and to the south-west is between Münster and Hamm. So our entire Rhineland–Westphalian industrial zone is most seriously threatened, in fact is already partially lost. South of Lippstadt the enemy is swinging towards Soest and in addition he is only 4 km from Kassel. A planned advance into Thuringia is now indicated. He is advancing towards Meiningen and meeting little resistance there either. Here and there minor successes by our reserve formations are reported but they make little impact. Larger-scale counter-operations are to be launched during the coming night but one must wait to see whether they lead to any alleviation.

During the course of discussion on the situation in the West the Führer again had a dramatic clash with Göring. Göring has once more been guilty of a series of irregularities and gradually this becomes infuriating. I cannot understand how the Führer has allowed this to go on for so long.

The single-combat victories scored by our Me 262s are highly satisfactory, thank God. Admittedly we can at present only put small numbers of these new fighters into action; where they have been in operation, however, they have had considerable success in shooting down enemy aircraft.

The enemy has made further progress in Hungary, even crossing the Reich frontier. The Lower Danube region is gradually becoming seriously threatened. Otherwise the entire Eastern Front was generally quiet.

The withdrawal of our troops from Küstrin did not take place as the Führer intended. On the Führer's orders Gruppenführer Reinefarth, who was commanding there, has been arrested by Himmler. It is said that he retreated without orders.

Sündermann visited Dr. Naumann this afternoon in order to ask a favour himself. He wants to continue to give directions to the press on my behalf as long as Dr. Dietrich is on leave. I have no wish to have him on my staff. I must now have high-grade men of character who will follow my instructions precisely and above all will remain stable in a crisis. In no sense is this the case with Sündermann. In any case I intend now to radicalise our entire propaganda and news policy. At the present stage of the war the sternest language is the best.

SUNDAY 1 APRIL 1945

(pp. 1–20, pp. 21–45 (?) missing)
Military Situation.
On the Eastern Front the Soviets continued to attack in strength from Hungary and Slovakia. We occupied a defensive position between the western end of Lake Balaton and the Drau southwards and the German frontier westwards protecting the Nagy Kanizsa oilfield; the Bolshevists exerted heavy pressure but without result. The enemy reached the German frontier south-west of Steinamanger. From the break-through area between Güns and Odenburg the Bolshevists pressed forward to points 10–20 km south and south-west of Wiener Neustadt. Here they were held by an army cadet school after severe fighting. Between Odenburg and the Neusiedlersee [Lake Fertöto] the enemy advanced along the western shore of the lake as far as Rust. Along the Slovakian–Hungarian frontier he penetrated farther across the Neutra and Waag towards Bratislava. In the fighting around Mährisch–Ostrau repeated heavy Soviet attacks were beaten off with a loss to the enemy of 72 tanks; we also improved our positions by counter-attack. Attacks on Breslau from the west failed. Soviet troop concentrations were observed in the Bunzlau area. The enemy continued to attack in Courland but there was no change in the situation.

The situation on the Lower Rhine has become more acute in that the enemy advancing north and north-westwards has greater freedom of movement and was able to reach Dingden and an area some 20 km south of Rheine. Leading enemy troops reached the Hamm–Münster railway. The Americans could only make an insignificant advance in the area south of Paderborn. In some cases they were driven back by counter-attack. Farther south enemy forces reached an area 4 km west of Kassel. Moving through Hersfeld the enemy reached the Werra in the region of Vacha. Between Fulda and Hersfeld the enemy was driven back by counter-attack at Schlitz. From the Gelnhausen area the enemy advanced to the Hanau–Fulda railway in the region of Bad Orb. Leading enemy tanks advanced from the Wertheim area and the Odenwald to the neighborhood of Würzburg and to the Tauber at Tauberbischofsheim. Attacking south-westwards they reached the Jagst valley and Mosbach. In the Neckar sector the enemy occupied Neckargemünd. From the Heidelberg area the enemy is attempting to roll up the front on the Upper Rhine in the direction of Karlsruhe. His leading troops reached the area of Wiesloch. Attempts to cross the river at Speyer were defeated. The enemy succeeded in forming a small bridgehead on the right bank of the Rhine at Germersheim.

No special reports from the Italian front.

Strong American air formations raided Brandenburg, Brunswick, Halle and towns in Thuringia. A British formation raided Hamburg. Some 500 American bombers from Italy raided Linz and Villach. A smaller twin-engined formation dropped bombs in the Innsbruck area. So far 42 enemy aircraft, mostly four-engined bombers, are reported shot down by Me 262s. Some 80 four-engined bombers raided Graz during the night.

Enemy estimates of German fighting morale differ. In some cases they refer to our men putting up fanatical resistance—this seems to be primarily the case in the Lower Rhine area—in others, however, they say that there is no longer any trace of resistance. As regards both military and moral resistance the behaviour of certain towns and cities has been excellent. Among these Aschaffenburg and Heidelberg receive special mention from the enemy. In Heidelberg the people are showing marked hostility to the Americans.

The situation in the West has deteriorated extraordinarily and at the moment must be regarded as really wretched. The enemy now has almost complete freedom of movement in the Lower Rhine area so that further surprises giving rise to great alarm are to be anticipated here. It is possible that by this evening the Ruhr will have been totally cut off from both sides.

About midday Kesselring telephones me and tells me that we shall probably have to wait three or four days before our large-scale counter-measures begin to get under way. Until then there can be no major shift of developments in our favour. Kesselring is nevertheless in good heart. He is assured and full of character in his estimate of the situation and there is not a trace of defeatism with him. He tells me also that the attitude of the civil population has somewhat improved under the influence of our propaganda. Müller is doing an excellent job. He has given Müller the widest powers so that he can operate with all the available propaganda resources in the western zone. Kesselring will now call me daily at midday to give me a brief situation report. I have the impression that he is fully in control of his staff and will not have dust thrown in his eyes. On Müller's suggestion he has had handbills distributed both to the troops and the civil population. On these handbills the civilians implore the soldiers to stand firm. These handbills are distributed to the soldiers by young people. In addition he has issued a call to the fighting troops explaining in a few sentences what is now at stake and why they must stand firm in all circumstances. I give Kesselring an exposé on the present political situation which is extraordinarily interesting to him. All our leading soldiers are now convinced that recourse must be had to political means of putting a stop to the well-nigh desperate development of the military situation. But that is easier said than done, primarily because on our side we have no high-class diplomatic representative available. Ribbentrop cannot be seriously considered in this category.

Our Werwolf activity has now produced a considerable scare in the enemy camp. They are now definitely afraid of a partisan-infested Germany which—so they say—could keep Europe in turmoil for years. Yet no move is being made towards abandonment of the downright crazy plans for the destruction of Germany. The German people are being told that they face a period of starvation lasting for years. The Americans, of all people, want to play the pedagogue, close German schools and take over education of the German people themselves. In addition the Morgenthau Plan will be pursued, under which Germany is to be turned into a potato field, German youth of military age is to be compulsorily deported abroad as slave labour and reparations are to be paid—in short anyone can see that it would be preferable to be slaughtered. We live in such crazy times that human reason counts for nothing. Reason has no say any more. The cynical threats made against us by the enemy beggar all description. They are neither fair nor do they accord with common sense. But what do men like Roosevelt and Churchill mind about that! They feel themselves at the height of their military triumph and think they need no longer take account of considerations of human reason.

However they are somewhat sobered by the behaviour of the Kremlin. The British and Americans have refused to recognise the Lublin Committee as the regular Polish government or allow it to participate in the San Francisco Conference. They give as their main reason the fact that Stalin has not kept his promise made at Yalta to reconstitute the Lublin Committee and also has allowed neither British and American correspondents nor UNRRA entry into Poland. Stalin will undoubtedly reply to that with some wily counter-move. On the previous day he had already made an appropriate declaration in TASS in such violent language that it could not be overlooked in Britain and America. The USA are now completely aware of the

hopelessness of the conference planned for San Francisco
and are advocating an adjournment. They know full well
that this conference will lead to great political hullabaloo,
particularly since the three votes for the Soviet Union conceded to Stalin at Yalta have called forth a storm of
protest in the American press. Domestically, therefore,
Roosevelt is in a fairly embarrassing political situation.
It is not the three votes conceded to the Soviets that are
so much taken amiss as the secrecy with which this tactical
manoeuvre was conducted. The American papers now refer
quite frankly to a conflict with Stalin hanging like a dark
shadow over the San Francisco Conference. Stalin has not
the smallest intention of taking a hand in the Pacific war.
As a result, it is said, and taking into account the potentialities for conflict in Europe, the third world war has
moved appreciably closer.

This debate is taken far more seriously in the United
States than in Britain. In Britain they are at present occupied in victory celebrations. In any case it is much in
Churchill's interest to divert the attention of the British
public from the extraordinarily critical potential political
crisis and concentrate it on military developments. In any
case the political crisis has developed so far that it now
provides adequate grounds for us to stand firm and make
not the smallest concession to enemy enticements to
cowardice and surrender.

The Soviets on their side are now trying to create *faits
accomplis* by means of military victories. They are advancing in Hungary while the Anglo-Americans are advancing
in the West. They have crossed the Austrian frontier on a
considerable scale and are now on the move towards Graz.
Stalin is said to have given the Red Army the aim of
capturing Vienna, Prague and even Berlin by 25 April. For
the next few weeks, therefore, we can be clear on one
thing: there is no question at present of any diminution of
the military crisis.

As far as Prague is concerned, it is an objective both of
the Anglo-Americans and of the Soviets. The Soviets, however, have already prepared the ground politically. Beneš

was in Moscow in the last few days. He is already forming his new government and is all set to move to Bohemia and Moravia. He has already left Moscow. This senile political globe-trotter now thinks that achievement of his infernal purposes is imminent.

This is the saddest Easter Day I have ever had in my life. From all corners of the Reich news causing fresh anxiety floods in throughout the day.

A prolonged series of air raids has wrought fearful devastation in the Reich during the last 24 hours. This time it was the turn especially of the city of Brandenburg.

I have a serious showdown with Lieutenant-Colonel Balzer who has recently evinced a somewhat defeatist attitude and caused me considerable vexation. I call him to order and think that, at least for the immediate future, I shall not have to complain about him any more.

By cutting the corners we have at last succeeded in getting the Werwolf station on the air for the first time on the first evening of the Easter holiday. The station transmits on the old Deutschlandsender wavelength and at considerable strength. The first programme was submitted to me in detail and I myself wrote an extraordinarily revolutionary exhortation in which I took not the smallest account of regular methods of conducting war or of wartime foreign policy. The programme will be carried by the Werwolf station this evening and then partially taken up by the regular Reich stations. The programme makes an excellent impression. It is inspired by a revolutionary spirit and will undoubtedly attract a large audience. I shall put through Werwolf programmes every evening and I hope that they will cement activists throughout the Reich into a firm community. It is really refreshing for once to be able to talk as one used to do during our struggle period. In the battle for the German people's freedom I intend to allot to the Werwolf station and the newspaper *Werwolf* the same role as I did to the newspaper *Der Angriff* during our struggle for power. The *Werwolf* is designedly addressed to the unflinching pertinacious political minority

which has always formed the steel tip of the popular leaden lance. The language it uses is well adapted to the present time and will also correspondingly . . .
[at this point probably 25 pages of the entry for 1 April 1945 are missing]

MONDAY 2 APRIL 1945

(pp. 21–33, pp. 1–20 missing)
. . . at last put some sense into . . .

The lengths to which the enemy is determined to go may be seen from the fact that he is now toying with the idea of setting up a provisional German government in the areas he occupies. If this took place we should be in considerable difficulties since the loss of confidence among the civil population is very great at the moment and, from the enemy's point of view, this seems to me to be the moment to produce an opposition regime which would give us a lot of trouble.

I know that the Werwolf movement is not being very active at the moment. Nevertheless I am carrying on propaganda for it energetically. I want gradually to get the organisation of the Werwolf movement into my own hands. Not only do I think myself suited to do it but I believe that the Werwolf must be led with spirit and enthusiasm. It must not become a mere organisation like the SD. There is no longer much profit in organisation now. Things have gone far too far for that.

Fresh hate programmes are being announced by the enemy. It is proposed, for instance, to cut down all German forests and transport the wood to England.

The cynicism of the Americans too is unparalleled. They have held a thanksgiving service in the ruins of Köln cathedral ending with the hymn "God bless America" sung by the congregation. What humiliations have we still to suffer before the moment of deliverance comes!

On their side, however, the Americans have their worries.

Both the prospects of the San Francisco Conference and even its date are now extraordinarily obscure. Senator Vandenberg, who has been nominated by Roosevelt as one of the delegates to this conference, has criticised Moscow's pretensions most severely. He had an interview with Roosevelt during which Roosevelt eventually divulged some of the secret Yalta agreements. These secret agreements have aroused extreme hostility among the American public. To counteract the poor prospects of the San Francisco Conference it is proposed that it be preceded by a meeting of the Big Five, at which Foreign Ministers of the enemy powers would be present. But Stalin is by no means in agreement with this proposal. Things have now gone so far that even the responsible *Times* refers to an open crisis. It accuses Stalin of refusing to join the Western security organisation, of being opposed to a new League of Nations, of wanting only bilateral treaties and so of bringing the third world war within sight. Accordingly, as *The Times* says, extraordinary difficulties arise which can hardly be overcome.

Moscow blandly declares that the three votes which the Soviet Union has demanded for the San Francisco Conference were conceded both by Roosevelt and Churchill at the Yalta Conference. In reality, therefore, the proceedings of the Yalta Conference were very different from what we were led to believe by the communiqué. U.S. public opinion is extraordinarily disillusioned over it, is attacking the Kremlin's policy most violently and holds Stalin responsible for the entire dilemma.

I am convinced that this potential political crisis could quickly be made to flare up if it was not continually being pushed into the background by the enemy's military victories. But how is it to be done when Roosevelt can announce some new victory daily? The Americans have now landed on the island of Okinawa, for instance. They burnt their fingers in doing so but what do they mind about that. Their potential is so adequate that they can afford such bloodlettings for as long as they like.

Easter Monday is filled with work from morning to

night. Except when one looks out of the window at the empty streets one does not realise that this is the Easter holiday.

During the last 24 hours, thank God, we have suffered no major damage from the air war. The Anglo-Americans have not been able to take off from England owing to unfavourable weather. Whatever the reason, the main thing is that we have had a certain amount of peace during the last 24 hours.

This evening it is reported that the enemy has gone over to the attack in the Arnhem–Nijmegen area as well. He is exerting extraordinarily heavy pressure here, clearly with the aim of overrunning the remnants of our position in Holland. In Westphalia he has advanced past Münster; he has not captured the city but has succeeded in encircling it. Rheine has so far beaten off the enemy assault. The Ruhr front has in general held; Hamm, however, has fallen into enemy hands. Soest has been recaptured by counter-attack. Our hurriedly organised front in the Teutoburger Wald has in general held. Very severe fighting is now taking place in Kassel. Gerland* will have to bring off his master-stroke here. The Americans have swung north from Eisenach and are reaching out for further major gains of ground. The Neckar front has in general held. It is pleasing to hear that even the Wehrmacht admits that Gauleiters Hellmuth and Gerland have conducted themselves superbly. They are organising one centre of resistance after another and as a result are creating a far better situation in their Gaus than in the other Gaus of the West. I would have expected this from Gerland anyway but as far as Hellmuth is concerned one can say: people rise to the occasion. Hellmuth has always been a most retiring unassuming Gauleiter in whom one had not too much confidence. Now, however, it is clear that there is more to him than one thought.

The American General Patton, who has been in command of the whole Rhineland offensive, now states for the

* Gauleiter of Mainfranken and Kurhessen.

first time that his blitz offensive has come to a halt. German troops are putting up furious resistance and only limited gains of ground are now reported, he says.

From Kassel comes the news that, like Mannheim, the city has offered its surrender over the telephone. I do not think this to be true. The news has been spread deliberately. The Americans obviously want to present these telephonic offers of surrender as a regular occurrence in order to persuade other cities to follow Mannheim's foul example.

In the East the situation in the Austro-Hungarian area has become most precarious in that the enemy has now succeeded in capturing Wiener Neustadt. We have been able to halt him south of Vienna. It is satisfactory, however, that Schörner has once again succeeded in general terms in beating off a heavy Soviet assault. His front is at present the most solid we have. In Breslau too all enemy attacks were beaten off. Hanke was given extraordinarily high praise at the Führer's briefing conference. He deserves it too. He is the outstanding commander among our fighting Gauleiters. A threat to Berlin arises from an extraordinarily heavy enemy concentration in the Cottbus area. It must be anticipated that he will launch an offensive from here.

Evenings are now invariably full of work and worry. For two days the British had not paid Berlin the compliment of their Mosquito raids, so that one was entitled to hope that their losses from our Me 262s had made them somewhat more cautious. This evening, however, they are back again at the regular time. We must not flatter ourselves, therefore, that these nerve-wracking evening raids on the capital have come to an end.

TUESDAY 3 APRIL 1945

(pp. 1–42)
Military Situation.

On the Eastern Front the main centre of fighting was again in Hungary where enemy pressure continues unabated.

A defensive position was formed around the Nagy Kanizsa area, running from the junction of the Mur and Drau in a general northerly direction along the western edge of Nagy Kanizsa to the level of Lake Balaton and thence swinging westwards. The enemy probed forward against this line from the north and penetrated it at a few places. At the same time he tried to outflank the switch line from the north.

Another line of defence was formed south of Steinamanger; it runs generally along the German-Hungarian frontier as far as Güns. Great activity on our side is noticeable in this area. The enemy was driven back in various places, in particular at St. Gotthard on the railway from Steinamanger to Graz and north of Steinamanger.

A defence line also exists in the Semmering area and there the enemy was unable to advance farther. On the other hand he succeeded in gaining further ground south and south-west of Wiener Neustadt. He crossed the Vienna–Bruck–Graz railway at Neunkirchen but was then held. Wiener Neustadt fell into enemy hands. From there the enemy advanced some 10–15 km northwards. His leading troops are now some 15 km north and south-west of Wiener Neustadt. The defensive front around Vienna is said to be very strong. Moving north from the Neusiedlersee the enemy reached Mannersdorf; the leading enemy troops were held, cut off and annihilated. From the northern shore of the Neusiedlersee a switch line runs to the eastern outskirts of Bratislava, along the eastern edge of the Little Carpathians, turns east at Tyrnau and then joins the Slovakian front. The Soviets made a local penetration at Tyrnau but all other attacks on this new line were beaten off.

The second main centre of fighting was in the Mährisch–Ostrau area where the enemy continued his heavy and uninterrupted attacks. He succeeded in making a deep penetration from the Schwarzwasser area; he crossed the Oppeln–Mährisch–Ostrau railway at Kreuzenort but was held by a strong counter-attack. The Bolshevists made a local break-in west of Ratibor. Otherwise all attacks were beaten off—generally by strong counter-attacks. It is reported that in this area the enemy has so far not used his main tank strength, so that a further reinforcement of his offensive must be expected. Violent Soviet attacks at Ziegenhals and Neisse all failed. The Soviets made small advances in certain housing blocks in Breslau but otherwise they were driven off everywhere.

No special operations all along the Oder front as far as Dievenow.

The enemy attacked the few remaining small German bridgeheads north and east of Danzig but there was no major change in the situation. No particular operations reported from the areas of Königsberg and Samland. Heavy Soviet attacks continued in Courland with no change in the situation.

On the Western Front the enemy attacked both northwards and eastwards on the Lower Rhine. From Enschede he reached Nordhorn, the eastern outskirts of Rheine, Ibbenbüren and Lengerich. Enemy detachments advancing on either side of Bielefeld encountered strong German resistance on the western edge of the Teutoburger Wald and could make no further progress. Equally, enemy forces advancing north towards Paderborn were stopped by strong

German counter-attacks. Hamm fell into enemy hands and from there he pushed on towards Soest. We still hold Soest itself.

In Army Group B's sector there was particularly sustained fighting on the Sieg front where the Americans, attacking northwards, encountered very strong German resistance. Nevertheless the town of Siegen was lost. In Sauerland violent fighting developed north-east of Winterberg, which was occupied by the enemy. South of Kassel the enemy crossed the Fulda at Melsungen and pushed forward to Eschwege. Between Eschwege and Eisenach leading enemy troops crossed the Werra at Kreuzburg. From the area of Fulda, which was occupied by the enemy, and the Rhön leading enemy troops pushed forward to the Meiningen region. Everywhere in this region there are still strong detachments of German troops who are now fighting their way eastwards. In the Aschaffenburg area the enemy reached Lohr, then turned south along the west bank of the Main and crossed the Main towards Würzburg. From the Bad Mergentheim area enemy advanced guards pressed on to the Würzburg–Nuremberg railway in the region south of Kitzingen. In the Neckar sector the enemy reached the area north of Heilbronn. Violent fighting is in progress at Bruchsal. The enemy advanced a little farther south from the Germersheim bridgehead.

Only local actions took place on the Italian front.

On the western battle front our air action against enemy tank concentrations and columns was successful. In all eleven enemy aircraft were shot down. Enemy air formations from Italy dropped bombs on Graz, Krems and St. Pölten. During the night 60 Mosquitos were over Berlin and 20 over Magdeburg.

Our Gauleiters both in the West and the East have acquired a bad habit: having lost their Gau, they defend themselves in long memoranda seeking to prove that they were in no way responsible. For instance there is yet

another of these exposés, this time from Grohé.* It is not
in the least convincing. Despite a series of pompous
declarations Grohé has not defended his Gau. He deserted
it before the civil population had been removed and now
wants to present himself as a great hero.

The behaviour of our Gauleiters and Kreisleiters in the
West has led to a great loss of confidence among the people.
The people thought that they could expect our Gauleiters
to fight and, if necessary, fall in action in their Gaus. In
no case has this happened. As a result it is more or less
all over with the Party in the West.

Grohé may lament about the highly confused command
relationships within the Wehrmacht but he had sufficient
powers to do something about it himself. The fact too that
not enough soldiers were available to parry the enemy
offensive is also partially his fault since he ought to have
helped to comb the rear areas for skrimshankers. He also
had sufficient powers to collect the numerous stragglers,
as was after all done on the Rhine. In short the Wehrmacht
cannot pin the blame for this disaster on the Party nor the
Party on the Wehrmacht; both carry a full measure of it
on their shoulders.

In any case the enemy has now become somewhat more
reticent about his victories. He pays the highest tribute to
our commanders in the West for their continued success
in organising resistance. London reports that the first co-
ordinated counter-attack has now been made in an effort
to relieve the Ruhr. Admittedly the Americans defeated it
but it was made with great fury.

Eisenhower has issued another proclamation to the
people of the occupied western districts or those about to
be occupied. Nothing fresh can be detected in this proclamation. Eisenhower is acting like a new German Kaiser.

Moreover it is simply not true that the entire population
of the West is submitting to the enemy. On the contrary the
Western powers report that the prisons are full of refractory elements with whom the occupation authorities

* Gauleiter of Köln-Aachen.

are unable to deal. The people of Frankfurt, however, seem to have been extraordinarily cowardly and servile. The enemy's reports on the subject make one blush. The Americans are said to have been received with large-scale demonstrations as they moved in. The Frankfurters' watchword was "Let's kiss and make friends." The Americans were quite prepared to kiss—particularly the Frankfurt women; as far as making friends is concerned, that is still some way off. Anyway the enemy's only intentions in the West are to despoil us, to starve the German people out and so exterminate it biologically. Nevertheless it makes one sick to read such reports. How can this be wondered at, however, when Sprenger* took off from Frankfurt before the enemy was even in sight and left the city to its fate. The only answer to this development is the Werwolf mentality. I therefore intend to advocate a Werwolf mentality not only over the Werwolf radio station but in a new German newspaper to be set up for the Werwolf. The Werwolf mentality idea is deliberately aimed at a ten per cent minority of activists among the German people. Provided they put in their word, however, these activists will carry the majority of the German people along with them.

I have a report from the Weser–Ems Gau showing a trend similar to that of previous reports from the West. It is the same picture of demoralisation in the Weser–Ems Gau. The soldiers collect in scattered groups, some of them throwing their weapons away. They are ruining the morale of the civil population in this Gau when it could have put up dogged resistance. For the first time the people's morale is badly affected. In some cases these groups of soldiers have even taken to looting. The watchword among them is "Home to mother." The Luftwaffe is prominent in these miserable goings-on, as must be re-emphasised. The Volkssturm and the Hitler Youth, the report says, occupied the defensive positions but they were largely unarmed, so not much could be expected of them. Seiffe, head of the Reich Propaganda Office, requests urgently that

* Gauleiter of Hessen-Nassau.

376

squads of military police be made available to him so that he can round up these miserable collections of retreating soldiers.

All these developments are giving British public opinion to hope that the Reich is in complete disintegration. They think that they will win a quick easy victory this way. The German people are thought to be absolutely ready to surrender; though the government may trumpet resistance and carry on, this would be out-weighed by spontaneous popular reaction; the German people is in process of exchanging the swastika for the white flag and so the West will have an easy time with them. In so far as this is true it is the fault of our own Party and Wehrmacht agencies. They have not proved equal to the present crisis. I hope, however, that I shall succeed in re-establishing the general war morale in the West as I did in the East a few weeks ago, though only by very great exertion. I am helped by the fact that I now have a clear information policy which is not confined to military war reporting but also very much takes in the political side.

As far as the political crisis of the war is concerned dissatisfaction with the Kremlin's policy is increasing among the American public. The San Francisco Conference is already written off almost everywhere. It is hoped to substitute a new Three-Power meeting for it. No one knows, however, whether Stalin will agree to this. Stalin is treating Roosevelt and Churchill like dunces and it is only to be hoped that this sort of provocation will gradually make the pot boil over in the Western enemy camp.

As far as the San Francisco Conference is concerned, it is already a thing of the past. It is thought that Churchill intends to fly to Moscow again to try to persuade Stalin to give way. The progress of the political crisis among our enemies depends on the next fortnight's developments. The main and deciding factor is whether we succeed in organising some form of resistance in the West again.

The Jews have applied for a seat at the San Francisco Conference. It is characteristic that their main demand is that anti-semitism be forbidden throughout the world.

Typically, having committed the most terrible crimes against mankind, the Jews would now like mankind to be forbidden even to think about them.

I have a report from Königsberg about the situation in that area. The unity between Party and Wehrmacht established by Kreisleiter Wagner has been more or less destroyed by the intervention of Koch. Kreisleiter Wagner has been demoted and is now in a subordinate post. Koch has taken charge of things himself using shirt-sleeve methods, probably out of jealousy of his Kreisleiter. He is now using in Königsberg the methods which did him so little credit in the Ukraine.*

All is at present quiet in the Protectorate [Bohemia/Moravia]. The Czechs have no thought of joining the partisan movement. Nevertheless the entire Czech public expects a German defeat daily. Germans in the Protectorate are desperately wondering when the German leaders will at last come to their senses, when they will learn from past mistakes and root out ruthlessly the obvious failures among the leaders. This question is being asked not only by Germans in the Protectorate but throughout the Reich. It is almost crippling to see how the lack of power of decision on personnel problems among the Reich leaders is gradually spreading discontent throughout the people like a creeping disease.

In the air war the only heavy air raids we have had to suffer have been from the south. No raids were made from England owing to bad weather. So this time it was Austria's turn only.

I am now working indefatigably to give the German press clear directions on the aims of our present war policy. Now that Dr. Dietrich is out of the way Sündermann is trying to take a hand in the direction of the press. I shall stop that, however, by cancelling Sündermann's reserved occupation status so that he can be made available for the

---

* Koch had been Reich Commissioner for the Ukraine and had been notorious for his brutality.

378

front. The German press now presents a thoroughly bellicose aspect. The gravity of the situation is not concealed;
readers, however, are given the arguments with which they
can come to terms with the present situation in their minds.
I am myself dictating guidelines for the German press
which are intended to set the standard for the immediate
future. They are as follows:

"1. The entire German news and propaganda policy
must now be devoted exclusively to re-establishing and
increasing the power of resistance, the war effort and
fighting morale both at the front and at home. To achieve
this aim all resources must be harnessed to produce a
direct and indirect impact on readers and audiences.
Anything which can be detrimental to this aim or runs
counter to it, even only passively, can have no place in
press or radio in these decisive days of our fateful
struggle. Anything which contributes to the achievement
of this great purpose should be expressly promoted and
henceforth be a central feature of our newscasting.

2. The main task of the press and radio is to make
clear to the German people that our Western enemies
are pursuing the same infamous purposes and the same
devilish annihilation plans against the German people
as are our Eastern enemies; the West is using ostensibly
more civilised methods only to deceive the German
people and entrap the feeble-minded. The brutal Anglo-
American air war is sufficient proof of our Western
enemies' bestiality and shows that all their ostensibly
conciliatory phrases are mere camouflage designed to
paralyse the German people in their stubborn defence
of their right to exist. Our task is to point out again and
again that Churchill and Roosevelt are just as merciless
as Stalin and will ruthlessly carry out their plans for
annihilation should the German people ever give way
and submit to the enemy yoke.

3. Deeds of heroism at the front and at home should be
given priority and embellished with comment. They
should not be presented as isolated examples but should

act as a stimulus for everybody and a challenge to the whole nation to emulate these shining examples of the struggle for our freedom.

4. The cultural section of our newspapers is not to become a little bourgeois refuge for war-weary brothers. These columns too must use every method to assist in reinforcing our national resistance and our war morale. The particular job of the cultural editor is to express in lofty varied language what has been said in the political section on the military and political struggle of the day. In these weeks superficial intellectual vapourings, divorced from the war as if it was "far away in Turkey," have no justification for appearance. A plethora of tasks and multifarious possibilities are now open to the cultural editor. Discussion of Clausewitz' writings, descriptions of the Second Punic War, comments on Mommsen's Roman History, dissertations on Frederick the Great's letters and writings, the careers of great warlike geniuses all through human history—these are only a few indications of the new tasks which will do more to promote our purpose than innocent entertaining anecdotes without political or moral content.

5. The local sections of our newspapers must subordinate themselves to these requirements. No measures of communal or local significance issuing from Party, State or Wehrmacht should be presented to the reader without simultaneously impressing upon him forcibly that our struggle for existence requires the mobilisation of all forces and the expenditure of all reserves of manpower and morale. Any sacrifice in the interests of war, however small and mundane, serves to concentrate our forces and increase our capacity for resistance and must be explained to the reader in this sense.

6. Newspaper publishers are recommended to pay particular attention to the advertisement section. All inopportune left-overs not in consonance with the spirit of the times should be eradicated."

The Führer is very much in agreement with the wording

of this directive. He is convinced that I shall now succeed in getting German press policy back on the rails.

I take leave of Fischer, hitherto Head of the German Press Section, who is going to the Wehrmacht. Fischer is most downcast over what has happened; I make clear to him, however, that I could not have acted otherwise than I actually have.

Meister Hahne, the first man to be decorated with the Knight's Cross to the War Service Cross, demonstrates to me a new gun on a captured mounting; he can assemble and make available for Berlin up to 200 of these guns from stocks available in Wehrmacht arsenals and arms production workshops. Hahne proposes that a careful check of Wehrmacht ordnance depots be made; they contain a mass of parts which could be assembled to produce new weapons. We must in fact now improvise in order even partially to make good the serious shortfall in production. That in arms production is the most important. Production at Alkett, for instance, is down by 50% and will fall even further next month. This is extraordinarily worrying and we must adopt new makeshift methods if we are to avoid the resulting calamity.

Once more a mass of new decrees and instructions issue from Bormann. Bormann has turned the Party Chancellery into a paper factory. Every day he sends out a mountain of letters and files which the Gauleiters, now involved in battle, no longer even have time to read. In some cases too it is totally useless stuff of no practical value in our struggle. Even in the Party we have no clear leadership in contact with the people.

As far as our situation in the West is concerned, we now have three major operations planned: one from Holland in the direction of Hamm under command of Colonel-General Student; General Bayerlein is to try to fight his way out of the Ruhr; an attempt is to be made to meet him with a counter-attack from outside. In Thuringia a new army under command of General Schulz, well known as having been decorated with the Swords, is to be formed from the units flooding into the area. This army is to take the enemy in flank and try to cut off considerable numbers of his units. Hausser has meanwhile been relieved of his command. He has definitely not stood the test. Obergruppenführer Steiner has been despatched to the Vienna area. He is to hold on there in all circumstances. The Führer has issued the strictest orders of the whole war for the defence of Vienna. Our soldiers must hold out here man for man and anyone who leaves his post is to be shot. It is hoped in this way to get the better of the critical developments in the Vienna area.

Schörner's stock stands very high with the Führer. He has beaten off attacks on the Mährisch–Ostrau industrial zone with the utmost courage. Schörner is our most outstanding army commander. Guderian has lost a great deal of credit with the Führer. Both in the Baranov and Hungarian areas he urged offensive action prematurely and so placed our operations at great risk, in fact made them impossible. The Führer has accordingly sent him on leave.

In the Führer's view the moment of decision is now upon us in the West. The Führer is indefatigable in urging the generals to resist and leave no stone unturned in order to throw fresh units into the western battle. He calls each individual army commander almost daily and points out to them what is at stake and what their duties and obligations are. In my view it would be better if the Führer addressed the people direct since here in fact are the grass-roots of resistance. Once the people were once more ready to resist, all the others would regain their old form. What both the people and the troops lack is the stirring word to rouse both man and woman. In the nature of things this stirring word can come only from the Führer. It is wrong, therefore, for the generals to think that I should speak instead of the Führer.

The situation in such that only a word from the Führer can relieve the crisis of morale in which the people is plunged at the moment. I regard it as a great mistake that the Führer does not speak. Even if at the moment we have no victory to which we can point, the Führer could still say something; it is not only in victory that one should speak but in misfortune as well. It is at present very difficult to get decisions from the Führer. He is occupied exclusively with the situation in the West and barely finds time for other problems. If, however, he succeeds in clearing up the situation in the West even partially, he will have done something which may decide the war.

At the daily briefing conferences the Luftwaffe comes in for the sharpest criticism from the Führer. Day after day Göring has to listen without being in a position to demur at all. Colonel-General Stumpff, for instance, refused to subordinate himself to Kesselring for the new operations planned in the West. The Führer called him sharply to order saying that the relative positions of Kesselring and Stumpff were similar to those of him and Schaub.

In the West, of course, it is now and for the immediate future a continuous process of muddling through. We are in the most critical and dangerous phase of this war and one sometimes has the impression that the German people, fighting at the height of the war crisis, has broken out in a sweat impossible for the non-expert to distinguish as the precursor of death or recovery.

The Führer has had very prolonged discussions with Obergruppenführer Kammler who now carries responsibility for the reform of the Luftwaffe. Kammler is doing excellently and great hopes are placed on him.

As far as the situation in the West this evening is concerned it has deteriorated only in Thuringia. Here the enemy has advanced as far as Gotha. At the moment we have nothing with which to oppose him since we do not wish to dissipate our offensive forces. Sauckel is working feverishly to put his Gau into a state of defence. In the Teutoburger Wald too the enemy has registered small gains of ground but they are of no great significance. Otherwise he is closing up all along the Western Front so that we must certainly reckon with further attacks in the next few weeks.

In the south-east the enemy has moved nearer Vienna. We are determined to hold here in all circumstances, cost what it may. Schörner, on the other hand, has beaten off all Soviet attacks made on his front—a really first-class heroic achievement. The Führer is extraordinarily pleased with Schörner's methods in the field. Schörner will undoubtedly be the next Field-Marshal and he has earned this promotion.

At this Tuesday's briefing conference the Führer was no longer so abusive of the generals. He is doing his utmost now to pull his military staff together, to inspire them with fresh courage and fill them with confidence for the future. He is tirelessly preaching a spirit of battle and resistance, as I am now doing in our Werwolf propaganda. My directive to the press has given him an opportunity to show the generals how such a job should be approached. The Führer is also extraordinarily pleased with my work on Werwolf. He said at the briefing conference that this is the way things must be done if the people are not to become a prey to despair.

This evening I dictate another call to the Werwolf movement in language reminiscent of that used in *Angriff* in the good old days of our struggle.

We have two air-raid alerts in Berlin this evening. So the enemy is not proposing to give us time off in the Reich capital. On the contrary the break has been only for reasons of weather and the series of air-raid alerts will undoubtedly not come to an end for the present.

[Entries for 4, 5 and 6 April 1945 are missing]

SATURDAY 7 APRIL 1945

[pp. 9–39, pp. 1–8 (Military Situation) missing.]
The British press has suddenly done a complete about-turn. It is now full of admiration for the German people's leadership and their power of resistance, for our military achievements and for the high morale maintained by the German nation in this fateful struggle. British generals are writing that it would not be fair to withhold admiration. Above all, according to the British, German tenacity is beyond all praise.

Our Werwolf activity is now being taken extraordinarily seriously in Anglo-American circles, so seriously that Eisenhower is said to be toying with the idea of using gas against Werwolf detachments. That would be entirely in line with Anglo-American conduct of war but it would not deter us in the slightest since we should then use appropriate counter-measures against Anglo-American soldiers.

Reuters carry an extraordinarily interesting politico-military report, for the first time giving a correct analysis of our present war policy. In particular the fact of our Werwolf activity is given proper emphasis among the general war clamour. The British realise that the Werwolf could be the germ of an extraordinarily dangerous instrument of German resistance to be maintained at any cost and for an unpredictable time.

People in London are more afraid than anything of the emergence of chaos in Germany which would put off pacification of Europe to the Greek Kalends. The Werwolf in particular is regarded as the germ of such a development which would, of course, upset the entire Anglo-American war concept.

The *Schwarze Korps* carries a sensational article which will undoubtedly do us a lot of damage. The article says quite openly that we no longer have any prospect of holding out militarily but that the idea must live on in all circumstances. Naturally this article has created a considerable stir primarily because it appears in the *Schwarze Korps* and is therefore taken as an expression of opinion from the diehard National-Socialist camp. The editors of the *Schwarze Korps* maintain that the article was included in the paper in error. I do not believe that. I am inclined to think that certain over-intellectual elements are entering a state of nirvana. I shall take most brutal steps against this.

Dr. Ley's leading article deals with the Werwolf question. It is quite impossible and I therefore had to reject it. Dr. Ley is now getting Kiehl, his press officer, to write a fresh article overnight, the first to appear in his name and to make sense. It would be more practical if Dr. Ley would have his articles written by his staff in future; then we should at least have some guarantee of eliminating the cruder absurdities.

The Americans have now formed a trades union in Aachen, hoping to curry favour with German workers. The inaugural meeting was a pretty colourless affair with no more than 40 men and women present. This cannot be said to be representative of the working class in the occupied areas.

Graf Krosigk writes me another pressing letter asking me to impress on the Führer the necessity for a more active foreign policy. He regards the war situation as so menacing that he concludes that we must act at once if it is not to be too late.

In this connection I have news from Bohle about the Foreign Office's activities in neutral countries. The Foreign Office is at present active both in Switzerland and Sweden and also in Spain. The results are fairly shattering. With Britain there is nothing whatsoever to be done at the moment. Under Churchill's leadership British policy proves to be totally intransigent. Churchill has now got it into his head that the German Reich must be destroyed and the German people annihilated. There is not the smallest loophole here. Soundings have shown that there is somewhat more to be done with the USA always provided that they are given possibilities of economic expansion in Europe. Roosevelt is nothing like so unapproachable as Churchill. A whole series of conditions are necessary, however, before one can even start talking to the USA. The most productive feelers have been those put out to the Soviet Union. However the Soviet Union demands East Prussia which is naturally an unacceptable requirement.

The Foreign Office has operated fairly ineptly in these negotiations. It has used the old routine diplomats who are of course not mentally attuned to presenting the National-Socialist viewpoint to the enemy. But what else can one expect from the Foreign Office! Ribbentrop is having pictures of himself published in the newspapers showing him in the trenches on the Oder front. Anyone seeing these pictures will at once conclude that the German Foreign Minister should now have something more important to do than trot round on the Oder front.

The Turkish government is now begging for a fair wind from Moscow. Saracoglu's* statements are cringingly servile. Stalin will soon give him the appropriate answer.

In any case the Kremlin now feels itself on top of the situation. The Soviets have earned good marks from the USA by abrogating their pact of friendship with Japan. This was an extraordinarily adroit tactical move by Stalin; his purpose was to take the wind out of the sails of Roosevelt's domestic opposition. In addition he proposes to take a hand in the East Asia conflict in order to be able to fish in troubled waters when the time arrives. The extent to which he is going is clear from an article in *Izvestia* attacking Japan and her predatory policy in extraordinarily

* The Turkish Prime Minister.

sharp terms. This is the way it begins and one knows how it will end. Anyway Roosevelt is entitled to be very pleased with the help Stalin is giving him at the moment.

Smuts* has made an extraordinarily gloomy speech at the Imperial Conference now sitting in London. He regards San Francisco as the last chance for civilised mankind. If San Francisco fails, then what we regard as cultured mankind would be doomed. A human catastrophe of unimaginable proportions would be the inevitable result. A third world war would be waged with new and even more devastating weapons. What remained of mankind would be neither worthy nor capable of existence.

A new conflict has now arisen in Poland in that the Soviets have arrested and deported 15 influential Polish politicians. The NKVD invited them to come for negotiations and then simply arrested them out of hand.† There is extraordinary consternation in London and Washington. Reuters' report on the subject is very candid.

In general it may be said that influential circles in London and Washington are becoming more and more uneasy over the Kremlin's imperialist policy. In London people are already saying that the future world outlook is frightful if the Kremlin persists in this policy. The military victories are completely overshadowed by these prospects. In Washington, however, these considerations are temporarily outweighed by Stalin's adroit move *vis-à-vis* Tokyo. The Japanese are in consternation. They comfort themselves with the thought that the Japanese-Soviet treaty runs until April 1946, but this is small consolation.

Otherwise the Soviet press is now attacking the rumours about separate peace negotiations between Moscow and Berlin. Their language is less violent than one might expect, however. Here too Stalin wishes to keep all doors open.

Developments in the Austro-Hungarian area continue to be most unfortunate. The removal of their armbands from

---

* Prime Minister of South Africa.

† On this episode see Z. Stypulkowski, *Invitation to Moscow* (1951).

the crack SS divisions has had a devastating effect. A number of SS officers were broken-hearted and shot themselves. Kersten, one of the Führer's aides who was with these divisions, was told by certain authoritative members of them that Berlin was finished as far as they were concerned, that they would allow themselves to be hewn in pieces for the Führer, that they were ready to go into the attack again wherever they were told but that the Führer would never see them again. It is a most tragic affair which brings tears to one's eyes. I am all for being strict and stern in our conduct of the war but please let it be so in all cases. The SS officers will not and cannot understand that the most atrocious shortcomings on the part of the Luftwaffe, which have resulted in practically the whole of the Reich going up in flames, should go unpunished, while a single failure on the part of these divisions, which otherwise have covered themselves with glory, is punished so savagely.

Once again the Luftwaffe can register the fiasco of its constructional and operational policy. The enemy has made extraordinarily heavy raids on Leipzig, Halle and Gera. Devastation upon devastation has been wrought on these urban areas. Things have now gone so far that these raids can no longer be recorded. The news of the air war can barely be unravelled.

Our suicide fighters were in action for the first time during this Saturday when the weather was only semi-favourable. Great success is expected from these missions but we will wait and see.

The evacuation problem is still most critical. In the West evacuation is in fact no longer practicable. As I had foreseen, the Führer's order cannot be carried out. No one now knows where people are to go. How can such extensive and thickly populated areas be emptied! As a result the evacuation problem in the West has been quietly shelved. In the East, on the other hand, it is a different matter. There are still large masses of people in the constricted East Prussian area. And now the question arises whether Vienna should be evacuated or not. I do not think that the Viennese population is showing the smallest desire to leave the city.

For the first time since the beginning of the war small riots have taken place in Berlin-Rahnsdorf. Two bakeries were invaded and loaves seized by 200 men and women. I have decided to take brutal measures against them at once, for such symptoms of weakness and incipient defeatism can in no circumstances be tolerated. Even if the food supply is not of the best at the moment, it is quite impossible to take such goings-on calmly or they would set an example and then we should be more or less lost. I am therefore demanding that the Berlin court martial take immediate proceedings against the ringleaders of this riot.

Colonel Fett from Field-Marshall Keitel's staff briefs me about the formation of the seven fresh divisions designated for our offensive in Thuringia. They consist of three divisions from the Labour Service and are primarily Peoples Grenadier Divisions. Their equipment is comparatively good, though they have no tanks. They will be made semi-mobile and will be equipped mainly with artillery, assault guns, carbines, machine guns and bazookas. They may achieve something since their manpower material is excellent. Cadres will be furnished by officers from the cadet schools. From the manpower point of view, therefore, the material of which these divisions are formed can be regarded as qualitatively satisfactory. The question is whether these divisions can be sufficiently welded together in so short a time as to form real fighting formations. As things are there must be some doubt about this. On the other hand it is hoped that the quality of men assembled in these divisions will do much to compensate for this. They come mainly from the 1928 class, which is of course excellent. This is a provisional arrangement which is being tried out for the first time and naturally implies great risk. The divisions should be ready for action by 20 April. Contrary to what the Führer thinks therefore, we cannot set any store by them in the next few days. We have to wait another fortnight and there is a danger that by that time the enemy will have reinforced his flanks so that these divisions will meet considerable resistance.

The capital's stock-taking does not show a great reduction this week, as I had feared. In general terms it has kept static though we have to record large shortfalls in certain sectors, particularly petrol and food, to say nothing of coal. Only small quantities of coal are arriving in Berlin. As a result I am introducing my planned restrictions on traffic and reductions in the supply of gas to private houses. These unpleasant measures have naturally led to great discontent among the public but I can do nothing else than introduce these measures in order to preserve what can still be preserved.

I have passed a weekend full of worry, of mental and material strain and also of doubt. I am most depressed over the Führer's action against the SS divisions which, of course, is extraordinarily humiliating for all SS officers including those in my entourage. One cannot imagine the state of mind in which they are now. I would so much like to help them but do not know what I can do. Perhaps I will make a personal approach to the Führer to ask him to mitigate these measures somewhat.

This afternoon I write a leading article headed "Resistance at any Price." In this article I use extremist language as also in an article on Werwolf. For the first time I discard to some extent my measured reserve. There is no object now in talking round the point. One must call a spade a spade even at the risk of the enemy making some use of what one says.

Bishop Galen of Münster has been interviewed by American journalists. Unexpectedly he attacked our Anglo-American enemies and their air terror. He is also afraid of the increasing bolshevisation of Germany. Mr. Bishop ought to have thought of this earlier. When we were giving warnings against bolshevisation he was always on the other side. He is a chameleon, or rather a Westphalian blockhead who always says the opposite of what public opinion thinks.

The evening situation report brings little good news. In the West the enemy has kept up the momentum of his advance. He is now some 15 km from Hildesheim and moving straight on Hannover. In addition he has passed through Bückeburg and is now in the region of Minden. So we in Berlin are gradually being threatened from the western side. South of Verden the enemy has swung towards Bremen. He is trying to capture a major port whatever happens. South of the Harz the situation is more or less unchanged. On the other hand in Thuringia the enemy has advanced to Erfurt and has captured Suhl and Zella-Mehlis, which is extremely distressing from the point of view of arms production. He is now west of Kitzingen and has advanced to Uffenheim and almost to Dinkelsbühl. He has dropped airborne troops in this area but it is hoped to deal with them. The situation is somewhat more favourable in the Heilbronn area and also in the Ruhr where Model's Army Group is fighting excellently. The situation in Holland has also been consolidated somewhat.

In the East Vienna is the critical point. The enemy has reached the city area on the south-west. He is outside St. Pölten. The south-eastern section of Vienna is already largely in his hands. Worse still, however, is the political situation which has emerged in Vienna as a result. Riots have taken place in the former red suburbs of the city and these has assumed such proportions that Schirach has been helpless and has had to place himself under the protection of the troops. That is typical of Schirach. He let things take their course and then takes refuge with the soldiers. I never expected anything else from him. Here is an example of the pernicious consequences of the Führer's lack of decision on matters of personnel policy. Schirach* has long been overdue for dismissal, but the Führer has not been able to make up his mind to despatch him to the wilderness. Now the severest measures must be taken to clean up the situation in Vienna. The Führer is still deter-

* Baldur von Schirach, former Reich Youth Leader, was Gauleiter of Vienna.

mined to hold the city come what may. The events taking
place in Vienna itself must not, of course, be over-
dramatised. Merely a rabble is responsible for these riots
and this rabble must be shot down. But things ought not
to have got so far. The case of Rahnsdorf in Berlin is an
example. The ringleaders were sentenced by the Peoples
Court this very afternoon. Three were condemned to death
—one man and two women. The case of one of the women
is less serious so that I have decided to pardon her. The
other two who were condemned to death I shall have
beheaded during the night. The people of Rahnsdorf will
be informed by placard that these two ringleaders have
been sentenced and executed; the rest of the Berlin population will be told over the wired broadcast with appropriate
comment. I think that this will have a most sobering effect.
In any case I am of the opinion that no more bakeries in
Berlin will be looted in the immediate future. This is how
one must proceed if one is to keep order in a city with
millions of inhabitants—and order is a prerequisite for
continuation of our resistance.

The only other unfavourable development reported
from the Eastern Front is in the Königsberg area where
the enemy has been able to penetrate to a greater depth.

During the course of the day our suicide fighters were in
action for the first time against enemy air raids. Successes
have not yet been counted but it seems that they were not
as great as had been hoped. It must not be forgotten, however, that this is the first trial and the experiment need
not yet be written off as a failure.

Magda has returned from Schwanenwerder for a visit to
Berlin. A somewhat melancholy evening during which one
piece of bad news after another descends on the house.
One sometimes wonders desperately where all this will lead.
The Führer must be expending an unparalleled amount of
nervous energy to keep his poise in this super-critical
situation. I still have hope, however, that he will get the
better of the situation. He has always known how to await
his moment with lofty calm. When the moment comes,
however, then he invariably jumps in with both feet.

SUNDAY 8 APRIL 1945

(pp. 1–39)

Military Situation.

In the East heavy enemy attacks were concentrated in the Vienna and Königsberg areas.

The situation in the Vienna area has deteriorated considerably. The Soviets advanced north-west and north from Baden and reached the Danube at Tulln. More numerous Soviet forces penetrated into the southern, western and northern suburbs of Vienna. The East Station, the Arsenal and the South Station were lost. The East Station and the Arsenal were recovered by counter-attack. Some of the inhabitants of the southern suburbs fought on the Soviet side against our own troops.

In the battle for Königsberg bolshevist reinforcements launched converging attacks and reached the Main Station. They also reached the south bank of the Pregel near its mouth. Penetrations on the eastern outskirts were dealt with by counter-attack.

On the Oder front two bridges which the enemy had captured were destroyed.

Otherwise no special developments on the Eastern Front.

On the Western Front the northern enemy grouping made further gains of ground. Enemy forces advanced through Rheine as far as Schapen and Lengerich. The enemy offensive towards Bremen reached Twistringen, Vilsen and the region west of Verden. American forces moved forward from their bridgehead on the east bank of the Weser south of Hameln, reaching Elze and a point just south of Hildesheim.

A fresh area of concentrated enemy effort is the southern edge of the Thüringer Wald where he attacked strongly towards Hildburghausen. He captured Themar and Schleusingen. From the Würzburg area the Americans pushed on north-east towards Schweinfurt and along the Würzburg–Nuremburg road to the region of Iphofen. Enemy armour drove through a gap in the front south of Mergentheim reaching Crailsheim and Jagstheim. Flank attacks are being made against them. No major change in the situation in the Heilbronn–Karlsruhe area.

In Sauerland and the Ruhr the enemy launched violent attacks on our forces between Oberhausen and Gelsenkirchen and in particular at Soest but he achieved local successes only at certain points.

Strong American bomber formations made daylight raids on north and north-west Germany, in particular on Neumünster, Lüneburg, Uelzen, Schwerin and Güstrow. So far six aircraft are reported shot down. Further reports of successes are not yet to hand. There was large-scale enemy fighter-bomber activity concentrated on Weissenfels, Gera and Weimar. Some 500 American four-engined bombers from Italy raided Innsbruck and Klagenfurt. During the night some 250 British bombers raided the Espenheim area. Eleven enemy aircraft were shot down.

In London a certain change of mood is noticeable in that people are no longer talking of an imminent end to the war but are resigned to a continuance of military operations. There has been a rude awakening from the illusionism of the Easter period when people expected the German surrender hourly. People are once again thinking in terms of three months before Germany is ground to the floor. I think that British public opinion will be by no means content with these constantly changing forecasts by British leaders. Obviously such short-sighted propaganda does not pay off in the long run. It merely keeps people's nerves on edge.

Anglo-American journalists working in the occupied regions are giving vent to the view that the German people will never capitulate. Only Hitler, Himmler or Goebbels, they say, could conclude a peace with Germany's enemies and they are in no way prepared to do so unless this peace was in the interests of the German people.

Anglo-American war reporters are gradually finding that the atmosphere in Germany is one of what they call stifling hatred and this naturally does not fail to make its impression on them. In addition, anxiety about the post-war period is growing in England day by day. The British people has become a people without hope. It was driven into this fateful war by Churchill and, looked at *à la longue*, will lose it whatever happens, whether it emerges victorious or not. In addition Britain has plunged Europe into the most frightful misery, not only her enemies but also friendly countries. The newspapers in the French capital, for instance, are now coming out with great headlines to the effect that Paris is facing starvation. Conditions in France seem to be beyond description. We have no need of our own reports to prove it; Anglo-American reports tell us enough.

The United Press reports sad news from Mülhausen in Thuringia. Our entire gold reserves amounting to hundreds of tons and vast art treasures, including the Nefertiti, have fallen into American hands in the salt mines there. I have always opposed the removal of gold and art treasures from Berlin but, despite my objections, Funk* refused to take advice. Probably he was talked into it by his staff and advisers who were desirous of moving to an ostensibly safe province, in other words Thuringia. Now by criminal dereliction of duty they have allowed the German people's most treasured possessions to fall into enemy hands. On enquiry from the Reichsbahn I learn that certain somewhat ineffectual steps had been taken for the priority move of the gold and art treasures from Thuringia to Berlin; remarkably enough they were not put into effect because of the

---

* Minister for Economic Affairs.

Easter holiday. One could tear one's hair out when one thinks that the Reichsbahn is having an Easter holiday while the enemy is looting our entire stock of gold. If I were the Führer I should know what has now to be done. I imagine, however, that those responsible will in no way be called to account. People in Germany now can do just what they like. There is no strong hand to take appropriate action against such crimes of neglect of duty.

Tokyo, the Japanese capital, has again been heavily raided by American bombers. It seems that these air raids are having a very bad effect on Japanese morale, since the Japanese are singing very small both to the Soviets and the Anglo-Americans. A Japanese statement, for instance, says that the Japanese have never done the Soviets any harm and that it is the job of the Soviets to reorganise Europe, whereas for East Asia this devolves on Japan. Thoughtfully there is no mention of us in this order of precedence. I have the impression that the Japanese have lost their traditional phlegm and self-assurance.

Suzuki's new Japanese government is composed of fairly unknown people. Suzuki himself is temporarily taking over the Foreign Ministry but it is thought that in a few days he will entrust foreign policy to Togo, the former Japanese Ambassador in Berlin. Togo is among the more pliable characters and there is nothing to be expected from him as far as we are concerned. The Japanese Embassy in Berlin admits that the new government is one to weigh the possibilities, perhaps even try out the ground. As far as Japanese war policy is concerned, therefore, one thing may be taken as certain: it would be the bloodiest irony in the history of this war if in the end Japan too was lost to us and we were left quite alone in the field.

Suzuki's first governmental statement is in general a strong and firm one. But one knows that story. Badoglio too initially made a robust war speech only to stab us in the back a few weeks later. So one must treat such declarations with much suspicion. Until one knows what the new Japanese government is actually doing, I shall not place any great hopes in it. The order of the day seems to be to remain very much on the watch to avoid being overtaken one day by unpleasant surprises.

Within the enemy coalition suspicion continues to grow. Stettinius, the American Foreign Minister, is at great pains to champion the San Francisco—or San Fiasco—Conference which is in considerable disarray before it has even opened. In a speech in New York he decried the panic rumours being spread about this conference and declared that the difficulties which have arisen between the Allies, though admittedly great, must be overcome. Otherwise Stettinius propounded totally vague peace aims for the coalition, of which one cannot make head nor tail. The conflict between the enemy powers revolves primarily round the question of the kidnapping of 15 Polish underground leaders. These underground leaders are simply no longer to be found. A guessing game is in progress in London and Washington as to where the Soviets have taken them. The suspicion is voiced that Moscow has laid hands on them in order to negotiate with them direct, bypassing the Anglo-Americans, and so produce a viable solution to the problem of reconstitution of the Lublin Committee. In that case the British and Americans would be completely outwitted and short-circuited in Poland.

From all these reports it can be deduced that there is fear and suspicion of each other within the enemy coalition but that it is the Soviet Union which is the object of the greatest fear and the greatest suspicion.

The Soviets have again got the upper hand through their military victories in the Vienna area. They are now fighting in the Vienna suburbs and slowly pushing forward to the centre. The Vienna suburbs have largely taken up arms on the side of the Red Army, resulting naturally in a fairly wretched state of affairs in Vienna. This is what we get from the so-called Viennese humour which, much against my will, we have always cosseted and extolled in our press and radio. The Führer appreciated the Viennese correctly. They are an odious crew, a mixture of Poles, Czechs, Jews and Germans. I think, however, that the Viennese would have been better kept in check had there been a decent and, above all, energetic political leader at the helm. Schirach was not the right man. But how often have I said that and how often has no one listened to me!

In the last 24 hours Anglo-American air raids have been mainly directed on airfields in the Mecklenburg, Hamburg and Holstein areas. In addition they attacked our hydrogenation plant at Pöhlberg.

The first use of our suicide fighters has not produced the success hoped for. The reason given is that the enemy bomber formations did not fly concentrated so that they had to be attacked individually. In addition our suicide fighters encountered such heavy defensive fire from enemy fighters that only in a few cases were they able to ram. But we must not lose courage as a result. This is only an initial trial which is to be repeated in the next few days, hopefully with better results.

The situation at the front has never been so bad. We have to all intents and purposes lost Vienna. The enemy has penetrated deep into Königsberg. The Anglo-Americans are not far from Braunschweig and Bremen. In short, on the map the Reich looks like a small strip running from Norway to Lake Comacchio. We have lost the most important areas of food supply and arms potential. The Führer must now launch our offensive in Thuringia as quickly as possible to give us room to breathe. In any case, with the potential available to us, we shall not be able to breathe much longer.

The Führer has now awarded Hanke the German Order in Gold. After Hierl, therefore, Hanke is the second German to receive this order, though in a lower class. As he told me over the telephone, Hanke is very pleased. He regards the situation in Breslau as extraordinarily critical. He does not know how much longer he can hold out. In any case this high honour is very much merited. He has done wonderfully and his pugnacious attitude has brought renown to the Party.

The Rahnsdorf affair* can now be considered com-

* See above pp. 390, 393.

pletely closed. The Rahnsdorf Kreisleiter called an open-air meeting at which he announced the draconian sentences passed and executed on the ringleaders. These sentences are regarded by the people of Rahnsdorf as a deliverance. I am convinced that the people of Berlin can always be persuaded to support maintenance of public law and order. Refractory elements must be routed. Experience shows that the sympathy of those in favour of law and order is enlisted thereby and they are in general the far greater majority.

The evening situation report contains the news that the main centre of fighting is in Lower Saxony. The enemy is now west and south of Hannover. Hildesheim has fallen into his hands. He is pressing on fast towards Bremen and is now west of Verden an der Aller. By throwing in reserve units attempts are being made to halt this advance which has again gathered breakneck speed. The enemy has crossed the Weser west and south of Göttingen. In general terms the situation in Thuringia is unchanged. Only at Hildburghausen were the Americans able to advance. Schweinfurt is threatened. Our troops are at present successfully resisting the American advance beyond Würzburg. All reports confirm that the Americans have suffered enormous losses; but they can afford them at the moment. Pforzheim has also fallen into enemy hands. On the other hand our position in Holland is holding out well. Our parachute troops are putting up extraordinarily courageous and dogged resistance there.

The main feature of the situation on the Eastern Front is the extraordinarily severe fighting in the centre of Vienna. The Soviets succeeded in crossing the Danube east of Vienna; otherwise they have moved in the direction of St. Pölten. Extraordinarily unpleasant incidents continue to occur among the population of Vienna, naturally increasing the difficulty of the situation for our units fighting there. Schirach can write that down on the debit side of his account. He is responsible for the behaviour of the people of Vienna and he cannot evade this responsibility. Schörner has launched an offensive to break up the enemy assembly areas. This offensive has made good progress. In Breslau the enemy attacked very heavily from all sides but in general was held. Nevertheless one must now begin to ask oneself the question how long this can go on. The enemy also made an extraordinarily heavy attack on Königsberg. Here the Soviets were able to penetrate to some depth.

An anxious evening once more; after the interval of the last few days the enemy renewed his Mosquito raids on the capital. We have become so used to these Mosquito raids that they have, so to speak, become part of the daily programme. On an evening when the British do not visit the Reich capital the people of Berlin feel that something is missing.

MONDAY 9 APRIL 1945

(pp. 1–10, "Military Situation" only)

Military Situation.

The centres of fighting on the Eastern Front were again the Vienna and Königsberg areas.

In Vienna, via the Kahlenberg and Frinzing the enemy reached the Franz-Joseph Station and the neighbourhood of the Danube Canal. In the west of the city too he penetrated farther in some places. Fierce house-to-house fighting is in progress east of Mariabrunn, at St. Veit und Mauer and on the south and south-eastern front of Vienna. The Bolshevists made only minor gains of ground at the Arsenal and in the Museum grounds. Enemy troops who had crossed at Nussdorf were driven back. On either side of the Vienna–St. Pölten road and railway Soviet forces reached an area 20 km east of St. Pölten. The enemy made numerous local attacks between the Drau and the Vienna battle zone but in general they were repulsed.

Along the frontier of the Protectorate numerous enemy attacks on the March sector were in general repulsed. In the western part of Slovakia bolshevist attacks northwards reached the Protectorate frontier in the area Holic–Trentschin.

South of Ratibor an enemy bridgehead was reduced by counter-attack; a local break-in on the western edge of Breslau was dealt with.

No special developments on the Neisse front.

The enemy continues to move west from the Danzig area. It is thought that Soviet forces released from this area are being transferred to the Stettin or Frankfurt fronts.

In the battle for Königsberg the enemy succeeded in making deep penetrations and cutting communications with Samland. With the enemy advancing from west, east and north the garrison of Königsberg is reduced to a small area.

No special actions in Courland.

On the Western Front enemy pressure in eastern Holland increased. Violent attacks on Deventer are in progress. They are being made primarily by Canadian formations. Leading enemy troops advancing north reached the Almelo–Zwolle–Meppel area. No special developments reported from the Lingen–Rheine area. In the area south of Bremen leading enemy troops made only a comparatively small advance. From Twistringen they moved along the railway as far as Bassum. The enemy advanced farther eastwards towards Hannover from the area between Nienburg and Minden. His leading troops are in the region of Neustadt bei Wunstorf, Stadthagen and Bückeburg. Enemy forces swung north from Hildesheim towards Lehrte, reaching a point south of the Weser–Elbe canal so that an attack on Hannover from west and south is now to be expected. Leading enemy troops are some 10–15 km north of Hildesheim, in other words 20–30 km south of Hannover. Another enemy grouping moved eastwards south of Hildesheim and reached the region of Bockenem between Hildesheim and Salzgitter. Other enemy forces reached Alfeld, Kreiensen and Einbeck. The Americans advanced into Göttingen where fierce fighting flared up, particularly in the barracks area. The enemy dropped parachute troops at Bad Sooden on the Werra and formed a bridgehead on the east bank. Fierce fighting is in progress here. No change in the situation in the areas Mühlhausen and Langensalza–Gotha. The enemy was driven out of Friedrichsroda by counter-attack. We also attacked at Tambach–Dietharz and inflicted severe losses on the enemy. The enemy is fanning out from Hildburghausen but he made only comparatively small gains of ground. From the area north of Schweinfurt the enemy advanced across the Fränkische Saale to Königshofen. The situation at Schweinfurt itself remained unchanged. East of Würzburg enemy forces crossed the Main at Volkach. Our counter-attacks against enemy forces which had pressed forward to Crailsheim made good progress. Our troops forced their way into Crailsheim and are now involved in heavy fighting on the Crailsheim–Mergentheim road. South of Bretten the enemy advanced through Mühlacker into Pforzheim.

The Americans made converging attacks on Army Group B (Ruhr area, Sauerland–Rothaargebirge) concentrating on the northern edge of the Ruhr, the Sieg front and the Rothaargebirge. In the Ruhr the enemy reached the northern outskirts of Oberhausen and also Castrop-Rauxel. He also gained some ground towards Dortmund. He reached the Unna–Soest railway on either side of Werl but here he was held by counter-attack. Enemy forces in action at Hitdorf and between Düsseldorf and Köln were annihilated in counter-attacks. The enemy made only small gains of ground on the Sieg front and in the Rothaargebirge; in many places he was held and driven back by counter-attack. It is reported, however, that the ammunition situation is becoming difficult on the German side.

No action reporter from the Italian front.

In the East enemy air activity was particularly heavy in the Vienna and Königsberg areas. A total of 18 Soviet aircraft were shot down. Over Reich territory some 1200 American four-engined bombers attacked industrial and transport targets in northern, central and southern Germany. Of these 350 operated over central and north-west Germany and another 350 over south and south-west Germany. Attacks were made on Schleiz, Sondershausen, Stadtroda, the Hannover–Hildesheim area, Plauen, Halberstadt, Stendal, Hof, Eger and certain airfields. Some bombs were dropped in the areas of Burg, Thale im Harz and Rathenow. Heavy enemy fighter activity was concentrated on the Nordhausen–Gera area. Some 500 American four-engined bombers from Italy attacked transport targets in the Innsbruck–Bolzano area. A smaller Soviet formation raided Brünn. Our fighters were not in action. Anti-aircraft shot down two enemy.

During the night there was much enemy long-distance night fighter activity with machine-gunning of transport targets over the whole Reich. Two strong British four-engined formations with Mosquito path-finders raided Hamburg, Lützkendorf and the Bernburg area. Mosquito raids were made on Lübeck, Travemünde, Dessau, Berlin and Munich. According to reports so far 20 enemy aircraft were shot down during the night.

ANNEXES

1 *Adolf Hitler's Proclamation to the people of Berlin on 22 April 1945*

(published in the first issue of the tabloid newspaper *Der Panzerbär* on 23 April 1945)

Grave Warning from the Führer
Mark well!

Anyone who proposes or even approves measures detrimental to our power of resistance is a traitor! He is to be shot or hanged immediately! This applies even if such measures have allegedly been ordered on the instructions of Reich Minister Dr. Goebbels, the Gauleiter, or even in the name of the Führer.

Führer's Headquarters, 22/4/1945

Signed: Adolf Hitler

2 *Letter from Dr. Joseph Goebbels to Harald Quandt, 28 April 1945*

Begun in the Führer's bunker   28 April 45

My dear Harald,

We are now confined to the Führer's bunker in the Reich Chancellery and are fighting for our lives and our honour. God alone knows what the outcome of this battle will be. I know, however, that we shall only come out of it, dead or alive, with honour and glory. I hardly think that we shall see each other again. Probably, therefore, these are the last lines you will ever receive from me. I expect from

407

you that, should you survive this war, you will do nothing but honour your mother and me. It is not essential that we remain alive in order to continue to influence our people. You may well be the only one able to continue our family tradition. Always act in such a way that we need not be ashamed of it. Germany will survive this fearful war but only if examples are set to our people enabling them to stand on their feet again. We wish to set such an example. You may be proud of having such a mother as yours. Yesterday the Führer gave her the Golden Party Badge which he has worn on his tunic for years and she deserves it. You should have only one duty in future: to show yourself worthy of the supreme sacrifice which we are ready and determined to make. I know that you will do it. Do not let yourself be disconcerted by the worldwide clamour which will now begin. One day the lies will crumble away of themselves and truth will triumph once more. That will be the moment when we shall tower over all, clean and spotless, as we have always striven to be and believed ourselves to be.

Farewell, my dear Harald. Whether we shall ever see each other again is in the lap of the gods. If we do not, may you always be proud of having belonged to a family which, even in misfortune, remained loyal to the very end to the Führer and his pure sacred cause.

All good things to you and my most heartfelt greetings
Your Papa

3 *Letter from Magda Goebbels to Harald Quandt, 28 April 1945*
Written in the Führer's Bunker   28 April 1945

My beloved Son,

We have now been here, in the Führer's bunker, for 6 days—Papa, your six little brothers and sisters and I—in order to bring our National-Socialist existence to the only possible and honourable conclusion. I do not know whether you will receive this letter. Perhaps there is still one human soul who will make it possible for me to send you my last greetings. You should know that I have remained here against Papa's will, that only last Sunday the Führer wanted to help me to escape from here. You know your mother—we are of the same blood, so I did not have to reflect for a moment. Our splendid concept is perishing and with it goes everything beautiful, admirable, noble and good that I have known in my life. The world which will succeed the Führer and National-Socialism is not worth living in and for this reason I have brought the children here too. They are too good for the life that will come after us and a gracious God will understand me if I myself give them release from it. You will go on living and I have one single request to make of you: never forget that you are a German, never do anything dishonourable and ensure that by your life our death is not in vain.

The children are wonderful. They make do in these very primitive conditions without any help. No matter whether they sleep on the floor, whether they can wash or not, whether they have anything to eat and so forth—never a word of complaint or a tear. Shell-bursts are shaking the bunker. The grown-ups protect the little ones, whose presence here is to this extent a blessing that from time to time they can get a smile from the Führer.

Yesterday evening the Führer took off his Golden Party Badge and pinned it on me. I am happy and proud. God grant that I retain the strength to do the last and most difficult thing. We have only one aim in life now—to remain loyal to the Führer unto death; that we should be able to end our life together with him is a gift of fate for which we would never have dared hope.

Harald, my dear—I give you the best that life has taught me: be true—true to yourself, true to mankind, true to your country—in every respect whatsoever.

(*New Sheet*)

It is hard to start a fresh sheet. Who knows whether I shall complete it but I wanted to give you much love, so much strength and take from you all sorrow at our loss. Be proud of us and try to remember us with pride and pleasure. Everyone must die one day and is it not better

to live a fine, honourable, brave but short life than drag
out a long life of humiliation?

The letter must go—Hanna Reitsch is taking it. She is
flying out once more. I embrace you with my warmest,
most heartfelt and most maternal love.

> My beloved son
> Live for Germany!
> Your Mother

4 *Appendix by Dr. Joseph Goebbels to Adolf Hitler's Will
and Testament, 29 April 1945*

[In his testament Hitler nominated Goebbels as
Chancellor under Dönitz as Head of State]

The Führer has ordered me to leave Berlin, should the
defence of the capital collapse, and act as a leading member
of a government nominated by him.

For the first time in my life I must categorically refuse
to comply with an order from the Führer. My wife and
children are at one with me in this refusal. Quite apart
from the fact that emotionally and for reasons of personal
loyalty we could never bring ourselves to desert the Führer
in this his direst moment, were I to do otherwise, for the
rest of my life I should consider myself an infamous
renegade and common blackguard; I should lose my self-
respect and the respect of his people which must be the
precondition of any further service by me to the future
shaping of the German nation and German Reich.

In the frenzy of betrayal in which the Führer is en-
veloped during these critical days of the war there must be
at least some to stand by him unconditionally and unto
death even if this entails contravening a formal order, however objectively reasonable, as set forth in his political
testament.

I think that I am thereby rendering the best service to
the future of the German people, for in the hard times to
come examples are more important than men. Men will
always be found to point the way to freedom for the
nation. Reconstitution of our national Germanic existence,

however, would not be possible were it not modeled on clear examples comprehensible to everyone. For these reasons I with my wife and in the name of my children, who are too young to make a statement themselves but who, if they were old enough, would adhere to my decision unreservedly, hereby declare my irrevocable decision not to leave the Reich capital, even should it fall; we prefer to bring to an end at the side of the Führer a life which for me personally has no further value unless I can use it in the service of the Führer and at his side.

Given in Berlin, 29 April 1945, 5:30

Dr. Goebbels.

5 *Official German Announcement of Hitler's Death, 1 May 1945*
(Broadcast)

It is reported from the Führer's Headquarters that this afternoon our Führer Adolf Hitler fell in his command post in the Reich Chancellery, fighting with his last breath for Germany against bolshevism. On 30 April the Führer had nominated Grand Admiral Dönitz as his successor.

CHRONOLOGY

1945

January

1   German advance from Komorn to relieve Budapest
7   Second German advance from Lake Balaton to relieve Budapest
11 Armistice in Greece
12 The Soviet 1st Ukrainian Front (Koniev) advances from the Baranov bridgehead and breaks through the German defences
13 The Soviet 3rd White Russian Front (Chernakovsky) goes over to the offensive at Pillkallen, East Prussia
14 The Soviet 1st White Russian Front (Zhukov) breaks through the German defences in Poland; the Soviet 2nd White Russian Front (Rokossovsky) takes the offensive from the Narev bridgehead towards Elbing
15 Further Soviet offensive directed on Cracow
17 Soviet units capture Czestochowa; the Germans evacuate Warsaw
18 Cracow evacuated by the Germans; beginning of breakthrough by 2nd Soviet White Russian Front (Rokossovsky); third German attempt to relieve Budapest from Lake Balaton
19 Soviet 1st White Russian Front (Zhukov) captures Lodz
21 Soviet 1st Ukrainian Front (Koniev) crosses into Silesia
22 Soviet troops capture Insterburg and Allenstein

23 Start of evacuation by sea of East Prussia and the Bay of Danzig
24 German withdrawal in Slovakia; Soviet 1st Ukrainian Front (Koniev) captures Oppeln and Gleiwitz; Himmler becomes Commander-in-Chief of Army Group Vistula; Soviet attacks at Libau (Courland) driven off
26 Soviet troops cut land communications with East Prussia; Soviets capture Kattowitz
27 Germans evacuate the Upper Silesian industrial zone
28 Soviet troops form bridgehead at Küstrin

February
 2 Ecuador declares war on Germany
 3 American air-raid on Berlin
 4 Start of Yalta conference between Stalin, Roosevelt and Churchill
 7 Garrison of Thorn fights its way back to the German lines
 8 Soviet 1st Ukrainian Front (Koniev) advances from Steinau and Leubus on Oder; 1st Canadian Army (Crerar) launches an offensive from the Nijmegen area; Paraguay declares war on Germany
10 Advance of Soviet 2nd White Russian Front (Rokossovsky) halted in Pomerania; garrison of Elbing fights its way back to the German lines; Liegnitz captured by Soviet troops; remnants of German–Hungarian garrison of Budapest surrender
12 End of Yalta Conference: co-ordination of military operations, division of Germany into zones of occupation, formation of an Allied Control Council, settlement on conference for formation of United Nations, agreement on a Polish government and the Polish–Soviet western frontier; Peru declares war on Germany
13 Anglo-American air attack on Dresden (repeated on 14 February)—devastation of Inner City—number of casualties officially estimated at 60,000
15 Breslau encircled; Uruguay declares war on Germany

414

16 Start of German counter-offensive at Stargard in Pomerania (cancelled on 18 February); Venezuela declares war on Germany

19 German troops in East Prussia re-establish land communications between Pillau and Königsberg; Himmler gains contact with Count Folke Bernadotte, President of the International Red Cross, in order to find out possibilities for a separate peace with the Western Powers

23 Soviet troops capture Posen; American 9th Army (Simpson) launches an offensive from its bridgeheads on the Roer; Turkey declares war on Germany

24 Soviet break-through in Pomerania; Egypt declares war on Germany

27 King Michael I of Rumania forced to appoint a communist government in Bucharest under Petru Groza

March

1 Start of German counter-attack in Lower Silesia leading to recapture of Lauban and Striegau

3 American 3rd Army (Patton) occupies Trier; Canadian troops capture Xanten

5 Graudenz surrenders

6 Start of German offensive at Lake Balaton in Hungary

7 American 1st Army (Hodges) captures Köln and pushes across the Rhine at Remagen

8 Start of secret negotiations in Switzerland between representatives of the Allied High Command and the German forces in Italy with a view to German surrender

9 Heavy American air-raid on Tokyo

10 Field Marshal Kesselring takes over command in the West from Field Marshal von Rundstedt; German troops evacuate Wesel

13 Start of Soviet offensive in the area of Heiligenbeil, East Prussia. Land communications to Königsberg severed

15 The Soviet 1st Ukrainian Front (Koniev) launches offensive in the area of Ratibor, Upper Silesia; German advance in Hungary halted

16 Soviet 2nd Ukrainian Front and 3rd Ukrainian Front (Tolbukhin) go over to the counter-offensive in Hungary

17 American 3rd Army (Patton) captures Koblenz

18 Kolberg captured by Soviet troops; start of Soviet offensive in Courland

19 Hitler issues "scorched earth" order calling for destruction of all industrial and supply installations in the Reich

20 Start of offensive by Tito's partisans in Dalmatia

22 American 3rd Army (Patton) crosses the Rhine at Oppenheim and advances east; German troops evacuate the last bridgeheads over the Drava at Siklos

23 Soviet troops break through German defence positions at Gotenhafen (Gdynia) and Danzig; British, American and Canadian troops advance across the Rhine from Venlo and occupy Wesel

25 American troops reach Germersheim, Ludwigshafen and Worms

26 American 1st Army (Hodges) drives through the Westerwald; American 3rd Army (Patton) occupies Darmstadt and reaches the Main

27 The Argentine declares war on Germany

28 Gotenhafen (Gdynia) captured by Soviet troops; Colonel-General Guderian "sent on leave" by Hitler; General Krebs takes over the affairs of the Army General Staff

29 German troops withdraw on to the Frische Nehrung; American troops occupy Frankfurt am Main

30 Danzig captured by Soviet troops; British troops occupy Emmerich and Bocholt

April

1 Start of evacuation of Hela Peninsula by German naval forces; American 1st Army (Hodges) links up

with American 9th Army (Simpson) in the Lippstadt area; main body of German Army Group B (Model) encircled in the Ruhr; French 1st Army (de Lattre de Tassigny) crosses the Rhine at Philippsburg

2 Soviet troops occupy the Hungarian oilfield of Nagy Kanisza

3 Münster occupied by Anglo-American troops

4 Soviet troops occupy Bratislava, Slovakia; last German troops withdraw from Hungary

5 Soviet 3rd Ukrainian Front (Tolbukhin) opens assault on Vienna. Last use of V2s in the West

6 Soviet 3rd White Russian Front (Vassilevsky) advances to the Frisches Haff; American 9th Army (Simpson) captures Hamm; Tito's partisans occupy Sarajevo

9 Garrison of Königsberg surrenders; start of major Anglo-American offensive in Upper Italy

10 American 9th Army (Simpson) occupies Essen and Hannover; the heavy cruiser *Admiral Scheer* sunk in Kiel by British bombers

12 President Roosevelt dies following a stroke; succeeded by Harry S. Truman

13 Vienna captured by Soviet troops

14 American attacks split up German forces in the Ruhr area

15 Destruction of a Soviet bridgehead at Magdeburg; start of Soviet offensive against industrial area of Mährisch–Ostrau; St. Pölten occupied by Soviet troops

16 Soviet 1st Ukrainian Front (Koniev) and 1st White Russian Front (Zhukor) launch assault on Berlin from the Neisse and Oder bridgeheads; German troops in the eastern Ruhr pocket cease resistance; British bombers sink the heavy cruiser *Lützow* in Swinemünde

17 Remainder of German forces in the Ruhr area surrender—325,000 prisoners

18 American troops capture Magdeburg and occupy Düsseldorf; American 3rd Army (Patton) advances into West Bohemia; last British air-raid on Berlin

CHRONOLOGY

19 Americans occupy Leipzig

20 Soviet 2nd White Russian Front (Rokossovsky) begins conquest of western Pomerania and Mecklenburg; Soviet artillery opens bombardment of Berlin

21 Soviet troops occupy Bautzen and Cottbus

22 French 1st Army (de Lattre de Tassigny) occupies Stuttgart

23 British troops move forward to Hamburg–Harburg; French troops occupy Mülheim, Baden; Hitler dismisses Göring from all his offices

24 German troops at Frankfurt on Oder surrounded; other German formations break through at Beelitz and withdraw across the Elbe. American and French troops occupy Ulm; in Italy the British capture Ferrara and the Americans La Spezia; through Count Bernadotte in Lübeck Himmler makes an offer of surrender to the Western Powers

25 Encirclement of Berlin complete; Pillau (East Prussia) captured by Soviet troops; American and Soviet troops meet at Torgau on the Elbe; in Upper Italy American and British troops cross the Po and occupy Mantua, Reggio and Parma; opening of San Francisco Conference to discuss "Charter of the United Nations"

26 Soviet troops occupy Brünn and Stettin; American troops occupy Bremen

27 Provisional Austrian government under Karl Renner formed in Vienna; French units occupy Ventimiglia and Bordighera on the Franco-Italian frontier; American troops occupy Genoa

28 German attempt by Wenck to relieve Berlin called off; Americans capture Augsburg; Mussolini and some of his entourage taken prisoner by Italian partisans at Dongo on the Swiss frontier and shot next day

29 The German army in Italy (von Vietinghoff) surrenders to Allied forces (Alexander); French troops occupy Friedrichshafen on Lake Constance; Hitler marries Eva Braun, signs his "political" and personal testament and nominates Dönitz as Reich President and Goebbels as Reich Chancellor

30 Hitler commits suicide in the bunker of the Reich Chancellery; Americans occupy Munich and Turin; Tito's partisans move into Trieste; sinkings by German U-boats since January reach 90,000 GRT

May

1 Grand Admiral Dönitz takes over as Head of State in accordance with Hitler's will; Goebbels and his wife commit suicide after killing their six children; Tito's partisans occupy the greater part of the territory of Trieste, Gorizia and Istria

2 The remnants of the garrison of Berlin surrender; the Soviets occupy Rostock; British and Soviet troops meet at Wismar

3 British troops move into Hamburg and the Americans into Innsbruck

4 German forces in Holland, North-west Germany and Denmark capitulate to Field-Marshal Montgomery

5 Graf Schwerin von Krosigk, nominated Foreign Minister by Dönitz, forms an acting Reich Government in Flensburg; rising by Czech resistance groups in Prague

6 Opening of major Soviet offensive against remnants of German Army Group Centre (Schörner) in Bohemia; Americans capture Pilsen and halt their advance; Breslau surrenders

7 Americans evacuate their bridgeheads over the Elbe; British troops occupy Wilhelmshaven, Cuxhaven and Emden; Colonel-General Jodl signs general surrender of the Wehrmacht in Reims

8 Soviet troops occupy Dresden

9 Field Marshal Keitel repeats signature of general capitulation in the Soviet headquarters at Karlshorst near Berlin

10 Soviet forces occupy Prague

11 Czechoslovak cabinet-in-exile returns to Prague from London

14 Heligoland occupied by British troops

23 Arrest of the Dönitz government and members of the

High Command of the German Armed Forces in Flensburg; Himmler commits suicide; Dutch cabinet-in-exile meets in The Hague

31 American Military Government orders dissolution of the Nazi Party by law.

June

5 The Allied Commanders-in-Chief (Zhukov, Eisenhower, Montgomery and de Lattre de Tassigny) issue declaration in Berlin announcing assumption of governmental authority in Germany by the Control Council formed of the Military Governors

9 Agreement concluded between Yugoslavia, the USA and Great Britain on temporary military administration in the Italian province of Venezia Giulia; Yugoslav units evacuate Trieste and Pola

10 Political parties allowed again in the Soviet-occupied zone of Germany

26 San Francisco Conference concluded with signature of United Nations Charter; Polish government announces "resettlement" of Germans from territories east of the Oder–Neisse line

28 Formation of communist Government of National Unity in Warsaw

July

1 Start of evacuation of Soviet zone of occupation by American and British troops; the Soviets accordingly occupy parts of Brandenburg, Saxony, Thuringia and Mecklenburg; American and British units move into the western sectors of Berlin

7 The Allies sign an agreement for four-power administration of Berlin; Saar Territory placed under French administration

11 First meeting of the Allied Commandants in Berlin

17 Start of Potsdam Conference between Truman, Stalin and Churchill (later Attlee)

August

2 End of Potsdam Conference; results: formation of
Control Council, agreement on reparations and dis-
mantling, transfer of German eastern territories as far
as Oder–Neisse line to Poland for "administration";
final peace treaty with Germany postponed until
formation of a central government.

GAZETTEER

The outline map of pages 1–li locates only the major sites mentioned in the military situation reports on the war in the air. The list below has been prepared for readers who wish to follow the movements of the land battle in closer detail on modern maps. The forms used by Goebbels, which have been followed in the text, are listed in alphabetical order together with their 1977 equivalents.

Altdamm	Dabie
Bahn	Banie
Bannerwitz	Babarów
Belgard	Białogard
Berent	Kościerzyna
Bielitz	Bielsko-Biala (formerly called Bielsko)
Breslau	Wrocław
Briesen	Wąbrzeźno
Bunzlau	Bolesławiec
Bütow	Bytów
Cammin	Kamień Pomorski (formerly called Kamień)
Cosel	Koźle
Danzig	Gdańsk
Dievenow	Dziwnów
Dramburg	Drawsko Pomorskie (formerly Drawsko)
Elbing	Elbląg
Falkenburg	Złocieniec
Friedrichswalde	Podlesie

Frisches Haff	Zalew Wiślany (Poland)
	Vislinskiy Zaliv (Russia)
Fürstenberg	Dalimierz
Glogau	Głogów
Goldberg	Złotoryja
Gollnow	Goleniów
Göritz	Górzyca
Gottswalde	Koswały
Grabow	Grabowo
Graudenz	Grudziądz
Greifenhangen	Gryfino
Grottkau	Grodków
Heiderode	Czersk
Heiligenbeil	Mamonovo
Hirschberg	Jelenia Góra
Jägerndorf	Krnov
Kallies	Kalisz Pomorski
Katscher	Kietrz
Kolberg	Kołobrzeg
Komorn	Komárno
Königsberg	Kaliningrad
Konitz	Chojnice
Kreuzenort	Krzyzanowice
Labes	Łobez
Latzig	Laski
Lauban	Lubań
Leobschütz	Głubczyce
Labiau	Polessk
Libau	Liep āja
Lichtenfeld	Lelkowo
Löwenberg	Lwówek Śląski
Mährisch–Ostrau	Moravská Ostrava
Mewe	Gniew
Mitau	Jelgava
Neuhäusel	Nové Zámky
Neukrug	Nowa Karczma
Neusiedlersee (lake)	Fertö
Neusohl	Banská Býstrica

Neuteich	Nowy Staw
Oliva	Oliwa
Pawlowitz	Pawłowice
Praust	Pruszcz Grański
Preekuln	Priekule
Plathe	Płoty
Polangen	Palanga
Pölitz	Police
Pollnow	Polanów
Putzig	Puck
Pyritz	Pyrzyce
Raab (river)	Rába
Ratibor	Racibórz
Reetz	Recz
Regenwalde	Resko
Rügenwalde	Darłowo
Schemnitz	Banská Štiavnica
Schlawe	Sławno
Schlochau	Człuków
Schöneck	Skarszewy
Schwarzheide	Stefanów
Schwarzwasser	Strumień
Schwedt	Świecie Kołobrzeskie
Stargard	Stargard Szczeciński
Stolp	Słupsk
Stuhlweissenberg	Székesfehérvár
Swinemünde	Świnoujście
Tiegenhof	Nowy Dwór Gdański
Treptow	Trzebiatów
Waag (river)	Váh (Czechoslovakia)
	Vág (Hungary)
Zachan	Suchań
Zehden	Cedynia
Ziegenhals	Głuchołazy
Zinten	Kornevo
Zitzewitz	Sycewice
Zobten	Sobótka
Zuckau	Żukowo

PLACE INDEX

PLACE INDEX

146, 180, 191, 199, 207,
219, 229, 247, 266, 276,
282, 292, 313, 323, 349,
373
Netherlands, 152, 173, 314,
336, 350, 370, 381, 392,
400, 403
Neuburg an der Donau, 277
Neuenahr, 81, 92
Neuhäusel, 313, 323, 335
Neukrug, 92
Neumünster, 395
Neunkirchen, 372
Neusiedlersee, 361, 372–73
Neusohl, 199, 229, 247, 256,
266, 276, 292, 323
Neuss, 24–25, 33, 35, 49, 59,
97
Neustadt (Silesia), 207, 256
Neustadt an der Weinstr., 200,
248
Neustadt (West Prussia), 146
Neustadt bei Wunstorf, 403
Neustettin, 4, 15, 22, 24, 34
Neuteich, 114
Neutra, 335, 349, 361
Neuwied, 35, 137, 248, 267,
275
New York, 140, 184, 194, 398
Newe, 44
Nidda, 336
Niederbreisig, 104, 137
Niederbrohl, 137
Nienburg, 46, 231, 403
Nienburg an der Weser, 268
Nienhagen, 46
Niers, 35
Nijmegen, 137, 370
Nikolas, 58, 103, 113
Nogat, 114
Nordhausen, 404
Nordhorn, 373
Norway, 73, 109, 109n., 196,
294, 399
Nürburgring, 105, 114
Nuremberg, xxix, 16, 20, 69,
193, 200, 209, 327, 374,
395

Obenheim, 248
Oberbach, 336, 350
Oberhausen, 395, 404
Oberkassel, 45, 220, 230, 248
Oberlahnstein, 283, 294
Oberpleis, 230
Obersalzberg, xxxviii, 2, 243
Oberwesel, 294
Odenburg, 349, 361
Odenwald, 351, 362
Oder, 4, 13n., 15, 35, 42, 45,
49, 58, 66, 80, 91, 96, 113,
146, 159, 180, 213, 228,
230, 254, 276, 289, 301,
335, 350, 373, 387, 394
Oderberg, 180
Offenbach, 294
Okinawa, 369
Oldenburg, 258
Oliva, 257, 276, 282
Oppau, 248
Oppeln, 45, 66, 80, 219, 373
Oppenheim, 267, 275
Oranienburg, 175–76
Orsoy, 67
Osien, 80
Oslo, 227, 236
Osnabrück, 105, 115, 171,
268, 284, 289
Osten, 336

Paderborn, 258, 315, 348, 350,
362, 373
Palatinate, 192
Palestine, 162–63
Papa, 282, 292
Paris, 396
Passau, 221
Pawlowitz, 180, 191
Peine, 46
Pellingen, 16
Phalz Forest, 257, 268
Pforzheim, 400, 404
Philippines, 261, 271
Pillau, 292, 313, 324
Pilsen, 69
Pirmasens, 257
Plathe, 58

PLACE INDEX

PLACE INDEX

PLACE INDEX

NAME INDEX

Acker, Achille van, Belgian Prime Minister 1945–6, 196

Albrecht, Alwin-Broder, personal aide (naval) to Hitler, 311

Alvensleben, Ludolf von, Lieutenant-General in Waffen-SS, Higher SS and Police Leader of Dresden, 79

Anfuso, Filipo, Italian Ambassador in Berlin, 330

Antonescu, Ion (1882–1946), Rumanian Marshal, Prime Minister 1940–4, executed as war criminal, 29n., 212n., 235

Antonescu, Mihai, Rumanian Deputy Prime Minister and Foreign Minister 1941–4, executed 1946, 235

Arent, Kukuli von, wife of Benno von Arent, the "Reich stage sculptor", 246

Arziszewski, Tomasz, Prime Minister of Polish government-in-exile in London 1944–5, 26, 212

August Wilhelm, Prince of Prussia (1722–58), brother of Frederick the Great, 226, 242

Badoglio, Pietro (1871–1956), Marshal, Italian Prime Minister 1943–4, 330, 397

Balzer, Rudolf, Lieutenant-Colonel, OKW Liaison Officer to Ministry of Propaganda, 141, 326, 366

Baruch, Bernard Mannes (1870–1965), American political economist, 196

Baumbach, Manfred, Luftwaffe Colonel, 241, 243, 244

Bayerlein, Fritz, Lieutenant-General, 381

Beneš, Eduard (1884–1948), President of Czechoslovak government-in-exile 1940–5, President of Czechoslovakia 1945–8, resigned 1948, 196, 365–66

Bidault, Georges, French Foreign Minister 1944–6, 1947–8, 1953–4, Prime Minister 1946, 1949, 1950, Deputy Prime Minister 1950, 1951, 1952, Minister of Defence 1951, 1952, 329

Binding, Regierungspräsident (Senior government representative) in Hildesheim, 151

Bismarck, Otto, Prince von, (1815–98), xxviii, 52

Bohle, Ernst Wilhelm, State Secretary (Permanent Secretary) of Foreign Office, Head of Overseas Organization and in that capacity the 43rd Nazi Party Gauleiter, SS-Obergruppenführer, sentenced to five years imprisonment in Nuremberg in 1949, 71, 74–75, 355, 386

NAME INDEX

Hadamovsky, Eugen, Head of Reich Propaganda Section of Nazi Party, Head of Reich Broadcasting, 33, 55

Haegert, Wilhelm, Head of Propaganda Section in the Propaganda Ministry, 100

Hahne, Franz, Obermeister, 214, 381

Hanke, Karl (1903–45), Gauleiter of Lower Silesia, designated Reichsführer-SS and Chief of the German Police in Hitler's will, killed by Czechs in June 1945 (?), 43, 51, 77, 224, 308, 333, 371, 399

Harris, Sir Arthur Travers, British Air Marshal, 148

Hartung, member of Gau headquarters Berlin, 272

Hauenschild, Bruno Ritter von (1896–1953), Lieutenant-General, Commandant of Berlin, 11, 63, 144, 150

Hauptmann, Gerhart (1862–1946), 356

Hausser, Paul, SS-Obergruppenführer, 20n., 346, 381

Heiber, Helmut, historian, biographer of Goebbels, xliv

Hellmuth, Dr. Otto, Gauleiter of Mainfranken, Regierungspräsident of Lower Franconia and Aschaffenburg, 370

Herostratus, 195

Hesse, Dr. Fritz, counsellor in the Foreign Office, 184, 190, 194, 237, 355

Hewel, Walther, Ambassador, Foreign Minister's Representative with the Führer and Reich Chancellor, 56, 237, 238

Hierl, Konstantin (1875–1955), Reich Labour Leader, Nazi Party Reichsleiter, member of cabinet 1934–45, 399

Hildebrandt, Friedrich, SS-Obergruppenführer, Gauleiter of Mecklenburg, Reichsstatthalter for Mecklenburg and Lübeck, 320–21

Himmler, Heinrich (1900–45), Reichsführer-SS, Reich Minister of the Interior, C-in-C of the Replacement Army and Chief of Army Equipment, committed suicide on 23 May 1945 after being recognised in a prisoner of war camp, xvii, xxi–xxii, xxiii, xxix, xxxii, 13 n., 20, 29n., 30n., 42n., 50, 79, 86–89, 126–27, 155–56, 168, 169, 178, 184, 235–36, 301, 305, 310, 343, 346, 359, 396

Hitler, Adolf (1889–1945), xvii–xl, 1, 2, 10, 13, 20n., 22, 28–31, 33, 42, 49–57, 64, 75, 87–88, 90, 94–95, 101, 102, 107, 109, 111, 116, 118, 123–35 passim, 138–39, 148, 152, 154–158, 165–69, 177–79, 184, 186, 189, 190, 194, 197, 204, 218, 225, 226, 237–46 passim, 249, 253–54, 258, 261, 263, 264, 280, 281, 286, 289, 290–91, 299–311 passim, 317, 319, 321, 327, 328, 330, 332, 339–47 passim, 352, 357, 358, 359, 380–83, 384, 386, 389–93, 396, 397, 398, 407–11

Hoffmann, Albert, SS-Gruppenführer, Gauleiter of Westphalia South, 175, 236

Hofmeister, Georg, Major-General, City Commandant of Berlin, 144

NAME INDEX

Reitsch, Hanna, test pilot, 410

Remer, Major, xxxii

Rendulic, Dr. Lothar, Colonel-General, 96

Reymann, Hellmuth, Lieutenant-General, Commandant of Berlin, 144, 150, 264

Ribbentrop, Joachim von (1893–1946), Ambassador in London 1936–8, Reich Foreign Minister 1938–45, executed in Nuremberg, xxviii, xxxi, xxxiii, xxxvi, xxxvii, xxxix, 57, 75, 79, 84, 88, 132, 184, 193, 216, 238, 259, 263, 280, 309, 355, 387

Roatta, Mario, Italian General, in 1943 Chief of Army Staff in Badoglio's Provisional Military Cabinet, 63, 85

Rodde-Hanau, Wilhelm, head of Reich propaganda in Hamburg, 357

Röhm, Ernst (1887–1934), Chief of Staff of the SA from 1931, Minister without Portfolio 1933, shot on 30 June 1934 during the "Röhm putsch", 305

Roosevelt, Franklin Delano (1882–1945), President of the United States, 1933–45, xxx, xxxviii, 9, 19, 26–27, 47, 54, 57, 71–72, 75, 108, 117, 133, 142–43, 161, 194, 196n., 202, 223, 233–34, 235, 241, 245, 252, 260–61, 270, 317, 319, 338, 364, 365, 369, 377, 379, 387

Rosenberg, Alfred (1893–1946), leader-writer for *Völkischer Beobachter* 1921, author of *Der Mythos des XX Jahrhunderts* (1930), head of Foreign Political Office of Nazi Party 1933, Reich Minister for the Occupied Eastern Territories 1941, executed in Nuremburg, 177, 197

Rshevskaya, Yelena, Soviet historian, xlvii

Rundstedt, Gerd von (1875–1953), Field Marshal, 7, 70, 107, 139, 156, 173, 184, 239–40, 304

Ryti, Risto, President of Finland 1940–4, arrested as collaborator but released in 1949, 48

Salazar, Antonio de Oliveira (1889–1970), Prime Minister of Portugal from 1936, 274

Saracoglu, Sükrü, Turkish Prime Minister 1942–6, 387

Sauckel, Fritz (1894–1946), Gauleiter and Reichsstatthalter of Thuringia, General Plenipotentiary for Employment of Labour from 1942, executed in Nuremberg, 289, 383

Saur, Karl-Otto, Head of Technical Branch in Ministry of Armaments, designated as Minister of Armaments in Hitler's will, 307, 309

Schach, Gerhard, office manager in Gau headquarters, Berlin, 32, 116, 154, 204

Scharnhorst, Gerhard Johann David von (1756–1813), 32, 134

Schaub, Julius, SS-Obergruppenführer, Personal Assistant to Hitler, 204, 311, 383

Schirach, Baldur von (1907–74), Reich Youth Leader 1933–1940, Gauleiter and Reichstatthalter of Vienna 1940–5, sen-

450

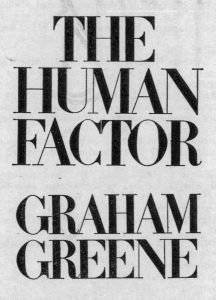

THE INTERNATIONAL BESTSELLER!

KG 200

J. D. GILMAN
AND
JOHN CLIVE

A Luftwaffe squadron that spoke perfect English.
If they'd succeeded, we'd all be speaking perfect German.

"This novel of aerial assassination, inspired
by actual historical events, booms right along to
an explosive finale."
Publishers Weekly

"Masterful . . . the implications are spine-chilling."
The Denver Post

Selected by 2 Book Clubs

Avon 39115/$2.25

KG 9-78

THE BIG BESTSELLERS
ARE AVON BOOKS

☐ The Human Factor Graham Greene	41491	$2.50
☐ The Insiders Rosemary Rogers	40576	$2.50
☐ Oliver's Story Erich Segal	42564	$2.25
☐ Prince of Eden Marilyn Harris	41905	$2.50
☐ The Thorn Birds Colleen McCullough	35741	$2.50
☐ The Amulet Michael McDowell	40584	$2.50
☐ Chinaman's Chance Ross Thomas	41517	$2.25
☐ Kingfisher Gerald Seymour	40592	$2.25
☐ The Trail of the Fox David Irving	40022	$2.50
☐ The Queen of the Night Marc Behm	39958	$1.95
☐ The Bermuda Triangle Charles Berlitz	38315	$2.25
☐ The Real Jesus Garner Ted Armstrong	40055	$2.25
☐ Lancelot Walker Percy	36582	$2.25
☐ Snowblind Robert Sabbag	44008	$2.50
☐ Catch Me: Kill Me William H. Hallahan	37986	$1.95
☐ A Capitol Crime Lawrence Meyer	37150	$1.95
☐ Fletch's Fortune Gregory Mcdonald	37978	$1.95
☐ Voyage Sterling Hayden	37200	$2.50
☐ Humboldt's Gift Saul Bellow	38810	$2.25
☐ Mindbridge Joe Haldeman	33605	$1.95
☐ The Surface of Earth Reynolds Price	29306	$1.95
☐ The Monkey Wrench Gang Edward Abbey	40857	$2.25
☐ Jonathan Livingston Seagull Richard Bach	44099	$1.95
☐ Working Studs Terkel	34660	$2.50
☐ Shardik Richard Adams	43752	$2.75
☐ Anya Susan Fromberg Schaeffer	25262	$1.95
☐ Watership Down Richard Adams	39586	$2.50

Available at better bookstores everywhere, or order direct from the publisher.

FIERCE COURAGE,
PULSATING SUSPENSE,
ELECTRIFYING HUMAN DRAMA!

BERLIN TUNNEL 21

The New Blockbuster by

DONALD LINDQUIST

Talking and plotting in Berlin cafés and
apartments, a brazen group mounts a perilous
challenge to the deadliest border on earth—the
Berlin Wall. An American, an artist, a male stud,
. . . a potential traitor . . . day after day they
survive cave-ins, floods, and paralyzing fear—
trapped in the explosive conflicts of love and hate,
bravery and cowardice, mercy and greed that
rock each man's soul—digging twenty feet
beneath the earth for something more
important than their lives!

COULD YOU, *WOULD* YOU, RISK ALL
FOR SOMEONE YOU LOVED?

BERLIN TUNNEL 21—where men and women discover
the ultimate price of freedom.

 AVON/36335/$2.25

TUN 3-78

IF THE MISSION WAS DEADLY, AND THE ODDS OF COMING BACK WERE A MILLION TO NOTHING, ONE ELITE SQUADRON GOT THE CALL...

THE HOMESTEAD GRAYS

James Wylie

The shattering, heroic novel based on the never-before-documented exploits of America's first black fighter squadron—a riveting epic of men singled out for annihilation by the Nazis and hatred by their own comrades.

WALKER: who downed a flaming string of Nazi planes and reaped Europe's sensual pleasures. **SKINNER:** an Olympian in Berlin in '36 who had a score to settle with "the master race." **ARCHIBALD:** who feared his sexual secret would explode and destroy them all.

"FLAMBOYANT ACES, VICIOUS DOGFIGHTS, PASSIONATE AFFAIRS"
The Washington Star

AVON 38604 / $1.95

AVON ◆ THE BEST IN BESTSELLING ENTERTAINMENT

☐ Tears of Gold Laurie McBain	41475	$2.50
☐ Always Trevor Meldal-Johnsen	41897	$2.50
☐ Atlanta Milt Macklin	43539	$2.50
☐ Mortal Encounter Patricia Sargent	41509	$2.25
☐ Final Entries 1945: The Diaries of Joseph Goebbels Prof. Hugh Trevor-Roper	42408	$2.75
☐ Shanna Kathleen E. Woodiwiss	38588	$2.25
☐ Self-Creation George Weinberg	43521	$2.50
☐ The Enchanted Land Jude Devereux	40063	$2.25
☐ Love Wild and Fair Bertrice Small	40030	$2.50
☐ Your Erroneous Zones Dr. Wayne W. Dyer	33373	$2.25
☐ Tara's Song Barbara Ferry Johnson	39123	$2.25
☐ The Homestead Grays James Wylie	38604	$1.95
☐ Hollywood's Irish Rose Nora Bernard	41061	$1.95
☐ Baal Robert R. McCammon	36319	$2.25
☐ Dream Babies James Fritzhand	35758	$2.25
☐ Fauna Denise Robins	37580	$2.25
☐ Monty: A Biography of Montgomery Clift Robert LaGuardia	37143	$2.25
☐ Majesty Robert Lacey	36327	$2.25
☐ Death Sails the Bay John R. Feegel	38570	$1.95
☐ Q & A Edwin Torres	36590	$1.95
☐ This Other Eden Marilyn Harris	36301	$2.25
☐ Emerald Fire Julia Grice	38596	$2.25
☐ Gypsy Lady Shirlee Busbee	36145	$1.95
☐ All My Sins Remembered Joe Haldeman	39321	$1.95
☐ ALIVE: The Story of the Andes Survivors Piers Paul Read	39164	$2.25
☐ The Flame and the Flower Kathleen E. Woodiwiss	35485	$2.25
☐ I'm OK—You're OK Thomas A. Harris, M.D.	28282	$2.25

Available at better bookstores everywhere, or order direct from the publisher.

AVON BOOKS, Mail Order Dept., 224 W. 57th St., New York, N.Y. 10019

Please send me the books checked above. I enclose $_____ (please include 50¢ per copy for postage and handling). Please use check or money order—sorry, no cash or C.O.D.'s. Allow 4-6 weeks for delivery.

Mr/Mrs/Miss _____

Address _____

City _____ State/Zip _____

BBBB 4-79

*She Was
Hunter
And
Hunted
In A*

MORTAL ENCOUNTER

Her father has been brutally murdered. And now Judith Weber, a beautiful young concert pianist, vows to find the men that killed him. Unable to trust anyone, Judith embarks alone on a deadly quest into a maze of missing photographs, cold-blooded murders, Alpine villages, brutal assassins, and ultimately, a trail of terror from the U.S. State Department to a nightmare that began over thirty years ago . . . and a horrifying secret in her own past—a secret that should have died with the Reich!

*A Heartstopping Novel
of International
Intrigue by*
PATRICIA SARGENT

 / 41509 / $2.25 / ME 3-79